Bicycles in American Highway Planning

Also by Bruce D. Epperson

Peddling Bicycles to America: The Rise of an Industry (McFarland, 2010)

Bicycles in American Highway Planning

The Critical Years of Policy-Making, 1969–1991

BRUCE D. EPPERSON

McFarland & Company, Inc., Publishers
Jefferson, North Carolina

LIBRARY OF CONGRESS CATALOGUING-IN-PUBLICATION DATA

Epperson, Bruce D., 1957–
Bicycles in American highway planning : the critical years of policy-making, 1969–1991 / Bruce D. Epperson.
p. cm.
Includes bibliographical references and index.

ISBN 978-0-7864-9495-8 (softcover : acid free paper) ♾

ISBN 978-1-4766-1679-7 (ebook)

1. Bicycle commuting—United States—History—20th century. 2. Bicycles—United States—History—20th century. 3. Highway planning—United States—History—20th century. 4. Transportation and state—United States—History—20th century. I. Title.

HE5737.E67 2014
388.3'4720973—dc23 2014038967

BRITISH LIBRARY CATALOGUING DATA ARE AVAILABLE

© 2014 Bruce D. Epperson. All rights reserved

No part of this book may be reproduced or transmitted in any form or by any means, electronic or mechanical, including photocopying or recording, or by any information storage and retrieval system, without permission in writing from the publisher.

Front cover images © 2014 iStock/Thinkstock

Printed in the United States of America

McFarland & Company, Inc., Publishers
Box 611, Jefferson, North Carolina 28640
www.mcfarlandpub.com

This book is dedicated to the memory of
Cecil Louis Troughton Smith (1899–1966),
a great writer, a great humanist, and a Great Man.

Table of Contents

Introduction

It appears that European transport historians have suddenly discovered the bicycle. In the last decade or so, a dozen or more scholarly articles, a book-length compendium of papers and an entire thematic issue of *The Journal of Transport History* have examined the history of European bicycle transportation. Several of the most recent articles originated from a workshop, *Re/Cycling Histories; Users and the Paths to Sustainability in Everyday Life*, held at the Rachel Carson Center in Munich in the spring of 2011. *Re/Cycling Histories* promised to be just the first of a series of conferences and workshops focusing broadly on the historical role of cycle transport in urban development, nation-building, and the evolution of class, gender, and race relations.[1]

This is not to say that the bicycle has gone unexamined. But such studies have primarily been what the technological historian Wiebe Bijker calls "internalist," focused on the mechanics of the bicycle itself to the near-total exclusion of its economic, social, and political context. The International Cycling History Conference (ICHC), first convened in Glasgow in 1990, has been held almost every year since, with its sixth North American visit scheduled for 2014. But the ICHC, with its roots in the British Veteran Cycle Club, has primarily concerned itself with either its mechanical evolution or the history of bicycle racing; out of about 340 papers presented during its first 20 years, only about 35 dealt with the bicycle's wider sociotechnical aspects as a transport mode, especially during the post–World War II era.[2]

On the other hand, the first VeloCity conference was sponsored by the General German Cyclist's Club (Allgemeiner Deutscher Fahrrad-Club, or ADFC) in 1980 with the specific intent to focus on bicycle transport and the politics of mobility enhancement. In 1984 it was hosted by the Greater London Council (GLC), and has since been held in a number of cities in Europe, North America and Asia. While a fertile ground for exchanging new ideas about how to use the bicycle to promote mobility (some believe it was the birthplace of the modern bike-share movement), cycle history has been a peripheral concern as its participants struggle with what they see as the urgent, immediate problems of urban sustainability.[3]

But in almost every case, whether one is talking about the latest article in the journal *Mobilities* or a plenary session of the most recent VeloCity conference, the term "bicycle transportation development" has almost always meant "bikeways development." Yet, the two are not necessarily synonymous. In fact, the authors of one recent European study found that up to the 1920s, and often well into the 1930s:

> Cycling organizations had neither promoted separating the traffic streams of horses, carts or pedestrians, nor campaigned for the construction of separate bicycle lanes, nor had they opposed cars. The clubs simply advocated to improve road surfaces for everyone.[4]

Other historians, including Anne Katrin Ebert and Manuel Stoffers, found that programs to develop bicycle facilities in the Netherlands were not systematically implemented until the mid–1970s. Tilman Bracher notes that in Germany, a decision was made in the early 1980s to move away from their decades-long "classical Radweg" approach of installing bicycle sidewalks alongside (or in conjunction with) pedestrian ways in favor of a more roadway-integrated strategy, especially at intersections, often by adapting designs first developed in the United States.

Those looking for a widespread, uniform adoption of bikeways technologies in Europe or a continuous history of steady, high-level bicycle use have been sorely disappointed by the new scholarship. The role the bicycle has played in European transportation development has proven to be surprisingly fine-gained, nationalistic, localized, and subject to rapid fluctuations in policy and external forces. There has been no historically enduring European bicycle Valhalla. If, as some American cycle advocates assert, a few now exist in northern Europe, they are of recent vintage and are the result of deliberate policy, hard work, and a lot of money.[5]

I do not intend to take a position on the hotly contested issue of whether bikeways are the *sine qua non* of bicycle transportation, nor will I even attempt to reach any conclusions about whether such facilities are good or bad. In 2014, few transportation researchers, engineers or even non-professional advocates would go so far as two American scholars did in 1971 when they wrote, "Our research has led us to the conclusion, that at least in the cities—*no bicycle paths, no bicycles*." However, there is a widely held assumption that the amount of cycle transport is, to a greater or lesser degree, correlated with the presence of purpose-built bicycle facilities. Whether that is true or not, the perception itself threatens to inject a degree of intrinsic bias into any historical analysis.[6]

What if facilities aren't necessary to create or sustain bicycle transportation? What if the decision to install or not install such facilities isn't primarily one affecting the overall magnitude of cycle use, but is instead an allocational issue? In other words, what if it is not so much a question of *whether* people will cycle, but *who* will cycle. Or, to put it squarely in the context of public policy, what if it is less a matter of *whether* cyclists will benefit from bikeways than it is an issue of *which* cyclists stand to gain? And finally, are there really, as is so often asserted, such powerful indigenous cultural, economic or geographic factors dividing Europe and America as to defy the most rigorous engineering treatments, yet so perishable that they cannot survive the transatlantic crossing?

These are questions that go to the heart of this book, because it is the story of bicycle transportation without bikeways. It is a detailed history of the origin and early development of bicycle planning in United States, a nation that has largely eschewed the construction of coordinated, interconnected networks of bikeways in its cities and along its rural highways. It focuses on the critical decision-making years, between 1969 and 1991, in an attempt to explain how each decision was reached, and why. Skeptics will retort that lacking the institutional support for a nationwide network of bikeways, America has no bicycle planning, nor does it have a bicycle transportation system. It is one of the primary aims of this book to rebut this assertion. The United States clearly has a system. It may be different from that in Europe, and depending on one's values and preferences it can be argued with equal veracity that it is either much better or vastly worse than Europe's. But it cannot be plausibly maintained that it does not exist.

Bicycle planning in America is unique in two respects. First, unlike in Europe, it didn't exist for almost a century until after the motor vehicle had already become the dominant form of surface transport. True, some scattered advocacy efforts had been made during the great bike boom of the 1890s, mostly to legitimize the bicycle's legal status, and utilitarian cycle use didn't evaporate with the appearance of the motorcar. But, after 1920, motor vehicle use increased extremely rapidly and displaced cycling's already diminished role as basic transport. Thus, no real attention was directed to utility cycling until the mid–1960s, when a confluence of economic and demographic factors led to a dramatic increase in the sales of adult cycles.[7] And second, as a result of this long dormancy, American bicycle planning is singularly unique in the extent to which it came to rely on the existing roadway system, in largely unaltered form, to provide for its basic infrastructure needs. Instead of planning for a universal system of bicycle infrastructure, it turned to spot roadway improvements and a reliance on cyclist roadway skills, enhanced through educational programs targeted at both bicyclists and motor vehicle drivers, to promote mutual safety, convenience and compatibility. Over the years, this strategy has become known as *vehicular cycling*, a contraction of its somewhat unwieldy, but more precise, original label, *vehicular integration of cycling*. This philosophy was summarized by the American Association of State Highway and Transportation Officials (AASHTO) in the second (1991) edition of its *Guide to the Development of New Bicycle Facilities*:

> Bicycle facility planning is commonly thought of as the effort undertaken to develop a separated bikeway system ... [in] fact, such systems can be unnecessarily expensive and do not provide for the vast majority of bicycle travel. Existing highways ... must serve as the base system to provide the travel needs of bicyclists.[8]

This is not to say that American bicycle planning has exclusively or rigidly developed along these lines. In fact, it has *never* adhered to any single ideology, instead following the eclectic "disjoint incrementalism" that has been such a notable feature of all city planning in the United States. Nevertheless, with the possible exception of Australia, no other nation relies so heavily on the integration of cycling into the normal traffic stream as a means to address its bicycle transportation goals. Vehicular cycling has become *the* indelible national characteristic of bicycle planning in America.

Given its importance, it is surprising that no one has yet attempted to document the history of bicycle planning in the United States, especially those aspects outside the subfield of bikeway engineering and design. In fact, it is only recently that historians have even attempted to narrate *any* of the recent history of bicycle use in America.[9] What little documentation that does exist is scattered, much of it is shamelessly self-interested, and all of it lacks adequate documentation, context, and background. This book seeks to correct this.

Within the cycling community itself, vehicular cycling is commonly thought of as a movement, a school, an ideology, even a lifestyle philosophy, one with a clearly identifiable canon developed by a handful of like-minded individuals working in unison within a definable time and place in history.[10] It is the second primary contention of this book that such a rigid, personality-centered mythology is mistaken. "Vehicular cycling" is, instead, a broad, amorphous, and incremental set of satisficing ("good enough") solutions developed over an indefinite period of time by a diverse range of individuals, cycling groups and governmental organizations working separately from each other to overcome a series of outwardly unrelated, often vaguely defined problems. Only occasionally did they work together in temporary, uneasy alliances; slightly more often they fought as opponents. Most of the time they worked independently of each other, developing their solutions in isolation, each as self-interested actors seeking incremental, "one-shot" remedies to what appeared to them at the time as a randomly occurring problem, crisis or opportunity.[11]

What eventually gave these uncoordinated, *ad hoc* activities enough commonality to resemble a coherent governmental and social policy called "vehicular cycling" were three overarching factors. First, even after the great 10-speed boom of 1969–73 ebbed, the number of adult (i.e., over age 16) cyclists remained higher than before, leading to a sharp increase in cyclist-motor vehicle conflicts, with correspondingly higher levels of cyclist injuries and deaths. Second, because of the revenue structure of the federal highway trust fund, the higher gas prices and tightened corporate average fuel economy (CAFE) standards required of automakers led to declines in highway funding after 1967.[12] Third, and directly related to this second factor, it became apparent by 1980 that governments at the state and federal level would not reallocate more than a token amount of their highway funding away from traditional roadbuilding to pay for transportation alternatives, including bicycle facilities, nor would local governments reapportion existing roadway space away from travel or parking lanes to give to cyclists.[13]

Given these three factors, the only possible options facing cycling advocates and the bicycle industry were to convince government to either: (1) actively intervene to reduce or eliminate casual bicycle use, in an attempt to return cycling to a pre–1967 condition; (2) remain neutral towards cycle use, but perform inexpensive spot roadway improvements to reduce cyclist risk, while at the same time encourage privately sponsored cyclist safety education programs; or (3) some combination of these two. The second alternative is the route that has been generally taken. However, all three alternatives have had their proponents in the cycling community, and each of these camps have, at one point or another, attempted to portray themselves as the "true" representatives of vehicular cycling.

A few communities, generally small and typically wealthy, did choose to embark on European-style facilities-intensive systems. However, as will be discussed later, planning critics disagree about whether these were developed as an end in themselves, or as a way to justify other, less egalitarian, planning goals.[14] In addition, as such cycle-exemplary cities as Davis, Boulder and Portland have become wealthier and less inclusive, some of the community values that originally motivated the installation of their systems have become less widely shared, and as a result there is less of a consensus about whether their residents want to make the personal transportation sacrifices necessary to ensure that these systems continue to function well as their cities (and regions) grow.

But the majority of cities and states never realistically expected that a massive infusion of federal money would somehow permit them to develop a system of pathways and lanes to duplicate and parallel their roadway systems. They either did what they could do in the way of spot improvements and quick fixes, using the resources available to them, or else they chose to ignore the problem entirely. Regardless of who took, or tried to take, a leadership role in the cycling community in the 1970s and '80s, no matter which organizations were successful or withered away, despite the books that were written or languished on editors' desks, and regardless of the name it came to be known by, the consensus approach to the problem of bicycle transportation in a society that chose neither to ban cycling nor to provide for it in a rational manner was to remain neutral, to try to incorporate as many small-scale roadway enhancements as possible without significantly increasing costs or adversely impacting motor vehicle convenience, and hope the cyclists could cure most of their own problems themselves. That is the essence of "bicycle planning, American-style." And American-style bicycle planning is synonymous with vehicular cycling.

Vehicular cycling exists not because someone invented it out of whole cloth, not because it was discovered or developed or compiled, but rather because it was inevitable. It was inevitable because it was the only thing left when all the other available options were eliminated. Vehicular cycling is not a policy; it is the absence of policy, *any* policy. French Premier Henri Queuille once defined politics as "the art of postponing decisions until they are no longer relevant." Vehicular cycling is the result of a political decision, one that was put off until it ceased to be relevant.[15]

* * *

This book is divided roughly into three parts. The first third is comprised of this Introduction, along with Chapters 1 and 2. Chapter 1 covers the pre-history of modern American bicycle advocacy, which was grounded in the good-roads movement of the 1890s, and the development of the American traffic planning professions that followed a couple of decades later. There is a widely held belief that the early American cyclists and their national organization, the League of American Wheelmen, were the driving force behind the good-roads movement, and along with the railroads, were the dominant political actors in shaping highway policy prior to 1910. I argue otherwise, maintaining that the league's highly visible, but very expensive and inefficient good roads campaign, was actually a means by which its leadership sought to contain the growing sectional, racial, and class divisions within its own organization. I believe that the league was never able to fully overcome cycling's origins as an elite hobby of wealthy young urban males from New England, and thus, it was ultimately forced to turn over its leadership in the good-roads movement to others before that movement matured into a fully effective social force.

Although little known, there was an alternative to the highway-centered approach of the L.A.W. Between 1898 and 1902 a movement for the construction of sidepaths briefly flourished, first as scattered local organizations in upstate New York, the twin cities of Minneapolis–St. Paul, Denver, and a few other localities. Under the leadership of businessman Charles T. Raymond, the local Niagara County (New York) Sidepath League expanded briefly into a nationwide organization in 1899, even publishing some 78 issues of its magazine, *Sidepaths*. However, it, and the movement it represented, soon faded into obscurity, a victim of restrictive public finance laws that greatly limited mandatory pay-to-ride sidepath fees; the hostility of the L.A.W., which believed sidepaths posed a threat to its good-roads agenda; and the overall decline in adult cycling after 1900. Had the L.A.W. leadership realized that its declining fortunes after 1898 were not a transitory phenomenon and chosen to link forces with the sidepath movement at its start instead of fighting it for almost a decade, who is to say if the subsequent experience in America might have been somewhat closer to that in northern Europe?

But given the rapid decline and fall of the L.A.W. after 1898–1900, the main accomplishments of the good-roads movement were not realized until the after the L.A.W. was forced to take a back seat to others. This was to have an impact a century later, as the league had great difficulty regaining its influence, even as a residual cultural force, in the development or spread of cycling-related highway policies when the great 10-speed boom of 1969–73 brought renewed attention to adult bicycle use.

I posit that a more important force in molding the highly individualistic, libertarian nature of American highway policy can to be found in the influence during the early automobile era of the first traffic planners such as William Phelps Eno, of New York, and Miller McClintock, of Los Angeles, who stressed education, enforcement and the rationalization of traffic regulations over a total reliance on "hard" engineering solutions to the problems of traffic safety. Eno developed simple but comprehensive traffic ordinances for New York and other large cities. McClintock applied social science methodologies to answer questions that are today taken for granted, such as finding the best method for directing drivers to make left turns, sifting through a half-dozen or more different procedures. For example, the now-familiar "Chicago turn," in which left-turning cars line up alongside the centerline of the street, was not his preferred alternative. He favored the "Philadelphia turn," in which the cars followed an L-shaped path, waiting in a "hold box" on the far right corner of the intersection until an all-red phase let them complete the second leg of their turn. He didn't get his wish: the Chicago turn prevailed because it could be implemented with only a signal light, and didn't need a traffic officer.

Unlike the era's civil engineers, who assumed that many, if not most, drivers would act incompetently or even deliberately anti-socially, Eno and McClintock believed that drivers could be habitualized into uniform, acceptable traffic behaviors requiring a minimum of capital facilities that could be used to guide, not coerce, cooperative habits. Although their skill-focused, social-science approach would, by the late 1930s, be overtaken by the "hard" approach of the highway engineers, their work left a unique legacy, especially in the field of "roadside" traffic safety, generally defined by highway engineers as everything other than the prevention of roadway car-on-car crashes. Unlike Europe, there always remained a residual belief among American traffic planners that a balanced "3-E" approach (engineering, education, and enforcement) to traffic safety could do more for less money than the highway engineer's approach of "idiot-proofing" roadways with ever-expanding amounts of clear-space and Armco barriers.

Chapter 2 turns to Europe and begins to narrow the focus more tightly on the central theme of bicycle-transport development. It is divided into two parts: one for the continental countries, and the other for Britain. The discussion of continental developments relies heavily on the recent research by European historians referred to earlier, especially for the period before 1970. Generally, the presence or absence of bicycle facilities in most of these nations depended to a great extent on the presence or absence of an influential national cycle club (or a tourists' organization closely identified with cyclists' needs). Those nations that had such a powerful organization to lobby for bicycle-specific taxing and spending policies usually got them, and those that did not had to do without. After World War II, especially after 1970, I conclude that the economics and politics of oil prices and oil import dependency played a key role in shaping alternative transportation policy in many continental nations.

Britain was unique in that it resisted the creation of bicycle facilities, less out of a national consensus than from the extraordinary propaganda skills of a single individual, George Herbert Stancer. Stancer was a professional journalist and magazine editor who, in 1919, left the financially troubled commercial magazine *Cycling* to become editor of the *CTC Gazette*, the magazine of the British Cyclists' Touring Club. At the same time, he became secretary of the club, managing it on a day-to-day basis. He realized that with the financial backing of a nationwide cycle club, he would be freed from the normal constraints of a commercial magazine publisher to earn a profit from subscription and advertising revenues each year. With one vote of the executive board, virtually unlimited funds of the club could be put at his disposal to cover budget shortfalls.

The downside of this system was that it required the club to maintain a flush treasury. That meant keeping membership high. Stancer's secret was to use the *CTC Gazette* to generate endless, grinding, and ultimately irresolvable conflicts. After being stirred up to a fever pitch, the only action frustrated readers could take was to join the CTC and hope the leadership could do something about it. While such controversy may have cost advertising revenues, it generated membership fees, so it guaranteed an available pool of subsidy funds for the magazine. In essence, the club became an annex to the magazine. The club's 30-year long war against bicycle paths was just one of a number of these membership campaigns in disguise. When Stancer died in 1964, the bicycle path battle evaporated almost overnight.

Stancer would become the ideological figurehead for the most radical wing of the 1970s vehicular cyclists, a Trotsky-like figure of vaguely revolutionary mythology, ideal for the job because, being dead, he was no longer in a position to disavow anything attributed to him by his erstwhile acolytes.

The second third of the book, comprised of Chapters 3 and 4, returns to America to cover the history of bicycle planning before, during, and immediately after the great 10-speed bike boom of 1969–73. There was a surprising amount of bicycle advocacy in the United States preceding the great boom, although most it was recreationally oriented and geographically concentrated within a few scattered regions of the country, such as the upper Midwest and New England. Individuals such as Bob Cleckner and Keith Kingbay made endless roadtrips to speak to YMCA gatherings and Rotarian lunches as early as 1960, pushing for bikeways and improved municipal ordinances. Similarly, the American Youth Hostels (AYH) was the most active bicycle-related organization in the early and mid–1960s, although its focus was on cycle touring as a way of promoting its network of inexpensive overnight lodging facilities and organized tours.

The primary reason that bicycle planning initially focused on the development of specialized, off-road bicycle paths and trails was not ideology, but money. The first large source of funding available to support any type of state or municipal cycling projects was the Land and Water Conservation Fund (LWCF) of the Bureau of Outdoor Recreation. Approved in 1965, it accepted applications starting in 1969 for bicycle and pedestrian facilities, but was discontinued after 1975. During this relatively brief period it was a lucrative funding source by the standards of bicycle planning, but was, as its name suggests, intended for the development of outdoor recreational facilities, and applications for bicycle facilities that overly emphasized a transportation function were often turned down. It was against this background that the early voices of protest against the shunting of cyclists off to infrequent, inconvenient, and often substandard specialized facilities began to be heard: Fred DeLong in 1970; Jim Konski and Clifford Franz in 1972; and John Forester, Morgan Groves, Harold C. Munn, Bill Wilkinson and others in 1973.

Some of the earliest tangible successes during this early period were realized in the area of legislative modifications, specifically to the model Uniform Vehicle Code (UVC). However, in many instances, while the proposals were first drawn up as early as 1973 and 1974, actually getting them approved by the national organization that controlled the UVC and then incorporated by legislatures into the traffic code for each individual state sometimes required as much as 20 years, and in the case of one or two states, never did occur.

Chapter 4 covers the exceptions to the rule. These were the small, generally young and affluent towns such as Davis, Boulder, and Portland that aggressively developed networks of semi-detached and/or fully separated bikeways. Although some recent historians have claimed that these cities (especially Davis) formed the vanguard of American bicycle planning, I argue that their successes resulted from unique circumstances that could not be transferred to other locations, were of limited duration, and often were implemented for reasons that had little to do with their actual contribution to their long-term transportation needs.

In the case of Davis, the bikeway system did fulfill the mission set out for it, but the changing demographics and economics of the city and its associated university probably meant that the bicycle will play a much smaller role in its civic life than previously. In any event, such cities as Davis, Boulder, Madison, and Portland have not served as viable role models for the meshing of bicycles into the overall transportation systems of the vast majority of American cities, which have chosen to rely on a broad vehicular cycling paradigm, either through intent, or more commonly, through simple benign neglect.

The final third of the book, Chapters 5 through 7, form much of its central narrative. Having initially moved assertively in the direction of bikeways development through the LWCF and the aggressive pro-facilities policies in Davis and a few other locations, planners and highway engineers encountered increasing fracturing and disenchantment within their own ranks starting in 1972 with the initial model of simply adopting and adapting European-origin solutions. The stage appeared set for an inevitable, slow evolution away from the formula of "a bicycle plan is a bikeways plan," starting with the first major nationwide planning study, *Safety and Locational Criteria for Bikeways*, published by the Federal Highway Administration in three volumes between 1975 and 1976. However, there then occurred the type of unexpected, external, and titanic force for which some historians spend their entire lives searching, but in vain.

The Food and Drug Administration (FDA) had, since 1969, been given the authority to regulate children's toys and other products after a rash of negligently treated, highly inflammable baby pajamas were discovered. In May 1972, the FDA, following a two-year-long safety investigation, issued a proposed "banning order" setting standards for the design and construction of new bicycles. Four days later, the FDA transferred authority for the promulgation of these rules over to a new agency that Congress had created, the Consumer Product Safety Commission (CPSC). Because of this rapid chain of events, nobody, not even the FDA and CPSC lawyers themselves, were entirely sure if the proposed new rules applied to all bicycles, or just bicycles intended for use by children. Poorly (and apparently hurriedly) drawn up, a critical reading of the initial draft of the new rules could be interpreted to mean that some important features of imported high-performance 10-speeds would have to be modified or eliminated.

Club cyclists, who up to this point had been largely indifferent to most government activities, exhibited behavior that can only be described as mass panic. Taking advantage of this, the most strident of the anti-bikeways cycling groups, heretofore marginalized, cleverly and successfully tied the two issues together to project their radical libertarian views into the mainstream. Although the CPSC rules were revised within a few months to the point where both *Bike World* magazine's Paul Hill (a lawyer) and *Bicycling* magazine's Fred DeLong (an engineer) agreed that the typical imported racing bicycle would comply if ten easily removable reflectors costing about a dollar were added, the dire threats that only "toy bikes" would survive the CPSC's efforts continued to reverberate into the late 1970s.

In less than two years, the norm for club cyclists became a vehement rejection of any type of government involvement in cycling except for some relatively weak measures that would discourage bicycle use by those with "inadequate" skill and strength, or those using "dangerous" (i.e., inexpensive) equipment. Mostly, these demands met with little enthusiasm from government transportation officials who did not want to divert their time, attention or money to alternative transportation efforts. Officials translated the club cyclists' calls into either a policy of benign neglect (by ignoring their demand to cull out "bad" bicyclists and, in the end, doing nothing) or hostility (by implementing their demands, but with equal fervor against both low-skill and club cyclists alike).

Faced with hostility and suspicion from their erstwhile constituents, government planners retreated to the development of educational programs for children and adults. This culminated in the "BikeEd '77" conference in Washington, D.C., in May 1977. While it did not achieve its stated goal of "hammering out ... a national strategy for bicycle education in the United States," to match that of Britain's National Cycle Proficiency Scheme, founded in 1947 (and today still going under the name "Bikeability"), it did have an immediate, if somewhat diffuse, impact on bicycle education programs.

Since then, there have been significant gains in the effectiveness and sophistication of both youth and adult education programs, but their penetration into the ranks of cyclists, especially adults, remains spotty. More recently, the private sector has moved into this area through the development and implementation of their own education programs, either under contract to a government agency, or less frequently, as a for-profit, fee-driven entrepreneurial venture. Self-education, in the form of books, or book/video or book/online combinations, has also grown greatly.

The era that opened with the start of the great 10-speed bike boom in 1969–70 began to close with the inauguration of the Reagan administration in early 1981 and the release of the *Guide to the Development of Bicycle Facilities* by the American Association of State Highway and Transportation Officials (AASHTO) a couple of months later. It reflected the victory of the vehicular cycling advocates: 31 pages long, only four of its pages were devoted to on-road facilities. The bulk was given over to off-road facilities, mostly trails. "Bicycles can be expected to ride on almost all roadways," it noted, then suggested that when funds were limited, secure bicycle parking was probably a more cost-effective alternative than trails or bike lanes. The *Guide*'s status quo presumption proved popular with state highway agencies and local public works departments. As urban planner James Staccy put it at a 1978 bicycle conference, "Given an equal choice between spending money on a facilities project or not, an official's decision is usually pretty easy to predict."[16]

Two little-recognized programs have greatly contributed to the professionalization and mainstreaming of alternative modes planning and engineering in the United States. The first is what I have coined America's "stealth bikeway program": the system of sidewalk curb cuts and widenings installed to accommodate wheelchairs and other mobility-impaired users first mandated in 1973 under section 503 of the Rehabilitation Act, and greatly augmented by the 1979 Americans with Disabilities Act (ADA). Although no hard-and-fast figures have been calculated, it is estimated that approximately $350 *billion* have been spent on sidewalk upgrades under section 503 and the ADA, as compared to $71.8 *million* spent on bicycle trails between 1969 and 1975 through the federal Land and Water Conservation Fund and $9 billion spent on bicycle and pedestrian projects of all types between 1992 and 2012 through the Transportation Enhancements program of the Federal Highway Administration.[17]

A second unexpected success has been that of bikes-on-bus (BoB) programs. As late as 1992, a federal study by one of the nation's leading experts on bike-transit intermodalism recommended that federal and state governments focus on bicycle parking instead of BoB-style carry-on services, because BoB would have only limited utility and would probably be met with such strong resistance from route schedulers, drivers, and mechanics that it would be difficult to implement at the typical municipal transit agency.[18]

Some 20 years later, over 400 transit services are fully or mostly equipped with relatively inexpensive front-mounted, fold-up, two- or three-bike racks available from a number of commercial suppliers. What happened? Two things. First, the technologically thorny problem of coming up with a good, cheap, easily removable rack was initially solved by imaginative transit agency mechanics, then brought to perfection by private firms who invested heavily in final development and testing. This was followed by aggressive marketing targeted at transit agency managements and unions. Second, the service proved to be a money maker: in a medium- to large-sized, low-density sunbelt city. BoB can improve off-peak farebox income by up to 20 percent on some low return peripheral routes.[19]

Bikes-on-bus clients are transit's bread and butter: blue-collar, auto-less males under 35 making their daily commute. Because these are largely involuntary, temporary cyclists who hope to soon acquire an automobile, they are not seen as a desirable target constituency by bicycle planners or advocates, and thus the implementation of BoB service has historically been driven by transit agencies without much input from cyclists.

Chapter 7 discusses the "unintended consequences" of America's vehicular cycling paradigm. In contrast to the successes of the section 503/ADA curb cut program and BoB, an unexpected failure has been the spectacular, and surprisingly consistent, inability of the bicycling community to put together an inclusive, nationwide organizational structure. The United States has never been able to assemble, let alone maintain, something similar to the Dutch ANWB, the German RadFahrer-Bund, or even the British CTC. The most successful of the American organizations, the League of American Bicyclists, the descendent of the old League of American Wheelmen, has survived by turning away from its membership club-activity model towards a more narrowly-defined political advocacy structure more akin to Greenpeace or the World Wildlife Federation. Its funding is roughly balanced into thirds, divided between memberships (individual, club, corporate, municipal); industry support; and project grant funding, increasingly through foundations focused on health, not transportation, such as the Robert Wood Johnson Foundation.

Probably less unexpected, given the vacuum left by almost 40 years of governmental benign neglect, has been the entrepreneurial commercialization of the vehicular cycling movement. How-to-ride-well textbooks started with John Forester's self-published *Effective Cycling* in 1975. Rodale Press brought out John S. Allen's *The Complete Book of Bicycle Commuting* in 1981. It is probably the best of the cycling texts, and with 20,000 printed, it is certainly the most successful to date. In spite of this, Rodale declined to issue a second edition, so Allen later bought back the rights, and in cooperation with a small publisher in Massachusetts, brought out a series of booklets, *Bicycling Street Smarts*, that condensed the earlier material. The unique thing about *Street Smarts* is that it has been sold to several state bicycle organizations in versions customized to the laws of their state. They then use it to teach their own structured, hands-on cycling courses.

Whether by coincidence or by imitation, *Street Smarts* has kicked off something of a cottage industry in developing and selling vehicular-cycling skills courses, either as audio-visual material, or as live, on-site courses. The British started to develop their National Cycle Proficiency Scheme in the 1930s, and began to implement it after World War II. The League of American Wheelmen started out with Forester's 33-hour Effective Cycling course, but when they shortened it and divided it into modules so it could be taught on weekends, Forester objected, and canceled their license. The league had little trouble developing their own version, which has been revised more-or-less continually over the years. The Royal Society for the Prevention of Accidents, the sponsor of the British National Cycle Proficiency Scheme, started offering a North American (i.e., keep right, not keep left) version of their program called Cyclecraft.

Compared to pedestrian safety and safe-routes-to-school programs, which are receiving millions of dollars in university research and development funds from health and safety foundations to, in the words of one administrator, help "develop, teach, measure, evaluate, re-develop, again and again and again," bicycle education is still largely the product of dedicated amateurs and is anecdotally oriented, the equivalent of going out on club rides with the proverbial "men who have ridden hard miles for many years."

The conclusion offers, in outline format, a summary of the lessons learned from the crucial "long two decades" between 1969, when the great 10-speed bike boom hit, and 1991, when AASHTO, the American Association of State Highway and Transportation Officials, made vehicular cycling the "official" policy of state highway departments by formalizing it into the second edition of its *Guide to the Development of New Bicycle Facilities*. The first edition, issued in 1982, had been almost devoid of standards covering bike lanes and other on-road bicycle facilities. At the time, it was explained that this was because these standards were too embryonic to permit codification in the publication of such an august body as AASHTO. But in the 1991 second edition the AASHTO editors flatly admitted that the section covering on-road facilities had been barely expanded because they were considered less practical and less desirable than emphasizing the use of the roadway itself by cyclists.

Times have changed. The 2012 edition of the AASHTO *Guide to the Development of Bicycle Facilities* was over 200 pages long, but the process of developing it had taken more than seven years, and neither the urban-oriented advocates of aggressive bicycle facilities development programs nor the more conservative, suburban/rural highway-based planners and engineers who had been satisfied with the 1991 and 1999 editions were entirely happy with the new product.[20]

By 2010, a competing organization, the National Association of City Transportation Officials (NACTO), had been established by several big-city public works directors as an alternative to what they saw as the hidebound and rural-highway oriented AASHTO. NACTO issued its own bicycle facility standards in 2011, which were far more extensive and liberal than the AASHTO standards, and planned to issue a volume of standards for "liveable" streets in 2013. In the NACTO livable street standards, the vehicular level of service standards would be subordinated to other urban quality-of-life priorities. The Federal Highway Administration shortly thereafter announced that they would no longer leave the promulgation of street and highway standards up to private organizations, but would start performing that function itself. The entire idea of a "professionals' consensus" about transportation standards had collapsed. To a small degree, a very small degree to be sure but a very definite one, the first cracks had appeared back in 1983 with one document, less than 40 pages long, entitled *Guide to the Development of Bicycle Facilities.*

* * *

It is an old aphorism, especially popular in academic circles, that the bitterness of any given dispute is inversely proportional to the actual value of the stakes involved. Never will you find a more truculent example than in American bicycle planning. Expressing approval or skepticism of some viewpoint or another, or even questioning a relatively minor ideological quibble or a detail of riding technique is enough to quite literally get one branded as suffering from a diagnosable mental illness.[21] In such a histrionic environment, it is a wonder that anyone was willing to even speak with me, let alone grant an interview or provide copies of historical documents.

However, a surprising number of brave souls were willing to do so, although in many cases my interviewee or correspondent was aware that I was skeptical of at least some of the viewpoints they held. Therefore, let me clearly state that *the appearance of an individual in this book, regardless of whether that person is cited in a document, quoted in an interview, or listed as a source of information, does not indicate that he or she agrees with what I have written.* The views contained herein are not their views. They are mine. Similarly, any errors or omissions are also mine alone.

To those providing documentation and other information, John S. Allen of Waltham, Massachusetts, must be singled out. He has amassed a considerable body of information on the history of the League of American Bicyclists (formerly the League of American Wheelmen). A former member of the league's board, he has collected much of this information because he has grown critical of the league's policy direction. While I am not unsympathetic to Mr. Allen's position, my previous work on the history of the American bicycle industry has led me to the conclusion that while it is not necessarily wrong, it is unrealistic and utopian. No nationwide bicycle club can ever succeed financially if it is estranged from the bicycle industry, and the bicycle industry will always be focused on expanding its potential consumer base. Moreover, a nationwide cycling organization cannot expect to be different from tennis, golf, or softball. Cycling will never be the mechanical equivalent of dressage, a self-consciously elite sport dedicated to maintaining its purity and sense of tradition.

Nevertheless, I thank John for recognizing that he is the custodian of records and documents belonging to others, and that he holds a moral, if not legal, duty to make them available to League of American Bicyclist members such as myself. Allen has published his "Biklg1965" series of documents and a second series of non-league documents related to the history of bikeways development in Davis, including the seminar paper presented by Robert Sommer and Dale Lott at Northwestern University Conference on Environmental Behavior in 1974.

David Henderson of the Miami Urban Area Metropolitan Planning Organization provided several valuable 1970s reports from the Federal Highway Administration, the National Highway Traffic Safety Administration, and the Florida Department of Transportation that were in the MPO's archives.

Many individuals were kind enough to grant me interviews, either in-person or by telephone: Tim Blumental, Dan Burden, the late Norman Clarke, Geoffrey Forester, the late Morgan Groves, Donna Lott, Ted Noguchi, Bob Sommer, Jay Townley, Dorris Taylor and Bill Wilkinson. Morgan Groves and Phyllis Harmon were interviewed by John S. Allen; Mr. Allen provided me with a transcript of the Groves interview with annotations added by former League of American Bicyclists boardmember William Hoffman, and he has posted the Phyllis Harmon interviews online as audio files.

John S. Allen, Zack Furness, James Green, P.E., Ross Petty, Jay Townley, John Williams and several others who wished to remain anonymous provided helpful information and corrections via letters and email. Manuel Stoffers invited me to participate at a panel session on the socio-political aspects of bicycle infrastructure at the annual meeting of the International Society for the History of Transport, Traffic, and Mobility (T2M) in Madrid in November 2012, at which time I was able to discuss many aspects of European cycle history with established authors including Manuel himself, Hans Buiter, Peter Cox, Anne Katrin Ebert, Martin Emanuel, Ruth Oldenziel. Since 1998, I have been able to attend seven of the annual International Cycling History Conferences, and several of the papers I have presented there have touched on various topics relating to various parts of this book.

Justin Marks, editor-in-chief of the *Transportation Law Review* at the Sturm College of Law at the University of Denver helped shape into final form my law review article, "The Great Schism: Federal Bicycle Safety Regulation and Unraveling of American Bicycle Planning" that appeared in the Summer 2010 issue of *TLJ*. Portions of that article appear in Chapter 5 of this book. In 2011, James Green, P.E., posted a rough, 40-page expansion of the *TLJ* article on his website, bicyclercconstruction.com. It elicited much valuable discussion and proved to be the germinal source of what would eventually grow and develop, nine generations later, into this book. Finally, many thanks to the library periodical departments of the University of Kansas and the University of Florida for their assistance in facilitating access to bicycle consumer and industry magazines of the 1970s and 1980s. Similarly, I am grateful for the help of the Alvin Sherman (main) and law libraries at Nova Southeastern University in Fort Lauderdale for giving me access to online and electronic databases and for helping track down hard-to-find bicycle-related magazine articles from several short-lived bicycle magazines of the early 1970s.

Abbreviations

AASHO—American Association of State Highway Officials. See AASHTO.

AASHTO—American Association of State Highway and Transportation Officials. Until the early 1970s, named the American Association of State Highway Officials (AASHO). Develops design and construction standards for roads, bicycle facilities and other transport infrastructure.

ABLA—Amateur Bicycle League of America. After 1976, the United States Cycling Federation (USCF), later Cycling USA. The sanctioning body for bicycle racing in the United States.

ADA—Americans with Disabilities Act.

ADAAG—*Americans with Disabilities Act Accessibility Guidelines* (1994–99). Successor document to the *Uniform Federal Accessibility Guidelines* (UFAG).

ANSI—American National Standards Institute. A non-profit organization that develops and publishes standards for a wide variety of processes and products, including bicycles. It is the North American affiliate of the International Standards Organization (ISO). See ISO.

ANWB—Nederlandsche Algemee Wielrijers Bond (Netherlands Tourists and Cyclists' Club.) Largest Dutch bicycle club.

ASCE—American Society of Civil Engineers. Parent organization of the Metropolitan Association of Urban Designers and Environmental Planners (MAUDEP), active between 1972 and about 1980. See MAUDEP.

BIA—Bicycle Institute of America. Before 1984, the promotional and public relations organization representing the American bicycle industry. Closely related to the industry's lobbying group, the Bicycle Manufacturers' Association (BMA). See BMA.

BMA—Bicycle Manufacturers' Association. Until 1984, represented the American industry on trade matters such as tariffs, product liability laws, etc.

BMA/6—*Safety Standards for Regular Bicycles*. A set of voluntary industry design and manufacturing standards issued by the BMA in 1972.

BoB *or* BOB—Bikes-on-Bus service. Originally offered in several different forms, BoB technology is now almost universally in the form of a multi-bicycle rack mounted under a bus's front windshield that folds when not in use.

BSTR—Bureau for Street Traffic Research. Research Institute established by Miller McClintock in 1925 at UCLA. Later moved to Harvard, then Yale.

CABO—California Association of Bicycling Organizations. A federation of bicycle clubs and other cycling organizations formed in 1972, active with the CalTrans bicycle advisory committee.

CalTrans—California Department of Transportation.

CBTP—Comprehensive Bicycle Transportation Program. A central feature of the seminal 1980 U.S. Dept. of Transportation document *Bicycle Planning for Energy Conservation*.

CF—Cykelfrämjandet (Society for the Promotion of Cycling). Swedish national cycle promotion and safety organization from about 1930 to about 1970. See KFC.

CPSC—Consumer Product Safety Commission. This agency, established in 1973, promulgated a set of bicycle product safety standards between 1973 and 1975 that had initially been written by the Food and Drug Administration (FDA). See FDA.

CPTSA—Child Protection and Toy Safety Act Amendments of 1969. Gave the Food and Drug Administration authority to regulate toys and other children's products. See FDA.

CTC—Cyclists' Touring Club. The largest cyclists' organization in the United Kingdom during the twentieth century.

DORA—Defence of the Realm Act. British legislation during World War I requiring cyclists to use taillights at night.

DOT—United States Department of Transportation. Also known as USDOT. Created in 1967.

EPA—Environmental Protection Agency.

FDA—Food and Drug Administration. This agency was given the authority to regulate toys and children's products, including bicycles, in 1969 by the CPTSA in response to a rash of highly flammable baby pajamas. All responsibility over products other than foods and drugs transferred to Consumer Product Safety Commission (CPSC) in May 1973.

FHSA—Federal Hazardous Substances Act. The FDA's original enabling legislation.

FHWA—Federal Highway Administration. A division of the federal Department of Transportation.

GLC—Greater London Council. A regional planning authority for the London urban area. Eliminated by the Thacher administration about 1992.

ICHC—International Cycling History Conference. A series of annual conferences focusing on the technical and social aspects of bicycle history. Originally loosely affiliated with the British Veteran Cycle Club, it now has an independent, international steering committee.

ISO—International Standards Organization. A non-profit organization that develops and publishes standards for a wide variety of processes and products. ISO formed a technical committee, TC-149, in 1973 to develop standards for bicycles and bicycle components. The American National Standards Institute (ANSI) is the standing American representative to ISO. See ANSI.

ITTE—Institute of Transportation and Traffic Engineering. A research institute located at the University of California's Berkeley and Los Angeles campuses.

ISTEA—Intermodal Surface Transportation Efficiency Act [of 1991]. An omnibus six-year act governing federal highway policy, procedure and funding. Followed by TEA-21 in 1997.

KFC—Kommitten för Svensk Cykelpropagananda (Committee for Swedish Cycle Promotion). Swedish national cycle promotion organization, 1930s–1950s.

L.A.B.—League of American Bicyclists. See L.A.W.

L.A.W.—League of American Wheelmen. A nationwide organization for bicycle enthusiasts, founded in 1880, but with several dormant periods. Active continually from early 1960s to present. Changed name to gender-neutral League of American Bicyclists (L.A.B.) in 1994.

LWCF—Land and Water Conservation Fund. Administered by the Bureau of Outdoor Recreation of Department of the Dept. of the Interior, it was the primary source of federal funds for bikeways between 1965 and 1975.

MAUDEP—Metropolitan Association of Urban Designers and Environmental Planners. Associated with the American Society of Civil Engineers (ASCE), this group sponsored a highly influential series of annual conferences on bicycle and pedestrian planning and engineering between 1972 and 1979.

MTC—Model Traffic Code. See NCUTLO.

MTO—Model Traffic Ordinance. A recommended set of local traffic laws, intended to parallel the state laws in the Uniform Vehicle Code and maintained by the same organization. See UVC and NCUTLO.

MUTCD—*Manual of Uniform Traffic Control Devices*. It is the standards book for roadway markings, signage, and traffic signals. It is maintained and published by a private, quasi-public organization, the National Committee on Uniform Traffic Control Devices (NCUTCD). See NCUTCD.

NACT—National Association of Cycle Trades. Britain's coordinating counsel for bicycle makers, bicycle parts makers, and allied trades.

NACTO—National Association of City Transportation Officials. Formed in 1995 by several large-city public works and transportation directors as an alternative to AASHTO, which was perceived as having a rural/suburban highway bias, NACTO has issued a set of bikeway standards in 2011 and plans to issue roadway standards for urban streets different from those in the AASHTO *Greenbook*.

NCC—National Committee on Cycling. Lobbying and policy coordination board for Britain's cycle trades, consumer groups, and national clubs.

NCUTCD—National Committee on Uniform Traffic Control Devices. The quasi-public organization that oversees the development and publication of the Manual of Uniform Traffic Control Devices (MUTCD). See MUTCD.

NCUTLO—National Committee on Uniform Traffic Laws and Ordinances. This non-profit organization maintained and published the statewide Uniform Vehicle Code and local Model Traffic Code. It suspended operations about 2009. See UVC and MTC.

NHTSA—National Highway Traffic Safety Administration. A division of the federal Department of Transportation.

OPEC—Organization of Petroleum Exporting Countries.

RSVO—Reichs-Strassen-Verkehrs-Ordnung. (Reichs Association for Bicycle Path Construction) Nazi-era quasi-governmental organization that provided matching funding to local governments.

STUFA—Study Group for Motorcar Road Construction. A German, non-profit, non-governmental organization, it disseminated bikeway standards in the 1920s.

TC-149—Technical Committee 149 (Bicycles) of the International Standards Organization (ISO). See ISO.

TE—Transportation Enhancements [Program]. A subdivision of the federal highway trust fund that supports nontraditional highway-related projects. It accounts for about 5 percent of highway construction funds. About 80 percent of TE funds are used for bicycle, pedestrian, and streetscaping projects.

TRB—Transportation Research Board. A private, non-profit organization affiliated with the National Academy of Sciences. A research organization, the TRB does not issue engineering or legislative standards, but does sponsor work that supports their development and improvement.

UBDC—Urban Bikeway Design Competition, *also* Urban Bikeway Design Collective. The Collective was the organizer of two bicycle plan competitions in 1973 and 1974, with compiled excerpts from the competition winners published with sponsorship from the Federal Highway Administration. The Collective evolved into a for-profit consultancy, the Urban Scientific and Educational Corporation (USER) about 1978. See USER.

UFAG—*Uniform Federal Accessibility Guidelines*. A set of accessibility guidelines for federal facilities published in response to section 504 of the Rehabilitation Act of 1973. Largely replaced by later ADA mandates, especially the *Americans with Disabilities Accessibilities Guidelines* (ADAAG). See ADAAG.

USER—Urban Scientific and Educational Corporation. A for-profit consulting firm formed by Lyle Brecht and Vince Darago in 1978. See UBDC.

UVC—Uniform Vehicle Code. A model statewide traffic code developed and maintained (until 2009) by the National Committee on Uniform Traffic Laws and Ordinances (NCUTLO). Its work will probably be taken over by the Federal Highway Administration. See NCUTLO.

ZfR—Zentralstelle für Radwege (Central Office for Bike Paths). Lead federal German agency coordinating bicycle facilities construction. Replaced by RSVO. See RSVO.

Chapter 1

Historical Antecedents: American Traffic Planning, 1870–1945

In Europe, the technological evolution of the bicycle flowed continuously from the foot-powered Draisine, through the front-wheel driven velocipede, to the high-wheeled ordinary to, in 1885, the chain-driven safety bicycle. But in the United States, the early history of the bicycle was broken into two distinct phases. The first was a brief, intense velocipede boom in 1868 and 1869, followed by a decade of commercial, technical and social abandonment. By the time the bicycle was reintroduced from England in 1877 in the form of the high-wheeled ordinary, few Americans remembered its predecessor, except as a dim memory. This discontinuity had a significant impact on its legal and social status, and on the standing of the clubs and advocacy groups formed to fight for cyclists' rights.

The early ordinaries and the first cyclists were overwhelmingly young, affluent and male. Although the earliest domestic bicycle, the Hartford-built "Columbia," at $90 was far less than the $120 of the typical imported English touring cycle, its price was still nearly three months' wages for the skilled machinists who built them. When the Boston Bicycle Club formed in February 1878, its 25 founding members were comprised of six merchants, four salesmen, four college students, three lawyers, three clerks, two corporate officers, an architect, a litterateur and a physician.[1] There was not a single workingman among the group. Organized upon military lines, the early bicycle clubs offered their members a chance to escape their typically sedentary lives and participate in an activity that recalled the rigors and romance of the recent Civil War with only a hint of its lethal potential.

A decade before the ordinary appeared, many towns and cities had reacted to the appearance of its predecessor, the velocipede, with restrictions and outright bans. These were not entirely unjustified. Cycling journalist Karl Kron (a pseudonym of New York City librarian Lyman H. Bagg), one of the few riders to participate in both the velocipede boom and the later high-wheeled era, recalled that the old velocipede was poorly suited for riding in the roadway, so most of his velocipede riding had been in the form of "running down the walks," or "taking a spin on the sidewalks," which were typically paved and, of course, free of horse manure. This had made velocipede riders decidedly unpopular with the citizenry, who demanded that they be kept off the walkways and out of the paths within public parks. When the ordinary made its appearance, the obvious wealth and regal bearing of its riders didn't help matters, and the old velocipede laws were quickly dusted off and applied to high-wheelers. In some cases they were even stretched to include the entire roadway, especially in parks or on bridges. In addition, the bicycle's novelty made its status as property unclear, making the prosecution of bicycle thieves difficult.[2]

Another form of abuse faced by the early cyclists was harassment and assault from teamsters and footmen who claimed that the sight and sound of bicycles frightened their horses. While this may have been true in isolated rural areas, urban horses were acclimatized to the noise and congestion of city street life. Urban clashes were more frequently real or perceived class conflicts. Teamsters were generally working-class immigrants, often Irish, Italian or Slav. Cyclists, on the other hand, were native-born, educated whites, and expected to be deferred to by their social inferiors in traffic as they were in everyday life. A successful teamster was not a timid man: road, loading dock and parking spaces were all limited, and strong vocal chords and quick fists were often the difference between a quick stop at the loading dock or a long and exhausting portage down the street.

Teamsters saw cyclists as effete dandies trying to dance through a street fight they didn't understand and from which they couldn't protect themselves. Increasingly through the 1880s, wealthy bicycle manufactures, such as Albert A. Pope of Boston and Hartford or Albert H. Overman of Chicopee Falls, Massachusetts, had to resort to paying for lawyers to defend wheelmen against bicycle bans or trumped-up citations, or to bring suit against abusive teamsters or their employers.[3]

Partially to help organize these increasingly numerous legal actions, representatives from thirty-one local clubs gathered at a cyclists' meet in Newport, Rhode Island, in May 1880, to form a new national organization, the League of American Wheelmen. The league deliberately held one of its early meets in New York in May 1883. The city had, since 1879, banned bicycles from Central Park and Riverside Drive. The local clubs applied for a permit to allow a parade of wheelmen in the park. It was quickly granted. A month after the meet, the park commissioners voted to allow L.A.W. members in Central Park between midnight and 9 a.m., and on Riverside Drive except between 3 and 7 p.m. Members were to be identified through a lapel pin, although wearing a club uniform proved to be the usual means. For all practical purposes, Riverside Drive restrictions ended, and it turned out to be the city's most popular cycling ground for the next quarter-century.[4]

After three years of limited Central Park admittance, the cyclists decided to take on all restrictions. One aldermanic candidate, Henry R. Beekman, said he would support equality between bicycling and equestrian rules if the local club would openly support his candidacy. They did, and Beekman won by ten thousand votes. He carried out his promise, but was stymied by city regulations that limited the powers of the park board. In the time-honored tradition of New York reformers whose efforts are blocked by the city's Byzantine bureaucracy, the cyclists tried an end run through the state capitol in Albany. The wheelmen proposed a law that defined a bicycle as a carriage and prohibited local regulations specific to cycles. It passed and went to Governor David Hill for his signature. City mayor Abram Hewitt demanded that Hill veto it.

Hewitt had been elected through the graces of a fragile coalition of the city's business elite and Tammany Hall, both terrified of the leading candidate, neo-socialist Henry George. However, Hewett, son-in-law of millionaire Peter Cooper, had proven both abrasive and incompetent. Almost immediately upon his election, he had alienated Tammany Hall, the business elite, the state legislature and the governor all at the same time. The L.A.W. told Hill it would help him in the next election and (more importantly) wouldn't help Hewitt, and the Governor whisked the new law off his desk. In 1886 the roads of Central Park were at last fully opened to cyclists.

But soon the league's main focus started shifting from legal rights to the promotion of better roads, for which it has since become legendary. But the reasons behind this involvement are neither as simple nor as straightforward as they have been traditionally portrayed.[5] First some background. The league was essentially a federation of clubs, comprised of local organizations which maintained their own charters, uniforms, and headquarters. In its early years, the state divisions were its most important units. Each was semi-autonomous, headed by a chief consul who oversaw a governing assembly of districts and local consuls. The local consuls were typically local club officers who themselves wielded considerable influence over state and national affairs. At the national level, the president and two vice-presidents comprised an executive committee, with ultimate authority vested in a National Board of Officers made up of representatives from among the state consuls, national officers and members of the standing committees.[6]

The two most powerful of the standing committees were the Committee of Rights and Privileges, which oversaw legal affairs, and the Racing Committee, formed in 1882. The issue of racing had always been particularly contentious. At first, the league tried to follow a strict policy of amateurism, mirroring the English tradition. As a practical matter, this was virtually impossible to enforce because the rules contained an exception clause allowing employees of bicycle firms to retain their amateur status. This made sense in the very early days of the industry, when almost anyone who was involved in cycling had some kind of job at an agency, in a factory, or with a cycling magazine. Factory foremen and clerks were often sent out to do riding demonstrations and informal races in small towns during the summer, when shop work was slow. But by the late 1880s, the "exhibition" exception was being openly flouted, with "shop hands" coming into the factory a couple of hours in the afternoon to sweep floors after a long morning out training on the road.[7]

Asked about a $200 bookkeeping entry for "racingmen," one company officer responded, "I guess a certain number of these young men who worked in the bicycle department were also racing men ... there were some pretty prominent riders who worked in the department." In addition to their regular wages, these "salesmen" demanded premiums for winning races and extra travel stipends. "We always objected to these expenses that were not really traveling expenses," explained a manager, "but our riders were never satisfied unless they were allowed ... they would not race, as a general thing [or] they might enter a race and not try to win."[8]

At the 1885 L.A.W convention, the chairman of the Racing Committee, Abbott Bassett, proposed that the word "amateur" be removed as a condition of league membership. His suggestion was received with immediate rejection and a resolution demanding that the Racing Committee initiate an investigation into the abuse of exceptions to the league's strict "no financial gain" amateurship policy. It uncovered evidence that virtually every prominent American racer was receiving some form of sponsorship support. The following February, the committee issued its report and a list of offending racers, specifically recommending that 28 be expelled, and several more be temporarily suspended.

In May, the promoters of the three biggest summer meets got together in Boston to found the American Cyclists' Union, a breakaway group organized for the purpose of sanctioning racing under international standards, which permitted amateurs to receive limited sponsorship and prize money. Karl Kron, in a magazine column, explained to his readers that winning a race

> has advertising value to the maker of the cycle upon which it is won. This fact renders extremely difficult the maintenance of any rule which tries to class in separate social grades the racers for glory and the racers for gain; and the attempts to maintain it cause a great deal of bitterness and acrimony to be displayed in public, and an endless

amount of hypocrisy, humbug, shilly-shally, sophistry, treachery, deceit, and downright lying to prevail in private.[9]

After 1886, amateurs were required to submit affidavits attesting to their status, although even the chairman of the LAW Racing Committee admitted that riders could "produce unlimited strange and mighty oaths" attesting to the fact that the rider "never, no never, did, could, would, had, or might receive one penny from any person or persons, directly or indirectly, as a result of his riding."[10]

This never-ending racing imbroglio was really just a manifestation of much deeper forces that were starting to pull the league apart. The first was the growing imbalance between its sectional interests. Originally, it was almost entirely a northeastern organization. In 1880, the year of its founding, 60 percent of the membership came from just two states, New York and Massachusetts, but at its peak in 1897, only 38 percent came from those states, with the Midwest (mainly Ohio and Illinois) contributing the largest proportion of any region. With much of the league's administrative structure decentralized into state divisions, it was easy for national issues, such as racing, to be turned into sectional disputes, and the editor of the Illinois division's magazine accused the Racing Committee of making the amateurism debate "a sectional fight between the East and the West."[11]

The second divisive force was the proletarianization of bicycling. As new wheel prices fell and a market for second-hand machines developed, clerks and tradesmen, then common laborers, took up cycling. Some L.A.W. members believed that this democratization was chasing away the gentile classes who had established the sport. Canadian bicycle historian Glen Norcliffe has documented the declining social prestige of the Montreal Bicycle Club between 1885 and 1895 by tracing the gradual conversion of the names on its annual group portrait from Anglophone to Francophone.[12]

In many cases, the new working-class cyclists were unable or unwilling to afford the trappings of the original elite clubs. By 1890, both the Boston and Massachusetts Bicycle Clubs, the first and second oldest in America, were bankrupt. About 1880, the Massachusetts club had purchased a lot on Newbury Street in the heart of the Back Bay and erected a three-story townhouse as a clubhouse. In 1889 it was sold to the Boston Art Club to avoid foreclosure.[13] In other cases, long-standing racial and ethnic animosities between different groups of working-class cyclists themselves created stress as clubs expanded and broadened.

As the price of bicycles fell dramatically after the mid–1890s, manufacturers expanded their network of agencies from exclusive company branch houses on downtown main streets to include neighborhood hardware stores and even the corner grocery. One large Chicago manufacturer of good, no-frills bicycles noticed a steady fall in sales in the deep south, bucking the trend in the Midwest and Great Plains states. They sent one of their managers to investigate. "It sounds odd to say it," reported the man upon his return, "[but] the Negro has killed the bicycle business in the south." Banned from the downtown bicycle and sporting goods stores, blacks could now buy them from a familiar retailer within their own neighborhoods on a cash-and-carry basis. Previously, their only option had been to give a deposit to a traveling drummer who might or might not deliver. But, discovered the Chicago man, "As soon as the Negro took to sporting a wheel, just that soon did the fad cease among the southern whites.... In New Orleans, in Birmingham and Nashville the business began to drop off perceptively."[14] Working class white southern cyclists were so bigoted that they wouldn't even ride in the same roadways as their black counterparts.

In the face of such divisive forces, the league needed a unifying issue. The good-roads campaign fit the bill perfectly. It was an issue that almost every cyclist could agree on, but was compatible with a decentralized power structure in which each state division could define its own particular needs. In Michigan, for example, wheelman Louis Bates had been lobbying since 1881 for a revised state law that would allow townships to collect at least part of their road taxes in cash instead of just two day's labor a year (one if the farmer brought a team of horses and a plow). In New York, cycle importer George Bidwell sought funds to permit his L.A.W. state counsel to prosecute negligent or corrupt county road supervisors.[15]

The good-roads movement also attracted new blood to the L.A.W. These new members were unencumbered with the emotional baggage of the league's past rivalries, largely because they weren't really all that interested in cycling. Horatio S. "By Gum" Earle was appointed chairman of the Michigan division's good-roads committee, then ran for, and was elected, its chief counsul a year later, despite the fact that he had never ridden a bicycle. Instead, he was a sales executive for an agricultural implement maker that also manufactured road-making equipment. When he ran for election as Michigan's chief consul, Earle proposed to eliminate the state racing committee entirely and replace it with a good-roads body. His campaign platform was that "there is no more sense in the L.A.W. running bicycle races than the poultry association staging cock fights or the dairy association, bull fights."[16] After he won, the division withdrew entirely from racing.

Sterling Elliott, the league's president in the mid–1890s, asserted that the L.A.W. wasn't even a bicycle club any more: "The League of American Wheelmen is fast getting to be a political party whose demands are equal rights and road improvement, and whose platform is made of broken rock and gravel."

However, many thought this was going too far, too fast: "There seems to be a desire on the part of some to drag the league into politics," cautioned the *Cincinnati Commercial Gazette,* "this is a mistake." Even John Wells, editor of *American Athlete*, warned that "though the membership is large and influential, the league would be but a small factor in the political working out of the end to be gained."[17]

At its national convention in June, 1888 the league voted to create a National Committee for Highway Improvement. At first, the committee simply enhanced the work that divisions in Massachusetts, New York, Michigan, New Jersey, and local clubs in Boston, Philadelphia and New York City were already doing. But in 1889, the Executive Committee drafted uniform legislation that it tried to push through in nine states calling for the creation of a state highway commission, optional cash taxation in rural areas, and the development of highway surveys and plans. It was crushed in every state. "The farmers must bear the expense while bicyclists and pleasure-riding citizens will reap the larger benefits," complained the Michigan Grange. "Give the farmer a fair price for his product and he will get to market all right without the aid of fancy roads and theoretical road makers," wrote one farmer.[18]

The league started to suspect it was in trouble. Although nobody realized it at first, a workable solution to the roads problem required a redistribution of money from cities to rural areas. Farmers demanded the right to pay their road tax in labor because they lived a largely cashless lifestyle. A small farmer and his family consumed or bartered as much as half of their annual production. A farmer who had to borrow money for equipment, land or seed, would likely show a profit only in extraordinarily bountiful times. Excess cash was used to retire debt or buy more land, not sit in a bank somewhere. Every cash dollar demanded of the farmer was the equivalent of two or three dollars in crops or land.

Better roads benefited the farmer who sold proportionally more of his output and consumed less, and therefore needed to haul more to the railhead. The call for good roads fueled farmers' fears that the railroads and big-city food processors, such as Heinz and Armour, would soon cut them out entirely and set up their own corporate farms. "I captivated the farmers completely," reported one wheelmen who spoke to a Grange meeting, "talked Good Roads, got the privilege of reading an essay on the subject, but they could not find time to devote any attention to Road Improvement; butter and cheese were the only questions."[19]

The only way to bring the two sides together was through a system of state-aid road funding that transferred money from city to township. To secure the allegiance of rural farmers, urban cyclists would have to promise to pay the bill. Some of the more astute league leaders realized it was time to change course.

"We must concentrate first on education, then agitation, and finally legislation," said league president James Dunn.[20] But for many of the original cyclists, stepping down out of the high saddle into the farmer's muddy field was a bitter pill to swallow. The first mass-distribution brochure to emerge from the league's mass-education campaign was Isaac B. Potter's *Gospel of Good Roads* in 1891. Potter's tract laid the blame for bad roads squarely on the farmer, portraying him as an ignorant rube and a Luddite fearful of any technological advance. In 1892, Potter was eased out of any leadership role in the coalition good-roads organization that displaced the L.A.W.[21]

Bicycle manufacturer Albert A. Pope recruited the most important outsider, General Roy Stone, a Civil War veteran and civil engineer from New York. Stone, who earned his engineering degree at West Point, came out of the French School of the Polytechnicians, a man of *Ponts et Chaussees*. Stone believed the federal government should be directly involved in roads, just as it had in the dredging of rivers, the digging of canals, and the construction of great harbors.

At Pope's behest, Stone drafted a proposal to take to Washington in May 1892 that was far more modest than the league's original 1889 nine-state proposal that had been crushed so badly. A national highway commission would function for two years. It would tabulate information, prepare an exhibit at the 1893 World's Columbian Exposition in Chicago, and draw up a national highways plan. The measure was introduced into Congress in June while thousands of cyclists milled around town during the L.A.W.'s annual convention.

The wheelmen soon went home, but Stone and league president Dunn stayed behind to lobby for the bill. It passed in the Senate once everyone agreed that no appropriation would be involved, which effectively foisted the problem off on the House. To everyone's surprise, all the resistance to the bill came from southern congressmen, not the farm-state Midwesterners and Westerners that had always run for office on a no-roads platform, and with whom Stone had in mind when he drafted it. On the last day of the session, Speaker Crisp refused to recognize the measure and it died when the session closed.[22]

Charles Crisp was the senior congressman from Georgia. When the wheelmen had been in town for their convention they had soundly defeated a measure proposed by Louisville member "Colonel" William Watts to amend the league constitution to restrict membership to whites. Appalled, *Bicycling World* editorialized that "we want every member and every dollar that is to be had. A black gentleman is infinitely superior to a white hoodlum." Unorganized and unprepared, the "Color Bar" delegates were apparently genuinely shocked that anyone would object to such an obvious and patently sensible suggestion and let their congressmen know they had been slighted before they left town. Any mention of the L.A.W. in the deep Democratic South instantly became pure poison.[23]

The problem had started back in the fall of 1891 when the Mercury Wheel Club of Wilmington, Delaware, an all-black, upper-middle class L.A.W. member club, sponsored a 10-mile road race and sent the results, in keeping with L.A.W. protocols, to *Wheel and Cycle Trades Review* for posting. There was apparently some sort of complaint, as Sterling Elliot, then head of the Massachusetts state division, wrote an editorial in the *L.A.W. Bulletin* explaining that African Americans were permitted under L.A.W. rules, acknowledging that there were black members, and stating that he believed that the rule should remain in its current form. A month later, in a column, the *Bulletin*'s editors noted that they had received many letters in response to Elliot's editorial, many in opposition.[24]

After the Washington, D.C., convention, Watts went back to Kentucky and immediately got a color bar inserted into the Kentucky state L.A.W. constitution. Six months later, he renewed the national constitutional amendment proposal at the league's national assembly. Watts and a member of the executive committee almost came to blows over Watts's derogatory language towards blacks.[25] A narrow majority of the delegates—108 to 101—voted to approve the measure, but constitutional amendments required a two-thirds majority. At the 1894 convention in Philadelphia, the southerners were organized and the issue made it all the way to a floor vote before going down. The 1895 convention was in Louisville and "Negro Exclusion" was the headline issue. It passed, 127 to 54, and the Massachusetts and New York delegations immediately withdrew.

Many of the financial backers and influential businessmen that the league had leaned on so far in its good-roads campaign ran for the exits. To salvage the movement, Stone set up the headquarters for a national Good Roads League in New York within three months after the Washington roads bill debacle. It held its organizational meeting at the Central Music Hall in Chicago on the evening of October 21, 1892 (the night before the opening of the Chicago's World's Fair), with an attendance of about 1,000. A board of directors was elected that represented a wide range of economic interests in better roads: bicycle-maker Pope, railroad executives Leland Stanford and August Belmont, carriage and wagon maker Clem Studebaker, and meatpacker Philip Armour. Missing were league representatives such as Isaac Potter or Sterling Elliot. The two ostensibly "independent" wheelmen representatives, Col. Charles Burnett and George P. Wetmore, were actually Pope retainers: Burnett was a Pope patent lawyer, and Wetmore was Pope's Illinois counselor. The control of the good roads movement was rapidly slipping out of the grasp of the L.A.W.[26]

The Good Roads League was itself a transitional organization, a victim of its own success. In late 1892, in what was essentially an administrative move, the House Agriculture Committee authorized the Department of Agriculture to set aside $10,000 for a roads office. In October 1893, when the new fiscal year started, the secretary of agriculture, Sterling Morton, established the roads bureau and hired Roy Stone as its first director. The minute Stone found out that he was hired, he closed up the headquarters of the Good Road League and moved it—files, furniture and all—to the Department of Agriculture building where he and stenographer Robert Grubbs became the entire Office of Road Inquiry (ORI). Historian Philip Mason notes that "after 1893 the Office of Road Inquiry replaced the League of American Wheelmen as the leader of the goods roads movement on the national level."[27]

For the first couple of years Stone stuck to his mandate and turned out research studies. By begging labor and materials, he even managed to get a demonstration road built at an Atlanta agricultural exposition in 1895. It was all of 150 feet long. The ORI survived from year-to-year only as a line item in the Agriculture Department budget. Every year Morton cut the allocation back, the league published the new figure, the members howled, and some of the cuts were restored.[28] It was the height of the bicycle boom and, at least for a little while, cyclists still had some clout left, especially within their respective state divisions.

What really changed the ORI and the entire good-roads movement was postal Rural Free Delivery (RFD). Back in 1891, John Wanamaker, President Harrison's postmaster general, had asked for $10,000 to develop an experimental RFD program to facilitate the delivery of first class mail and small packages to roadside mailboxes of farmers, saving them the trouble of having to run into town to pick up their mail. It could be argued that Wanamaker, scion of the Philadelphia and New York department store family, had a slight conflict of interest in the matter, but the idea was immensely popular with farm organizations. But before it could be implemented, Harrison was out, Grover Cleveland was in, and Wilson A. Bissell, Cleveland's new Postmaster General, quashed it, even after Congress doubled, then tripled, the appropriation for the experimental program. Bissell believed that RFD would give "certain big eastern merchants" (i.e., Wanamaker) too much of an advantage over local shopkeepers.

Both the wheelmen and Stone at the Office of Road Inquiry realized that this was an issue that could bridge the interests of cyclists and farmers, so they pushed hard for the idea. In 1895, Bissell stepped down and was replaced by William Wilson. Wilson was skeptical of RFD's practicality, but knew that Congress had given his department an explicit order and he wasn't going to risk his head over something he didn't feel that strongly about. As it turned out, the test was a smashing success and by mid–1897, over 40 pilot routes were in place.[29]

Congress and Wilson's office were deluged with requests for new routes. To prevent chaos, the post office developed a procedure that required applicants to petition their congressmen for service. The post office then sent out an inspector to survey the route. There were two requirements: a minimum of 100 persons along a 14- to 16-mile loop, and a route with roads passable during every month of the year. Suddenly, farmers had a reason to worry about the quality of the road in front of their house. At the same time, Stone revived an old idea that the states be allowed to use loans from post office savings banks to finance road improvements.[30] Previously cool to the idea, the post office now thought that it looked like a good way to promote RFD and make some money in the process. The post office was now in the roads business, and helping distribute the L.A.W.-sponsored magazine *Good Roads* and Stone's ORI circulars now sounded like a good investment. The L.A.W., which up to this point had been stonewalled in getting approval for second-class postal rates for *Good Roads*, the *L.A.W. Bulletin* and publications like the *Gospel of Good Roads*, suddenly found itself welcome at the Postmaster General's office.

But the corrosiveness of its internal politics had, over time, eaten into the league. Although nobody realized it at the time, the 1895 Louisville convention, the one where African-American cyclists had been barred, leading to the withdrawal of the New York and Massachusetts divisions, was the beginning of the end. The color bar, regional antagonisms, and near-daily embarrassments over racing issues (including revelations over fixes, fake amateurs, deliberate take-downs, and smear campaigns in the racing committee) continued to darken Sterling Elliot's overweening political ambition to make the league a political party with a scope extending beyond mere cycling matters. "Some of the greatest political parties have made mistakes," he said, trying to sweep the controversies under the rug. "It cannot be expected that an organization comprised chiefly of young men should be entirely free from error."[31]

While still financially flush, the league was flying apart from its own centripetal force as various social classes, sectional groups, business interests, and others spun off in their own directions. Horatio Earle, the former state consul, now a Michigan highway commissioner, wrote in his diary, "My candid estimation is that the L.A.W. is to grow smaller and smaller each year until there will be no divisions, probably only a secretary paid and he too will have other business."[32] Membership peaked in January 1898 at 103,298. The following June, a *New York Times* headline announced: "Steady Decline in the League of American Wheelmen Membership Still Unchecked." In only six months, membership had fallen over 10 percent, to about 90,000. By August it had shrunk to 81,300. It fell below 50,000 in early 1900. By 1904 it was an old-timers club for former ordinary riders run off Abbot Bassett's kitchen table. It died along with him in 1924.[33]

* * *

The league's efforts to secure equal rights to the road, and to make those roads as good as possible, have traditionally been considered the cyclists' legacy to American highway policy. But recent research by scholars Ross Petty, Evan Frist and James Longhurst has shed new light on a long-forgotten chapter in American cycling history: an organized, nationwide sidepath movement. It even had its own biweekly magazine, *Sidepaths*, published for 78 issues during the early 1900s in upstate New York.[34]

Even before the league's good-roads movement picked up steam in the early 1890s, urban cyclists had renewed the demands of their velocipede progenitors a generation before for access to some alternative to the crowded, muddy, dung-covered urban streets of the era: cement sidewalks or sidepaths made from crushed gravel, kiln-fired bentonite clay (the stuff baseball infields are made of) or cinders. They were to be financed from a combination of public expenditures, private subscriptions, and user fees. For example, the Coney Island Cycle Path, built between 1895 and 1898, was an early example of such a project. Running alongside the Ocean Parkway in Brooklyn from near Prospect Park on the north to Coney Island on the south, five-and-a-half miles long, was built with $6,500 in public funds and $3,500 raised by local cycle clubs.

Originally proposed in 1892, construction was not started in earnest until mid–1895, after the Brooklyn Good Roads Committee lobbied the Brooklyn Parks Commission to allocate the necessary $10,000 in construction funds, then raised the money on its own as an inducement to get work underway. Finished over the winter of 1895–96, the original, or westside path, had its formal opening on June 28, 1896. That summer it carried up to 32,000 riders a day. Soon after, Timothy Woodruff was appointed Brooklyn parks commissioner and promised that the construction of a "return," or eastside pathway would be completed in late 1896 or early 1897.[35]

However, his promise was tied to the enactment of a new state law that allowed the Brooklyn park commission to treat the Ocean Parkway as literally a parkway: a linear park over which the commission had the power to enact and enforce rules. A comprehensive set of 18 ordinances was issued in 1898. Rule number eight specified that cyclists were to use the sidepaths exclusively.

There was a split within the ranks of the New York state division of the L.A.W. over rule eight. The roadway surface in the center of Ocean Parkway was decidedly inferior to that of the sidepaths, so many cyclists had little objection to the rule. In fact, many L.A.W. members, who were also members of the local Brooklyn cycle club, volunteered to act as part of a special cycling police corps to enforce the park regulations. But the official position of the L.A.W.'s state Committee on Streets and Highway was that the right to road must be something that had to be fought for on ideological grounds, even if holding fast to that position created a short-term detriment to cyclists. Isaac B. Potter, for example, was the original chairman of the Brooklyn Good Roads Committee that raised the seed money, but resigned after 1893 as the organization became increasingly focused on the Ocean Parkway sidepaths to the exclusion of more general roadway issues.[36]

But the state L.A.W. division could not always bind its membership to its position; Timothy Woodruff became the Republican candidate for lieutenant governor in 1896, and his support among cyclists was highly active.[37] It appears that while the L.A.W. local divisions had the ability to rally the membership and local clubs to their good-roads creed, they could do so only so long as they could tie that ideology to pragmatic gains. The league could not sell good roads by pointing to some distant shining city on a hill; it had to appeal to its membership based on demonstrable, tangible gains. Cyclists wanted better places to ride, and the good-roads movement succeeded only so long as it held out the promise of being the most efficient and most comprehensive way of achieving that end.

While not as spectacular as Brooklyn, other cities joined the side-path movement in the mid–1890s: Chicago followed a year after Brooklyn built the first half of Ocean Parkway, as did Seattle. Denver built a 50-mile path to Palmer Lake, south of town. Minneapolis built six miles of sidepath using private money and public workers and equipment.[38]

With such widespread, but scattered use, it was only a matter of time before someone attempted to organize sidepath development efforts through a national organization, the Sidepath League, in a manner similar to how the L.A.W. was attempting to organize good-roads efforts. It was also inevitable that the Sidepath League's work would come into conflict with L.A.W.'s emphasis on universal access to more and better roads.

Charles T. Raymond was an active wheelman and businessman in Niagara County, New York. He helped organized the Niagara County Sidepath League in 1890, which built short stretches of pathways near Niagara Falls, New York, paid from club memberships. Although the Niagara Sidepath League's paths were open to all, this approach seemed unfair to Raymond, who believed that "what all use, all should pay for." He drafted a state law permitting Niagara County to levy a bicycle tax to build sidepaths. It was approved by the legislature in 1895, but required review and approval by the mayors of Niagara Falls and Lockport, which it failed to secure. It was successfully reintroduced in 1896.

With this success in hand, Raymond followed with another legislative proposal to implement a statewide taxing scheme. The L.A.W. vigorously opposed the bill. Isaac B. Potter wrote: "A special cycle path can be asked for with justice and reason only in those cases where our road officers have failed to provide a roadway of such quality as to make it fit for the use of all classes of travelers."[39] The bill was defeated, as was another the following year, also opposed by the L.A.W. As historian James Longhurst notes, "Division among cyclists diluted their clout, and few counties followed Niagara's lead in securing meaningful sidepath legislation before 1898."

About 50 miles away from Niagara Falls, Monroe County, where the city of Rochester is located, proposed a $1 tax on all bicycles. Seen as a tax on all cyclists to pay for facilities that only some might use, the proposal was subject to vociferous criticism. It was replaced with a voluntary association that attempted to raise the necessary money through subscriptions.

By 1899, six New York counties were operating under a hodgepodge of laws that provided for various sidepath construction and financing schemes, ranging from no funding mechanism at all to voluntary contributions to fee-to-use license systems. The state legislature brought uniformity to the system through the General Sidepath Act of 1899, which authorized a county court, upon a petition of 50 wheelmen, to designate a single-purpose pathway commission, empowered to construct and maintain sidepaths along any public road or street. However, such construction had to have the approval of the applicable general elected body, such as city commission or county commission. Instead of such typical road financing mechanisms as a general property tax or abutment levy (an assessment imposed on adjacent property owners based on the number of feet their land fronted on a new or improved roadway), the 1899 law was based on a flat annual user fee. Cyclists who purchased a yearly license fee set by the county (at least 50 cents) received a visible badge or emblem (usually a headbadge) that allowed them to use the pathway system.

As we will see in the next chapter, similar systems were enacted in northern Europe, especially in the Netherlands, Germany and the low countries. Badges or colored rings that could be slipped onto the handlebars were the most common proof of payment utilized. As was also the case in Europe, Longhurt's research indicates that the user fee plan outlined in the New York State statute encountered "varying levels of success in a bicycle-mad world." He discovered ten counties that invoked their power to create a sidepath commission and establish a voluntary user fee. While Monroe County raised enough money through this method to allocate $11,143 in 1900 for labor, materials and four salaried positions for path building, Fulton County spent only $1,465, Seneca Falls $1,055, and Warren County, $300.[40]

This method was not limited to New York State. In 1896, two Minneapolis cycle paths were built using funds raised through membership fees in a local Cycle Path Association. The 1898 annual report of the city engineer indicated that the city had constructed about 13 miles of paths within town and another nine miles out to nearby Lake Minnetonka. The following year, 28 miles had been completed within the city. These had an in-season use of about 25,000 cyclists per day.[41]

In 1900, Minnesota enacted legislation permitting a user-fee sidepath commission in the three largest counties in the state. Both Minneapolis and St. Paul chose to create sidepath commissions, sell 50-cent headbadge licenses, and charge a one dollar fine for using the pathway system without a license. A year later, the Cycle Path Association in St. Paul disbanded and transferred its funds to the county sidepath commission, and it appears its Minneapolis counterpart did likewise at about the same time.

By 1902, the St. Paul association and commission had built 115 miles of path used by 12,000 cyclists, financed through a combination of club dues, sidepath tags, and government subsidies. Minneapolis had built 72 miles of sidepaths by 1906. However, the transfer of authority from private to public hands appears not to have been able to stem the decline in interest in cycling prevalent across the nation after 1900. Minneapolis sold 26,000 tags in 1900 and 30,300 in 1901. This was followed by a gradual decay: 25,000 in 1902 and 20,000 in 1903. According to historian Ross Petty, at this point sales collapsed; reportedly, only 701 by 1909.[42]

The New York user-fee model was not the only method tried. In 1899, Oregon enacted legislation permitting ten of its 33 counties to enact a general bicycle tax of $1.25. The funds were paid onto a "Path Fund" used to construct or repair "such suitable paths for the use of bicycles and pedestrians as may be determined upon by the county court or board of county commissioners." However, these facilities were required to be situated within already existing highway rights-of-way.

But in less than two years, the Oregon law was challenged by J. A. Ellis, whose bicycle was seized after he failed to pay the $1.25 fee required by Multnomah County and a $1 fine imposed for his delinquency. The crucial issue to be resolved by the Oregon Supreme Court was: "Is the bicycle assessment a user fee or a tax?" The court ruled that it was a tax, because it was not directly related to either the costs of regulating bicycle use or the highway costs and burdens that bicycles imposed on society. In other words, it was a means of raising revenue, not a method of reimbursing identifiable costs. Under Oregon law, as was true in most states, that made it a tax, not a user fee.

That determination had powerful implications. Because the enabling legislation only authorized the bicycle tax in ten of 33 counties in Oregon, it failed the "special laws" provision of the state's constitution. It prohibited laws that only applied to some specifically named people or places, but not others. (It is okay to pass a law that applies a tax to any big city; it is not okay to pass a law that only applies a tax, by name, to Portland.) Likewise, the statute violated the state constitution's requirement for "uniform and equal" taxation, because it taxed all bicycles the same $1.25, regardless of their value. And finally, it ran afoul of the constitution's prohibition on double taxation, because cyclists in the ten designated counties had to pay the bicycle tax *and* the regular county personal property tax on their wheels.[43]

A few months later, the Supreme Court of Pennsylvania not only struck down a sidepath tax, but the idea of sidepath commissioners as well. The Commonwealth had enacted an 1899 law very similar to New York's. Upon the petition of a specified number of wheelmen, the county commission was required to appoint a sidepath commission of wheelmen and begin collecting an annual sidepath tax not to exceed one dollar, the funds to be deposed in a separate account for the betterment of cyclists and pedestrians. In Erie County, the procedure was followed, the sidepath commission duly appointed, but the county commission refused to levy the tax. The sidepath commissioners sued to compel the county commission to follow the law. Instead, the state supreme court struck down the law.[44]

In Pennsylvania, as in most states at this time, control over the roads was reserved to townships and township-road supervisors, and the state constitution prohibited the state or counties from making an end-run around the township supervisors by appointing a "special commission." If the sidepath commissions envisioned in the sidepath law were intended to partially supersede the authority of the township road supervisors, the court said, they were special commissions, and thus the law was void as a violation of the state constitution.

If, on the other hand, the sidepath commission was not a "special commission" but instead a general county office, that is, a delegation of the county commission's own authority with powers commensurate to that that of the county commission, then the sidepath commissioners had to be elected, not appointed. In authorizing the sidepath commissioners to exercise plenary powers equal to that of the county commission while being merely appointed subordinates of the county commission, the statute again voided the law as a violation of the state constitution. Thus, regardless of how you interpreted the sidepath law, it failed one or the other provision of the state constitution.

The court noted that "both parties to this controversy have expressed regret, and probably with justice, that so desirable an improvement in the public roads should fail," but noted that "there should be little difficulty in the framing and passage of an act empowering the regular county township authorities to make the desired changes in the public roads, and providing by assessment, or tolls, or otherwise, for the necessary expense."

However generous the sentiments of the Pennsylvania Supreme Court were, the inherent problems of defining the powers of elected or appointed citizen highway commissions, let alone something as specific as a sidepath commission, proved to be so intractable, even after World War II, that neither the federal government nor the states ever successfully created a citizen highway commission with anything more than mere advisory powers. As authority grew ever more centralized, away from the township and county levels to state and federal departments, authority after the Federal Highway Act of 1916 became lodged within the executive branch of state and the federal governments, not in citizen legislative boards or commissions.[45]

At nearly the same time the Oregon and Pennsylvania state statutes were being struck down, a local ordinance in the town of Hoquiam, Washington, was voided. It was a straightforward tax, requiring anyone riding on the streets of Hoquaim to purchase a license for one dollar. There was apparently no exception clause for non-residents who were merely passing through town, nor did the ordinance make any mention of specific uses for the revenues raised. The town asserted that its general powers "to establish, lay open, alter, widen, extend, keep open, improve and repair streets" authorized it to levy the tax. The Supreme Court of Washington disagreed. Hoquaim can make and enforce reasonable regulations to govern bicycle use, but the public ways are open to all, said the court, and a town "is without power, therefore, to require a license fee as a prerequisite to ride a bicycle thereon." The court did specifically note, however, that its opinion did not cover the situation when the state legislature had specifically authorized cities and towns to levy such taxes, a hypothetical upon which it declined to speculate.[46]

In every case examined by James Longhurst when a state enabling statute permitted a blanket bicycle tax on the county level, either no county ever did actually impose a tax or it was struck down by the courts. Only the semi-voluntary user-fee emblem system was both enacted and sustained. This is not to say that the semi-voluntary system always failed or that its results were mediocre. For example, Ross Petty notes that in 1900, the St. Paul Cycle Path Association had 2,300 members, but an estimated 7,500 cyclists were using the cycle paths built with the funds it raised through membership dues.[47]

But by 1907 most of the sidepath commissions had disbanded. One problem was the growing problem of maintenance; as the systems grew, a larger proportion of funds were needed to maintain what had already been built. Township supervisors and state highway departments proved just as reluctant to maintain sidepaths as they had been to build them in the first place. In the end, road construction proved to be the greatest threat to the sidepaths. As highways were widened and (usually unpaved) shoulders added, the sidepaths became the cheapest and easiest place to install the expansions. In a few cases, paved road shoulders did replace the sidepaths, but more often, as minimum standard lane widths grew from eight to ten or eleven feet, and grassy run-off areas added between the roadway and adjacent drainage ditches, the sidepaths were simply asphalted over or plowed under. As will be seen in the following chapter, much the same thing happened in Europe, only 40 years later, after World War II.

The American sidepath movement was never as large or as widespread as the League of American Wheelmen and the good-roads movement, but it does provide some important lessons. *First*, there was an alternative to the league's good-roads narrative. While the L.A.W. had, at one time, over a hundred thousand members, a gigantic budget, and a dozen or so magazines on the national, state and local levels, the Sidepath League published at least 72 issues of its magazine *Sidepaths* in upstate New York between 1898 and 1902. *Second*, there was confusion and uncertainty among cycling's leadership about the relationship between the good-roads and sidepath movements. Were they antagonists or colleagues? The first (west) sidepath of Brooklyn's Ocean Parkway was sponsored by the Brooklyn Good Roads Committee, but its first president, Isaac B. Potter, stopped participating when it became apparent that it was focusing almost exclusively on the Ocean Parkway pathways, and would accede to Timothy Woodruff's plans to implement rule number eight restricting bicycle use to the sidepaths.

Further complicating the dynamics of the path v. roads conflict was that the sidepath movement did not become effective until after 1899, by which time the league was in decline, and cycling had ceased to be an elite activity. Increasingly, the interest of league members—or, to be more accurate, former members—in the good-roads movement came from their motoring activities, not from cycling, which they had abandoned in favor of motorcycles and automobiles. As membership slid from over 100,000 in 1898 to one-tenth that number in 1902, the L.A.W. leadership desperately sought ways to open its tent to riders it would have shunned a decade before, including pathway users.[48]

In 1898, the league's policy towards pathways had been to support "the construction of cycle-paths in those parts of the country where roads are not found and cannot reasonably be looked for in the near future." But, as James Longhurst notes, after 1900, sidepath advocacy and the good-roads movement existed side-by-side in the *L.A.W Bulletin*: "Within five years this country will possess a system of side-paths that will extend almost everywhere." Alas, the biggest price the league paid for being late to the game was that it realized neither aim: it had been squeezed out the good-roads movement by 1902, and by ignoring the sidepath movement until it was too late, it never gave it any real chance at life.[49]

* * *

If the "American-ness" in American cycling, the cultural legacy of vehicular cycling, can't be found among the cyclists themselves, then where *did* it come from? I argue that it originated in the rise of urban traffic control in the 1920s, during the early days of the motor vehicle. The United States has traditionally exhibited a unique approach to traffic control, one that extends back a century to the dawn of the automobile age. The first American traffic engineers were a disparate mix of amateur enthusiasts, architects, urban planners, and city administrators. What they shared was a common perception that traffic management was a social problem.[50] Probably the most famous of these early pioneers was William Phelps Eno. Born in 1858, he was an eccentric New York millionaire who gave up a lucrative real estate career in 1895 to devote himself to studying and writing traffic codes, first for carriages, later for automobiles.

In 1899, he convinced the City of New York to adopt a 50-paragraph code which, among other things, mandated a "keep right" rule for the first time in its history. "Order out of chaos" became his mantra, and the publication, dissemination, and enforcement of clear and unambiguous rules became his method. In 1920 he wrote *The Science of Highway Traffic Regulation*, which spelled out his basic philosophy. Effective traffic regulation was 95 percent public education and only 5 percent enforcement, he explained, because "it is easy to control a trained army, but next to impossible to control a mob."[51]

The key, he believed, was one set of regulations for all users. For example, horse-drawn vehicles, being slower, should logically be kept closer to the right-hand curb, but there was no reason to give them right-of-way preference at intersections. Some municipalities gave automobiles and horse-drawn wagons equality, while others—sometimes even adjacent cities—granted them right-of-way priority at cross-streets.[52] Differential traffic rules should, Eno argued, always be based on divergent movements or travel paths, not on vehicle identity, unless absolutely necessary. This emphasis on universality, to the point of legalistic rigidity, is a key point among some adherents of contemporary vehicular cycling, typified in the straightforward, if somewhat reductionist, neologism: "Same Road—Same Rights—Same Rules," popular among some club cyclists.[53]

Although Eno had published seven books by the mid–1920s, it was Miller McClintock who ended up exercising the most influence over American traffic planners before World War II. He had received his doctorate in public administration from Harvard in 1924 with a dissertation entitled "The Street Traffic Problem." He moved west to teach at what would soon become the University of California at Los Angeles (UCLA) and establish its Bureau for Street Traffic Research (BSTR). In 1925, McGraw-Hill published a revised version of his dissertation as *Street Traffic Control*. It was the best-selling text on traffic management for the next two decades. Like Eno before him, McClintock believed that *traffic* management was fundamentally a question of *driver* management, that

> one [is] somewhat amazed that so little restriction has been placed on drivers.... There are three general requirements: first that he be mentally and physically qualified to operate a motor vehicle; second, that he shall know the laws governing the operation of a vehicle; and third, that he shall understand the operation of a vehicle and prove it."[54]

The primary difference between Eno and McClintock is that while Eno relied mainly upon regulatory control, McClintock advocated a combination of regulatory and physical optimization. Like Eno, he believed that better laws would lead to a more efficient use of the street space, and in 1924 the Los Angeles Traffic Commission hired him to re-write the city's traffic code. Enacted in January 1925, McClintock's code, which regulated the movements of autos, pedestrians and streetcars, greatly facilitated traffic movements in the downtown area without the need to make large-scale capital improvements, and the Traffic Commission claimed this as one of its greatest achievements for several decades.[55]

However, McClintock was not reluctant to advise the installation of spot roadway improvements to help relieve bottlenecks, channelize traffic paths, and facilitate control. Today, such coordinated local improvements are known as Transportation System Management (TSM). Additional examples included the installation of safety islands for waiting streetcar passengers or road-crossing pedestrians; widening the radius of intersection corners to prevent right-turning streetcars from "pinching" autos against the curb; and improved signalization schemes.

On the other hand, McClintock's regulatory proposals were far less proscriptive than Eno's, and more adaptable to the physical problem presented. For example, he listed five different ways that cities were regulating intersection left turns, only one of which relied on today's method of placing the stack of waiting cars adjacent to the centerline of the street! "The real test of any regulation," he wrote, "is to be found in whether or not it does the work better than any other method."

His own preferred technique was to have left-turners perform a two-stage, L-shaped turn by first having a traffic patrolman send them straight through the intersection to a "hold box" on the far right-hand side of the intersection, then, after all the straight-through traffic had passed, releasing them to make the second stage of the turn onto the cross street. This so-called "Philadelphia System" turn eventually lost out to today's one-stage "Chicago System" turn, mostly because the Chicago turn needed only a traffic light, while the Philadelphia system required a police officer.[56]

But by the 1930s, the social-science based approach of Eno and McClintock was on the decline. The highway engineer, trained in civil engineering, not the social-science oriented public administrator, started to emerge as the dominant figure. Traffic planners sought to exercise social control to achieve a better, more skillful, more cooperative driver, but the new highway engineers simply assumed that drivers would act incompetently, inattentively or even antisocially, and incorporated these assumptions into their designs. To the extent their highway departments could afford it, they insisted that roadways be built to match their low expectations of driver skill. Texas highway engineer Charles Simons wrote that given modern "smooth, level twenty-foot highways, with no physical obstacles, no curves, no ditches and a wide, sloping right-of-way, engineering cannot be held at fault. Engineering made the road as technically perfect as it could be and, if accidents occur, they must result from other causes."[57]

But safety advocate John Maher countered that even given perfect infrastructure, "No engineering approach to the highway safety problem is complete without the admission that the human equation holds the ultimate key to its solution." As early as 1915, the private, non-profit National Safety Council (until then primarily focused on industrial safety) coined an easy-to-remember slogan for its new auto safety campaign, "The 3-Es": Engineering, Education and Enforcement. Its instructional program was led during the 1920s and '30s by two educators, E. George Payne and Albert W. Whitney. The latter wrote a seminal book on the psychological aspects of motor vehicle control, and how motoring behavior can be manipulated for the better (by governments, schools and safety councils) or worse (car ads, sensational movies).[58]

Shortly after Whitney's book was published in 1936, the two parted ways, mostly because Whitney, unlike Payne, believed that education alone was insufficient to rectify the problems of negligent and antisocial driver behavior. An insurance executive, he believed that economic incentives and disincentives had to be added to the mix. Except in the most extreme circumstances where legal (i.e., criminal) sanctions were called for, these economic cues need not be delivered by the government, but could be imposed by the private sector, in the form of higher or lower insurance rates. The only part government need play would be to mandate universal liability insurance coverage for all auto owners.[59]

In 1926, McClintock moved the BSTR from California to Harvard. Initially welcomed by Harvard president A. Lawrence Lowell, the climate grew frosty as street traffic control was pushed aside by the growing power and prestige of the highway engineers, and McClintock was warned in 1936 by Lowell's successor, James B. Conant, that he "had considerable doubt as to the advisability of having this Bureau connected with the University." In 1939, McClintock moved the BSIR to Yale, but resigned in 1947 to take over as president of the Mutual Radio Network.[60]

The brief reign of the "traffic engineer" had yielded to the much longer era of the "highway engineer." The attempt to achieve "driver perfectibility" or even "good driver citizenship" was replaced by the preeminence of the road designer, with residual supporting roles for the "3-E" safety councils, mostly to work with insurance companies on promoting high school drivers' education programs and to lobby for legislation to identify and remove habitual offenders from the road. As transportation historian David Blanke explains:

> Engineering and education methods required little federal oversight and reinforced the business model logic that worked so well for industry [in promoting industrial safety]. Moreover, engineering and education solutions did little to offend existing drivers, a powerful public faction. Politicians might avoid the condemnation of millions, who feared the loss of their automotive freedoms, while appearing concerned (and downright scientific) in their reliance on these hidden professionals.[61]

But a half-century later this same controversy would flare again in the sphere of bicycle planning. Was the bicycle planner analogous to Eno and McClintock's "street traffic planner," a social reformer of cyclists, or a post–1930 "highway engineer," who assumed incompetence (or, to be more precise, a diverse and unpredictable range of competencies) within the target audience, and planned and built accordingly?

* * *

The above suggests that that transportation engineering and land use planning in the United States, even as early as 1930, had already been given over to highway development and a decentralized, suburban city form. This is indeed probably true. With the exception of a few older, eastern cities such as New York, Philadelphia, and Boston, both motorization and suburbanization had become the consensus strategies of urban planners, elected officials, and city residents (at least those with the franchise) no later than 1930, and in many cases as early as 1920.

Between 1910 and 1920, population growth within the 29 largest American cities averaged 25 percent, while growth at or around their fringes averaged 33 percent. The figures for the 1920s were 24 and 33 percent, respectively. Almost every significant American city started to experience faster annual growth along its fringe than in its core area between 1920 and 1929, and many were already at this point by the start of the decade. Thus, suburbanization was a fact even before auto use became widespread (the mid- to late 1920s), mainly because most cities' inner core areas had become so overcrowded relative to their supporting infrastructure. The automobile's most significant impact was not in the displacement of land, but in the displacement of other forms of transport. Between 1910 and 1920, the number of horses in New York City decreased from

128,000 to 56,000; in Chicago from 68,000 to 30,000; in Baltimore from 15,000 to 7,000; and in Cleveland from 16,000 to 4,000. The change was not in personally owned animals, but from drayage; that is, horses used to pull streetcars and commercial wagons.[62]

Most of the large cities reacted to downtown densification by preparing sophisticated regional transit plans to deal with both growth and decentralization. But as historian Mark Foster notes, "The pattern of decision-making revealed remarkable consistency among the various cities: exacerbation of local traffic problems, preparation of a plan, intense debate, then conscious rejection of the plan."[63] The common weakness of these plans was that they had to be, by necessity, large in scale and unitary in their implementation. A quarter of a subway line did not deliver one-quarter of the benefit of the entire line; it would be lucky to deliver any benefit at all. Guideway transit is not incremental; such projects are largely all-or-nothing propositions. Approving a large-scale, integrated transit plan locks decisionmakers and citizens into an expensive, long-term commitment, and both citizens and their political representatives in the United States have traditionally shunned such obligations.

On the other hand, a road-based transportation system is flexible and incremental, if ultimately inefficient at buildout. A road can be built as a two-lane gravel street one year, paved a couple of years later, and widened a few years after that. If there is a recession or some other exigency, delaying the next phase of the improvement does not negate the advantages realized from previous sunk costs. Moreover, much of the operating costs for maintenance, stormwater removal, accident response, snow clearance and so on can be dispersed throughout the general budgets of a number of different local governments and thereby understated or obscured.[64]

Various conspiracy theories have, and continue to be, advanced over the years to explain the replacement of transit with automobile modes in the United States, but as one historian observes, "There appeared to be little reason for automobile executives to sabotage street railways consciously; by ignoring them and simply working for legislation beneficial to their own interests, they were [by the 1930s] winning control of urban transportation." The irony was this combination of automobilization and suburbanization worked, by serendipity, to increase road safety. Peter Norton and Clay McShane both have noted widespread popular protest movements in the 1920s arising from the frequency and severity of child street injuries and fatalities caused by auto collisions. However, only McShane goes on to observe that Los Angeles had a much lower rate of child pedestrian fatalities than New York and many other eastern cities. Moreover, such fatalities steadily dropped in most cities nationwide throughout the 1930s for the same reason as Los Angeles's lower base rate: suburbanization.

"Suburban homes with yards, a housing style more common in the U.S. provided an alternative play space," he notes.[65]

But there was a downside. As the more upwardly mobile members of the early emigrant groups living in the closer-in, first-ring neighborhoods joined the movement to the suburbs, new immigrants and the poor and aged members of older groups were left to fend for themselves. This is reflected in the relative death rates for children and the elderly in the years of rapid motorization and suburbanization. In 1914, vehicle deaths per 100,000 members of the age cohort were 2.5 for those under age five, and 5.7 for those from five to 14. For those 65 to 74 it was 9.3. By 1920, the children's rates increased to 8.6 and 14.6, respectively, but this was outpaced by elderly deaths at 27.0. In 1930, the children's rates had leveled at 13.0 and 14.7, but for the seniors it was an incredible 72.5, about the same as the all-ages death rate for tuberculosis.[66]

Disproportionately, children moved with their parents out to the suburbs, while the elderly stayed in their life-long homes in the close-in residential first-ring areas surrounding the original downtown. As McShane notes: "The cost of automobility was the reduced social control of traditional street users, which destroyed the livability of inner-city neighborhoods designed in the pre-automobile years."[67] The protests of the 1920s did not repeat themselves because, other than the elderly hangers-on, the new residents had formerly occupied even worse tenement neighborhoods in the heart of the core zone itself. For them, the first-ring residential neighborhoods, made newly affordable by the exodus of their former occupants out to the suburbs, was something to celebrate, not protest against.

However, that did nothing to change the fact that these neighborhoods were now more dangerous for their children than for the children of the former residents, those who were now living out in the suburbs. Things were still better than in the core tenement districts they left behind, which were often left to those on the very bottom of the ladder, people of color. In many cases these slums went untouched until the Title I and Title III programs of the Federal Housing Act of 1949 provided the funds and the legal muscle to act against the slumlords, and even then the remedy was usually only to raze everything and rebuild commercial or civic projects. Despite such notorious failures as the Pruitt-Igoe slab blocks in St. Louis or the Schuylkyll Falls towers in Philadelphia, most of the replacement housing was typically dispersed out to the first ring suburbs, not the closer-in urban neighborhoods one to four miles from the central business district.[68]

But because more of the households in the older middle-ring neighborhoods were elderly "stay-oners," fewer of them had children. And as time went on more of these households lacked anybody: by 1940, the Urban Land Institute found that nearly one-third of all privately owned lots within the city limits of large urban areas were vacant, presumably old residential blocks cleared for future downtown commercial expansion but which now had "doubtful" prospects for development, because the department stores and offices had started shuttering their downtown locations, following their customers out to the new fringe suburbs or edge cities.[69]

If there is a lesson to be learned here, it is that there is rarely such thing as a universally beneficial or a universally destructive transportation or land use policy. Almost always, the effects are allocational: some gain, others lose. The fundamental question that needs to be asked is not "is it good or bad?" but "Who Gets?" and "Who Pays?"

CHAPTER 2

Historical Antecedents: European Bicycle Planning, 1890–1990

Other than in the United Kingdom, the history of bicycle planning in Europe is virtually synonymous with the history of bicycle facilities development. Bicycle lanes running down the center of the roadway existed in Bremen, Germany, as early as 1897. It is believed that these were inspired by earlier, similar facilities that had been installed somewhere in Belgium. By 1910, on-road bicycle lanes existed in Hamburg, Hanover, and several other northern German cities in the now familiar each-edge-of-the-road configuration. As cities increasingly asphalt-paved their roads, many of these lanes were left in their original cinder-covered or macadamized condition.[1]

The city of Magdeburg and its municipal engineer, Dr. Carl Henneking, were influential in the early development and dissemination of bikeway technology. Working with a local organization founded in 1898, the Magdeburger verein für Radfhrwege (Magdeburg Cycle Path Association), Henneking experimented with various configurations throughout the 1920s. In the end, his preferred solution was one in which the entire roadway was asphalt-paved, then separate lanes delineated with curbstones, effectively creating sidepaths.

By 1926, the Association had established a 285-km (177 mi.) network of cycle paths.[2] Most of it was paid for through an annual user fee. Upon payment, a cyclist received a colored ring that he or she placed on their handlebar, permitting them to use the pathway system. Each year the ring color changed. "The creation of specially conceived paths for bicycles is the only real solution to the annually escalating problem of creating safe traffic conditions for cycles and pedestrians," Henneking asserted. His Magdeburg design was disseminated throughout northern Europe in 1927 by the Study Group for Motorcar Road Construction (STUFA) and the German bicycle industry. Financing, however, proved to be a major impediment. After publishing Dr. Henneking's STUFA report, the federal government and the bicycle industry association established the Zentralstelle für Radwege (Central Office for Bike Paths, ZfR) which attempted to replicate the Magdeburg model in other cities. Adherence to the colored-ring system had been, at best, merely satisfactory in Magdeburg. It was, at heart, just an adequately supported voluntary system. Applied elsewhere, it eventually failed, especially after the left-leaning Workers' Cyclists Union, Solidarity (the nation's largest cycling club, with about 200,000–300,000 members), balked at the scheme. A national bicycle tax was proposed in 1928 by STUFA to pay for bicycle paths, but afraid of alienating Solidarity and its leftist supporters, the Ministry of Transportation took no action. Nevertheless, the ZfR eventually managed to coordinate the development of about 2,500 km (1,500 mi.) of bicycle facilities.[3]

The ZfR was eliminated when the Nazis assumed power in 1933. They replaced it with a new Reichs-Strassen-Verkehrs-Ordnung (Reichs Association for Bicycle Path Construction, RSVO). Ostensibly a non-profit organization, the RSVO was actually a quasi-governmental agency. It was placed under the direction of roadway engineer Hans-Joachim Schacht. Between 1934 and 1939, the RSVO coordinated the construction of about 6,000 km (3,600 mi.) of bicycle paths, almost all of which were paid for by local or regional governments with the assistance of federal matching funds.[4]

Tilman Bracher, a Berlin transportation consultant, believes the German "Radweg" (sidepath) construction program was instituted as part of the nation's unemployment relief efforts of the 1920s and 1930s. On the other hand, transport historian Volker Briese asserts they were built primarily to promote speedy traffic:

> German motives for the construction of paths, especially in the thirties, were different from the reasons given in other countries, from the information available. For example, neither in Holland or Denmark was the demand for cycle paths connected to the fostering of motor vehicle transport. Maybe this is the reason why in these two countries cycle paths remained preserved after WW II, instead of being destroyed, as they were in Germany in the seventies, to allow for car parking. It sounds more believable that in other countries paths were really built for the comfort and safety of cyclists.[5]

The development of cycle facilities in the Netherlands, while initially occurring at almost the same time as in Germany, eventually turned in a very different direction. But at first this was not the case. As Manuel Stoffers notes, "Although the reputation of the Netherlands as cycling country dates back to the interwar period, only after the Second World War did the Dutch deviation from the general European pattern of bicycle use become more marked."[6]

As was the case in Magdeburg, it was a cycling organization, this time a nationwide club, the Nederlandsche Algemee Wielrijers Bond (Netherlands Tourists and Cyclists' Club, ANWB), and not a government agency that took the lead role in the planning and constructing of bicycle facilities in the early years. The ANWB began forming local "bicycle path associations" in 1914 to work with area bicycle clubs to sponsor the construction of facilities, mostly for use by upper-middle-class cyclotourists. By the early 1920s it formed a central "Roads Commission" and hired its own roadway engineer, A. E. Redelé, to coordinate the activities of these local associations.[7]

The turning point came in the 1920s. After their nation's defeat in the Great War, German cycle manufacturers began exporting low-cost bicycles to the Netherlands for sale in guilders, a more stable currency than the inflation-prone deutschemark. Between 1919 and 1925 the average price of a bicycle in the Netherlands fell from 129 to 61 guilders. At the same time, the basic fare on Amsterdam's tramways increased from the equivalent of five cents to 15 cents.[8]

Even more importantly, in 1924 the Dutch government imposed a new bicycle tax, despite one magazine's prediction that it would be "the most unpopular tax ever levied." It had no relation to bicycle facilities or even highway expenditures; it was intended purely as a general revenue enhancement tool. It was a flat three guilders per bike and thus highly regressive when applied to the inexpensive imported utility bicycles of the working classes. Amsterdam and other large cities already had developed an acute case of bicycle theft (close to 10,000 per year); thieves now switched to the safer and more convenient alternative of stealing the bronze medallion that indicated that a bike's owner had paid that year's tax.[9]

One Amsterdam police officer complained that he and his colleagues had rarely encountered a law "that was more unpopular with the public." Confiscated bicycles were taken to the former warehouse of the Dutch East India Company until their owners could pay the fine and retrieve them, and one observer noted that the vast storehouse started to look "like a bicycle auction." When revenues turned out to be more than double the original projections, its unpopularity grew to into a clamor and, in 1926, the government was forced to propose changes.

The flat rate per bike would be cut and, more importantly, the income would be earmarked for a special road fund, towards which other users, primarily motorists, would also pay. The ANWB pressured the government to set aside some of this money for bicycle facilities. In exchange, they agreed not to oppose the restructuring of the tax which, under the original legislation, was due to expire in 1930. The government agreed to this in 1926, formalizing the rules three years later.[10] Even then, there is disagreement as to whether Dutch cyclists got a fair deal. Ton Welleman, former Waterstaat roadway engineer and coordinator of the Dutch Cycling Council, notes:

> Between 1900 and 1940, the number of bicycles grew from 100,000 to four million.... The government considered all these bicycles primarily as a source of income. A major part of the road plans was therefore financed from bicycle taxes. The construction of cycle tracks along some of the national highways could be regarded as "bicycle policy." However, this happened mainly to decrease the hindrance that the many cyclists caused for a few car drivers![11]

By 1938, the Netherlands had a total federal road network of 1,884 km (1,168 mi.), of which 51 percent had been installed with sidepath-style bicycle facilities. State and provincial roads, generally secondary highways and farm-to-market roads, extended for about another 10,350 km (6,400 mi.), of which about 23 percent were installed with bicycle facilities. Moreover, about 37 percent of the nation's total bicycle path system was unassociated with the roadway system. That is, they were not sidepaths, but were instead separate paved trails planned and built primarily to meet the needs of cycle tourists and other recreationalists.[12]

Their users tended to come from farther up the socioeconomic spectrum than the sidepath utility cyclists. After the war, these higher-status cyclists would be the ones who prevented the wholesale dismantling of bike lanes and the conversion of sidepaths to car parking zones. In addition, because almost 40 percent of the Dutch system was located completely off roadway rights-of-way, there would never occur the corrosive class conflict between automobile and cycling interests that would render the British Cyclists' Touring Club largely irrelevant after the mid- to late 1930s.[13]

In April 1941, Arthur Seyss-Inquart, the Austrian-born occupation Nazi administrator for the Netherlands, along with Anton Mussert, the leader of the NSB (the Dutch fascist party), announced the repeal of the bicycle tax. Before the war, the NSB had campaigned for the end of the tax, but the NSB was even less popular than the tax; in the last parliamentary election held before the German invasion, it garnered only 4 percent of the vote. Nevertheless, NSB members cycled around with placards boasting: "All of Holland Is Happy; Now We Cycle Free."[14]

In Sweden, planners dealt with many of the social and political changes that were to play an important role in shaping American bicycle planning in the 1960s and '70s, only a half-century earlier. By the mid–1920s, City of Stockholm administrators were using planned suburbanization to address alarmingly low housing standards, high rents, and inner-city overcrowding. The new residential suburbs were built in coordination with tram and bus lines into the center city. But to an unexpected degree, the new residents found these inadequate and turned to bicycle use, as road engineer Gustav Dahlberg explained in 1933:

> Especially in the larger cities and the industrial towns, workers and civil servants of different categories strive for the opportunity to live in suburbs outside the workplace, but still in its neighborhood. The high rents and lack of suitable dwellings inside the cities, moreover, force the economically less well-off to live outside or in the vicinity of the outer parts of the cities. In many cases, they then use the tramways, omnibuses or suburban trains for their daily journeys between the city and their homes, but this is often uncomfortable, and, in the long run, the journeys are too costly for people of lesser means. For them, the bicycle is often the only alternative.[15]

Thus, beginning in the late 1920s, bicycle lanes were established on the access roads into Stockholm. As was the case in Germany, the provision of bicycle facilities was the result of both "push" and "pull" factors. The primary "pull" factor was improved roadway safety through reduced bicycle-motor vehicle accidents, while the main "push" factor was the promise of increased roadway throughput brought about by removing slow-moving cyclists.

In the 1936 Regional Plan for Greater Stockholm, engineer Einar Nordendahl wrote that "the construction of separate cycle and pedestrian lanes is largely motivated by the desire to free the road from such traffic elements that reduce both its traffic capacity and safety. This is particularly the case with pedal cyclists." In 1930, the percentage of total traffic between Stockholm center and its working-class suburbs to the south comprised of cyclists was 5 percent. By 1938 this had increased to 20 percent and peaked in 1943 at 43 percent. The proportion of cyclists to the more affluent suburbs to the west and northeast was somewhat lower (peaking at about 25 percent), but the timeline was virtually identical.[16]

Within the center city itself, however, no provision was made for bicycle use, and cyclists were expected to share the streets with other traffic modes. Bicycle traffic was not mentioned in either the 1928 or 1930 Stockholm city plan, mostly because the narrow streets in the center city area did not allow for the construction of bicycle lanes. This appears to have been a consensus decision, as it was not opposed by the Society for the Promotion of Cycling in Sweden (CF), although the CF did unsuccessfully lobby for a "ring road" of bicycle lanes around the outskirts of the inner city in 1938.

As a result of the rapidly increasing bicycle use and lack of facilities within inner-city Stockholm, cyclists gained a reputation as unruly and incompetent roadway users. Facilities were seen as a solution to this problem, but one that was not available within the center city. The alternative was to regulate or improve cyclist behavior. Initially, more intense regulation was proposed by the city's traffic department in the form of roadway prohibitions, bicycle registration and mandatory operators' licenses. These were opposed by the CF, who instead implemented a bottom-up grass-roots program of education, promotion, and public outreach. "According to the CF, the self-control of bicyclists, instead of top-down control, was the way to ensure their safe traffic behavior," notes historian Martin Emanuel.[17] Thus emerged a tense triangle of traffic engineers, city administrators, and cycle advocates. Each pulled in their own direction to resolve the problem of a city center with no bicycle facilities that was being force-fed an oversupply of bicycles from the suburbs—the result of an inadequate, overpriced transit agency and a system of radial bikeways that could efficiently pump cyclists in and out—but only as far as the city limits. No solution appeared in sight up to the start of the Second World War, when, of course, all civilian concerns were moved to the back burner.

Finland's early development of bicycle facilities is unique in that it was planned as an alternative to roadbuilding, at least in its two most northerly and least populated counties: Norrbotten and Västerbotten.[18] The first known bicycle trail was built between 1900 and 1912 along the Ljungan River in Västernorrland to support timber floating operations. In the 1930s, the Swedish Parliament approved the construction of almost 8,500 km (5,300 mi.) of rural bike trails in the two northern counties. About 90 percent were built under the direction of the Swedish Forest Service, with the remainder to be privately-built, publicly-subsidized trails running across private timber land, but open to public use. These trails served two main purposes. First, because of the worldwide depression, Sweden was experiencing high unemployment. The construction contracts were issued in short 400–800 meter (quarter- to half-mile) segments so that local residents (typically families) could bid on the work. Contracts paid 10 to 20 percent less than market rate construction work, and the trails thus derisively gained the name "Starvation Strings." But for many agricultural villages they were, for months at a time, the only source of cash income. Secondly, they were built to facilitate the mobility of forestry-related activities, such as the movement of foresters, game wardens, fire-fighters, and the itinerant residents of logging camps. All were constructed to specifications appropriate to these requirements, mostly using packed earth over a bed of spruce or juniper boughs and plank culverts.

A second wave of bike trail construction occurred in the 1940s, this time predominantly in Norrbotten County. The fear of forest destruction from German fire-bombs was the driving force behind this plan, which focused on the need to rapidly move fire-fighting crews into hot zones and to build and staff lookout towers. Of the 3,532 km (2,190 mi.) of trails contained in the 1930s and 1941 plans for Norrbotten, 950 km (590 mi.) were ultimately built, with the final projects concluding in the early 1950s. Figures for Västernorrland are not available, but are probably smaller because it was not included in the 1941 plan. Only a few scattered remnants of these trails remain; many have been incorporated into paved forest access roads.

* * *

In the United Kingdom, the mass use of the bicycle did not begin until the 1920s. There was little or no bicycle planning by the start of World War II, after which the exigencies of war and its subsequent financial crisis delayed implementation for almost another two decades. By and large, this lengthy delay can be attributed to the deliberate efforts of a single organization, the Cyclists' Touring Club (CTC), and its secretary, George Herbert Stancer.[19]

For almost a decade before becoming CTC secretary, Stancer had been the editor of the commercial magazine *Cycling*, but by 1919, it, along with the rest of the British cycle industry, was feeling the effects of the postwar economic recession. When he moved to the CTC in 1920 he was less interested in the club than its journal, the *CTC Gazette*. By combining the roles of CTC Secretary and *Gazette* editor, he was able to draw on the resources of the club to support the journal. Most of Stancer's time, and an inordinate amount of the club's money, went into the *Gazette*. By 1935, it rivaled any commercial publication, averaging 40 heavily illustrated pages per month, but it also cost over £3,100 a year to produce, the equivalent of 6,000 annual memberships. The CTC was a small organization, comprising only about 34,000 members in 1939, minuscule when compared to the UK domestic annual bicycle market of 1.4 *million* units.[20]

The CTC had originally been a middle-class, bourgeois club. Cycle ownership remained out of reach of the working classes until after the Great War. As cycling became democratized, the club's membership shrank to 7,000 by 1918. Stancer found that one of the best ways to grow readership (and, by extension, subscription and advertising revenues) was to generate controversy and conflict—preferably irresolvable conflict. "CTC membership offered few clear benefits to the growing numbers of working-class cyclists until it started campaigning on the wider issues of rights for all road issues," observes British cycle historian Peter Cox. Whether this new advocacy was motivated by its actual benefit to proletarian cyclists, or simply because of its emotional appeal in the wake of the 1926 General Strike (thus guaranteeing a loyal readership for the *Gazette*) is more problematic. Cox notes that when "viewed from the outside, if judged solely on what they appear to be concerned with," then the CTC campaigns of the 1930s "appear almost absurd." However, he maintains that "only by understanding the actors involved and their social locations do they become intelligible." For example, when Stancer died in 1962 the Club discontinued the *Gazette* in less than a year.[21]

A prime example of Stancer's penchant for such emotive, class-based conflict was his 31-year campaign against rear cycle taillights. During World War I, auto headlights were dimmed by blackout slits, so the Defence of the Realm Act

(DORA) required cyclists to carry a red taillight. In 1921 DORA expired, but Parliament proposed reinstating the taillight provision.[22] Although British auto electrics (including headlights) were world-famous for their undependability and weak output, Stancer and the *Gazette* strongly campaigned against the new act.

"At that time, the CTC was still fighting to prevent regulations that would, eventually, force cyclists to use rear red lights," says current CTC staffer Chris Peck. "[They] believed that cars should at night be obliged to travel at a speed which would enable them to stop should they encounter another user in the road—it should be their responsibility to notice the unlit road user, not the responsibility of the cyclist."[23] The CTC was able to fend off the taillight law for eight years, eventually compromising on a red rear reflector ordinance in 1928. Finally, in 1945, the same year Stancer retired as *CTC Gazette* editor, the government made taillights mandatory.[24]

Britain's first cycle-path, two-and-a-half miles long, was constructed alongside what was then Western Avenue (now A40 highway) in London in December 1934. It, too, was opposed by Stancer. "In 1934 the CTC was dead against cycle tracks of all kinds," Peck notes, "we were still very much of the mind that we should try and recapture the roads from the motorists." The *Gazette* carried elegant diagrams of intersection turning maneuvers intended to show that cycle tracks would increase accidents. "Cycle paths would tend to degrade the pastime, reduce the number of cyclists, and to strike a blow at the cycle manufacturing and distribution trades from which they would never recover," Stancer huffed in one editorial.[25]

Instead of special tracks for cycles, the club called for the development of that new idea coming out of Germany and Italy: motorways. The first, the M1, opened in 1959. The idea would boomerang against the club by the 1960s, as the motorway program began to divert so much highway funding from the upkeep of regular surface roads—the "A" and "B" highways—that the latter soon became woefully inadequate, to the detriment of cyclists. In 1963, the club sent a formal letter to the Ministry of Transport asking that bicycle facilities be required on primary highways, on bridges, and on major urban roadways.[26]

In 1937, representatives from the CTC testified before a House of Lords select committee that universal cycle proficiency training for children and young adults was urgently needed. The committee agreed and put this in its final report. However, the war intervened and it was not until 1947 that a national scheme for training and testing children in cycling proficiency was actually realized—starting with one class, at one school. The program was not fully implemented until 1958. In this aspect, the British foreshadowed some aspects of later American efforts toward institutionalizing vehicular cycling as a government policy.

However, when it comes to the planning and construction of bicycle facilities, cycle historian Peter Cox points out that Stancer and the CTC were only able to delay bicycle facilities construction until the late 1930s, and concludes that the fact "that cycleways were not constructed [in the UK] was an historic accident imposed by the intervention of war and the chronic state of public finance in its aftermath."[27]

Had Britain's economy, more interconnected with that of the United States than other European nations, not been so adversely affected by the Great Depression, and then had it not been bankrupted by the costs of the World War II, Cox believes that England's construction program of cycleways may have looked much more like that in Germany or even the Netherlands than it did.

* * *

"Before the Second World War, continental Europe was the principle destination for students of traffic engineering and town planning," notes Swedish historian Per Lundin, who observes that continental planners tended to visit the Ebenezer Howard–inspired Letchworth or Welwyn Garden City in Britain for ideas on town planning. The United States was considered a relative backwater. But after the war, America became everybody's center of attention. "The shift in attention to the United States in the mid–1950s was due to one thing: the automobile," says Lundin. Traffic engineering was no longer a factor to be incorporated into city planning; it had *become* city planning.[28]

Between 1945 and 1982 Germany pursued a contradictory cycle transportation policy. On one hand, planner and cycle historian Tilman Bracher notes that the "classical Radweg" approach had been "popular among [local] politicians and transport planners since the 1920s as it reserved road space for cars," and that as late as the 1980s "classical Radweg schemes [were] still commonly implemented." On the other hand, Radwegs were just as frequently torn up to make way for automobile parking or (more often) slowly and surreptitiously converted over through lax or nonexistent parking enforcement.[29]

In 1982, a set of semi-official planning recommendations resulted from an ongoing cooperative process by government agencies and cycling groups. It advocated moving away from a total dependence on Radwegs toward a more roadway-integrated approach, especially at intersections. In other words, the report recommended more vehicular-oriented standards akin to those that the American Association of State Highway and Transportation Officials (AASHTO) had issued the year before in their *Guide to the Development of Bicycle Facilities*. As a field test, a federal government transport department tried to implement the recommendations in two different types of cities: those that, so far, had installed no provisions for cyclists, and those that had already been extensively provided with Radwegs.[30]

The "clean slate" towns were given an integrated "bicycle-friendly" approach, generally comprised of encouragement and safety education programs, widespread traffic calming measures, cycling-oriented roadway spot improvements, and relaxation of roadway-use restrictions. The result? "In the end, local public reaction and implementation problems became the major impediments," Bracher reported. "It took a long time to reduce resistance to the 'imported experts on bicycle planning' [and the] unconventional measures ... were not immediately adopted."

In Erlangen, the "classical Radweg" town, some sidepaths were abolished at intersections, and the cyclists merged into the roadway. The results were generally no better than for the "clean slate" trials. "In practice," Bracher admitted at the time, "[local] implementation is progressing half-heartedly. Even in a cycle-friendly city, much resistance has to be overcome!" In other tests, where Radwegs were replaced with on-road bicycle lanes, only about half of the cyclists approved of the change, although they almost invariably resulted in a statistically meaningful drop in the number and severity of accidents.[31]

In the Netherlands, the immediate postwar crisis was not a shortage of bikeways, but a shortage of bicycles. By the spring of 1945, half of the Netherlands' four million bicycles had been stolen or destroyed by the occupation authorities. Amsterdam was left with approximately 160,000 bicycles, less than half its pre-war inventory. Starting back in mid–1942 and accelerating greatly in 1944, the military authorities began confiscating bicycles for use by the German army and in civilian factory complexes in Germany as gasoline and other consumables started to run out. As the army retreated in 1945, it abandoned them, and many were collected and returned to use. The Dutch plant of the French Simplex firm, lacking the raw material necessary to make new bicycles, turned to refurbishing these confiscated bikes, eventually putting over 60,000 back on the road. The bike tax was never reinstated, although the architects of its repeal never knew that. Seyss-Inquart, the occupation administrator, was hanged at Nuremberg and Anton Mussert, head of the Dutch NSB party, was shot by a firing squad in 1949.[32]

Explaining why the Netherlands became such a robust cycling society during the postwar period, while, say, Germany and Denmark did not, has lately become something of a happy hunting ground for transport historians and social scientists, largely because clear cause-and-effect explanations have proven elusive, as Ruth Oldenziel and Adri Albert de la Bruhéze explain:

> The causal relationship between the rates of automobility and urban visions was not always close, however. In the Netherlands, where automobility came late and the tourist organizations reinforced a classless image of cycling, policymakers considered bicycles facts of life; in Denmark where automobility grew quickly, policymakers

> nevertheless assigned equal rights to cyclists and motorists. Like in the Netherlands, in Germany cars came rather late, yet policies sought to tame cyclists early on. Levels of automobility then cannot solely account for the differences. Visions about the future better explain the treatment of cyclists.[33]

The problem here, of course, is that it assumes that "vision" is both linear and unidirectional: somebody has a "vision" of an automobile-based or car-free culture and the power to implement it consistently over thirty, forty or fifty years. However, rarely does reality sit still long enough for such a clear snapshot to be taken, and amorphous attributions like "vision" allow many causality problems to be swept under the rug.

As Manuel Stoffers points out, the difference in the Netherlands after the war wasn't that bicycle use decreased, but that it dropped less than elsewhere. However, not even that is true across the board. In Amsterdam, the cycling mode share dropped from about 83 percent in 1950 to 30 percent in 1970; in Eindoven, about 75 percent to 36 percent; in Enschede, 87 percent to 47 percent. (But keep in mind that we are still talking about some substantial numbers here, especially before the early 1960s: by one estimate there were five to six hundred thousand bicycles in Amsterdam in 1955, when it had a population of 900,000. In 1958, 8,000 bikes were confiscated by the police just for illegal parking.[34])

In Stockholm, the cycling share fell from 86 percent in 1950 to 12 percent in 1970; 55 percent to 14 percent in Hannover; 52 percent to 17 percent in Antwerp. The Dutch decline ceased abruptly during the period 1970–75, and unlike Stockholm, Antwerp, London and Manchester, where the post–'70s upturn flattened or turned down again after 1985, it kept on increasing, with one exception, Eindoven.[35]

After World War II, all of western Europe had turned its attention to implementing a 1950 joint European highway plan known as the "E-network," designed largely along American superhighway lines. However, most nations lacked the money to actually build it; by 1967, only about 6,700 km (4,150 mi) had been completed, mostly in the form of upgrades to existing roadways. In the Netherlands, the pace of development increased dramatically when an engineer named Bert Beukers took over the roadbuilding department of the Waterstaat. Educated at Miller McClintock's old BSIR program at Yale (which, by this time, had evolved into a fairly standard highway civil engineering program), he overcame the bureaucratic resistance to his "American approach" within the Ministry of Spatial Planning and Environment by starting his own urban planning program in the Waterstaat. In 1968 he scrapped the previous 1958 national plan, which called for 1,200 km (740 mi) of new high-speed roads, replacing it with a 3,600 km (2,230 mi) grid of superhighways.[36]

Some did object. The most famous protest movement was the famous "white bikes" of the anarchist Provo movement. It is probably one of the most misunderstood chapters in the history of bicycle activism. The eventful day was July 28, 1965. The idea of a pick-up/drop-off "bike share" system wasn't new: a similar "red bike" program had been in place inside Amsterdam's sprawling NDSM shipyard for several years, and two of the Provos, Robert Grootveld and Luud Schimmelpennink, had previously worked at NDSM.

There were only three bikes at the opening ceremony, and they weren't ready to go that afternoon because the white paint wasn't yet dry. The whole thing would have been easy to write off as farce; a bit of bad street theatre. It got hardly any newspaper mention that morning. The whole scheme was on the fast (bike) path to oblivion. Then the police blundered in. The chief of the district police station, listening to Grootvelt ramble on that afternoon, actually told one reporter, "I'll leave them be. They want us to interfere, but as long as traffic isn't hindered, it appears best not to interfere." With the three bikes not yet usable, the Provos led them off by bike to wait for the paint to dry and then set them out. But that evening, two officers confiscated the bikes under a 1928 ordinance that required all bikes parked in public to be locked.[37]

The press had a field day. Grootveld later admitted that the biggest logistical defect in the plan was that the Provos didn't have a central depot for storage, repair and distribution, so they had to fall back on spontaneous outdoor "happenings" to drum up support for the donation of bikes. They would be fixed up and painted on the spot, then moved to staging sites for use. Three days after the White Bike program's "launch," the Provos were having a donation "happening" when a police car pulled up and, with little or no provocation, one of the cops started beating on a Provo bike mechanic, Roel van Duijn, with a nightstick. Pictures of the police attempting to club van Duijn while he tried to shield himself with a half-painted bicycle made the next morning's papers.

Hundreds of bikes poured in and were put out on the street, only to be seized by the police as fast as they were staged. Several of the Saturday night donation happenings turned into near-riots. In March 1966, the Provos almost disrupted the marriage procession of Crown Princess Beatrix by flinging bicycles in the path of her horse-drawn carriage and screaming, "Where is my bicycle!" (The chief of police would later lose his job for his ham-handed management of the Provo protests, and the mayor would be defeated in his reelection bid a couple of years after that.)

In June 1966, the Provos—now a registered political party—gained a seat on the Amsterdam City Council. However, they could not get an official white bicycle plan approved, losing 37–2 when a program proposal was finally put to a vote in October 1967. Historian Pete Jordan calls the Amsterdam White Bike program "an urban myth." "Aside from the few dozen old White bikes that the

Provos had distributed in 1965," Jordan concluded after interviewing former Provo leaders from the era, "the Provos' White Bicycles Plan never came close to fruition ... indeed, there *had been no* collection points, there *had been no* control, and there had been no certainty because there simply *had been no* operating White Bicycles Plan."[38]

As a result of this White Bike mythologizing, more than a dozen bicycle cities later experimented with free or coin-operated share-a-bike programs. La Rochelle, France ("Yellow Bike"), in 1973 and Cambridge, England ("Green Bike"), in 1993 tried completely unfettered systems. Everyone admits that Cambridge lost all 300 of its bikes in a couple of days. La Rochelle put on a braver face, claiming that its program was a success, despite in-house records that suggests almost all the originally staged bikes also disappeared within a few weeks, and the system kept going as long as it did only because the city kept pumping replacements out on the street.[39]

These failures led Copenhagen to try a coin-operated system in 1995. "There have been many difficult experiences since then," admitted transportation consultant Thomas Krag in 2002. The deposit was 20 kroner, about three U.S. dollars, and the bikes were permitted only within the center-city area. Despite this precaution, Copenhagen ended up losing about 1,100 bikes by 2002. "Only with a significant input of public money and practical support could the program be realized," adds Krag. Due to theft of both the bikes *and* the coin boxes, the program had to be suspended by 2004.[40]

The coin-op system was also tried by a number of American cities in the 1990s, including Portland, Spokane, Tucson, Madison, Victoria, Boulder, Tampa, Olympia, and Fresno. All were spectacular failures. "We put about one hundred bikes out and they all disappeared," recalled the Tucson program coordinator. "The truth is it didn't work. It's terrible to see them all disappear." Portland was the biggest loser: between its launch in 1994 and the disbanding of the program in October 1997, Portland YellowBike lost over 1,000 bikes. It is very likely that as many as 25,000 bicycles were lost worldwide in a Quixotic attempt to emulate a program that never existed, except in the popular imagination.[41]

In the Netherlands, unlike the United States, a policy decision had been made early on that the new motorways would not be pushed through into cities, but would end at peripheral ring roads. (The sole exception was the Hague.) Thus, "anti-asphalt" protests tended to be debates about damage to the rural landscape. The ANWB, for example, played a pivotal role in the dissemination of American roadbuilding techniques through an annual "European course for traffic engineers," which it developed with the Organisation Mondiale du Tourisme et de l'Automobile (OTA), an association of European touring and automobile clubs. The OTA offered summer classes in its "European course" through the early 1970s, when it disbanded due to differences on energy and environmental policy between its automobile clubs and touring organizations.[42]

The moderating influence of non-automobile interests within the ANWB as it grew into the nation's most powerful automobile lobby helped blunt the American roadbuilding exuberance of Waterstaat engineers such as Bert Beukers, but what finally pulled the plug on the E-network highway plan, both in the Netherlands and across all of Europe, wasn't white bicycles or bourgeoisie cyclo-tourist clubs. It was the staggering increase in the price of oil during the 1970s. In October 1973, the Organization of Petroleum Exporting Countries (OPEC) organized a boycott of most western nations after the Yom Kippur war. British Petroleum (BP) was majority-owned by the British government. BP, in turn, held 40 percent of Royal Dutch Shell, the Netherlands national oil company.

A month after the war, British Prime Minister Edward Heath instructed BP officials to order Shell to give British firms delivery priority over everyone except its own Dutch customers, regardless of contractual obligations. Shell refused. Heath threatened to nationalize BP and cancel all of Shell's exploratory leases in the then-new North Sea Brent oil field. Shell still refused. Heath's own bureaucrats, with cooler heads, essentially refused to execute Heath's retaliatory orders. Two months later, OPEC eased the restrictions—except for the Netherlands, which had sold aid to Israel. The European Community authorized clandestine relief shipments of oil to the Netherlands. France, busy trying to sell jet fighters to several OPEC members, hemmed and hawed. The Netherlands, provider of 40 percent of France's natural gas, threatened to shut off the pipeline at the border. The oil transshipments went through.[43] Generally, it was a very ugly time.

The Netherlands quickly developed a whole new transport plan, and it didn't say very much about superhighways. Moreover, they stuck to it for the next 40 years. Through a gradual process of scaling back new highway development and increasing bicycle projects—generally refined versions of same type of facilities that Dr. Henneking devised in 1927—expenditures for bicycle projects amounted to 10 percent of the surface transport budget by the mid–'80s.

There are dissenters, however, who assert that this economic "it's the price of oil, stupid" theory is both oversimplified and reductionist. Ton Welleman, the Netherlands roadway engineer who became coordinator of the Dutch Cycling Council, points out: "And this is crucial. The bicycle was old fashioned, a vehicle for the poor, but cycling *was* recognized as a mode of transport that is a part of life.... In the Netherlands, transport policy meant a pro–car policy, but in general *not* an anti-bicycle policy. That was wise: at that time [1950–75] there were, after all, hardly any alternative modes of transport available for most of the Dutch. Mass motoring did not even start until about 1960, and the role of public transport was minimal even then."[44]

Thomas Krag, the traffic consultant from Denmark, echoes this: "What distinguishes Denmark from many other European countries, with Holland being the main exception, is that cycling never disappeared as a normal travel mode. The decrease was big, but the bicycle was still visible in urban traffic even when at its lowest. That changed around 1975." Joost Vahl, an engineer for the City of Delft, recalls undertaking a series of what he later called "outlandish stunts," actually controlled field experiments, in the early 1970s that ultimately resulted in the development of the Netherland's famous *woonerven*, or residential street-yards. Vahl and his compatriots staged bike accidents ("we wanted to know if car drivers would stop and help or pass by"), and built false road construction sites ("when the streets are broken up for repair, everything was functioning perfectly with half the space"). From these experiments, Vahl was able to estimate how to get cars and people to interact in non-destructive ways, and what the outer limits of frustration tolerance and social control were. The now-widely replicated *woonerven* designs were the result. The essence of the *woonerven* is to communicate that the street—almost always a residential side street—belongs to the residents of the block, that it is an extension of their front garden areas, and that cars are permitted to use it only as a guest. The result is a deliberate confusion of right of way, of proper directional path, of what will happen in the next five seconds. Dutch traffic engineers found that traditional traffic calming measures such as chicanes, neck-downs and speed humps slowed traffic by about ten miles per hour. *Woonerven* slowed traffic *to less than* ten miles per hour.[45]

On the other hand, some Dutch bicycle advocates maintain that the nation's federal transport policy, in regards to bicycling itself, was ambivalent all the way up to 1980–82. For example, although the Ministry of Transport and Public Works introduced a fund for the construction of rural bike paths in 1975, and eventually spent 500 million guilders (roughly 480 million dollars, or 380 million euros, both adjusted to 2013 equivalents), the fund was eliminated in 1985 when the ministry announced that the backlog of needed projects was fulfilled and that henceforth local and regional governments had the necessary resources to address future demand. But in May 1989, the seven-year-old Lubbers coalition government collapsed over the issue of whether to cut tax breaks for auto commuters and allocate the resulting revenues to alternative transport programs. The replacement government was more liberal, and revised national transport and environmental plans drawn up in 1990 were more assertive about reducing auto use, especially in urban areas and within towns.[46]

Bicycle parking continues as one of the nation's greatest problems. Indoor garages are the only real guarantee against theft. In Amsterdam, the police estimate that between 120,000 and 180,000 bicycles a year are stolen, yet the number of neighborhood garages shrank from 234 in 1975 to 155 in 1981, to 116 in 1988, to probably no more than 80 today—not surprising in a city where modified metal shipping containers have sometimes been pressed into service as emergency short-term housing units. In 2011, the Amsterdam Bicycle Processing center received 55,000 bicycles, most impounded, but some abandoned, stolen or derelict.[47]

In Sweden, planners anticipated the turn to automobilization, but were still caught out by its speed and intensity. The 1952 Stockholm city plan, like its pre-war predecessors, continued to focus on the construction of new residential suburbs, and added a subway system to augment the transit network. But the planners did not anticipate the rapid growth in automobile tripmaking that did not begin or end in the center city, but traveled exclusively between suburbs. A new 1960 plan relied much more heavily on motorways, many constructed out of the old pre-war suburb-to-center city access roads. The new motorways made no provision for bicycle facilities, because the role of cycling was foreseen as limited to tripmaking within each individual residential suburb, primarily by women (shopping) and children (school-related), and not for suburb-to-center city or intersuburban trips. At the same time, Martin Emanuel asserts that Sweden's traffic planners and its national cycle organizations, the Society for the Promotion of Cycling in Sweden (CF) and the Committee for Swedish Cycle Promotion (KSC) together abandoned the idea of individual cyclist competency as the base upon which to build bicycle planning:

> During the 1950s, the "individual-psychological" explanatory model of traffic safety was challenged by another model focusing on planning as a means to avoid accidents. In this discourse, responsibility was transferred from the individual road user to the planner, and, in the end, to the state. Traffic accidents were the result of "bad planning," but could be avoided with an "idiot-proof" traffic environment.... Being "idiot-proof," however, downplayed the role of education and manners. Road safety and had been professionalized and deindividualized, and materialized in infrastructure.[48]

This was an echo of the same process that traffic planning and engineering went through in America during the 1920s and 1930s. Planning, a sociological tool focused on improving the performance of the individual operator, gave way to engineering, which strove to maximize the performance of the infrastructure in the face of anticipated low-skill user behaviors. Swedish cyclists would either use Radweg-type facilities or secondary streets to travel between their homes and suburban centers. The CF all but abandoned efforts to promote urban cycling and educate cyclists about high-traffic mixed-use roadway conditions, and returned to its roots as a cyclotouring organization. In 1949, 29 percent of

Stockholm's summertime suburban-city work trips were taken bicycle; by 1961 this had fallen to 4 percent, with the wintertime share of trips at 9 percent (1949) and 4 percent (1961).

* * *

In 1947, Britain's move toward nationwide bicycle training and testing for children resumed when the first test group of seven schoolboys went through a class held in an indoor school gym. Gradually, as staff was trained, more and larger classes were held, mostly in school parking lots. The process was overseen by the Royal Society for the Prevention of Accidents (RoSPA), with the manual and most of the volunteer instructors provided by the CTC. In 1956, the Ministry of Transport published a "Report on Child Cyclists" that essentially said the same things as its 1936–38 prewar report, which had largely been prepared by the CTC. The development of the program accelerated after this and became fully operational around 1958.

There appears to have been little provision made for bicycle traffic in the British planned "new towns." The earliest, Letchworth (1904) and Welwyn Garden City (1919), both privately developed, probably had no need for them; the towns were geographically small, self-contained, and the growth of car ownership in the U.K. lagged at least 20 years behind the U.S. It was assumed that the roadway system would be primarily used by pedestrians and bicycles, except for lorries in the industrial districts that were a feature of both.[49]

In the first of the postwar planned new towns, Harlow and Stevenage (both 1945–48), fairly extensive bicycle and pedestrian networks were installed. The engineering was especially inspired in Stevenage, which gained notoriety for the "Stevenage Circle," a rotary junction of Gunnels Wood Road and Six Hills Way that included fully grade-separated bicycle and pedestrian components (the bicycle and pedestrian ways, in turn, were separated from each other). In addition to its engineering, the Stevenage Circle is just as famous for an incident that took place in 1967. E. C. Claxton, the chief engineer for the Stevenage Development Corporation, gave a bikeways-related presentation before the venerable Royal Society for the Encouragement of the Arts, Manufacturers and Commerce on the evening of November 15, 1967. Presiding was the flamboyant Ernest Marples, Tory minister of parliament and former minister of transport.[50]

Marples had left his cabinet post a couple of years before under something of a cloud for his aggressive towing of illegally (and many claimed, legally) parked cars in the city of London, which, as a national, not municipal, official he apparently lacked the authority to do. (The architecture critic Reyner Banham also accused him of placing "Do not Enter" signs at both ends of certain side streets in the city containing the homes of his friends.) After engineer Claxton finished his presentation, Marples offered his own comments, appropriate of nothing that had gone on before:

> I am quite certain that we will never get the pedal cycle back on any scale unless it is segregated from ordinary forms of traffic.... Man is conditioned by original sin, and once you put him in a motor car you multiply that original sin by the number of horses underneath the bonnet! If you put an 18-year-old in a Jaguar you have given him more power than he is capable of using wisely. As Lord Acton said, distrust power more than vice.[51]

Leslie Warner, then-secretary of the CTC was in the audience, as was Alan Gayfer, editor of *Cycling*. Marples "conditioned by original sin" argument was mocked over and over again in editorials in *Cycling* and *CycleTouring*. Marples wanted his paths to protect hapless cyclists from bloodthirsty fang-toothed teenagers in sports cars. Vampires in Jags! Overlooked was Caxton's reply to Marples's comments. The situation had nothing to do with evil. It was simply a matter of reaching an appropriate engineering definition of "free-flowing" traffic, from both a psychological and a physical standpoint:

> Our chairman has reminded us that we all have a lot of evil in all of us. I don't believe, however, that the motorist becomes more evil when he gets behind the steering wheel. The pedestrian probably hits people a thousand times while the motor car only hits someone once. If you go through a crowded throng on your way to get a ticket at a booking hall, count the number of times you are hit.[52]

A decade later, Marples's "conditioned by sin" argument would be repeated by the American advocate John Forester under his most famous (and outrageous) ideological expostulation, the "cyclist inferiority complex."[53]

The British national government's infrastructure policy remained ambivalent. For example, when the new town of Milton Keynes was planned in 1968, no provision at all was made for bicycle use. After the first OPEC oil crisis of 1973, an attempt was made to graft on a cycle network to the semi-completed infrastructure network using a system of "redways" (essentially Radwegs that merge onto the roadways to become bike lanes at intersections). They were heavily criticized by local cyclists and not extended as the town continued to expand. On the other hand, a "new town" expansion of Peterborough, started in 1970, did incorporate bicycle provision from the beginning of planning.[54]

In 1977, the Department of Transport issued a Transport White Paper inaugurating a new Innovatory Projects Budget that underwrote much of the cost of experimental cycling schemes undertaken by participating local governments. By 1992, about 80 projects had been installed. In 1981, the program was expanded to allow localities to apply for funds to install unified networks of facilities, not just single installations. Although slow to get started, the program of the Greater London Council (GLC) promised to be the largest network of urban facilities in the United Kingdom, and the GLC actually budgeted 1 percent of its total capital expenditures on cycle facilities (many of them parking related). Margaret Thacher, however, personally detested the GLC (it was feared as a bastion of social liberalism) and her administration ordered its dissolution in 1986. The development of its bicycle facilities network, along with many other GLC regional efforts, died with it.[55]

Since the 1990s, bicycle planning efforts in the UK have mirrored those in the United States: incremental, localized, dependent on short-term budget priorities. In the mid–1990s, the national government began the Cycle Challenge Project, which invited bids for local-public/private partnerships, with matching funds provided by the national government up to a total of £2 million for cycling projects that did not require heavy infrastructure investments.

A typical project was in Nottingham. It involved establishing a local government program to develop and administrate what would be called Transportation Management Associations (TMA) in the U.S. The building owners in an office park installed bicycle parking, showers, short stretches of connecting sidewalks, an emergency take-home shuttle service, and paid an existing employee on a half-time basis to manage the program, for which the building owner was reimbursed. The difference in Nottingham from the typical American TMA was that the British program, following the funding mandate, gave priority to bicycle use where American TMAs primarily stress transit, vanpool and carpool enhancements. As was the case in American TMAs, some installations succeeded well, others were not heavily utilized. (The reasons for success or failure largely conformed to those described in Robert Cervero's seminal study of TMAs, *Suburban Gridlock*.[56])

The national government also launched its National Cycle Network, comprised mostly of signed rural roads and abandoned canal towpaths and railroad grades, financed mostly by lottery funds. While there are now 12,000 miles of NCN routes, it is acknowledged that these are primarily recreational, rural facilities of varying quality that do little to ameliorate urban transport problems. Gil Harrison of SusTrans, the non-profit organization that manages the NCN, admits:

> We would love to see an NCN of the same standard as the routes in Holland and Germany but that would require government commitment and investment. In those countries the governments invest between £10 and £15 per head of population compared to English governments whose average input is less than £2.[57]

As a result of this funding limitation, the two main cycle advocacy groups, the CTC and the Bicycle Association, recommended that the national Department of Transportation not adopt what they called the "Dutch Model" of planning within urban areas. Instead, they recommended the following hierarchy of planning strategies:

1. Traffic reduction
2. Traffic calming
3. Junction treatment and traffic management
4. Redistribution of the carriageway
5. Segregation—cycle lanes and cycle tracks

And except for modifying "traffic calming" to read "speed reduction," this was the recommendation that the Department of Transportation included in its 2008 cycle infrastructure design guidelines.[58]

It is apparent that in Britain, as in the United States, cyclists and highway engineers together worked in tandem to respond to a situation where an inevitable and apparently unalterable shortage of funds made the implementation of a grand, large-scale bikeways program a permanent impossibility. Instead, they forged a compromise that exchanged the cyclists' moderating their demands for capital-intensive roadway improvements in return for the engineers' assurances that they would deliver cost-feasible changes in roadway geometrics and operations. Unlike the U.S., the U.K. highway engineers were willing to cede some significant performance changes, yielding such sacred cows as freedom of route choice and universal rapid speeds for motor vehicle drivers, things that few, if any American highway engineers (or politicians) would be willing to give away in exchange for anything. It remains to be seen if the promises of the British road engineers were sincere.

Probably the most significant postwar development continued to be the revitalization of the U.K.'s national cycle proficiency scheme, now called *Bikeability*. It is summarized by the CTC and Cycling England, the advisory body to the British Department of Transport, thusly:

> In 2006, Cycling England began piloting *Bikeability*, the new consumer brand-name for the Cycle Training National Standard, the new Cycling Proficiency for the 21st Century. With research having shown a 50 percent decline in cycling over just one generation, *Bikeability* was launched with the aim of training and encouraging more young people to cycle by ensuring that no child leaves primary school without the chance to receive on-road cycle training. *Bikeability* includes on-road training at Levels 2 and 3 and the scheme is marketed to adults as well as children. Meanwhile, Cycling England's Bike Club initiative (coordinated by the CTC Charitable Trust, UK Youth and ContinYou) began to develop new cycling clubs and cycling opportunities in after-school and youth club settings' and corporate sponsorship enabled the programme to extend to Scotland, Wales and Northern Ireland.[59]

Broken into three modules for various ages, and with a voluntary participation section for adults, it is the largest cycle-education program in any of the western nations. The adult version of *Bikeability* was added in 2008 with the introduction of John Franklin's revised book *CycleCraft*. The United Kingdom is probably the exemplar of the broad, inclusive, non-ideological mainstream of vehicular cycling on the national level: a well-organized, uniform scheme of cyclist skills enhancement combined with supportive, but fragmented, incremental, and localized policies of facilities development.

One would think that British highway engineering would be the most significant influence on Australian bicycle planning, but according to architect and Convenor of the Australian Bicycle User Research Group, Michael Yeates, this is not so. The greatest influence over bikeway policy was exercised by former Denver bicycle planner James Mackay when he spoke on the topic of "Bicycle Facility Signs and Pavement Markings in the USA" at the Eighth Velo-City Conference in 1995. The Australian Bicycle User Research Group was so impressed with what he said that Mackay was invited to speak on the same topic at a conference the following year in Australia. While acknowledging that "many traffic engineers and beginner cyclists want all cycling to take place off street," Mackay believed that such physical separation "creates the illusion that motorists and cyclists don't need to keep track of each other." It is the act of "keeping track of each other": motorists scanning for cyclists when turning or entering arterial streets, and cyclists looking for these cars, that Mackay believed was the key to cycling safety.[60]

So what Mackay implemented in Denver in those corridors where full-width bike lanes were not possible (which was most of the center city) was a system of pavement markings, similar to those located within bike lanes, but without the formal lane stripe running parallel to the edge of the road. The intent was to highlight those locations where motorists should expect cyclists to be found, while making it clear that there was no requirement that either cyclists or motorists use a specific portion of the roadway. The Bicycle Federation of Australia was attracted to Mackay's solution primarily because its leadership had become convinced that a key element was the reduction of urban traffic speeds:

> The question that increasingly arises therefore is whether a cycling-friendly city or town requires any separate facilities for the safety of cyclists if the traffic speed is safe. The answer appears increasingly to be that separate facilities or road-sharing facilities [i.e., bike lanes] are needed to provide more space for the cyclist but that safety and increased usage are much more dependent on traffic speed.[61]

Paradoxically, the primary problem with this method is that it attempts, in Yeates's words, to use the "positive endorsement of cyclists in narrow traffic lanes [to] provide both legitimacy for the cyclists and the opportunity for cyclists to provide a mobile speed management role." In other words, Yeates's group did not think it was necessary to link the installation of these markings to any additional engineeering measures to reduce the government's default speed limits of 50 kph (37 mph) in suburban and commercial areas, and 40 kph (25 mph) in residential and central business districts. The presence of the cyclists themselves would act to lower automobile speeds.

Traffic engineers proved to be far less amenable to the idea of using cyclists as rolling speed limiters, and they were equally cool to the idea of imposing blanket speed reductions. As a result, the Australian national cycling plan fundamentally disaggregated responsibility for bicycle policy to the state and local level. At the risk of overgeneralization, Australian bicycle planning in 2009 was much like that in the United States or the United Kingdom. Largely broad and aspirational, it emphasized the need to keep as many roadway corridors as possible open and available for cycle use while at the same time developing trails, paths and other off-road facilities, all given severe budgetary limitations.

In practice, much Australian bicycle planning was refocused after 2003 by the death of a pedestrian and a casual cyclist as result of collisions with participants in the "Beach Highway Death Ride," one of a number of large group or "bunch" rides in the Melbourne metro area. The state police documented several of these semi-organized weekly rides along beachside highways around Melbourne containing up to 200 riders and traveling at sustained speeds of 30 mph. Bayside, a suburb of Melbourne, drafted a plan to address bunch riding. Three frequent participants in the Hell Ride, Burridge, Lajbcygier and Lema, submitted a response to the city that, in essence, recommended that the authorities instead accommodate the needs and desires of the bunch riders and acknowledge their athletic superiority. In 2009, the Victoria Police commissioned a study from Monash University to examine the causes of bunch riding and other sociopathic cycling activities and recommend ways to curb it. Since that time, largely due to anger over the death of the elderly pedestrian and the arrogant and dismissive tone of the "Hell Riders'" report, addressing the problem of sociopathic cycling has become one of the highest priorities in Australian national bicycle policy.[62]

Chapter 3

Early American Bicycle Planning, 1965–1975

World War II left Britain economically devastated. The nation had thrown everything it had into the war effort: over a quarter of Britain's Gross National Product between 1938 and 1945 had gone into war material. Worse, even after Germany and Japan surrendered, the government failed to demobilize in a vain attempt to keep its empire together and to maintain the façade of a great–power status it no longer possessed. In 1937, the nation had spent £6 million per year on defense. Between 1946 and 1950 it averaged £209 million a year. Except for gasoline and tires, no household consumer rationing was needed during the war itself, but eggs, butter, meat, clothing, sugar and coal were all regulated at one point or another between 1945 and 1950, with a few controls extending to 1954.

In addition to the diversion of economic resources to national defense, civilian consumer goods were limited by the need to give priority to exports to pay off the nation's huge dollar-denominated foreign debt. The Marshall Plan, which paid for the rebuilding of much of Western Europe, had almost no impact in Britain because 97 percent of its cash grants went to repay debt, not to repair damage or buy goods and equipment. After struggling for years, the chancellor of the Exchequer finally devalued the pound in September 1949 from $4.03 to $2.80, effectively reducing the price of British-made goods by a third in the United States. The British government pressured domestic industries to increase output as rapidly as possible, and to send it overseas. The auto industry (especially the British Motor Corporation, later British Leyland) was all but ordered to export 75 percent of its output, mostly to the U.S. However, both governments recognized that a thriving market for British automobiles in the U.S. would take years to establish. On the other hand, similar targets for the bicycle industry could be met in just a few months. The American market was ripe for the picking because it had been shielded behind a protective tariff wall for well over half a century, since its earliest days. The American cycle import tariff was cut from

30 to 7.5 percent. Imports jumped from 18,500 units in 1947 to 408,000 in 1953, while the sale of American-made bicycles fell almost 50 percent.[1]

The American bicycle industry soon decided the only way to offset its shrinking slice of the market was to expand the entire pie by cultivating new adult riders. "The thing we fought more in the 1950s than any other thing in the industry was to encourage people to continue riding after the age of sixteen," recalled Norman Clarke, president of the Columbia Manufacturing Company and, at that time, also president of the Bicycle Institute of America (BIA), the industry promotion group. "The way we did it was two things—promote it, and recognize that the clunkers we were making were too big and much too heavy for adults." The industry also wanted to flatten out its intensely seasonal sales cycle. "About 45 percent of our output was sold for Christmas at that time," Clarke notes, resulting in the need for an annual layoff that started sometime between Thanksgiving and New Years Day, depending on sales. In many years, layoff notices would go out the week before Christmas—a "terrible time to let people go," Clarke recalled.[2]

The efforts of the BIA were given an unexpected boost by the sudden fame of Dr. Paul Dudley White. Dr. White was a cardiologist, a dedicated cyclist, and a long-time member of the American Youth Hostels (AYH), the favored organization of the minuscule number of serious American cyclotourists of the 1950s. In 1956, President Eisenhower suffered a near-fatal heart attack and White was brought in as his cardiologist. At that time, the standard treatment was months of near-immobilized bed rest. White was an apostate—he recommended mild, then increasingly strenuous exercise, weight loss, absolutely no smoking, and moderate alcohol consumption. Golf, Eisenhower's passion, was useless, White told him—not enough of what we today call "aerobic" exercise. Cycling, White said, would be perfect. He could ride in reasonable privacy and security at Camp David or his farm in Pennsylvania. "Perhaps you might not have had a heart attack had you cycled regularly," White told a grumpy Eisenhower.[3]

The bicycle industry went bonkers. "Boy, we've got something here!" Clarke recalls his fellow bicycle executives exclaiming when they heard the news of Dr. White's sudden national fame. "[After it was over] we took him [White] to all of our conventions, paid his bills [and] dedicated the first bicycle path in New England around the Charles River basin to him, and had one on Nantucket built that we paid for." Earlier, in 1951, the League of American Wheelmen (L.A.W.) had been revived with the help of BIA funding, but until the mid–1960s it was almost exclusively a federation of clubs around Chicago and in the upper Midwest region.[4]

Dan Burden, who would later found Bikecentennial (1973) and the Bicycle

Federation (1976), first became an amateur activist in his home town of Columbus, Ohio, about 1963, mostly promoting rides through the local chapter of the AYH. That would have been typical for an AYH local chapter of the era. Although best known for its hostels—cheap overnight accommodations for bikers, hikers and skiers, often made from rehabilitated farmhouses or urban townhouses—and its multi-week European tours, the bread-and-butter of most local chapters was actually their short, weekend classes and supported ("sagged") tours, where cyclists or hikers had their gear trucked from one overnight stop to the next.[5]

Columbus resident Charles Siple and his son Greg had taken a two-day, 200-mile, out-and-back ride along the Scioto River valley together in 1962. They repeated it the next year, when two friends joined, and every following Mothers' Day weekend, with the tour growing each time. Burden first participated in 1964, when it had about 45 riders. "I didn't think there were forty-five people in Ohio who *had* 10-speeds," Greg Siple later recalled. By now, the ride was getting too big to hold as an informal, by-word-of-mouth event, so Burden connected the Siples with Charles Pace and the Columbus AYH. By 1967, Charlie Pace became the permanent ride coordinator and the Columbus AYH event sponsor of what was now known as TOSRV, the Tour of the Scioto River Valley. Pace and the Columbus AYH would continue in these roles for nearly 30 years, although the sheer size of the undertaking eventually required that the event be spun off as its own freestanding non-profit corporation. "Back then, it really was the AYH playing a huge role," Burden recalls of the mid–1960s, "although the real advocacy started with recreation. The active transportation side ... didn't get a good launch until the early 1970s."[6]

Burden believes that the first professional cycle advocate in America was a man named Bob Cleckner, who also started with the AYH during the mid–1960s in and around the Chicago/Milwaukee area. "Bob was the first full-time paid professional in America to go around and really try to drum up interest in this stuff, starting with bike lanes," Burden told an interviewer in 2012, "he was my inspiration. He was getting *paid* to go around the country and get adults to stop thinking of bicycling as something that was just for children." Jay Townley, then a vice-president at Schwinn, recalled that Cleckner was hired by the BIA in 1969 or 1970 "as a full time bicycle and bicycling advocate. Bob traveled nationwide and lobbied congress as well as selected state capitals." Cleckner worked together with Keith Kingbay, who had formerly worked for Schwinn for 17 years as parts and service manager.[7]

"Frank V. Schwinn paid for Keith Kingbay to work for BIA and Bob and Keith carried out much the same advocacy functions," explained Townley. "Bob and Keith coordinated their efforts and for a time this gave BIA two full-time bicycle and bicycling advocates." Schwinn withdrew from the BIA in 1968 in a disagreement over the role that mass-market retailers should play in the organization, but continued to work with the BIA on an almost daily basis. To avoid forcing the BIA to furlough Kingbay due to lack of funding, Schwinn rehired him in a new position, cycling activities manager. "Bob continued to be the full-time advocate for the BIA and Keith represented the L.A.W.—again paid for by Frank V. Schwinn," explains Townley.

The league had experienced a checkered history since its initial demise in 1924. It was resurrected as largely a federation of Chicagoland bicycle clubs by Jack Hansen, president of Chicago Cycle Supply, a distributor of parts and accessories affiliated with Schwinn. The new L.A.W., with financial contributions from Hansen's firm, Schwinn, and the BIA, continued a modest existence until Hansen's death in February 1955, at which point it again faded out of the picture. It was again revived in 1964, still as a loosely-knit consortium of mostly upper Midwest and New England clubs until the great 10-speed bike boom hit in 1970. Individual memberships increased from about 250 to around 4,500. Indirect memberships, that is, individuals who belonged to a local club that was formally affiliated with the league, rose from somewhere around 6,000 to 75,000.[8]

This continued until 1973, when Horace Huffman negotiated a more formal, long-term support agreement with the L.A.W. "I'm not sure if Keith convinced Frank V. Schwinn that it was better for the advocacy message if he represented the L.A.W. or if Frank thought it was better," recalled Townley, "but for many years [after 1968] Keith wore a red blazer with an L.A.W. patch on the pocket with the permission of the L.A.W. board of directors and told audiences that he represented the League."[9]

Although Greg Siple may have only been half-joking when he expressed surprise at finding 45 people in the state of Ohio with 10-speeds in 1964, Columbia Bicycle's Norman Clarke estimated that by 1965, a third of his firm's total production of 650,000 was in the form of multi-geared bicycles: "3-speeds and 5-speeds, some 10-speeds." It would also appear that the industry was well on its way to freeing itself from its dependence on the Christmas tree for survival. However, it soon found itself blindsided.[10]

In early 1963, Schwinn's west-coast distributor reported that teens were buying used 20-inch wheel bikes and retrofitting them with "banana" saddles and high-rise handlebars intended for bicycle polo. An independent west coast distributor had custom-ordered 500 factory-made versions from Huffman Manufacturing's Azusa, California, plant under the label name "Penguin." Al Fritz, a Schwinn vice-president, decided to make up five hundred of their own for their southern California dealers. When Frank Schwinn saw the prototype (which Fritz had the foresight to name the more aggressive-sounding "Stingray") he thought his man had gone nuts, but Schwinn sold 45,000 in just six months. They eventually made over two million before the craze started to ebb in 1968. Then, just as suddenly, the Stingray craze was replaced by the great 10-speed bike boom of 1969–73. Domestic sales shot up from 35 per 1000 persons in 1969 to 72 in 1973. Almost all of this was in the form of adult, lightweight, multi-geared bicycles.

Many theories have been offered to explain the great boom. The most plausible is that a combination of postwar demographics and Stingray economics crashed into each other starting in 1969. Stingrays had all but pushed out middleweight and lightweight one- and three-speeds as the bicycle of choice for sub-teens and teens by 1965. While middleweights and lightweights could be adapted for use by young adults, Stingrays were strictly kid's stuff, so as their owners grew up out of their teens, they had to buy new bicycles if they wanted to keep riding. At the same time, these Stingray boys and girls, members of the peak birth years of the postwar baby boom, were moving into young adulthood in record numbers. Thus, a convergence of two factors: (1) young adults, who wanted bicycles, were increasing in record numbers; and (2) the bikes they already had suddenly turned, like so many Cinderella carriages, into useless pumpkins.[11] Because they were young, open to new ideas, and less risk-adverse, they were more likely to walk past the upright-handlebar one- and three-speeds to the ten-speed section and ask, "What's this?"

* * *

Besides the Charles River and Nantucket facilities already mentioned (both components of larger redevelopment projects), the first effort at some sort of bicycle planning in the United States appears to have been in the village of Homestead, Florida, about thirty miles south of Miami. Between 1961 and 1963, Homestead designated and signed a network of secondary, lightly traveled streets to connect residential areas with "schools, playgrounds, shopping centers, ball parks, and other centers of activities." Although city planners told *Bicycling* magazine's Peter Hoffman that they were not intended to divert "the experienced cyclist, capable of riding long distances," but were, instead, meant for "the newcomer, the weekend cyclist, the family with children," they were still attractive enough to serious sport cyclists to induce the League of American Wheelmen to select Homestead as the site of their 1969 National mid–Winter Rendezvous, even though it was, at that time, a small farm town, the last stop before Everglades National Park and the Overseas Highway to Key West.[12]

Homestead's experiment worked largely because of its unique situation. With a mild year-round climate, it had more bikes per capita than comparable towns. It was an old town (for south Florida) that had been laid out in a tight gridiron plan for small bungalows. However, it had gone largely undeveloped due to World War I and the subsequent collapse of the Florida land boom. When development restarted in the 1950s, it was in the form of ranch houses spanning two or three of the original 1914 lots, resulting in many quiet, untracked streets. Finally, it was a small, tightly-knit community centered around an adjacent air base. When Chicago, which had a disconnected set of lakeside trails left over from the 1950s, tried to copy the idea, it found it had to build separated paths to close all the gaps in the network, and a 64-mile system in the affluent Milwaukee suburb of Waukesha was entirely comprised of paved pathways.[13]

The Waukesha facility was actually laid out in 1939, but wasn't constructed until Bob Cleckner and the Milwaukee AYH urged the county to apply for federal funding. In 1965, Congress created the Land and Water Conservation Fund (LWCF), and starting in fiscal year 1969 local governments could apply for bicycle projects that met the LWCF's basic function to "assist state and federal agencies in meeting present and future outdoor recreation demands."

The LWCF quickly became a prolific source of money for bicycle facilities. Between 1969 and 1975, roughly $71.75 million, about eight percent of all LWCF funds, were spent on bicycle programs. The Waukesha facility was typical of many built during this era: separated from the roadway system, usually running through a park or along a waterway, with little transportation potential. That was the problem with the LWCF: its legislative purpose was to promote outdoor recreation, not just bicycle or pedestrian paths, and many bikeway funding requests were rejected by the Bureau of Outdoor Recreation (BOR) because they overly emphasized transportation. The expiration of the LWCF in 1975 led to the cessation of most new large-scale bike path projects.[14]

Many in the bicycle industry hoped that Section 217 of the Federal Highway Act of 1973, which, for the first time, allowed (but did not require) states to use a portion of their roadway funds for pedestrian and bicycle facilities, would rectify this. It didn't, because states were loath to divert funds from roadway projects. This points out just how unique the LWCF was in the history of American bicycle planning: it was the last program in which aid flowed directly from the federal government to the local level. All subsequent programs followed the federal transportation funding model, which was state based.

At the time the federal-aid road system was created in 1916, the federal Bureau of Public Roads (BPR) had promised state highway departments that it would not go into the business of building roads directly, but would limit itself to channeling its funding authority through them. The BPR would set standards and provide funding, but it would be the state highway commissions who would actually control construction and run the highways when they were built. After much controversy, this structure was maintained when President Eisenhower created the highway trust fund to build the interstates. The state-highway-centered structure of American road development typically meant that urban transport received short shrift, because urban areas often needed repairs, rehabilitations, transit accommodations, and other spot improvements of the type Miller McClintock had talked about thirty years before, which were small, hard, slow and not very profitable for contractors. State highway engineers wanted to build highways. In fact, their professional competency was measured on how much highway they could build per dollar. Diversions, such as including sidewalks, transit islands or bicycle facilities, simply dragged down their efficiency ratio.[15]

Although cities and counties in almost every state requested bicycle project funding under Section 217, by 1979, only 28 state highway departments had even bothered to forward an application on to the federal Department of Transportation. Total requests between 1973 and 1979 amounted to $26 million, and projects actually funded came to only $2.7 million for the six-year period, an annual rate about one-tenth of that for the LWCF.[16]

The BIA had responded to the LWCF by surveying local parks and recreation departments, then compiling a best-practices manual in 1965 as *Bike Trails and Facilities—A Guide to their Design, Construction and Operation*, probably the first bicycle planning document published in significant numbers in the United States. Similarly, the BIA and the BOR organized the nation's first bike-ped conference, the "National Trails Symposium," in Chicago, in June 1971.[17] There was very little to contrast between American and European bicycle planning at this stage, because the focus in America was so overwhelmingly recreational. However, there was emerging the first inchoate strands of what would soon weave together to form vehicular cycling.

Fred DeLong was the technical editor of *Bicycling*, America's largest cycling magazine. An engineer, he was a technical consultant and project coordinator for the BIA and, starting in 1973, the U.S. delegate to technical committee TC-149 (bicycles) of the International Standards Organization (ISO).[18] He had also been the L.A.W.'s safety coordinator since about 1967, and in this capacity had written a booklet, *Bicycle Safety and Proficiency Tests* for the BIA and the league. Although it wasn't sophisticated by today's standards, it did keep schools, scout troops, and fraternal organizations from teaching bad technique at a time when instructing new cyclists to ride on the right side of the road was considered sufficiently controversial to warrant study and commentary by the National Safety Council. On the other hand, it was well written, illustrated and produced. It was featured in the French trade magazine *Le Cycle*, which reproduced several of its pages. In an editorial, *Le Cycle* suggested that this was the type of consumer-targeted project that the French cyclemakers' group should be considering. A shorter write-up also appeared in the British magazine *CycleTouring*, successor to the *CTC Gazette*.[19]

At about this time, DeLong had also developed his own version of a proficiency course for the Philadelphia Council of the AYH. At first a somewhat rudimentary course for relative beginners, it was soon expanded and improved. (DeLong even experimented with a mobile set of simulated railroad crossings to teach cyclists how to cross angled train and streetcar tracks. It could be adjusted from 45 to 15 degrees.) *Bicycling* began serializing excerpts from it in 1970. By 1972, *Bicycling* had run fourteen or fifteen such installments, and it now included such advanced topics as roadway placement on narrow, high-speed roads and column (paceline) riding. In 1974, after further refinement, an overview of it appeared in his book *DeLong's Guide to Bicycles and Bicycling*.[20]

The basic difference between the DeLong program and John Forester's later Effective Cycling was largely a matter of emphasis. DeLong stressed the tools generally needed by recreational cyclists for rural touring; Forester concentrated on suburban commuting. As DeLong wrote, the "prime requisite for safe and efficient cycling is the ability to maintain perfect balance without a swerving path ... the competent cyclist needs less than 24 inches of space, particularly if there is no curb. Having learned to maintain a smooth and steady path for long distances, you can ride relaxed in this lane knowing you can maintain a true course," especially in a paceline or group of cyclists. But for Forester, the *sine qua non* of competent cycling was the ability to make a vehicular left turn in heavy traffic.[21] After observing dense urban traffic in French cities, DeLong became convinced that there was no such thing as specialized commuter riding: if one was a trained road touring cycling, one already had the full toolbox needed to handle urban riding. After one of his Paris visits, DeLong wrote:

> The most striking thing was that we noticed many young bicycle riders taking part successfully in the traffic mix. Apparently they had been taught from the start how to handle themselves in traffic. *The needed skills don't belong only to seasoned experts.* They can be learned by children of 10 or 12 years.[22]

The difference boiled down to a question of whose behavior was intended to be changed through the educational program. DeLong's program was internally focused: it concentrated on improving the cyclist's ability to use his or her bicycle. Forester's program, on the other hand, was external: it stressed the cyclist's ability to gain mastery over *the other road users* around him in any particular situation. "How do you handle motorists when you change lanes?" Forester asked. "Are you confident, or are you betrayed by uncertainty ... yes, you'll never do it right until you feel deep down inside that you are as important as motorists."[23]

Although he made part of his living as a technical consultant to the BIA, DeLong grew worried very early after the start of the great 10-speed bike boom that the industry was starting to place too much of its emphasis on bike trails. "The bicycle is a legitimate vehicle which has a right to use the public highways," he wrote in 1972. "Bike paths can be helpful, but bike paths in all too many instances suffer their own problems ... the cycle path movement can lead to entrapment of the cyclist in a limited sphere."[24] He had become convinced of this on

> several recent trips in Paris and about 2,500 miles throughout France [which] brought into focus the concept of "all roads for all users" ... if cyclists can be trained to ride skillfully and motorists trained to accept cyclists' rights to the road when it does not interfere, we already have millions of miles of bike paths for our use in the U.S.A.[25]

The first widely disseminated bicycle-planning report was *Bikeway Planning Criteria and Guidelines*, prepared by the Institute of Transportation and Traffic Engineering of the University of California at Los Angeles (UCLA-ITTE) in April 1972 and republished in November of that year by the Federal Highway Administration. As will be discussed in greater detail in a later section, the report did not represent a full cross-section of expert opinion as to what constituted state-of-the-art bicycle planning, nor was it intended to do so. It was prepared in response to a specific California legislative mandate to investigate "alternatives to bicycling on public streets and highways," and much of the work was done by two faculty members at the University of California–Davis who had written an early research paper reprinted in an April 1971 issue of the *Congressional Record*. That paper, "Bikeways in Action," concluded that "just as one cannot have a railroad without tracks, or a bus system without highways, so one needs special facilities and regulations for bicycle traffic."[26]

Bikeway Planning Criteria and Guidelines was predicated on the need for physical separation between motor vehicles and bicycles, commenting at one point that "it should be emphasized that the efficacy of the various at-grade intersection designs presented in this section depends to a large extent on cyclists staying in their defined rights-of-way." For example, its designs were based on cyclists making two-stage left turns at intersections, much like Miller McClintock's "Philadelphia System" left turn of the 1920s. This presumption was retained in *Bikeway Planning Criteria and Guidelines* in spite of the fact that after six years of research and experimentation in Davis, the report's contributors admitted that "more often than not, [Davis] cyclists make left turns on the basis of convenience rather than following the right angle method," and that while "the Davis city officials were very favorable to the bicycle paths, however, to a man they commented about the intersection problems" inherent to forced two-stage left turns.[27]

Just why these planners continued to advocate a set of solutions that had, in practice, already been rejected by both users and the practicing engineers responsible for administering, enforcing and maintaining them is a topic that must be left for later. (Suffice it for now to say that the UC-Davis planner/authors were more interested in promoting a new class of strictly utilitarian cyclists than they were in accommodating the utilitarian tripmaking of already-existing enthusiast cyclists.) The point here is that when astute local planners attempted to implement the UCLA-ITTE model to their own municipalities, they quickly realized something was wrong.

In June 1973, Ralph Hirsch, an associate professor of urban planning at Drexel University, performed a pilot bicycle commuting study for downtown Philadelphia. Using regular transportation modeling methods, he estimated that 3 percent of automobile work trips to the center city could be diverted to bicycles, about 7,200 one-way trips. However, when he attempted to plot a network of bicycle facilities he was forced to admit:

> Experience with bike lanes and other bikeways elsewhere suggests that cyclists tend to prefer the shorter, more direct routes, even if these are more heavily traveled, to longer, more circuitous routes.... Each corridor is approximately 1 to 1½ miles wide, so that a bikelane established to serve its residents would not require an excessive detour ... particular corridors have been selected not because they necessarily include a good potential bikelane within them, but rather because they illustrate the principle by which potential demand for a bikelane can be estimated.[28]

In other words, after establishing a demand potential of 7,200 one-way bike trips, Hirsch was forced to lay down a network of bicycle facilities in corridors where he knew they could not be built, because if he situated them only in those corridors where their construction was feasible, then that pool of 7,200 trips dropped to unacceptably low levels. This was because the bikeway network became so loosely woven that the trip lengths for most origin-to destination combinations stretched out too long. His initial simulation model, like the assumption of the Davis planners, presumed that cyclists were like railroad trains, and could only follow bicycle facilities. If limited to a network of only feasible, realistic facilities, then the additional distances added by the diverting from bikeway to bikeway stretched out the total trip length for each cyclist to the point where cycling offered no advantages over other modes.

Ultimately, Hirsh should have dropped the "railroad track" assumption and let his model free up cyclists to travel over unaltered roadways that they would pick-and-choose through a combination of directness and some kind of compatibility or selection criteria. But that was a fairly subtle idea (the realization that car drivers regularly deviated from shortest path/fastest path out of discomfort or intimidation, especially from freeways, was fairly new, and not well understood), and would not be tackled quantitatively for bicycle use for another 20 years or so.

In his 1973 plan, Hirsch simply (and straightforwardly) admitted that he was stumped by his own results. Where everyone else had set out to do a *bikeways* plan from the start, Hirsch had at least tried to do a *bicycle* plan, but in the home stretch fell back into the familiar assumptions of a facilities-dependent model (the "railroad track" myth). In the end, he failed to grasp the distinction, although he did recognize that his own plan was generating an internal contradiction somewhere that he could not explain. In fact, without realizing it, the Philadelphia commuter plan was the first hard evidence that bikeway-dependent plans didn't work. It just wasn't possible to lay down a network of facilities based solely on ease of implementation (ignoring projected use or any other demand criteria), then derive a set of use projections from the network that would justify its construction. Shuttling cyclists back and forth between bikeways that had been laid down simply because they were the lowest-hanging fruit on the tree just increased travel distances to the point where all the simulated travelers chose some other mode. Cyclists either ignored the bikeway system, cycling straight from A to B on the regular roadway network, or they left their bicycles at home and drove.

Bicycle facilities planning, like any other form of transportation planning, had to start with the demand projections based on pure, as-the-arrow-flies desire lines, then make its facilities recommendations based on those lines. Even if the resulting facilities map yielded infeasible projects, at least it was honest. Traditional transportation planners are used to working with a set of goals, opportunities and constraints that, in the end, yield a null solution set. The typical answer is to wait a few years, try again, and see if any circumstances have changed.[29]

The UC-Davis planners were wrong: bicycles aren't railroad engines. They don't run on guideways called bikeways. In fact, they don't need any transport facility at all, as anyone who has cut through a parking lot or across a park can attest. Also, without a guarantee of sufficient, irrevocable funds to implement the entire planned network in a short period of time (say, ten years or less), a bikeways plan is meaningless, because partial or compromised implementation will simply result in a return to the status quo.

Distinguishing between a bikeways plan and a bicycle plan came to be *the* critical watershed concept in the history of American bicycle planning. (In some circles, the distinction is *still* not fully appreciated.) Further complicating matters is the fact that in America, mainstream planning is often used as a way of delaying or avoiding, not facilitating, government action. In the coming decades, very few government agencies would take the facilities elements of their own bicycle plans seriously. There was rarely the money, dedication, or leadership needed to implement safe and useful bicycle networks. But as was starting to dawn on Ralph Hirsch, and would become clear later on to a younger generation of brasher, more irreverent planners, the facilities element really wasn't where the action was at in the typical bicycle plan. It was just there in case some kind of miracle should fall out of the sky. And in urban planning since 1980, miracles have been few and far between.

* * *

In May 1973, 13 months after the state of California issued *Bikeway Planning Criteria and Guidelines*, the U.S. Department of Transportation (USDOT) hosted the "Bicycles USA" conference at its Transportation Systems Center in Cambridge, Massachusetts. The majority of the of the presentations were stock bike-trail material, but a young technician for the National Park Service, who had been assigned a presentation on "bicycle trails, their construction and use," prefaced his remarks by stating:

> I strongly disagree with those who suggest that biking be limited to exclusive bike trails and bike lanes. So much more can be done for so many more bikers through the development of procedures for creating safe bike routes along urban streets. I think that trails should be provided under two conditions only: (1) as the only alternative for safe bicycling in an area either parallel to a major highway or connecting two or more major points; or, (2) to provide a unique recreational facility.[30]

By the end of the decade, that young technician, Bill Wilkinson, would be the executive director of the BIA, but only after spending most of intervening years working within the federal Department of Transportation on bicycle and pedestrian matters.

Shortly before Wilkinson addressed the "Bicycles USA" conference, the city of Santa Barbara, California, had issued a request for proposals to do "a small study" on bicycle accidents in the city. Dr. Kenneth Cross was a principal at a Southern California research firm named Anacapa Sciences. They bid on the project and won. "We did a pretty conventional study," Cross later recalled, "it was just about the same thing everyone else had done."[31]

When they finished, Santa Barbara gave Anacapa a follow-up contract to develop a bike-safety program based on the data collected so far. "The problem was that I couldn't define good, hard, definite educational objectives," Cross remembers. Frustrated, he started physically sorting the accident reports into stacks of similar accident types. The number of piles ended up being surprisingly small—less than a handful. He then broke down each stack into subtypes. "I ended up with a very crude typology. As I recall, we identified ten accident types that accounted for 90 percent of all accidents." Given the available data, that was the best he could do: "All I had at the time was ... traffic accident forms. As you know, they don't have complete information, but ... it gave us insights into the different types of accidents."

Cross discovered that "there's not a very high correlation between ways bicyclists have assumed car-bike collisions occur and the ways they actually occur." Busy streets weren't the problem; it was cross-movements that mattered—turns by cars, and vehicles entering and exiting the traffic stream. The resulting school safety program stressed hazard identification, and downplayed the teaching of manual skills. "I think there will be a movement away from training in bicycle handling skills," Cross predicted at the time. "Vehicle handling skills and deficiencies don't seem to be important problems." There was one exception to this, however: on-road training: "I personally would like to see lots of on-road training, because I think it is the highest fidelity training you can get."

In 1974, the National Highway Traffic Safety Administration (NHTSA) awarded Anacapa Sciences a contract for a similar, but much larger, study. "[They] wanted an accident typology and I had a rudimentary typology," Cross explained. The study required three years, with the preliminary results not ready until May 1977. Meanwhile, in 1975, Ralph Hirsch, through a nonprofit organization he directed, the Bicycle and Pedestrian Transportation Research Center, sought financial support for a program "to combine the Ken Cross approach to hazard recognition with the Fred DeLong approach to cycle proficiency training ... the best available training in on-the-road bicycle proficiency."[32]

That same year, the Kamehameha Schools, outside Honolulu, began what was undoubtedly the most advanced bicycle training program in the country. The Kamehameha Schools is a privately endowed high school serving the needs of native Hawaiian and part–Hawaiian students. To ensure proper maintenance and operational uniformity, the school decided to use its own bicycles, purchasing twelve Fuji and Gitane 10-speeds. Over the course of thirty 45-minute daily classes, students were taught on-the-road skills. They also learned bicycle maintenance, using special "drone" bicycles, such as 10-speeds cut down to only their power trains or front- and rear-brakes. Students were eventually taught to ride in heavy traffic and on rollers. Despite the breath and intensity of the program, set-up costs ran to only about $5,000, and operational costs (not including staff salaries) were covered by a five dollar per student "lab" fee. By 1980, almost 500 students had taken the program.[33]

In December 1972, the Metropolitan Association of Urban Designers and Environmental Planners (MAUDEP), an affiliate of the American Society of Civil Engineers (ASCE), held the first annual MAUDEP Bicycle-Pedestrian Planning and Design Conference in San Francisco. A featured speaker was Jim

Konski, ASCE's vice-president, an ex–bicycle racer, still-avid cyclist, and regular contributor to *Bicycling* and other publications.

Konski argued that "the transportation and utility aspects [of cycling] are only offsprings of the prime factors," which were its recreational and sporting aspects. "A properly designed bicycle is a high precision instrument that requires skill and knowledge to use ... [because] a person is traveling by bicycle at about 20 miles per hour." Such a device, in the hands of a skilled user, could not be accommodated on an exclusive facility unless it had been designed and built to such high standards that it cost "about 70 percent of what a two-lane secondary highway would cost."

Konski found that the biggest problem thus far in promoting a sound, nationwide program was that, while public officials were willing to accept "the bicycle as a real thing," he believed "they have not been able to grasp its full potential." Likewise, the public did not appreciate to what extent a trained cyclist on a precision bicycle was capable of achieving. "The prospect of bicycling for solving some of our urban transportation problems, as well as better health, environmental and recreational needs, is highly dependent upon the development of what I call 'better bicyclism,'" he stated. "Bicyclism," he explained, was defined as "the art and practice of bicycling."[34]

Developing "better bicyclism" required public support for racing, or at least an active culture of club-level performance cycling along the lines of youth-league football or soccer: "Why is it important to advance the sport of racing if we are to provide bike routes and paths? Because if the public understands the sport and learns why the serious cyclist does the things that he does, the individual, though he may not be interested or capable of racing, will be better able to apply this knowledge." He asserted that so far, most "bike paths or bike trails or whatever you want to call them," had been failures. "Why? The answer is simple ... [they] did not have a sufficient knowledge of bicyclism."

Thus, Konski recommended that all aspects of cycling, from the development of engineering standards for bikeways, to accident research, to the preparation and training of regional and Olympic racing teams, should be vested in "a [single] national agency or organization with strong leadership ... by people who fully understand both bicyclism and the transportation disciplines."

Here was the basic outline of a new and uniquely American style of bicycle planning. Its emphasis on the use of the existing roadway system and cyclists' traffic skills was borrowed from the urban experience of France and England. As both DeLong and Konski pointed out, "bicyclism" needed a system of proficiency education and training. But most importantly, this nascent "American System" was firmly grounded within a recreational or sporting context. Few, if any, participants were expected to be strictly utilitarian cyclists; transportation was an ancillary activity that enthusiasts would participate in because it gave them another reason to ride.

If any single characteristic could be said to define a unique "American" style of bicycle planning, this would be it: the assumption that its constituency would always be made up of utilitarian trip-makers drawn from an existing pool of recreational cyclists. In other words, it was presumed from the start that planners couldn't make utility riders out of non-cyclists on the basis of pure economics. Potential cyclists simply could not be induced to respond to time and cost considerations in the same way as transit riders or auto drivers. Bicycle planning would always require an exogenous "pull" factor—an interest in cycling.

This was verified by Eric Hirst of the Oak Ridge National Laboratories who prepared a report, *Energy Use for Bicycling*, a few months after Konski's speech. After doing some econometric modeling, Hirst concluded that if the appropriate value-of-time factors were included, bicycle commuting was economically superior to car use only if the commute distance was no more than a mile each way, the commuter earned no more than $1.10 per hour ($4.80 to $6.30 in 2013 dollars), or the cyclist actually enjoyed the activity, so their time in the saddle was perceived as a benefit, not a cost.

The average commute at that time was easily over three miles long (19 minutes by car for a suburb-to-suburb commute; 25 minutes for a core-to-core commute; and 35 minutes for a suburb-to-core trip), so Hirst's model essentially predicted two distinct classes of cyclists. The first was involuntary utilitarians, who rode because they had no access to a car or suburban transit, or couldn't afford expensive downtown parking; the second group was voluntary enthusiasts who saw their daily journey to work as an opportunity get in some more saddle time.[35]

The idea that bicycle use would have to settle for the existing roadway system and rely on improving cyclists' skill in moving within the traffic stream had no name, no identifier, no "hook." (Even Konski quickly gave up on "bicyclism.") But in late 1974, Harold C. ("Hal") Munn, a CalTrans engineer and active member of the Los Angeles Wheelmen, read a paper before a meeting of the American Society of Civil Engineers. "Most of the bikeway thinking to date has been directed towards finding ways to separate bicycles from the normal flow of vehicular traffic," he noted. Whether one thought this was good or bad was largely a moot question, because the simple truth was that separate facilities *wouldn't* be built because they *couldn't* be built:

> Time and experience are bringing us back to reality. There is simply no way to create separate bikeway systems to any significant extent in 20th Century urban America ... the pressure to provide additional capacity for motor vehicle has been unrelenting on nearly every roadway in the nation. Until very recently, reserving space on the

> road for bicycles was the last thing on anyone's mind.... Can traffic engineers and public officials provide for, and then persuade, the motoring public to accept some minimum provision for bicycle use of the public roads? The possibilities at present are very limited.[36]

Therefore, Munn concluded, "The bicyclist will have no choice but to mix with motorized traffic," and as a result, for "transportation purposes it is more realistic and productive to think in terms of integrating the bicycle into the normal flow of vehicular traffic." It was therefore necessary to convince adult cyclists "to operate their bicycles as they do their automobiles." His paper, published the following year in the *Transportation Engineering Journal*, was the first to refer to the "vehicular integration" of cycling, or as it eventually became known, "vehicular cycling."

The definition of what constitutes "vehicular cycling" has been contested ground for forty years, and continues to be vigorously debated. For the sake of consistency, when I refer to vehicular cycling, what I mean is a broad, generalized approach to bicycle planning grounded in three general assumptions or principles:

1. Most cycling will be carried out on the existing roadway system, if for no other reason than programs to build specialized bicycle facilities will never be given the adequate, consistent levels of funding needed to make them workable except in a few special communities.
2. Almost all utility cycling is, and will continue to be, done by willing, if not enthusiastic recreational cyclists as an extension of their pre-existing interest in cycling. This assumption is highly questionable. It is poorly supported by the available quantitative data, if not actually refuted by it. It is, nevertheless, a foundational presumption of vehicular cycling across the entire ideological spectrum and so it is included here.
3. Educational programs are the most cost-effective way to increase cyclist safety, even if they may not be attractive to the population as a whole. Whether this is a sound assumption depends primarily on the veracity of Point No. 2 above. After all, if most utility cyclists do not like to bicycle, and do it only out of extreme need or coercion, then it is, of course, unrealistic to expect that they can be persuaded to take the time or trouble to improve their skills through educational programs.

Generally, I am talking about "vehicular cycling" as *something that government does, not something that cyclists do.* It is a government policy, or rather, an interrelated set of government policies. However, there is nothing that prevents individuals, nongovernmental organizations, and for profit corporations from participating in the formulation, implementation, or change in these policies.

Vehicular cycling, in the way that I use it in this book, is not an educational program, a cycling philosophy, or a cycling method. Whether one believes that a cyclist should ride 18 inches or six feet out from the curb; or whether a cyclist should queue up with the cars at a red light or work his or her way up to the front of the line; or whether one should turn left from the traffic lane or within the crosswalk is largely irrelevant as to whether one is *really* talking about vehicular cycling, or has wandered off on some irrelevant (or heretical) topic. It is of no interest as far as *this* book is concerned.

As will be discussed later, there are dozens of different books, pamphlets, videos, and educational programs for teaching (sub)urban bicycle use, all of which profess to show the student how to do so, and do it in a way dramatically different from any other program, sharing in common only an emphatic certainty of the disaster that will befall the hapless student should they pay the least attention to anything in any of the others' approach. They all, of course, assert with equal veracity and great gusto their sole, true legitimacy to the label of "vehicular cycling." On the other hand, what they do equally share, as their central purpose, is the mission of instructing the cyclist to ride in an environment largely devoid of exclusive facilities or extensive roadway modifications to accommodate their presence. The essence of vehicular cycling is not situated in these various educational programs, nor in the ideological squabbles behind their fragmented diversity. The essence of vehicular cycling is in what they share: a consensus that their graduates are going to go out and use a roadway system that is unmodified or unimproved to accommodate their use, and that they must be prepared for this. For all their bickering fragmentation, they have been anointed by the powers-to-be as the solution. They *are* the system.

* * *

Probably the earliest success in American bicycle advocacy was in the area of legislative changes. Most state traffic laws followed the Uniform Vehicle Code (UVC), maintained by a non-profit organization called the National Committee on Uniform Traffic Laws and Ordinances (NCUTLO). However, states rarely updated their own laws in perfect synchronicity with each new revision of the model code, so in almost every case a state's traffic statutes were a hodgepodge of new and old versions of the UVC. Moreover, while no state was required to adhere to the UVC, a state that started to diverge too far from the currently adopted version ran the risk that automobile insurance companies would raise rates or pull out of the state.

California bicycle clubs had formed a statewide interest group in 1972 called the California Association of Bicycling Organizations (CABO). To keep it going, its expenses were underwritten by the L.A.W. and the Bicycle Institute of America. In April 1973, CABO convinced Senator James Mills to introduce Senate Concurrent Resolution 47 (SCR-47) to form a State Bikeways Committee and report back on needed legislative changes by early 1975. Members were selected in late 1973 and committee meetings began in early 1974. In the fall of 1974, a series of public meetings was held in various venues around the state. The final report was prepared between October 1974 and February 1975. John Forester was selected as CABO's representative.[37]

But the real driving force behind SCR-47 was its chairman, Richard Rogers, who had just been appointed to direct CalTrans's office of bicycle facilities. He was himself a skilled cyclist, in addition to being an able administrator, and he realized that one of the primary problems was that the language in state statute requiring cyclists to "ride as near the right-hand curb on the edge of the roadway as practicable." This language, taken from the UVC, was ambiguous when it came to such things as left turns and overtaking slower vehicles because the UVC did not define a bicycle as a vehicle, but only gave them the rights and duties of a vehicle, a status that was itself rather obscure and open to self-interested interpretation.

Contrary to the widespread belief that the "all rights and duties" language was intended to create a separate class of traffic laws for cyclists within Chapter 11 of the UVC (the model traffic code of state laws), the exclusion of bicycles from the definition of "vehicle" (subsection 1–184) had actually been intended to exempt bicycles from the recommended *penalty schedule* in Chapter 17, the UVC's Model Traffic Ordinance (MTO) for local governments.

In an era when most cyclists were children, the goal was to make bicycle traffic violators subject to either a local fine of $5 or confiscation of the bicycle under the MTO. Presumably, child offenders would be given the largely symbolic fine, while adult offenders would have their cycles seized. Ironically, one side effect of making bicycles vehicles was to incorporate the "$5 or confiscation" penalty schedule into the UVC itself in 1983, but soon thereafter, in most states, confiscation was eliminated because it was held to be an unconstitutional seizure under the fifth amendment to confiscate a bicycle as a penalty for a simple traffic violation.[38]

In August 1974, Rogers took the unusual step of seeking a formal interpretation from the California Attorney General's office as to the "ride to the right" language, and whether it over-rode the more general language in the traffic code that applied to such things as left turns, overtaking slower vehicles and obstructions, and so on in California statutes.

Meanwhile, three months after the California Statewide Bicycle Committee was formed, the NCUTLO itself decided to act. In March 1974, its important subcommittee on operations named a five-member panel to prepare a report recommending changes to the UVC to improve its relevance in an era when many more cyclists were adults. The panel would report back to the operations subcommittee, which would then winnow down the changes it thought appropriate to the full national committee. That body could either approve some or all of the changes for inclusion in the next edition of the UVC; reject them; or recommend that they be put to a vote before the full membership, about 140 members.

The members were Harold Michael of Purdue University (Chairman); Marie Birnbaum, director of the bike-ped office at the USDOT; Morgan Groves, executive director of the L.A.W.; Ken Pulver of the Reno Police Department; and Larry Wuellner of the Missouri AAA. (The Missouri auto club was, somewhat surprisingly at this early stage, a progressive force in developing bicycle and pedestrian safety education programs.) The NCUTLO shipped each member what Morgan Groves later described as a "truckload" of materials preliminary to the panel's October 1974 meeting. Afterward, they wrote up their recommendations in a 122-page report that was released in late January 1975, about two weeks before the corresponding California report.[39]

The Michael Panel's report contained three primary recommendations. The first was that a bicycle should be included within the definition of a "vehicle" and that the old, tortuous "all rights and duties" language in section 11-1202 be dropped. If a particular section of the code did not inherently apply to bicycles, it should be changed to read "motor vehicle" or otherwise altered to indicate those classes of vehicles to which it did apply. Actually, this was a more complex change than it sounds at first. Up to 1938, the UVC had given bicycles the responsibility to follow traffic laws, but none of its rights, including (according to an opinion offered by the Oregon legislative policy staff) the normal right-of-way accorded to all other vehicles at intersections and traffic control devices.[40] From 1938 to 1974, section 11-1202 gave a bicycle rider all the rights and all the duties of a vehicle except when specifically countermanded in a given section and "except as to those provisions of [the UVC] which by their nature can have no application." However, bicycles continued to be excluded from the definition of a vehicle itself. The question of whether any given reference in the UVC "by its nature" could have "no application" (and just who had the power to make that call) was always rather fuzzy. For the panel to specifically include bicycles within the section 1-134 definition of "vehicle," then insert contravening language in every situation where it was clearly inappropriate (for example, in sections dealing with the transfer of titles or prohibiting vehicles with solid tires from driving on highways) required changing about 32 different sections of the code.[41]

But it was two other recommendations of the Michael Panel that were the most controversial. They advocated striking the "ride to the right" (section 11-1205[a]) and "mandatory sidepath" (section 11-1205[c]) regulations. The panel made a number of other, more technical recommendations, including changes clarifying the sections regulating bicycle racing, bicycle parking, and required nighttime equipment. They also recommended *against* a number of changes, proposing no specific regulations controlling bicycle lane use, bicycle paths at highways crossings, the use of the entire lane by cyclists, right turn conflicts, or bicycle-specific speed limits.

Returning to the "ride to the right" rule, the panel explained:

> UVC § 11-301(b) [already] requires all vehicles proceeding at less than the normal speed of traffic at the time and place and under the conditions then existing to stay in the right hand lane, or as close as practicable to the right-hand curb or edge of the roadway, except when passing or preparing for a left turn.... This is all that is needed. Some members of the Panel expressed concern that a bicycle could ride anywhere in the right lane, and where this is the only lane available, this would hold up traffic unnecessarily. Others noted that such an obstruction is no more than any other slow moving vehicle would cause when there is only one lane for the direction of traffic, and that the bicyclist should have no greater duty to pull over than any other driver of a slow moving vehicle.... Nevertheless, it should be left to the bicyclist to determine when he should pull over on the basis of his perception of what is safe and reasonable. If he has a good reason for not pulling over, he should be allowed to stay out in the lane, and the law should not suggest to other drivers that they have a legal right to substitute their judgment for the bicyclists and demand that he pull over.

The Michael Panel thus concluded that UVC § 11-1205(a) should be deleted in its entirety from the code.[42] Similarly, when it came to the "mandatory sidepath" section:

> The consensus of the Panel following discussion was that if a trail is safe and convenient, it will be used without the necessity of a law mandating its use.... There is no more of a need for a law requiring bicyclists to use bike lanes than there is a law requiring bus drivers to use bus lanes. While bicycle paths do separate the bicycle and motor vehicle traffic, such paths create new and possibly more serious safety problems at intersections. The Panel was not convinced that requiring bicyclists to use a bike path adjacent to a roadway provides greater safety.[43]

While supportive of the redefinition of a bicycle as a vehicle and most of the technical changes, NCUTLO's subcommittee on operations was so horrified by the idea of removing the "ride to the right" section that it refused to even consider reporting it out to the full national committee. On the other hand, it did reluctantly report out the recommendation to eliminate the mandatory side-path rule, but the national committee, at its July 1974 meeting, approved only the amendment redefining the bicycle as a vehicle.[44]

Meanwhile, in California, Richard Rogers had gotten his answer from the state attorney general's office about what California's version of the "ride to the right" rule (section 21202) meant. Its wording was virtually identical to that in the UVC. Noting that the state's vehicle code allowed vehicles to move left for turns, to overtake slower vehicles, and to avoid obstacles, the attorney general observed that

> as a result of the enactment of section 21202, any person operating a bicycle on a two-way roadway must operate his bicycle as close as practicable to the right-hand curb. The bicycle operator apparently has no discretion to operate his bicycle in any other place, and this would seem to take precedence over those statutes cited above which permit drivers to move to the left in certain specified situations. Indeed, this interpretation would be in accordance with the familiar rule of statutory construction that a special statute which deals with a particular subject takes precedence over a general statute covering the same subject. In addition, it is certainly possible to argue that section 21202 precludes making left turns from the left turn pocket, or passing on the left, or moving to the left to avoid hazards, because the statute does not specifically provide for those hazards.[45]

However, the attorney general admitted that this interpretation had a big problem: it was nonsensical. It couldn't be made to work. "Such a construction would be both unreasonable and absurd," said the opinion. Therefore, the "ride to the right" law would have to be interpreted differently than normal, in a manner that would make it most consistent with other traffic regulations, while doing the least to circumvent its literal language.[46] Therefore, it should be interpreted to mean that cyclists could deviate from the right-hand edge of the road to make left turns, to overtake, and to avoid obstacles, because there were ordinances that specifically directed motor vehicle operators to do these things, and the code said that bicyclists had all the rights and duties of motor vehicle operators unless a provision "by its nature" was inapplicable.

Riding two abreast, on the other hand, was a different matter because there was no corresponding motor vehicle section: "However, it is our opinion that if two bicyclists are riding abreast of one another, both of whom are on the roadway, the one on the left would be in violation ... when bicyclists are operating on the roadway, they should ride in single file." This requirement was independent of any "obstructing traffic" law, so riding single file was required regardless of whether any other traffic was present. The attorney general suggested that the committee recommend to the legislature that the left turn, overtaking, and obstacle exceptions be incorporated into state statutes in order to avoid any confusion by judges and law enforcement officers in the future.[47]

Rogers and his committee essentially split the difference between the California Attorney General's recommendation and the strategy taken by the Michael Panel. Rather than simply recommend that the "ride to the right" provision be eliminated, as did Michael's NCUTLO panel, or include only exceptions for left turns, overtaking, and obstacle dodging, as the attorney general wanted them to do, they recommended that the state's law be modified to include *six* exceptions:

1. To permit a left turn at intersections or mid-block, such as into a driveway.
2. To avoid a hazardous condition.
3. To occupy a lane when it is too narrow to permit motor vehicles to overtake.
4. To pass a motor vehicle or bicycle.
5. When moving at the prevailing speed of traffic.
6. To travel two abreast when traffic is not impeded.

California state law did not mention "sidepaths," only "bikelanes." There was a sharp dissention in the committee between (reportedly two) members who wanted bikelane use to be made mandatory and (reportedly another two) members who equally strongly felt that all references to bikelanes in the statutes should be deleted. By a 5–4 vote, the committee's moderate center recommended a law that essentially applied the "ride to the right" exceptions to bike lanes, but without the "taking the lane" condition for narrow lanes. That is, cyclists were required to use the bike lane except to turn left, avoid obstacles, etc.

The committee also made what was probably its most important recommendation. It urged the addition of a new section of the code to limit the power of local governments to bicycle-related ordinances that dealt only with registration, parking and bikeway use. All other traffic laws were reserved to the California state code; localities could not unilaterally ban bicycles or enact non-uniform regulations. This was diametrically opposed to the then-current version of the UVC, which rather schizophrenically granted states and cities equal authority to create overlapping regulations for bicycles.[48] In 1975, the California legislature approved the SCR-47 recommendations made by Rogers's committee.

Returning to the nationwide model laws, after the main NCUTLO meetings in which the mandatory sidepath and "ride to the right" issues were defeated, Groves stepped down and was replaced by Bruce Burgess of the Bicycle Federation. From that point on, he and Ralph Hirsch, the legislative director of the L.A.W., carried the struggle forward. Generally, those who supported striking the mandatory sidepath rule were more optimistic than those who wanted to eliminate the "ride to the right" rule. Edward Kearney, chairman of NCUTLO's subcommittee on operations, and John English, its director of research, both approved of the sidepath amendment, although Kearney, a cyclist himself, was unenthusiastic about eliminating the "ride to the right" rule. The most important strategic change Burgess and Hirsch made was to abandon the earlier NCUTLO committee's strategy of totally eliminating the "ride to the right" rule and switching to the same "list of exceptions" approach that had worked for Richard Rogers at California's SCR-47 committee.

Burgess, together with the L.A.W.'s Ralph Hirsch, began a four-year lobbying campaign, mostly on the state level. Kearney's pessimism notwithstanding, it was the "ride to the right" rule that yielded first. In 1979 NCUTLO approved a change to section 11-1205(a) adding the same six exceptions that SCR-47 had developed in 1974–75, although the language used to define each exception was not always the same. However, it again rejected any change to the mandatory sidepath rule. A year earlier, the operations subcommittee had unanimously recommended dropping it after viewing a Burgess-prepared "horror show" of slides depicting inadequate, unmaintained, and dangerous sidepaths. In 1979, the same year it approved the "ride to the right" modification, 43 members of the national committee voted to eliminate the mandatory sidepath rule, a majority, but approvals required 50 ayes. The matter was, by standing rule, distributed to all 140 NCUTLO members for a mail-in vote. It received 71 votes; 86 were required. Burgess was still a NCUTLO member (with Hirsch as his alternate) in 1983 when NCUTLO finally voted to approve the amendment.[49]

By the mid–1980s, the California Association of Bicycle Organizations was having trouble meeting its costs. It elected to become part of the [California] Planning and Conservation League, a consortium of environmental lobbying groups based in Sacramento. The PCL has repeatedly had to fight to preserve the state-preemption clause that CABO gained in 1975, the law that limits local regulations to bicycle parking, registration and off-road use, thereby blocking local bike bans and road limitations. PCL has also fought for the provision of bicycle facilities such as secure parking, shower, and locker rooms, which have been frequently omitted from new developments in spite of state and local mandates requiring them.[50]

A coda: In 2008, the National Committee on Uniform Traffic Laws and Ordinances, the organization responsible for maintaining the UVC, rather suddenly announced that it was disbanding. It made no arrangements for succession or for delegating its functions to any other organization. It did not explain why it was disbanding. The most likely explanation is that the Federal Highway Administration had informed NCUTLO that it intended to make the UVC amendment process subject to notice-and-comment rulemaking under the Code of Federal Regulations. It had already done this with the Manual of Uniform Traffic Control Devices in 1982, allowing the National Committee on Uniform Traffic Control Devices, a similar private, non-profit organization, to carry on its coordinating and supervisory functions, but with each step subject to the federal Administrative Procedures Act and all the administrative documents subject to the Freedom of Information Act. In 2012, Secretary of Transportation Ray LaHood, expressing similar reservations over AASHTO—he specifically mentioned his unhappiness over the glacial pace and conservative recommendations generated to date in the process of updating the *Guide to the Development of New Bicycle Facilities*, suggested that it may be time to do the same for that venerable organization.

CHAPTER 4

The Dutch Challenge: Third-Stream Bicycle Planning, 1967–1974

Meanwhile, the small city of Davis, California, was moving ahead on a very different course. Davis, about 60 miles east of San Francisco, had, since 1907, been the site of the University of California's agricultural research station. In 1943, the state highway department relocated Highway 40 (later I-80) from its old route that took it through the center of downtown, making it a bypass southwest of the state agricultural farm and the town. Since then, Davis has been unburdened with regional traffic; the town did not grow over to the other side of I-80 until the 1970s.[1]

After World War II, the crush of post-war G.I. Bill students started to overwhelm the Berkeley campus, so the state upgraded Davis to an independent university in 1959 and put it on a crash construction program. Unusually spread out (a legacy of its agricultural school days; some buildings were almost a mile apart) and lacking an adequate campus transportation system, the new university's first chancellor, Emil Marak, requested in 1961, "I have asked our architects to plan for a bicycle-riding, treelined campus," and advised new students to bring a bicycle with them.[2]

Some historians argue that Davis's "bicycle city" reputation is as much symbol as substance. The issue is less the university (photographs from the 1950s and early 1960s consistently show an unusually large number of bicycles parked around, even for a university campus) than the city itself. The agricultural research station had been located in Davis because it was the northern anchor of the state's famous "inland empire," a huge, rich valley of produce, grains, and specialty crops such as tomatoes, avocados and nuts. Although in the 1950s Davis was still primarily a farm town, a 1956 proposal to build a tomato cannery sailed through the land use approval process, but to shock at city hall, it met vehement citizen opposition that held it up for years and required four referenda. The cannery's developers eventually prevailed and it was built in 1961. Opposition centered around the university's liberal arts and sciences faculty. From that point on, the lines were drawn: the older, traditional town, grounded in its agricultural-service sector, versus the younger "ivory tower" university community, with the ag-school standing uneasily on the sidelines.

The city's bikeway movement began in 1963, when faculty members Frank and Eve Child returned from a sabbatical in the Netherlands at almost exactly the same time the police were starting a crackdown on errant cyclists and the city council was enacting several new get-tough laws on riders. (There is disagreement about whether these were motivated by legitimate safety concerns or were part of a "town vs. gown" political skirmish. What little available evidence there is does not strongly support the latter.[3])

Assisted by Dale and Donna Lott, who arrived from Seattle in 1965, the Childs made bicycle use an important quality-of-life issue in municipal elections in 1964 and 1966, with an openly sympathetic slate of candidates elected in 1966. Bicycle facilities were a relatively cheap and highly visible way of proving that the old order had been overthrown, and that Davis was no longer a farm town with an agricultural school; it was now a small city with a full-fledged liberal arts and sciences university, one with aspirations to acquiring the cosmopolitan culture of a Berkeley, Cambridge, or Palo Alto.

A supportive city public works director, Dave Pelz, asked the university's staff for advice on implementing the new mandate, and the Lotts, Robert (Bob) Sommer, Melvin Ramey, William Adams, and graduate students Bonnie Kroll and Wes Lum, among others, created an informal research group to evaluate bicycle use and the design of facilities. Their work, which started in 1966, was highly experimental, and placed an emphasis on modifying the street system to facilitate utilitarian bicycle trips, often by cyclists of limited ability. "The city streets became our laboratory," recalled Sommer many years later. Donna Lott agrees: "Much of what we did was trial-and-error. We put things down. We took them up. We improved it and tried again."[4]

Bob Sommer traveled to Christchurch, New Zealand, to inspect the facilities there. Once known as "The Copenhagen of the Pacific," he found nearly disused old routes, and a pending proposal to ban bicycles from the central business district. Much the same was true when he visited Boston. Time appeared to be passing the bicycle by. "Such incidents generated a fear in me that if environmental supports were not developed and implemented for bicycle transportation, bikes would be squeezed out of urban areas," he remembered.[5]

It is clear that most of the university study group looked to European, particularly Dutch, techniques as a template. Frank Child, who had lived in the

Netherlands for several years, preferred the Amsterdam model, which stressed the complete separation of bicycles and motor vehicles, even to the point of placing bicycle lanes behind parked cars or grassed medians. While such designs improved most cyclists' perceived comfort in mid-block, they frequently created visibility problems and added conflict points at intersections.[6]

Bob Sommer and Dale Lott also pointed out the ambiguity inherent in the idea of a bike lane "which many automobile drivers interpret to mean 'Bikes Stay Inside' rather than 'Car Stay Out.'" But in the early years of their work, this is often the result for which the Davis Group was aiming. The Davis municipal traffic code in the late 1960s and early 1970s required cyclists to make what Miller McClintock had called in the 1930s a "Philadelphia Style" two-stage left turn. But Sommer and Lott themselves admitted that "most cyclists do not use the recommended two-stage right-angle procedure for making a left turn at a major intersection ... more often than not, cyclists make left turns on the basis of convenience rather than follow the right angle method." And after evaluating the Davis designs in 1972, Deleuw, Cather and Co. was even blunter, observing that those cyclists who made a Davis-style left turn from the bike lane had to cross the travel lines of all vehicle "approach movements except the right turn coming from the opposite approach." As a result, this "level of conflict, particularly with straight-through movements, generally requires the left-turning cyclist to wait through almost two complete [traffic signal] cycle phases, [so] cyclists generally execute a number of illegal forms of left turns which allow them to maintain momentum through the intersection."[7]

Even as this was being written, the Federal Highway Administration was taking a more skeptical view of such "forced" right-angle turns, and by the time of its multi-volume *Safety and Locational Criteria for Bikeways* (1975–76), it was actively cautioning against the practice, recommending instead that bike lanes be ended in advance of intersections and that cyclists be given the choice of either making a "Chicago-Style" left turn in the same manner as cars, or crossing in two legs within the crosswalks in the manner of a pedestrian.

Many of the Davis researchers preferred the design of "protected" or "sandwich" bike lanes where the motor vehicle and bicycle travel lanes were separated by a row of parallel-parked cars, parking lot bumpers placed end-to-end, or grass median strips. The Davis city engineers came to prefer the "Oregon" design, which placed the bike lane in the now-standard position between the curb and the motor vehicle travel lane. "To a man, they commented about the intersection problems," noted Dale Lott and Sommer, "the paths provided safety while riding parallel to the curb but did not help much at intersections." Ted Noguchi, the city traffic engineer at Palo Alto, went to Davis in 1972 to assess the work being done there "but I did not find it especially helpful, as the underlying conditions were quite different, the biggest difference being the amount of off-street parking needed to be removed to make a system work." David Takemoto-Werts, the Davis bicycle coordinator in 2005, noted that these "ill-fated designs were phased out long ago, [but] some facilities design decisions made decades ago were not so easy to remedy."[8] The research group believed that many of the operational problems they observed could be addressed by placing additional restrictions on motorized traffic, eliminating on-street parking, converting streets to one-way operation, or installing separate traffic-signal phases just for bicycles.

The first work at UC-Davis resulted in a stridently pro-bikeway report published in the *Congressional Record* in April, 1971. "Just as one cannot have a railroad without tracks or a bus system without highways," it concluded, "one needs special facilities and regulations for bicycle traffic ... *no bike paths, no bicycles*." That summer, the California legislature asked CalTrans to undertake a study that both explored "alternatives to bicycling on public streets and highways" and studied "the most feasible and least expensive methods by which existing and future public streets and thoroughfares can more safety accommodate bicycle riders." The Institute of Transportation and Traffic Engineering at the University of California-Los Angeles (UCLA-ITTE) integrated these somewhat mutually exclusive goals into "A Study of Bicycle Path Effectiveness," focusing on "providing bicycle facilities within street rights-of way," that is, on bike lanes and sidewalk-style bike paths.[9]

Its final report, *Bikeway Planning Criteria and Guidelines*, they adopted several Davis designs, such as their "sandwich" bike lane, and the use of small berms to separate travel lanes from bike lanes in intersections to force cyclists to make two-step, right-angle, pedestrian-style left turns. This probably shouldn't be surprising, as much of the work was done in Davis, and UC-Davis's Mel Ramey was a co-author. Ramey recalls:

> I was in my office and received a call from my department chair. The people at UCLA-ITTE wanted someone at Davis to send a proposal to the Federal Highway Administration. The UCLA people had no expertise in this area and knew the Davis faculty were interested in bikes. I had been a transportation planner in graduate school and had done rail and highway planning, and I was an assistant professor who needed grants.[10]

The implication is that most, if not all, of the work on the "UCLA" report was actually done in Davis by the UC-Davis research group, although the primary authors were listed as Gary Fisher of UCLA and Mel Ramey of UC-Davis.[11]

Bob Sommer acknowledged that the design cyclist the Davis group had in mind was the average junior-high-school bicycle user:

> Laws, practices and policies pertaining to cycling must take into account that the largest number of riders are under the age of 16. This does not mean that all bike

> laws, like TV shows, should be written for ten-year olds ... [but] one cannot pretend that the bikeway struggle is between two groups of purists—touring cyclists and amateur ecologists—and ignore the millions of school age cyclists as non-persons.[12]

Some experienced cyclists had complained that riding bikeways at roadway-like speeds was "a 1,000 times more dangerous than riding on the roadway." His response was equally brusque: slow down or hang up the bike. "Arguments against laws and policies of the bike reformers ... are motivated explicitly by self interest," he retorted. "It is true that a bikeway system intended to provide safe riding for children will crimp the style of more experienced riders ... [but] the old solutions based on a small number of experienced and competent individuals no longer are effective." Donna Lott was just as blunt: "None of us had ridden in a double century or ever would. We liked to do our daily travel around town by bike, and wanted to preserve that feature of life in Davis."[13]

Traditionally, American bicycle planners have been portrayed as belonging to one of two philosophical groups: either pro-bikeways inclusionists, or radical-libertarian "Effective Cyclists." This analytical dichotomy has created a great deal of historical confusion and distortion. This is because there were not *two*, but *three* distinct schools of bicycle planning in the United States in the early 1970s.

First, there was a broad, ill-defined mainstream, then as now, largely pragmatic, eclectic, and incremental. At this very early stage, its strategy could best be described as "try a little bit of everything." Second, there was a rapidly emerging cadre of vehicular cyclists. They were diverse, leaderless, lacking in ideology, and often unaware of each other's existence. About the only thing they shared was youth, a passionate interest in cycling, and a desire to become involved in government. (This latter would change; an explanation is forthcoming.) Finally, there was an active third-stream comprised of egalitarianists such as the Davis Group, Michael Everett in Tennessee, Ken Kolsbun in Santa Barbara, and others.

The third-streamers openly advocated policies that specifically targeted the weakest and most vulnerable bicyclists and involuntary users who rode strictly out of need, not choice. Together, these comprised cycling's lowest common denominator, and for the third stream planners, they formed the yardstick by which to measure success or failure. If high-end recreational cyclists couldn't live with their solutions, well, there were lots of other sports in the world they could turn to. As one Netherlands traffic engineer remarked, replying to a question at an American workshop about that nation's post-seventies bicycle planning program:

> What do "enthusiast cyclists" think? What *is* an "enthusiast cyclist?" Cycling is just something you do. You have to get from point A to point B, so you get on your bike

and you ride. It's like a toothbrush. You get up, you brush your teeth. What's the big deal? Do you subscribe to *Toothbrush Times*? Join a toothbrush club?[14]

Some ardently pro-bikeway advocates have asserted that Sommer and Lott's 1971 *Congressional Record* report formed the bedrock of American bicycle planning. For example, Davis historians Ted Buehler and Susan Handy claim that "the bike lane standards established by Davis were adopted as part of the state highway code and in 1974 by the Federal Highway Administration."[15] The written record does not bear this out. Instead, the work of the Davis research group appears to have been an evolutionary dead-end. While Davis's Dutch-influenced facilities did exist briefly alongside later designs developed elsewhere, they died out with amazing rapidity. As early as 1974, the Federal Highway Administration's (FHWA) preliminary survey document *Bikeways—State of the Art*—noted that bike lanes "which employ positive barriers to protect the lanes make it difficult for cyclists to cross the street at mid-block ... as a result they tend to produce bi-directional use with the attendant problems of both bike/bike conflicts in the lane and bicycle/motor vehicle traffic steam conflicts at intersections and driveway crossings ... because of these kinds of problems, employment of the protected lane concept is becoming less frequent."[16]

Many of the Davis bikeway designs were further downgraded to "not recommended" by the time the final two reports in the FHWA series, *Safety and Locational Criteria for Bicycle Facilities,* were completed in 1976.[17] The "Oregon" design, with the bikeway placed to the right of the automobile travel lanes—preferably on roadways without parallel parking that could lead to "dooring"—became the universally preferred standard. Even the city of Davis changed with the times, as municipal bicycle coordinator David Takemoto-Weerts recounted in 1998:

> Because Davis pioneered the bike lane and other bicycle facilities in this country, it is not surprising that some facilities were less successful than others. One such example was the construction of "protected" bike lanes where motor vehicle and bicycle traffic was separated by a raised buffer or curbing ... [the] benefits of such facilities were soon found to be outweighed by the many such hazards created for their users. Most such well intentioned, but ill-fated designs were phased out years ago.[18]

Buehler and Handy admit that "eventually, all lanes [in Davis] were converted to the now-familiar configuration of the bike lane between the moving cars and parked cars." Moreover, "Davis was slow to adopt designs invented elsewhere ... [although] bicycle design infrastructure was still evolving.... Not a single multi-use path had been built [by 2000] with state-required clear zones or bollard markings. Early on, it was reasoned that these innovations were not needed for Davis. Davis had a high enough number of bicyclists and light car traffic."[19]

In 1975, civil engineer Robert Wortman observed that "in some respects, the history of bikeway design is analogous with the evolution of freeway and expressway design in the United States during the period of the 1950s and the 1960s." After World War II, the rapid construction of freeways, then the interstate highway system, pushed the envelope of highway design. Starting with German autobahns, the "highway design was undergoing rapid advancements due to due to a better understanding of traffic operations on these roadways." By the 1960s, it was recognized that some of the original designs "resulted in conditions that constituted roadway hazards." Wortman concluded that "the current state of bikeway design might be compared with highway design of the mid–1960s period. As was the case for the original freeways, a critical review of facilities only a decade old could often be justified."[20]

Bob Sommer recalls that "basically, the research by the Davis folks ended about 1972, and after that the money came into the field, and the Eastern engineering firms that had the connections got the money. So after that we all went back to our respective areas of interest." But a frequently overlooked part of the Davis research group's work was that only a relatively small part of it actually dealt directly with the design and implementation of bicycle facilities. Articles appeared in journals or published conference proceedings all through the 1970s on such disparate topics as transportation engineering, citizen participation in urban planning, survey methodologies, exercise physiology (optimal pedaling speeds and techniques), and even the possible averse impacts of Los Angeles smog on the participants at the upcoming 1980 Olympics. Bob Sommer again:

> Because so little research on this work had been done on this topic, [cycling] investigators were able to pursue their specialized interests. Bill Adams used stationary bikes to test energy expenditure at different inclines. Mel Ramey modeled standards for one and two-way paths ... for Mel it was the chance to collaborate with psychologists and exercise psychologists about environment supports for cycling.... One student for his M.A. thesis put up cameras on the top of the 5-story dormitory building to study the left turns on Russell boulevard. Another student investigated the "shy distance" from bicycle riders left by motorists driving at different speeds.[21]

Much of this data contradicted the anecdotal information and hoary legends that passed for the conventional wisdom so carefully passed from one generation of club cyclists to another, or from racing coaches to their riders. Thus, it threatened to subvert the social pecking order within the American club structure that had been inherited from England and Europe. It is small wonder that black-wool-clad cycling elders derided such "white coat" data, even when it had nothing to do with roadway construction.

Moreover, in the past, mainstream engineers and planners knew little about cycling, so lawyers involved in accident liability cases had little choice but to turn to the most knowledgeable of the club cyclists for use as expert witnesses in their cases. This could be a lucrative occupational sideline. A handful made a career out of it. But as researchers like the UC-Davis group professionalized bicycle science, power and prestige passed away from the club cycling elders, who stuck fast to their lifeline that "only a real cyclist can know cycling," even if that "real cyclist" lacked any of the basic educational or occupational rudiments of engineering, physics, epidemiology, statistics, forensic science, or transportation planning familiar to other experts in transportation, sports performance, or public works.[22] Knowledge is power, and with the application of standardized research techniques, scholars and professionals now controlled the information, with accompanying photographs, tables and graphs. The club cycling elders had their scars, their legends, and their woolies. It wasn't quite the same.

In the old days, the club cycling elders could turn their folk expertise into money. But after bicycle engineering became professionalized, the same expert one would call for a car, truck or train crash would be the person to consult for a bicycle accident. There was no longer any room for the home-brewed "bicycle transportation engineer." The most important legacy left by the Davis research group wasn't their facility designs, it was the heightened benchmark of professionalism in the field of bicycle transportation.[23]

* * *

As Davis grew into a medium sized city, its rigid growth control measures forced many, if not most, university employees into homes outside the city limits greatly increasing traffic during the morning and evening rush hours. The city's increasing reluctance to openly restrict automobile accessibility, in the opinion of Ted Buehler, Susan Handy, Bob Sommer, and David Takemoto-Wertz, became one factor that led to a decrease in the city's "bike culture."

Similarly, those organizations based on the idea of advocating for bikeways, not just cycling in general, did not survive much past the end of the great bicycle boom in 1973–74. In 1972, the Bicycle Institute of America decided not to fund the most strident of the pro-bikeways groups, the "Friends of Bikeology." Horace Huffman reported to his fellow industry executives: "*Bikeology:* We've visited Ken Kolsbun in Santa Barbara three times and reviewed his efforts. He wants to be major force, but it's largely a one-man effort at present and he's groping for direction." The BIA decided instead to throw its support behind the League of American Wheelmen. Two years later, Kolsbun wrote an editorial in *Bicycling* calling the league "an anti-bikeway movement," complaining, in part, that it was not taking the bicycle seriously as "a replacement for the car." By mid–1975, Bikeology was a spent force, and Kolsbun had moved on to other forms of environmental activism.[24]

In addition, the hyperbole of the Davis group needs to be placed in context. As previously noted, the Davis bikeway program was conceived and carried out in a hyper-politicized environment in which bicycles merely symbolized other issues, some of which could not be discussed in public. For example, at one point in 1977, Bob Sommer and another UC-Davis sociology professor, John Finley Scott, became embroiled in a dispute over the conversion of an abandoned railroad right-of-way in rural Yolo County well outside of town. Scott opposed the conversion, arguing that it would be better to plow it under and use it for orchards than turn it into a multi-use trail for low-skill "hypothetical" cyclists. He was always particularly incensed by Davis's efforts to encourage more women to bicycle, as he saw them as "killers" of dedicated, high-skill cyclists due to their "simple ineptitude." (In fact, women—except at the very highest skill levels, where the difference is slight—have a vastly lower accident rate than men.[25])

In 1965, Scott had written a now-infamous sociology journal article examining college sororities, which he concluded were largely factories for grooming women to find rich husbands, as they lacked the innate ability to do much else with their lives:

> Many girls, whose parents hope will marry "the right kind of man," lack the intellectual fortitude (because they learn the techniques for hypergamy instead) to meet the increasingly severe performance standards of high-status private colleges, even if their parents could afford the tuition. Co-educational schools of high repute, whether public or private, are characterized by a high sex ratio (a preponderance of men); those of low repute by a low sex ratio; and the social strata represented by the students are consistent with the academic reputation. Thus the disposition of nubile girls to feminine charm, which brings them profound rewards, and their indisposition to abstract thought, excludes many of them from one fine source of high-status men.[26]

In an interview, one female UC-Davis sociology department research associate from the 1970s related how women graduate students were quietly advised to not let Scott sit on their dissertation review committees.[27]

Sommer responded that "to someone unaware of the history of the bicycle movement, it would seem improbable that any group of cyclists would oppose a bill to encourage recreational riding facilities. The explanation is that [Scott does] not represent the much larger constituency of amateur, nonorganized casual recreational riders." But even Sommer noted with amazement that "not representing the interests of one's fellow riders is one thing; opposing their interests is another." The far right wing of the vehicular cycling crowd could never entirely escape the faint odor of misogyny.[28]

But overall, there was a clear trend away from Davis's categorical approach throughout the 1970s. It was the FHWA's *Safety and Locational Criteria for Bicycle Facilities* that proved to be the template for American bicycle planning, not the more exotic of the Davis designs.[29] In the end, the Davis group and the Friends of Bikeology were no more able to forge a planning consensus based on a progressive agenda of purging recreational elites then radical libertarian cyclists could later create one based around a strict meritocracy. American bicycle planning would always be incremental, fragmented, pragmatic, and broadly inclusive. To the extent that any interest group tried to base its agenda on either redistributive or exclusionary principles, it would be doomed to frustration and failure.

Yet, the third stream itself cannot be considered a failure, as it did make one vital contribution to American bicycle planning, even if an unintended one. The basic reason the work of Bob Sommer, Dale and Donna Lott, Mel Ramey and their associates has colored the thinking of two generations of bicycle planners is that *it gave them a purpose*. For so many, their work was a lifeboat in an unfriendly sea, an opportunity to advance a clear theoretical framework and find practical applications for it, and to advance the general well-being of their communities. At least it was something, *anything*, beyond merely taking already adequate and motivated cyclists and making them a little better. One does not need to go very far to the right of center of the broad spectrum of vehicular cycling before the whole idea of bicycle planning as a government activity becomes irrelevant. Although flawed in theory and execution, this facet of the third-streamers' work has to be considered some kind of victory, even if on promise alone.

By the mid–1980s the progressivist left would be gone, with American bicycle planning comprised of a vehicular cycling mainstream, almost unclassifiable in its diversity outside of a consensus on the need to improve cyclist skill and an acknowledgment (grudging, cheerful, or merely resigned) that the roadway system, mostly in an unaltered form, would have to suffice. More ironically, by the new millennium, many were arguing that Davis wasn't even a progressive town anymore—just a rich one. "Davis has a reputation as liberal bastion," wrote Daniel Weintraub of the Sacramento *Bee*, "but the city is truly conservative, fighting change with every ounce of its political body.... Davis remains a mostly white enclave for wealthy, highly educated people ... the children who grow up in Davis cannot afford to live in town once they leave their parents' home, but their parents refuse to consider just about any project to build more homes."

The university had grown so frustrated in its search to find housing for its graduate students and employees that it developed its own residential village for 4,000 students, faculty and staff right on campus, where it was beyond the reach of the city's land use controls. The median price for a single-family house in 2009 had ballooned to $550,000. Many, if not most, university non-tenured employees by now lived outside of town, and to a large extent, the town itself had become a wealthy suburb of Sacramento, 16 miles away. The university had no bus system until 1992, except for a student-run co-op shuttle started in 1968 that used old British double-decker buses. That year, the university acquired the co-op, modernized and expanded the system, and made it free, paying for it through parking fees generated from two huge new parking garages built about 2002 at a cost of $30 million. In 2004, Tim Bustos, the city's bicycle and pedestrian coordinator, told an interviewer that "we've really done as much as we can do for bicycle facilities. Unlike a lot of cities in California, we've really approached buildout."[30]

Similarly, observers of the Vanity Fair that is Boulder howled with laughter when GO Boulder, the municipal transportation program, announced that it had achieved a 21 bicycle commuting rate. "Nobody buys [that] mode share," commented one locally-based bicycle industry analyst. Martha Roskowski, GO Boulder's alternative transportation program manager, initially defended the number, then admitted that it was something of a statistical fluke. Around 65 percent of the city's workforce can't afford to live in town, so they commute in from elsewhere, while over a third of Boulder residents (not counting students) are so wealthy (or retired) that they don't work. The survey only covered residents (again excluding the 30,000 students who reside in university housing), ignoring the majority of the workforce who commute.

So out of perhaps 130,000 individuals located within the city limits during a typical weekday—working or not—the survey represented a pool of around 54,000. Boulder actually has the chutzpah to hold up its exclusionary land use policies as an exemplar for maintaining a compact and "bikeable" city, and any suggestion that it also does a very good job of ensuring that it is only accessible to students, the ultra-rich or those with enough influence at the University of Colorado to get them into one of its housing facilities is dismissed out of hand as the grumblings of right-wing, anti-environmental malcontents.[31]

Much the same situation exists in Portland. In 1973, the Oregon legislature enacted Senate Bill 100, a statewide land-use planning law that, among other things, required cities to designate an urban growth boundary and restrict infrastructure development outside this line. Portland enacted a very tight boundary of 229,000 acres in 1979, and by 2008 had expanded it by only 25,000 acres, a growth rate of about 0.16 percent per year. In 2004 Oregon voters enacted Measure 37, which changed state statutes. A property rights measure, it granted vested rights to owners of land outside the growth boundary who could demonstrate that their property held historical rights to a higher intensity of use at the time they acquired it. Alternatively, the government could compensate the landowners for their loss. In 2007, another referendum, Measure 7, scaled back the extent of any given landowner's potential vested rights.[32]

In a head-to-head comparison of two similarly-sized metro areas, Portland

and Charlotte, North Carolina, Yizhao Yang found that most housing and demographic measures were very similar: average homeowner age (P: 46.7 years, C: 47.7); length of residential tenure (P: 122 months, C: 108); family income (P: $63,000, C: $65,000); race (P: 90 percent white, C: 76 percent); high school graduation (P: 90 percent, C: 83 percent). The biggest differences were in housing density (P: 3.2 dwelling units per acre, C: 1.2), street grid connectivity (P: 25 intersections/sq. mi.; C: 13), and average block length (P: 263 ft., C: 465). Comparing satisfaction of the residents of the two cities, Yang found only one clear result: "In Charlotte, compact and mixed-use environmental features were clearly considered undesirable at both neighborhood and block scales. In Portland, however, higher neighborhood level densities and stronger land use mix characteristics contributed to residents' positive neighborhood assessments."[33]

Yang puzzled over the tendency of respondents in both cities to report lower levels of satisfaction if they lived in neighborhoods of medium density, apparently unaware that Donald Appleyard had encountered an identical phenomenon in his massive, landmark 1981 study, *Liveable Streets*. However, Yang came to the same conclusion Appleyard did: it was a statistical anomaly caused by housing mobility. Residents of medium density neighborhoods—regardless of whether they are "medium density" as measured by the standards of Appleyard's San Francisco and London, or Yang's Portland and Charlotte—are more often in transition either upward (to the suburbs or high-rise housing), or downward (into elderly housing or the homes of relatives).[34]

When the "Appleyard Syndrome" is explained away, Yang's data yields a fairly clear example of the "Tiebout Effect," named after the economist Charles Tiebout and his seminal 1956 paper, "A Pure Theory of Local Expenditures."[35] Avoiding the theoretical details, Tiebout theorized that residents treated the costs and benefits of their cities much like any other consumer good, and in response the cities themselves acted like competing, profit-maximizing producers. "The consumer-voter may be viewed as picking that community which best satisfies his preference pattern," Tiebout concluded, "the greater the number of communities and the greater the variance among them, the closer the consumer will come to fully realizing his preference."

The cities, in turn, compete to capture the "best" residents and firms, that is, the wealthiest ones. But since there are not that many rich people to go around, the next best policy is to make your citizenry as uniform as possible, so they all end up paying about the same level of taxes and all demand the same type of services. A library will serve 200 people as well as 50, so it is a good thing if everyone in town is a college graduate and wants to go to the library. If all your citizens are young married couples, there will be widespread support for good schools. If the citizenry is predominantly older and retired, then fewer amenities, more police, and lower taxes are typical. Theoretically, at least, citizens will "shop" for cities the same way they shop for groceries. Boulder is just flat-out rich. Charlotte and Portland are alike in their level of affluence, but very different in the type of person they attract. The typical Portland person would be unhappy in Charlotte, and vice versa. In fact Jane Duckwall of the *Charlotte Observer* quoted one former Portlander as saying, "We are thrilled that we have left the massive amount of bikes on the road in Portland ... [they] have taken over the street." She and her family loved their new home in suburban Charlotte, a "normal" place where they could drive around on the streets without interference.[36]

As Carl Abbott and Joy Margheim observe, the city of Portland has turned its growth boundary into a form of iconography disconnected to its actual legal and planning functions. The boundary is the site of performance art pieces, photo montages, the subject of poetry and song lyrics, and even a travelogue on hiking its entire 260-mile perimeter. They note that:

> As Portland's UGB has taken on an imaginative identity in addition to the legal identity codified in legislation, administrative rules, and court decision, it has also become a part of the city's sense of itself. As the regulation has become a text, it has become part of the mental imagery by which observers and residents understand a regional sense of place.... Metro executive David Bragdon agrees that it is perhaps "better appreciated as a symbol than for its functional value."[37]

The city spent $143 million between 1993 and 2008 to build its bicycle network, roughly the cost of one freeway interchange reconstruction. These were, not coincidentally, the years when the growth boundary was under its most intense legal and political attack. Like the boundary, cycling has created an urban identity that extends far beyond the realities of its economic or transportation impact. In 2006, the city commissioned a study that concluded that cycling-related businesses generated $63 million a year. The bicycle community was ecstatic until a Portland State University economist pointed out that this was roughly the same economic contribution that one sizeable car dealership would make.[38]

But cities like Boulder and Davis have continued to pour money into their bicycling programs, even after undergraduates have, to a large extent, abandoned on-campus dormitories in lieu of private apartments, and have essentially become commuters, pouring in each morning in busses, on scooters and, of course, in cars. Nobody can name the largest car dealership in Boulder or Davis, but as a way of hanging onto that hip small-city cachet, there isn't anything that gives you more bang for the buck than a nationally recognized bikeway system.

The Portland urban growth boundary has had one massive effect on spatial dynamics. Constrained by the boundary, growth has gone across the Columbia

River, to Vancouver, in Washington State. So much of Portland's economic livelihood now depends on trans-movement with Vancouver that the two neighboring states' DOTs have been actively pushing the federal government to fund a new $4.5 *billion* dollar bridge across the Columbia. A transportation and land use policy based around a $143 million infrastructure outlay that, in turn, results in a set of spillover effects that requires a fix 25 times more expensive than the original investment is not one that has escaped notice.

Portland cyclists are split on the big I-5 bridge, called the Columbia River Crossing: some oppose it, fearing that it will lead to more Vancouver-based cars; others, complaining of the old, overcrowded existing river crossing, point to the new span's state-of-the-art bike, pedestrian and transit facilities. As this is being written (late 2013) the odds are against the Crossing; the Washington State Senate rejected a bill allocating initial funding for the project as too expensive. The bridge's surface rail component was widely unpopular on the Washington State side, both because it increased the cost of the bridge and because it obligated metro Vancouver to develop a rail system to connect to the existing Portland light-rail network, a multi-billion dollar commitment. Vancouver residents wanted the bridge to make it easier to drive into Portland, not so they could pay higher taxes for the privilege of schlepping in every morning on packed rail cars to allow Portlanders to enjoy the privilege of riding their bikes down the middle of semi-deserted streets.[39]

In addition, the computer models were very sketchy in projecting exactly how many drivers would actually pay to cross on the Columbia River Crossing, and how many would divert to the existing I-205 bridge. The same model had so dramatically overestimated the toll revenues from the rebuilt Tacoma Narrows bridge south of Seattle that by 2012 the state of Washington was worried that the bonds that paid for the work couldn't be paid off on time. The suggestion of one Portland commissioner that the uncertainty be removed by simply going ahead and start levying a toll immediately on the existing I-5 bridge, then sit back and see what happened, did not go over very well on the Washington State side.[40]

In 2009, a research team from Purdue University, the Harvard School of Public Health and the Rails-to-Trails Conservancy evaluated the nationwide distribution of funds allocated and actually spent on bicycle and pedestrian projects under the federal Transportation Enhancements (TE) program between 1992 and 2004. (The enhancements program is a subcategory of the federal highway trust fund. It makes available to the states 80/20 matching financing for a wide variety of non-traditional transportation-related projects. Bicycle facilities, sidewalks, pedestrian over- and under passes, and highway landscaping make up about 88 percent of TE allocations.) A total of $3.17 billion in federal funds was obligated during the 12-year study period to 10,012 projects.[41]

In the funding of completed (not just allocated) bicycle and pedestrian projects, large metropolitan areas received less than half the per-capita funding of suburban and exurban areas ($0.62 vs. $1.41). Counties with lower levels of educational attainment also had lower levels of funding per capita. Similarly, counties with persistent poverty were less likely to have been allocated funds, and less likely to have had the funds they were already allocated processed all the way through to implementation. In general, the poorer, less well-educated and closer to the urban core a jurisdiction was, the less likely that it would get an equal share of TE allocations, and the smaller its chances of turning the allocations into actual finished projects.

The Purdue/Harvard/RTC study was rigorous, its evidence robust—and disturbing. The Transportation Enhancements program, created in 1991 as part of the ISTEA highway act, was running into deep structural obstacles in getting transportation-related facilities placed into the dense, inner-city areas of older, larger urban areas. It has been more successful in developing recreationally-oriented facilities in smaller, wealthier communities; either suburbs or freestanding exurbs like Davis and Boulder. In essence, the TE bike/ped program has made the rich richer and the poor poorer; it has not placed bicycle facilities in inner-city areas, as their installation has been difficult-to-impossible because of right-of-way needs and the necessity of significantly rebuilding the adjacent road. TE inner-city projects have also encountered government bureaucracies that are less skilled, honest, or able to work with DOTs or metropolitan planning organizations (MPO) than their suburban counterparts. In many cases, central cities want to run the project and be compensated for the management; while DOTs and MPOs would rather have the cities step aside and let an outside contractor do everything while the DOT or MPO audits the paperwork. The upshot is that TE money has gone into fully separated trails for cities already used to working with other suburbs in a regional governance system, and who are willing to spend the money for their annual upkeep and repair.

In Davis, after the bus system was acquired in 1992 and the new garages were built, the share of cycling trips to campus plunged from 75 to 45 percent. The bicycling mode split for all journey-to-work trips throughout the city fell from 29 percent in 1980 to 15 percent in 2000. Transit trips to work citywide during the same period increased slightly, from 13 to 18 percent, but the big gainer was auto trips, increasing from 58 percent to 70 percent. "There is no evidence that Davis's leaders were particularly disturbed by the decline," write Buehler and Handy, "no planning documents since 1991 at the city or campus level indicate an effort to change mode share."

But the university did start to closely monitor the travel patterns in and out of its campus after 2005. The bicycle mode split of the original demographic group targeted by the Davis research, university undergraduates, held steady, wavering only slightly from year to year between 45 and 47 percent (46.5 in 2011), with the bus system the second-runner at 28 to 30 percent (29.0 in 2011). That generally fell as one went down the scale to graduates (50.2 bike, 4.9 bus in 2011) to faculty (37.7 bike, 1.8 bus) to staff (21.5 bike, 4.1 bus).

The biggest demographic change over the years was not in transportation, but land use. By 2011, 6.4 percent of UC-Davis faculty did not travel to the traditional campus. Their work site was either at a location in Davis not within the old campus, or in about half of these cases, was at a work site that was not even in the city of Davis. Overwhelmingly, they did not live in Davis proper, but did live in the surrounding county. The same was true for 7.3 percent of UC-Davis staff. When asked in a survey why they stopped riding after their mandatory on-campus freshman year, the overwhelming response of juniors and seniors was, "I moved too far away to find a place to live." And indeed, while the median (50th percentile) residential distance from campus for undergraduates in 2011 was slightly more than 1.5 miles and an impressive 2.6 miles for faculty, it was 10 miles for staff, reflecting the split of the town into threes: students in state-owned housing; well-paid and long-residing faculty members; and hourly staff and support personnel who must live far away, typically in the west-side Sacramento suburbs, some 12 to 15 miles away.[42]

Responding to an editorial in a local newspaper written by Bob Sommer entitled "Where have all the Cyclists Gone?," campus bicycle coordinator David Takemoto-Wertz listed eight reasons why bicycling was declining. Of these, the majority—including the free transit system, increased student affluence, the retirement of the city's bicycle-era public works staff, and more dispersed housing patterns of students and employees—all seemed imply that the decline was determined by exogenous factors and were, therefore, inevitable. In 2006, the city commission decided against eliminating two travel lanes on Fifth Street, a major east-west arterial just north of campus, to provide for bike lanes and protected left-turn pockets. Mayor Sue Greenwald said that the problem was the concerns of residents on the edge of the city that they would not be able to get through mid-town without getting stuck in perpetual traffic jams. "The city and campus continue to grow and attract a more diverse population with different origins, lifestyles, careers, and workplaces. These newcomers do not necessarily share the same vision as long-time residents," rues Takemoto-Weerts.[43]

CHAPTER 5

Backlash, 1973–1977

A review of cycling magazines before 1973 indicates just how little interest there was among sporting cyclists in the development of bicycle planning. John Forester of the California Association of Bicycling Organizations noted in 1974 that "[the] non-competitive cycling magazines have, in general, been quite gentle with bikelanes."[1]

Sport cycling was predominantly a rural activity engaged in by suburban participants, so mandatory urban sidepath laws were typically not a front-burner issue. Their pressing concern was the rising number of spot blockages that were rendering an increasing proportion of secondary roads and highways unusable. "Maybe the bicycle has been endorsed by all good people," said Clifford Franz of the League of American Wheelmen at the first MAUDEP conference in 1972, "but it has received only token support ... compare the position of the bicyclist now with that of ten years ago. Bicyclists are excluded from many bridges, endangered at cloverleaf intersections, cut off at freeways. In short, bicyclists' needs are invariably forgotten." In such cases, the addition (or opening) of a sidepath to circumvent a bottleneck like a bridge, tunnel, or interchange was sometimes seen as a workable compromise. Thus, there was not the visceral antipathy against specialized facilities that would later be seen in some quarters. The result, in the early 1970s, was a decidedly equivocal stance. This would soon change, due to a rather improbable confluence of factors.[2]

* * *

In 1970, Ted Noguchi was the traffic engineer of Palo Alto, California, a suburb of San Francisco that was the home of Stanford University. With the bike boom and increasing enrollments at the university, bicycle ownership had increased more than five-fold over the last six years. Complaints and accidents were both rapidly piling up. "I went to Davis to assess the work being done there," he recalls, "but that was not especially helpful, as the conditions were quite different." The roads in Palo Alto were narrower and busier, but "the biggest difference was on-street parking and the need to remove it to install any system." The original proposal put before the city commission ("Plan A") affected parking in front of 5,600 homes and removed 231 commercial-area stalls. Angry residents and business owners besieged city hall. "We had anticipated that," Noguchi says. "It was built into the process—the plans were prepared from the start in the anticipation that they would be modified."[3]

But by the time Noguchi ended up with "Plan E," he was less in search of the optimal plan than one with the least parking impact. "Parking considerations did determine the ultimate configuration," he admits. (Plan E affected only 741 homes.) Moreover, he was not permitted to eliminate traffic lanes. "If we could have cut the number of traffic lanes down to one [each way], we could have used [today's bike lane designs]." Instead, some arterials relied on sidewalk-style sidepaths. "I would have preferred another solution," Noguchi says in hindsight. To his credit, Michael Everett notes that "the sidewalk bikeways in Palo Alto [were] constructed for, and apparently heavily used by, the children of that town."[4]

The real problem was that the city council had earlier approved a poorly-drafted ordinance that made their status unclear. Section 8 of Ordinance 2652, approved several months before "Plan A" was even presented to the commission, made the use of bike lanes and bike paths mandatory in those locations where designated by signage. Section 7 of the same ordinance made it illegal to ride on the sidewalks in most areas of the city. The ordinance drafters also apparently wanted to include language that allowed the city to post signage to override this blanket sidewalk prohibition at specific locations. But instead of doing this in a separate section, they tried to throw it into the language of Section 8. As a result, the wording of Section 8 became so muddled that under its literal language, the only thing signage could be used for was to make the use of paths, lanes and sidewalks mandatory; it included no permissive element.[5]

"Making the use of the system mandatory was not initially intended, especially the use of the sidewalks," Noguchi says. This was caught and reversed several months later, and when it passed, it "really wasn't an issue and didn't make much of a difference. I didn't think it was necessary back in 1972."[6]

The system did not generate a great deal of controversy at the time it was installed. *Bicycling* ran a generally positive report in July 1972, before it was completed in October. The article did not mention any mandatory use requirement. In December, Jack Murphy, executive director of the San Francisco Bicycle Coalition, addressed a bicycle planning conference on bikeway concerns in the area, specifically noting that "there is always the possibility that cyclists might be required to use, on a given street or in a given area, facilities ... that are not adequate," but he did not mention Palo Alto, suggesting that while the mandatory-use provision may have been on the books, it was not being regularly enforced against adult cyclists.[7]

This appears to be verified by Forester's account of how he came to be involved in cycle advocacy:

> I was driving to work one morning and I saw along my route to work they had put up a whole lot of little signs, like parking signs, about one foot by a foot and a half, every several hundred feet along the road. They said bicycles must use the sidewalk.... I wasn't going to ride on the sidewalk and risk myself. And I persuaded them to give me a ticket.[8]

It appears that the signs actually said "Bicycles Must Ride This Way on Sidewalk" on one side and "Bicycles Prohibited this Direction" on the back. A 2003 plan prepared for the city of Palo Alto illustrated one of these by-now ancient fixtures and explained, "Many years ago the city signed these sidewalks as bike paths. The signs attempted to ameliorate one of the negative impacts of sidewalk riding, i.e., wrong-way riding, by installing the message 'bicycles prohibited this direction.'" The plan recommended they be removed and they were taken out in 2004. Thus, it appears the intent of the city was to allow cyclists to use the sidewalk, not force them to use the sidewalk.[9]

In February 1973, Forester wrote a magazine article for *Bike World* sharply critical of the new system. However, unlike Fred DeLong's comments the previous November in *Bicycling*, his article tended to be digressive and hard to follow in places. "He was an arcane technical kind of guy without much in the way of persuasive skills," explained Morgan Groves, then the League of American Wheelman executive director. All too often, in an effort to make himself understood, he would resort to theatrics that would descend into histrionics. "He can't argue without being rude," his father, the author C.S. Forester, complained to a friend in 1949, when Forester was just nineteen. But he also was being deliberately vague about such things as whether he had actually been personally impacted by the new system (notice that he said he didn't see them until he *drove* past them one day); or whether he had really been ticketed by the Palo Alto police or had to go to them and *ask* them to issue him a violation ("I *persuaded* them to give me a ticket"); or whether he had actually been required to ride on the sidewalk at all by the literal language of the sidewalk signage. In a November 1973 letter to L.A.W. executive director Morgan Groves, Forester indicated that he had never ridden on the Palo Alto bikeway system until he and his partner, Dorris Taylor, had taken a recent reconnaissance run over them.[10]

"He used to call me at home, late, and harass me," Noguchi recalls. "He didn't really have anything concrete to discuss, he just wanted to rail at me. I didn't think that was appropriate." Forester once wrote, "Practically everybody except cyclists combine ignorance, selfish interest, and superstition."[11] Although a follower of Jim Konski's "all cycling is sport cycling" and Harold Munn's "vehicular integration of cycling" philosophies, he was primarily inspired by the Cyclists' Touring Club's George Herbert Stancer, a man who, over the course of a life that ended in 1962, had not shied away from the melodramatic. Stancer's willingness to subordinate the best interests of the CTC to advance his own journalistic career, and his love of controversy for its own sake, have already been noted.

These incidents appear to have made an impression on Forester. Born a British citizen (he moved to the United States with his family in 1940 when he was ten, becoming a citizen in 1951) he was an avid reader of English cycling publications from the mid–1940s on. Stancer's experience convinced him, first, that compromise was never warranted if you had other options, and second, it was more important to base your support on a small group of hard-core followers than on a larger body of more casual participants.[12]

While Forester tended to be personally inflexible and uncompromising, at this early stage in his career as an advocate his ideas were still in flux, leading to thundering pronouncements of categorical imperatives that nevertheless tended to drift over time. For example, his initial response to Noguchi's Palo Alto bikeways plan was to demand the removal of sidepaths and bikelanes, but to do this he was willing to press for another type of specialized facility, what would eventually become known as "bicycle boulevards":

> Now I'm going to introduce what may become the best idea of all these—bicycle boulevards.... Cyclists like boulevards, despite the traffic, because they go to desired locations, are wide enough for all, protected by stop signs against side street traffic, have traffic signals adjusted in their favor, and aren't impeded by the residential thicket of stop signs.... If you give cyclists streets with all the characteristics of a boulevard, they'll use it for sure. But, you object, it would then be a boulevard, full of motor traffic on an unplanned route. Here's where the invention enters. Keep the stop signs that presently impede traffic, maybe add a few more, but mark each one with an additional "BIKES GO" sign. Also mark the side street stop signs with an additional "BICYCLE CROSS TRAFFIC DOES NOT STOP" notice ... frankly this is a special rule for cyclists.[13]

Although he personally had abandoned "bicycle boulevards" by 1976, the idea itself caught on and became the backbone of Palo Alto's bikeway system, replacing most, if not all, of the earlier 1972–73 facilities.[14]

The bicycle boulevards were the first manifestation of Forester's decade-long search for a way deal with a potentially fatal logical conflict inherent to his Effective Cycling program's philosophy. When Morgan Groves's NCUTLO subcommittee recommended in early 1975 that the Uniform Vehicle Code be amended to include bicycles among the class of "vehicles," Forester had objected, ostensibly because he feared it would make bicycles subject to laws that had previously only applied to *motor* vehicles. Examples included sections of the UVC prohibiting tailgating (thus outlawing paceline riding) and the section on "street racing," which, if applied to bicycles, would outlaw club time trials, century runs or any other ride in which the participants had to finish within a given deadline. However, Groves and his partners on the panel had gone through the UVC section-by-section and dealt with every one of these concerns, going so far as to almost completely re-write the section defining "street racing."[15]

In actuality, Forester preferred the older language because it let him have it both ways: he could cling to his flamboyant, absolutist "same road, same rules" doctrine while at the same time selectively choosing which laws a cyclist had to adhere to and which could be ignored. The older language in section 11-1202 of the UVC stated that bicycles were entitled to all the rights and bound to all the duties of vehicles, except for those "which by their nature can have no application." This created an inherent ambiguity when it came to determining exactly which "rights and duties of a vehicle" applied to bicycles. Were these "rights and duties" fixed or contingent? That is, could they vary from time to time or from one set of circumstances to another?[16] Did the "which by their nature can have no application" language mean that each section of the vehicle code was subject to an objective or subjective interpretation? If subjective, that would mean that any law that the cyclist himself decided "by its nature" didn't "reasonably" apply at a particular time, place, or set of circumstances could be ignored without violating the law.[17]

In particular, Forester believed that stop signs "naturally" didn't apply to highly experienced club cyclists. Therefore, they could roll through them, treating them like yield signs. "His actual riding behavior was pretty bad," observed Morgan Groves. "I once followed him through the streets of Washington, D.C., after a meeting and he just sailed through the stop signs. He knew so much that he felt the rules really didn't apply to him. I wasn't much impressed."[18]

He had originally tried to finesse his way around this "don't have to stop" / "follow all the rules" contradiction with the bicycle boulevards. When Ted Noguchi and Ellen Fletcher co-opted that idea, thereby making it anathema in the Effective Cycling canon, he shifted to his concept of subjective interpretation. Unfortunately, by their nature, traffic ordinances do not lend themselves to subjective interpretation, and such interpretations are rarely, if ever, accepted as a defense to a moving violation. ("Your Honor, I stopped for that stop sign to the extent I believed was appropriate for a cyclist of my degree of skill and experience to meet the intent of the law.") In fact, the opposite is true: traffic laws as a whole are a class of what are called strict liability violations. Normally, an element of any criminal-type infraction is intent; one cannot normally commit a criminal violation by accident. A necessary element in a criminal conviction is the need to prove that the accused intended to break the law. Traffic laws are an exception. You may not have intended to speed, but you did, so now you have to pay the ticket. Your violation can be merely negligent and still be valid.

Traffic law is almost always objective: the driver does not get to decide what is or is not reasonable behavior given the language of the code. Instead, its parameters are either interpreted in the code book itself, or by prior case law, or if all else fails, to a general "reasonableness" standard. But who gets to define "reasonable?"

Forester appealed his Palo Alto ticket, and was staggered when he lost. "The court paid no attention to the facts of the case, nor to my arguments and I assure you that they were well stated in understandable English and logical sequence," he complained to Morgan Groves.[19] Actually, in a way, he was right. The court didn't pay any attention to his facts of the case, and it was Quixotic for Forester to believe it would.

"Rationality" and "reasonableness" are very specific terms of art in law. Basic rationality asks, "Does an ordinance have a rational relationship to any legitimate or articulable government interest?" "Rational relationship" in turn, asks:

> Is there any currently existing set of facts, or any *conceivable future set of facts* that can establish a rational relationship between the ordinance and an arguably legitimate government purpose; "legitimate" meaning that it is not arbitrary, discriminatory, or demonstrably irrelevant to the policy the legislation is free to adopt.[20]

In short, "where legislation is challenged, the inquiry must be restricted to the issue of whether *any* state of facts, either existing or which could be assumed, affords support for the ordinance."[21]

That's a very broad standard. It says that if you want to beat a government ordinance based on its lack of technical merit, you must prove that the ordinance is not only inferior to your alternative *here and now*, but it will continue to be inferior given any conceivable future state of affairs the government agency can envision. Why? Simple: "A legislative choice is not subject to courtroom fact finding."[22] You can argue that an ordinance was passed through a flawed procedure. You can argue that an ordinance conflicts with another, pre-existing ordinance, or with a higher state or federal law. But you can't argue against a law simply based on the grounds that it's technically flawed. The government need only reply that under some conceivable future set of facts and circumstances, it may prove beneficial.

The logic behind this is that the typical appellate judge is not an expert in roadway engineering, chemistry, linear programming, fluid dynamics, atomic physics, or a million other subjects, so she is not going to try to decide any of these matters based on the relative technical merits proffered by either side. If the agency or city followed proper due process, it is presumed that they have relied upon the expertise needed to decide the matter wisely, and certainly they are the ones who have to live with the consequences of their actions. Don't like what the city has done? That's why they have elections.

It was the loss of his appellate argument, combined with Alan Gayfer's excoriation in the pages of the British magazine *Cycling* of Ernest Marple's brainless "man is conditioned by original sin" comments at the Royal Society in 1967 that led Forester to his "cyclist inferiority complex," essentially a fanciful pop-sociology resurrection of the short-lived 1930s ideology known as Technocracy. How can you define "reasonableness" on what the average citizen thinks (or even the average American cyclist thinks) when 98 percent of them are blithering idiots? That's like having an election to decide what the yield strength of T-6061 aluminum frame tubing ought to be. The social order has become too complicated to be understood by politicians or their constituents. Control must be placed in the hands of honest, selfless engineers and scientists.

Eventually, Forester went so far out as to try to assign a DSM-IV code number to the cyclist inferiority complex from the *Diagnostic and Statistical Manual of Mental Disorders*. Even within the ranks of the effective cyclists, some though this was all going a little far. Karen Missavage, one of the very first certified Effective Cycling instructors, cautioned: "Not all bicyclists know how to run stop signs safely, and permitting individual interpretation of traffic regulations based on vehicle type has many threatening implications," such as the tendency for motor vehicles to start mimicking cyclist behavior, the alienating of motorists, and complications in accident liability.[23]

To return back to 1973, what little response Forester's February *Bike World* article criticizing Ted Noguchi's bikeway system did receive was generally positive, but its muted response showed just how low a priority the "bikeways" issue had among club cyclists. Also, at this time, *Bike World* was still mostly a West Coast regional magazine, trying to crack into the national market by positioning itself as an edgier alternative to the establishment *Bicycling*. As a result, Forester hadn't gained many adherents, and those he had persuaded usually focused more on mandatory sidepath than laws on the installation of the facilities themselves.

All that changed in October 1973.

* * *

In 1970, the Bicycle Manufacturers Association and the Bicycle Institute of America had developed a set of voluntary industry standards called BMA/6 to standardize the design and construction of "regular" bicycles, which it defined as those with wheels 20 inches or more in diameter, or intended for riders over

100 pounds. BMA/6 was issued in anticipation of a federal government report under preparation by the National Committee on Product Safety (NCPS). The outcome of a large-scale, three-year study, the BMA feared the NCPS report would be sharply critical of the industry for failing to develop adequate product safety standards in general, and in particular for not adopting minimum rules for lights and reflectors.[24]

Fred DeLong approved of BMA/6 when it came out, writing in *Bicycling* that "bikes have been designed to attract the fancies of children, and sound engineering has often been disregarded." He applauded BMA/6's prohibition of such dangerous fads as steering wheel–shaped handlebars and extended chopper forks. Echoing a recent French regulation, BMA/6 also mandated the addition of pedal reflectors and a white front reflector to the traditional red rear reflector.[25]

In March 1972, the U.S. Food and Drug Administration (FDA), which had jurisdiction over bicycles through a 1969 amendment to the Federal Hazardous Substances Act (FHSA) giving it the authority to regulate the sale of toys and related children's products like baby cribs and pajamas, issued its own report on bicycle accidents, including a review of BMA/6. Among other things, it recommended strengthening standards for nighttime conspicuity, suggesting that reflective systems should not only make a bicycle visible at night, but should also make it readily identifiable in outline as a bicycle.[26]

In May 1973, the FDA issued a draft "banning order" covering any bicycle intended for use by children. Based loosely on BMA/6, the regulation in effect prohibited the sale of all "hazardous" bicycles, then established the minimum criteria a bicycle must meet to avoid being considered hazardous. It did not specify how a bicycle "intended for use by children" would be differentiated from one meant for adults, but the order did contain sections covering quick-release wheel hubs and derailleur gear systems, strongly suggesting the FDA had more than sidewalk bikes in mind.

Four days later, all authority over these regulations were transferred to a new agency, the Consumer Product Safety Commission (CPSC), created by Congress a year earlier under legislation drafted in response to the same 1970 NCPS final report that had been critical of BMA/6. The staff of the senate committee that drafted the CPSC's enabling legislation had been highly critical of the FDA's existing procedures, which it found "marked by too much timidity and inordinate delay." However, due to a quirk in the 1969 amendment that gave the FDA authority over toys and children's products, the new CPSC legislation actually had more *stringent* rulemaking provisions when it came to bicycles, a fact that would not come to light for several years.[27]

The first major article in the cycling press on the new regulations, by April and Don Stockard, appeared in the July 1973 issue of *Bicycling*. Based on interviews with Paul Hoffman, a CPSC attorney, and BIA staffer James Hayes, the Stockards predicted that the banning order would soon be expanded to include adult bicycles, and asserted that the BIA favored this change. "We have found no biker as yet who supports it," they wrote, "only the Bicycling Institute of America has stood out in support." They quoted Hayes as saying: "It is fine as far as it goes, but it doesn't go far enough."[28]

The Stockards were wrong on both counts. It was true the CPSC staff was debating whether it was feasible to distinguish between a bicycle intended for children from one for adults, but there was no way that Hoffman could say anything definite, because the CPSC itself was still a long way from reaching a decision on the matter. In February 1974—seven months *after* the article—CPSC Assistant General Counsel David Schmeltzer wrote the Commission's chairman that it was "questionable" whether "a regulation applicable to all bicycles, without a distinction made between children's and adult bicycles, could sustain a court challenge," and added that he personally believed "a court would rule that a regulation issued under the [old FDA law] covering all bicycles is illegal."[29]

Moreover, the industry was clearly *not* in favor of changing the banning order to include adult bicycles, because it was not in favor of *any* banning order. A month before the *Bicycling* article appeared, the BMA had petitioned the CPSC to junk the entire FDA-based proposal. Instead, it wanted the CPSC to start over again under its own, new enabling legislation. True, the new law did allow the commission to continue down the FDA procedural road because the first draft had been issued before the transfer, but whether it was *required* to do so would later become a source of contention.[30]

Regardless, the BIA wanted the banning order dropped for three reasons. First, it had invested a lot of time, effort and money in BMA/6 and didn't want to walk away from the industry standard. However, depending on how the CPSC drew the line between a child's bicycle and an adult bicycle, BMA/6 threatened to create a regulatory nightmare. Recall that BMA/6 covered all bicycles with wheels 20-inches and larger, and those intended for riders over 100 pounds, so-called "regular" bicycles. The smaller and lighter bicycles not included in BMA/6 were considered "sidewalk" bicycles. However, BMA/6 made no pretense of considering this a child/adult distinction, as many bicycles in the "regular" category with 20 and 22-inch wheels were clearly designed with children in mind. The BMA firmly believed the CPSC lacked the power to regulate adult bicycles under the old FDA law. Their lawyer, Thomas Shannon, told a Congressional subcommittee, the act "only governs toys or other articles *intended* for use by children."[31] But even had the CPSC acquiesced to the industry, unless it used a definition of "child's bicycle" that matched the BMA/6 definition of "sidewalk bicycle," the banning order would leave a conflicting hash of BMA/6 and CPSC rules. There would be *three* different regulatory classifications: no BMA/6, but the banning order, for very small sidewalk bicycles; both BMA/6 and the banning order covering regular bicycles still small enough to be considered by the CPSC as intended for children; and BMA/6, but no CPSC, for large bicycles meant only for adults. Moreover, firms like Schwinn, which both imported and manufactured bicycles, faced additional problems because their European and Japanese suppliers preferred the standards being promulgated by the Geneva-based International Standards Organization (ISO). ISO had created a task group (TC-149) in 1973 dedicated to the development of bicycle standards. ISO's representative in North America, the American National Standards Institute (ANSI), soon followed suit with its own group. Fred DeLong was the Americans' representative. "The European nations wanted to use the ISO standards being developed by TC-149," recalled Jay Townley, former Schwinn vice-president. "Anyone who both imported and built domestically had a great interest in maximizing compatibility between the ISO-ANSI standards and government regulations." The best thing for all manufacturers, both foreign and domestic, was simply to ignore the dichotomy of "child's bike/adult's bike" and come up with one set of workable specifications that all bicycles (except for small, cheap toy bikes) could meet. While domestic-only makers ideally preferred a set of rules based on BMA/6, Townley says that "compatibility was the real issue."[32]

A second reason the BIA wanted the proposed FDA regulations scrapped was because banning orders were not product safety standards—they only defined a "hazardous bicycle," and the industry wanted a full set of safety specifications to protect itself from product liability lawsuits. "It is, at best, legally questionable whether the [old FDA rules] enables the promulgation of complex, highly technical product standards," cautioned BIA/BMA counsel Shannon. "Nowhere in the act or in the legislative history did Congress indicate any intention to grant authority to set prescriptive standards such as those now proposed for the bicycle industry." Shannon did not, of course, admit that lawsuits were the concern—he instead maintained that the banning order could create an "all-or-nothing" situation where flexible mitigation measures such as repairs, upgrades or partial replacements were not permitted. However, the industry had rarely resorted to such measures in the past, and their use was highly speculative.[33]

Third, and most importantly, the bicycle industry wanted preemption. To prevent a manufacturer from having to meet one set of product safety standards in one state and another in a second state, Congress determined that once the CPSC issued its standards, those rules took precedence over state law. The old FDA banning orders did not have preemptive effect. Norman Clarke of the

Columbia Bicycle Company recalled that during just one year, 1973, over 400 bicycle-related laws and ordinances were introduced in state legislatures, and the BIA eventually had to dedicate a staffer, administrative assistant, and fax machine full time just to responding to state bicycle safety legislation.[34]

The BIA was especially concerned about rules for nighttime conspicuity. After the original 1972 FDA report calling for better nighttime visibility was issued, the 3M Company developed a reflective tire sidewall for bicycles. It wanted the BMA to include these as mandatory equipment in BMA/6, but the industry refused, because they were expensive. Instead, the BMA came up with a "10-reflector system" with front, rear, wheel and pedal reflectors that cost about a dollar per bicycle, and this was very near to what the FDA subsequently put in its banning order. The tire companies and 3M tried to do an end-around the federal rules by going to the states. At one point in the spring of 1974, 38 separate bills in 23 states were pending dealing with some aspect of bicycle lighting or reflectorization requirements.[35]

Jay Townley explained the problem to a federal congressional committee:

> We have three demonstration bicycles to illustrate the conflict we face ... [this] bicycle cannot be sold in Rhode Island now; in New York after May and in Nebraska after January.... The second bicycle, we will call our Rhode Island unit ... cannot be sold in California now; New York after May, Nebraska after January, and Illinois now.... This third bike, we call our New York unit because it complies with the current regulation there for reflectorized tires, but it cannot be sold in California.... All three of these bicycles do meet the federal regulations.[36]

Forester's first published piece was the February 1973 *Bike World* article on the Palo Alto bikeway system. Digressive and somewhat obtuse, it was largely ignored. It also suffered from being followed by longer, better constructed articles on the same topic in *Bicycling* by Jim Konski in June and Fred DeLong in July. The DeLong article in particular generated a large response.[37]

But a second Forester *Bike World* article, "Toy Bike Syndrome," published the following October after the release of the draft product safety rules, did get a lot of attention. Forester alleged a vast conspiracy between the government and American bicycle manufacturers to use bike paths and safety regulations to shut out high-quality imported European racing bicycles, force proficient cyclists off the roads, and create a monopoly for cheap, department-store bikes. Claiming that he spoke for the "true cyclist," Forester cried: "We are driven off the roads, forced to drive dangerously, and will soon be compelled to ride toy bicycles." He called the CPSC "ignorant bureaucrats," the BMA member firms "cycling's old enemies, the American manufacturers of toy bicycles," and the new bike-boom era cyclists "the intellectually dissatisfied middle classes," who "have a basic aversion to machines."[38]

Forester's article reflected a polemical style that frequently alienated potential friends and allies. "He was prone to inflammatory comments," notes Townley. Dorris Taylor, Forester's partner at the time, admits that "style-wise, there were things that could have been different ... he knew he was always right." At a national bicycle planning conference later that year, Forester told the audience that when the chairman of his city's bikeway committee had been struck by a car "we all laughed uproariously. We'd have laughed harder had he been injured seriously," and described his own cycling technique as "outrunning all those police cars." Morgan Groves at the L.A.W. cautioned him that "you run the risk of a kind of pointless martyrdom unless you can join forces with people with similar concerns, develop a consensus, some realistic strategies and workable tactics." Even the *Bike World* editors felt it necessary to distance themselves from Forester's overwrought article, stating that "we have no right to accuse the government of collusion with the Bicycle Manufacturer's Association ... it is no use writing sarcastic words about supposed sneaky tricks between the BMA and the Federal government."[39]

It was the fear that the BMA would try to shut out the high-priced foreign racing bicycles prized by enthusiasts that club cyclists really latched onto. "What they plan to enforce will wreck havoc on the sophisticated and expensive bikes that many of us ride" wrote one worried L.A.W. board member to Morgan Groves. Groves himself believed that the BMA wanted to use the FDA rules to gain an advantage over imports in the highly competitive market for low-priced department store bikes, but doubted that the BMA had any interest in trying to manipulate the high-end specialty bike-shop market. But not only cyclists were taken in. A team of Brookings Institution researchers asserted in 1976 that the bicycle regulations were an "egregious example" of a trade association's attempt to restrict foreign competition. The only source they cited was "Toy Bike Syndrome."[40]

An author of one of the more popular cycling books of the era, Dick Teresi, recounted how

> the BMA put pressure on the Commission [the CPSC] to write a provision into the federal standards that would require the front wheels of bicycles to be factory installed instead of being shipped disassembled and then installed by the dealer. Shipping bikes with the front wheel unattached is a way that foreign manufacturers reduce crate size by one third and keep their shipping costs down. Most American bike companies ship their bikes with both wheels installed.... The bike industry has pressed for the provision because it would freeze out imports, said Richard O. Simpson, chairman of the commission according to *Business Week*.[41]

Much here is either incorrect or deceptive. The CPSC rules stated that they applied only to a bicycle "in the condition that the consumer would normally receive the bicycle." Therefore, the condition in which a manufacturer shipped a bicycle to a distributor or retailer was irrelevant, *unless* the retailer turned around and sold it to the final customer in that same condition. In other words, the CPSC rules did not apply to delivery condition unless the store sold it to the customer "in the box."

It is true that BMA/6 required BMA member firms to ship their bicycles with front and rear wheels installed, in anticipation of "in the box" sales, and as one L.A.W. member wrote to Morgan Groves, "Many stores who encourage 'in the carton' bicycle sales will [only] assemble for an additional five dollars." Many cheaper imported bicycles that competed against BMA members for the department store trade did come with the front wheel detached. The first draft of the FDA/CPSC rules dealt with this by requiring that any bicycle delivered to the final customer "in the box" must include all the tools required for assembly beyond the standard household screwdrivers, pliers, and an air pump. That is, if an importer shipped with the front wheel detached, he also had to include a ⅜-inch or ⅝-inch wrench for the front wheel nuts. In the end, the final CPSC rules got around this by requiring assembly standards that all but mandated the retailer assemble the bicycle himself, mooting any controversy about whether the BMA/6 standard should be adopted.[42]

Moreover, as Norman Clarke, former president of the Columbia Bicycle Company (one of the BMA member firms), pointed out, BMA/6 was not always followed. "We did ship some of our 26-inch English racers and 27-inch racing bicycles with the front wheel detached, because if you left them on, the box was too big to ship by UPS [United Parcel Service]," requiring them to be sent to dealers via truck lines, which at this time was much more expensive. "This was generally done only for bike shops and other retailers that assembled [each bicycle]." Finally, no such article as Teresi refers to appears in either *Business Week*'s annual index, the *Reader's Guide to Periodic Literature*, or *Gales Index to Business and Economic Literature* for the years 1973 or 1974.[43]

Ross Petty, a lawyer and cycle historian, looked into this "protectionist theory" in the 1980s. He recalls Forester "calling me and sending me a pile of papers," trying to persuade him of an industry-CPSC conspiracy. Petty's conclusion? There was "little evidence to support the allegation," because most foreign-made bicycles (whether from Europe or Asia) "readily could be modified to satisfy the standard." A decade later, Petty was even blunter in stating that "commentators have criticized [the CPSC] rule as being a blatant attempt to restrict foreign competition. This criticism is misplaced." While there was, about this time, some concern with "cheap, imported bicycles that were unsafe and [gave] the industry a bad name," this was not an important factor, because firms knew that Japan "could easily make a bike to satisfy the CPSC standard, so if the goal was to exclude imported bicycles, this goal would necessarily fail." In fact, many, if not most, European manufacturers supported the idea of product safety standards, but as noted previously, they preferred an ISO-ANSI framework.[44] Like the BMA, their primary motivation was state law preemption.

Raleigh of America (a wholly-owned subsidiary of British Raleigh), the Chambre Syndicale du Cycle (the French cyclemakers' association), and the Syndicate des Fabricants d'Equipments et de Pieces Pour Cycle et Motocycles (the association of French cycle parts manufacturers), all wrote Congress supporting the Schwinn-BMA petition to re-start the rulemaking process under the CPSA. Raleigh stated that it "specifically supports Schwinn's primary recommendation that the [FDA proposal] be repealed in its entirety and that concurrently all existing regulations issued under that Act be transferred to the authority of the [CPSC]." The French associations echoed the BMA concerns that "accurately portray the difficulties presently encountered by bicycle manufacturers as a consequence of state regulations." They added that "the difficulties are compounded for foreign manufacturers that confront language, communication and transportation problems beyond those borne by domestic manufacturers."[45] However, the protectionist theory had become so widespread among club cyclists of the era as to amount to an article of faith.

Forester's "Toy Bike Syndrome" became a seminal article. Coming immediately after Ralph Nader's expose of corporate greed and rapacity in the auto industry, and the increasingly lurid theories spun around the death of President Kennedy by Mark Lane and Harold Weisburg, his article successfully turned the "bikeway issue" from a rather arcane municipal engineering spat into American cycling's version of the Dreyfus Affair. "You have shown that as presently executed, they [bikeways] are more dangerous," Morgan Groves cautioned Forester, "but I do not think it is logical to jump from the fact you have proven to a rigid anti-bikeways position ... if cycling enthusiasts neglect the interests of beginners, we all lose." Forester couldn't disagree more: "The only persons who have ever demonstrated the viability of cycling in America are schoolchildren and expert cyclists," he said, "a program to encourage cycling can be successful only if it encompasses all those features that *expert* cyclists have already found necessary."[46]

Morgan Groves warned league president Carroll Quimby in the summer of 1973 that the FDA "proposal needs serious study, as there are both good and bad points in it." He recommended they "make some input before the regulations are fully adopted." In fact, as he admitted to John Forester, "If the L.A.W. does nothing else in the coming year but develop a bikeways and safety platform, we will have accomplished as much as the preceding 8 years."[47] This would not be easy, however:

> Developing the platform and carrying through with rational action may be extremely difficult. As you note, the industry people are still afflicted with the toy mentality. Furthermore, they want to use the F.D.A. regs to restrict foreign competition. The L.A.W. is in a precarious position in that the industry has put up some money to establish a central office, and I am sure they are going to resent our opposing their views. The only answer is going to lie in building our membership to the point that we can be completely free to oppose them whenever necessary.[48]

"The L.A.W. needs to be able to maintain its independence and opportunity to oppose, where appropriate, the desires of the industry," Groves told his executive board. To put his plan into action, Groves formed an expert policy committee to deal with such technical matters as product safety rules and bikeway specifications. In November 1973, he wrote Forester inviting "you, Fred DeLong, Dr. Bond, Floyd Frazine, Jim Konski and any others with the background and interest to work on an official position for adoption by the league. Fred is interested, and the need is critical. I think the platform should represent the whole range of cyclists, from the fat lady to Fast Eddy."[49]

Forester agreed, writing Groves, "I'll be very glad to work with the others." Groves later thanked Forester for his contribution, telling him that "your work, along with Fred DeLong, Dr. Bond, Carroll Quimby, and many others, has been invaluable to bicycling as a whole." But by that time the "Toy Bike Syndrome" article had come out, and he went on to advise Forester: "I think the battle has to be fought rationally, and it does no good to write off as enemies the people and institutions who disagree on specific points. Even the BIA and the BMA (which have some grievous faults) can and should be our allies on particular points. We should give them hell, but we should pat them on the back where possible, too." Up to December 1973, John Forester probably had no stronger supporter or enabler than Morgan Groves at the L.A.W., but where Groves wanted to restructure the relationship between American club cyclists and the American bicycle industry, Forester wanted to destroy it, and the industry as well.[50]

In July 1974, the CPSC promulgated what it hoped would be the final version of the bicycle regulations. Rejecting the BIA petition to scrap the banning order and start over, it announced it would continue under the old FDA-based process. However, arguing that any product that could foreseeably be regularly *used* by children was a product *intended* for children, it extended the banning order to all bicycles. But after reviewing the new draft rules, Fred DeLong concluded that "a standard Fuji, Raleigh Professional, Schwinn Paramount or Peugeot PX-10 with reflectors added would pass the specifications."[51]

The CPSC claimed they couldn't scrap the old FDA procedure because its enabling legislation required them continue with existing rulemaking already underway unless they could prove the proposals written by the FDA were inadequate to eliminate or reduce the risk of injury. "Congress said 'you must first look to the [old FDA legislation] and you must regulate under that act unless you lack sufficient authority to get the job done,'" explained CPSC chairman Richard Simpson. "Well, we had the authority to ban, to write a standard. We had the authority to enforce. We had the authority to do something."[52] However, as always, there were hidden agendas.

In truth, the CPSC, supposedly the model for a new generation of fast, cheap, and efficient federal rulemaking, was getting politically killed. New regulations on swimming pool slides required 570 days; matchbooks, 974; and lawnmowers, 1,670.[53] The CPSC was under pressure to promulgate standards quickly and inexpensively without having to water them down. Chairman Simpson complained to Congress:

> We have encountered what we believe, at least what many believe, to be undue delay. There is due process and there is "never." Some of these procedures seem like they end up being "never." We are not suggesting you should remove the due process procedures, but we have some that we are following on bicycles and fireworks that look like they might never be ended.[54]

In August 1974, Schwinn, the BMA, Bendix, Raleigh and Shimano submitted formal, written objections to the July final rules, invoking their right to a public hearing. The CPSC, citing the highly streamlined procedures under the 1969 toy and children's products amendments, denied the request. But the CPSC had misread its own enabling legislation. As a result, denying the public hearing was a statutory violation. It is unclear whether the CPSC staff knew at this point whether they had erred. Some later actions suggest they may have.[55]

The following December, the CPSC again postponed the effective date of the rules, this time indefinitely. Throughout the first half of 1975, commission staff met with industry representatives and toured bicycle and component factories in an attempt to iron out differences. "They made many visits," recalled Townley. "Schwinn was the most frequent, but there were also visits to and from China, Japan, Europe, and with ISO and ANSI ... we ended up in a position where we could determine our own best way to meet the CPSC mandates—using performance specifications, not design restrictions." Ironically, Townley believes that it was this high level of cooperation that helped fuel the conspiracy theories.[56]

Because he chose to work within this cooperative process, Forester accused DeLong of being bought off by government and the industry. "The CPSC obtained the services of Fred DeLong to advise it about changes that would get the cyclists off its back," he later wrote. "DeLong [was] a well-known cyclist with a long history of friendship with the bicycle manufacturers." According to

Forester, only DeLong's unique technical knowledge made it possible for the CPSC to secretly modify the original FDA banning order to the point where it could feasibly cover adult bicycles. "Fred should have told the CPSC ... that he would have nothing to do with it," he wrote, "instead, Fred jumped right in."[57]

DeLong, for his part, grew increasingly exasperated at what he saw as Forester's *ad hominem* attacks. "I've been trying to take the attitude of, let's be calm about this, because it's not as bad as it sounds," he told *Bike World*. "These misinterpretations that get out in the magazine and blast everything are just confusing the issue.... I've been told that my reputation has gone to hell because I've been working with these people."

"You mean John Forester's article?" asked the *Bike World* interviewer.

"There's no question about it," replied DeLong. "My son races, and I've got Gitanes and Raleigh Professionals and Paramounts, all of which will be affected by this and I'm not going to back down and accept something that would ruin good equipment." In the end, Townley recalls, "DeLong and Forester came to dislike each other intensely."[58]

As early as October 1973, Forester had already decided to sue the CPSC; his participation in the many workshops and public meetings was intended solely to elicit statements and admissions that he hoped could later be used in court. As a result, the public input process came to resemble a form of kabuki theater, with Forester trying to trap the CPSC staff with trick questions and the staff giving increasingly bland, evasive answers.[59]

Forester filed first in San Francisco, followed by James Berryhill and the Atlanta-based Southern Bicycle League (who filled jointly), followed by eight industry plaintiffs, including the BMA and Schwinn. At the time, Jay Townley said his firm filed only to meet evidentiary and procedural requirements. When asked if the firm actually planned to challenge the regulations, he responded with a flat "no."[60]

The bicycle rules took effect in May 1976, about 18 months later than the original timeline proposed back in 1973. Schwinn, the last of the industry plaintiffs, had withdrawn from the suit in December 1975, leaving only Forester and Berryhill. David Schmeltzer, of the CPSC legal staff, explained that the industry plaintiffs had either been seeking extensions to the effective date or refinements to the standards, and these had been "granted or ironed out." Townley agreed: "We ended up in a position where we could determine our own way to meet the regulation ... [so] we backed off." He recalled a meeting he attended in Milan in the spring of 1976. "Tullio [Campagnolo, the famous bicycle component-maker] was not happy—he was quite upset—but by the end we had assured him, showing him plans and specifications, that it could be done with minor changes.

This was true throughout the industry—Shimano, Huret, SunTour, all of them." The bicycle makers, both foreign and domestic, withdrew, leaving the field to the advocates for whom they no longer had much, if any, empathy.[61]

Looking for an objective point of view, *Bike World* asked Paul Hill, a lawyer, researcher at Omaha's Creighton University Law School, avid cyclist, and later a widely published author in bicycle law, to review the case. He concluded that "as far as the average rider is concerned, the only rule of consequence to him apparently will be the reflectors requirement," and recommended that "we stop quibbling over it." He warned that "we may be past the point of CPSC rules or nothing. We may instead have CPSC rules or bizarre and conflicting state and local laws." After examining the oft-repeated claim that a FDA-based banning order could not be applied to adult bicycles, Hill cautioned: "I do not think the CPSC is as vulnerable on this point as some cyclists feel."[62]

Oral arguments were heard in October 1976. Ironically, most of the plaintiffs' arguments were those originally raised by the BMA: (1) the old FDA rules allowed only outright product bans, not product specifications; (2) they permitted only the specification of prohibited features and could not be used to create positive rules defining what a good bicycle was; (3) they were limited to items intended for use by children and could not be used to regulate adult products; (4) the rulemaking process violated the plaintiffs' Constitutional due process protections; and (5) the sixteen rules actually promulgated were so technically flawed that they were ineffective in eliminating cyclist injuries.

Berryhill argued against the tortured procedural history of the rules on Constitutional grounds, not as mere statutory violations.[63] This proved to be a strategic blunder even the court itself eventually called into question. Forester's strongest argument was that the FHSA's "products intended for children" language couldn't be stretched to cover bicycles clearly meant for adults, and thus the CPSC could only regulate small, cheap toy bicycles. However, he dissipated most of his time, effort, and brief pages on what were essentially pointless digressions.

For obscure reasons, the 10-reflector rule became his *bète noire*. His position on nighttime conspicuity changed repeatedly over the course of the litigation. Back in 1973, he had demanded no federal conspicuity standards at all, claiming that "we'd be better off neglected." However, in his opening brief he admitted that the Commission did have the authority to regulate children's bicycles, but argued that the standard should have mandated a front headlight requirement instead of reflectors.

He apparently believed it was more likely the court would restrict the Commission's jurisdiction to children's products then void the rules completely. Following his hunch, he hoped he could convince the court to change the conspicuity requirement from reflectors to lights. If he was successful, then children's bicycles would need to be equipped with a headlight, while adult bicycles would go unregulated. He may have come closest to revealing his strategy in a 2002 memoir of the case, when he wrote that "the manufacturers were terrified that they might be required to provide lighting systems," and that "for the kind of bicycles that the BMA sold, provision of a lighting system that would continue to function under childish use would probably double the cost of the bicycle."[64]

Forester seemed to be aiming for some type of domestic bicycle tariff, one that would serve the dual purpose of driving American cyclemakers out of business while making bicycles too expensive for the casual, occasional or indifferent cyclists he loathed so much. Forester hoped to use the CPSC ruling to turn the clock back to an idyllic, pre–bike boom era. "Before 1970, cyclists were able to operate on the road," his former partner, Dorris Taylor, explains. "Government started making rules and regulations.... John saw [it as] catering to the least common denominator." However, in his last reply brief, Forester appeared to return to his original position that the bicycle rules should contain no nighttime conspicuity standards at all.[65]

The D.C. Circuit Court of Appeals rendered its opinion in June 1977. As seemed to be true for everything else related to this matter, the stated issues weren't the real issues and the outcome may, in fact, have been negotiated months before. On paper, the CPSC came out ahead. The bicycle regulations were legal, they could be applied to both children's and adult bicycles, and 12 of the 16 rules were valid, although four were found to be "arbitrary and capricious" and were remanded back to the CPSC for further consideration.[66] Both sides declared victory.

Here's what really happened: when the industry plaintiffs settled and withdrew in the fall of 1975, they took all their lawyers and experts with them. They knew where the real Achilles' heel of the CPSC's case was, but because their clients no longer had a stake in the matter, it wasn't their place to meddle.[67] However, Washington is a small town and soon the word got around. The real issues were highly technical and never directly addressed by either side.[68]

As discussed earlier, the rulemaking procedures under the old FDA legislation were very lengthy and demanding, with one exception—toys. This was the so-called "1262(e) exception," the one inserted in 1969 in reaction to a rash of fake "fireproof" infant pajamas. It allowed the FDA to make rules for children's products without formal public hearings. It also required any potential rule challenger to meet an "arbitrary, capricious and an abuse of discretion" standard. On the other hand, the rules for toys and other children's products under the new CPSC legislation were the same as any other product: a public hearing was required, the CPSC had to publish express findings of need for each rule, and court challenges were based on a lower "substantial evidence as contained in the record" standard.

The CPSC asserted that because the FDA had issued the initial draft of the bicycle rules four days before the changeover to the CPSC, the 1262(e) exception applied. They were wrong. Transfer language in the CPSA overrode the 1262(e) exemption. The informal public meeting in September 1974 did not meet the standards of a public hearing, and the objections filed by the bicycle manufacturers had not been considered rule challenges requiring administrative adjudication, as they should have. Also, the technical challenges Forester raised in his lawsuit did not have to show that the CPSC had acted in an arbitrary and capricious manner. He only had to prove that, based on a preponderance of evidence in the record, each rule was improperly or inadequately promulgated. However, Forester didn't raise this argument, and framed his technical arguments assuming an "arbitrary and capricious" standard, so strictly speaking, the court had to consider them as they were presented.[69]

At this point things get murky. It appears that the court's preference would have been to throw out the CPSC's case entirely and remand all the rules back to the Commission based on its mistaken reading of the 1262(e) exception and have it start over under the CPSC rulemaking procedure. But on the other hand, it had little sympathy for Forester and Berryhill's two core arguments: the rules were technically flawed, and the government could not regulate adult bicycles under a law meant for children's products. As to the former, it is well-settled law that a court will not consider the technical merits of a rule provided that the adoption procedure was followed. The courts are simply not equipped to make fine-grained technical engineering judgments. In addition, while the CPSC didn't follow the rulemaking procedure exactly, it did spend a lot of time and energy building a consensus among the cyclemakers both foreign and domestic, on what the rules should be. The cyclemakers were satisfied with them because Congress had amended the law in 1976 to give rules initiated under the old FDA system the same type of preemptive power that CPSC rules had. There would be no single-state laws mandating 3M reflective tires on new bicycles.

As to the latter, that issue had recently been addressed in another case known as *R. B. Jarts*, concerning lawn darts. It had held that a product normally intended for adult use could be regulated as a toy if it was "reasonably foreseeable that the product would be subject to more than incidental or exceptional use by children," a situation that applied without much difficulty to bicycles of all types.[70]

But above all, the court was anxious to issue a written decision that clarified what the phrase "unreasonable risk of personal injury or illness" meant. This was a very minor point in the *Forester* case, but several lower courts were backed up, waiting for guidance on this issue. If this court simply issued a sweeping rejection of the bicycle rules, it could be a year or more before it got another chance to make a ruling that provided a definition of "unreasonable risk."[71] In short, the court didn't want the CPSC to get away with its disingenuous 1262(e) arguments, but on the other hand it didn't want to just throw out the case, either, because it needed to rule on an issue of seemingly minor importance in order to clear up a logjam backing up in its lower courts.

So it appears that the court told the CPSC to go back to the bicycle makers that had previously dropped out and forge a consensus as to how many of the 16 rules, based upon a lower "preponderance of evidence in the formal record" standard they could all live with. Townley is circumspect in acknowledging the extent to which Schwinn and the other firms were involved in the case after they had withdrawn, noting only: "Schwinn was ready in 1975 to meet all the CPSC requirements—including the ones that were thrown out."[72]

It is probably no coincidence that the four rules remanded back to the CPSC were of greater concern to foreign firms, and all were still being negotiated by ISO's technical committee TC-149. The caliper brake rules, which the BMA had argued from the start should be covered by ISO standards were struck, as was the protrusion rule (the one that had angered Tullio Campagnolo so much), the handlebar width rule (it had the potential to block some models of Italian Cinelli and Japanese SR drop bars), and the pedal tread rule (which could have outlawed the replaceable aluminum bodies of high-end racing pedals). Once it had this information, the court then reviewed the technical merit of all 16 CPSC rules, ostensibly using an "arbitrary and capricious" standard, and remanded the sacrificial lambs back to the Commission.

R. B. Jarts already settled the issue as to whether the CPSC could cover adult bicycles under a law meant to regulate toys. Finally, as to the issue the court needed to rule on (whether a precise statistical showing of the impact of a new rule was required to justify ameliorating an "unreasonable risk"), it said that the CPSC was under no obligation to develop a "body count" of the injuries expected to be reduced. Forester had argued something rather different, that each standard had to eliminate *entirely* a specific hazard, a contention the court swept away with the admonition that "he has misread both the requirements of the [law] and the relevant standard of review."[73]

The CPSC case, like the appeal of the Palo Alto bikeways citation, revealed the great weakness in Forester's strategic approach. Bicycle transportation was (and is) a multi-disciplinary field, calling upon skills from a wide range of disparate disciplines: civil engineering, mechanical engineering, kinesiology, epidemiology, landscape architecture, and urban planning, which is itself an interdisciplinary study. Forester believed that he could carve out from each of these subjects only that narrow part relevant to bicycle use and become an expert in it, ignoring the rest of each discipline. In 1993, he told a questioner that not only was he the inventor of the field of "bicycle transportation engineering," he was the world's only practitioner of it. Asked "would you include adequate skills and knowledge of the law as one of the requirements to be a cycling transportation engineer?" he replied, "Adequate skills in that portion of the law which is traffic and [that] applies to the operation of bicycles."[74]

But as he discovered, you cannot simply carve out a narrow sliver of "the law" and become an expert in it, just as you cannot carve out a sliver of civil engineering or any other sophisticated profession. For all anyone knew (or still does), his technical arguments in regards to the 16 CPSC rules may have been correct. However—and this is the important part—they were also utterly irrelevant. *Forester v. CPSC* was never about the quality of the CPSC's 16 rules. It was about the quality of the administrative procedure used to promulgate them. Being in a state of utter incomprehension as to how the promulgation process worked, his Cassandra-like warnings about the technical impact of the rules was just so much shouting into a vast, windy canyon.

The CPSC never reissued any of the four standards remanded back to it, and the rest of the bicycle rules have gone unrevised, falling into obsolescence over the years. Ross Petty, who has closely examined their safety impact, twice concluded that they have been ineffective in reducing bicycle accidents and injuries. Jay Townley argues that the only thing the controversy accomplished was to make Forester notorious: "If it hadn't been for the CPSC case, Forester would have ended up some obscure bike club president somewhere."[75]

A few months after the conclusion of the CPSC lawsuit, Darryl Skrabak, *Bicycling*'s government affairs editor, wrote what amounted to a eulogy on the era of bike club-government cooperation:

> A remarkable transformation has occurred in the attitude of bicycle activists toward government. Only a few years ago bicyclists clamored for official attention. When that attention was granted in the form of new programs and projects for the benefit of bicycling, the activists congratulated themselves.... Today the response of these same activists to similar government attention is often much different. There is suspicion, even hostility: "Uh, oh, what are they doing to us now?" These days bicycle advocates seem to spend much of their energy attempting to fight off government "assistance."[76]

The club cyclists' new motto could best be summed up in John Forester's crotchety complaint: "We're better off neglected."[77]

* * *

The origins of *Effective Cycling*, the book, are murky, as Forester has given differing accounts, all lacking in specifics. Beginning in January 1974, the California Statewide Bicycle Committee, SCR-47, undertook a yearlong investigation into cycling conditions in the state. As part of its work, the committee formed a subcommittee on bicycle safety education, including Forester. For the most part, the work of this subcommittee duplicated that of a simultaneous Traffic Safety Education Task Force and Bicycle Safety Education Resource Panel convened by the State Department of Education (DOE).

Forester's subcommittee, which was almost entirely a one-man effort, focused on adult education programs, as the DOE task force had already done much of the work creating the foundation for a statewide children's education program. Among the cycle proficiency courses that Forester collected for evaluation was Fred DeLong's old American Youth Hostels program, which DeLong and Ralph Hirsch were in the process of updating. They were seeking grant funding from the League of American Wheelmen and other organizations in order to distribute it nationally. Other safety programs collected were Ken Cross's Anacapa Sciences hazard-recognition system, the result of his 1973 study. Cross himself gave a presentation before the committee on his ongoing nationwide NHTSA-funded follow-up to the Santa Monica study.

Ultimately, only a few paragraphs of the subcommittee's work found its way in the SCR-47 final report, but it did give Forester the opportunity to collect a lot of information at the expense of the State of California, the California Association of Bicycling Organizations (CABO), and CABO's sponsors, the L.A.W. and the BIA.[78]

In June 1975, Forester volunteered to teach a course at Foothills Community College in suburban San Francisco, and he subsequently referred to the material he assembled for this course as the "first edition" of his book, although it may never have been gathered together or bound in any form. The first actual book, the so-called "second edition," a 266-page, mimeographed, comb-bound, self-published volume, first appeared in November 1975.[79]

When he was later accused of plagiarizing DeLong's AYH material, Forester only replied that he "had no need for DeLong's information" because he already knew everything anyway, and that he "considered DeLong to be an engineer of low competence."[80] On the other hand, Morgan Groves, L.A.W. executive director in the early 1970s, told an interviewer in 2009: "Forester had a first-rate idea, but needed the temperance of someone like DeLong, who had been doing things like this right back through the 1950s." Dan Burden says that "his [DeLong's] work preceded John Forester's Effective Cycling program by about four years.... DeLong helped raise awareness about the technical side of adult bicycling—how to brake, how to turn, how to set up your bike—he really put the science into it.[81]

James McCullagh, editor of *Bicycling*, said in 1978: "Forester claims ... *Effec-*

tive Cycling consists of everything you really need ... [but] some 15 years ago in Philadelphia, Technical Editor Fred DeLong, in conjunction with the American Youth Hostels, had a similar cycling proficiency program ... cyclists' mistakes were analyzed and corrected on the spot. Then the group was led into increasingly heavy traffic with no protection except their newly learned skills. [They] had participants from 8 to 70 and no mishaps."[82] Jay Townley believes the book sold only because Forester had gained such notoriety through the CPSC case as the *infant terrible* of American cycling. "Maybe he would have written that book of his," Townley admits, "but it never would have gone beyond the mimeograph stage."[83]

In 2004, Robert Hurst wrote a book, *The Art of Urban Cycling*, in which he explicitly sought to adapt *Effective Cycling* to inner city conditions. That he felt "obliged" to address Forester's *Effective Cycling* principles in the introduction of his book "and then so often afterward is testament to its power," he wrote. On the other hand, he was concerned that "one of the big problems" with Effective Cycling "or any principle of cycling for that matter," is that it fails to take into account adequately "the complexities, details, and chaos of the city." This is debatable, of course. John S. Allen, who has become a something of an elder statesman within the world of vehicular cycling, for example, believes that Forester's *Effective Cycling* book was, for him, especially useful in improving his riding in the type of constricted traffic situations he encountered in nearby Boston.[84] To some extent, Hurst appears to object less to what *Effective Cycling* actually says than the big-brother-ish way it tends to be said:

> Forester's advice is usually quite sound, [but] a large number of cyclists have added a militant, confrontational tone to the framework of his message. They have taken the vehicular-cycling principle and bastardized it. Through their riding habits in traffic, which are often deliberately, theatrically antagonistic, they seek to make some kind of point to their special audience of road users. One is never quite sure what their point is—something about the rights of their road. Their riding often becomes little more than a passive aggressive acting out.... What a waste of a good bike ride.[85]

Forester was apoplectic. This was a heretofore unheard of crisis—someone who wasn't trying to *attack* the holy canon, but instead *rewrite* it! "Hurst invents imaginary defects in vehicular cycling," he wrote in a review. It is important to note that Forester is not only accusing Hurst of misrepresenting his book *Effective Cycling*, but of misinterpreting the entirety of vehicular cycling, which is rather like accusing one of misrepresenting the entire discipline of philosophy or economics.

Forester dealt with the "Hurst issue" by resorting to that most ancient of remedies—excommunication. "Hurst's cycling is not vehicular cycling," Forester wrote, "his style of cycling is not the activity that he argues vehicular cycling to be."[86] As I have just suggested, the problem is not cycling, but semiotics. Both Hurst and Forester treat "vehicular cycling" and "Effective Cycling" as synonymous. But in fact, they are different. In its literal meaning, Effective Cycling is both the title of a book and a trademark for a proprietary cycle education program based on that book, and a second work, *Bicycle Transportation*. In its ordinary usage among cycle advocates, Effective Cycling is a subset of the broader class of riding techniques called "vehicular cycling," which, in turn, is one of a number of schools (or philosophies, or approaches) to bicycle planning. To be an adherent of Effective Cycling is to be an adherent of vehicular cycling, but as Robert Hurst demonstrates well with his *The Art of Cycling*, one can be an adherent of vehicular cycling while rejecting some or all of the beliefs of Effective Cycling. This is because Effective Cycling is a closed system.

The best definition of a closed system is the one used by George Orwell: "Everything that is not required is prohibited." No question exists for which the answer is "it depends." Every situation has a solution that embodies the One Best Way. There is no room for ambiguity, relativism, or individual interpretation. Of course, the problem with any closed belief system is that it invariably declines into groupthink, another Orwellian term, and when it becomes identified with a single individual, groupthink can further degenerate into a prophetic cult of personality, frequently millennial in outlook. David Bromley, who has spent the last twenty years studying such millennialist cults as the Branch Davidians, the People's Temple, the Solar Temples and Japan's Aum Shinrinko, notes: "Prophetic movements stand in resistance to the established social order. They challenge its legitimacy by creating a vision of an alternative order.... For their part, prophetic movements sacrilize their ideologies, their missions as a transcendental mandate, and their organizations as representations of an ultimate reality." It is interesting to note that by 2007, Forester was introducing himself to lay audiences as "me, John Forester, the leader of the vehicular cyclists."[87]

But keep in mind the evidence to the contrary: the bicycle proficiency course developed by Fred DeLong in 1969, and his warnings in *Bicycling* in 1972 and 1973 that bikeways "suffer their own problems" qualify as nascent movements towards "vehicular cycling," and they predate *any* involvement by Forester in bicycle advocacy. The same is true for the "bicyclism" declaration of James Koniski at the San Francisco MAUDEP conference in 1972. Bill Wilkinson's warning that "more can be done for so many more bikers" by improving urban streets than by restricting cyclists to bikeways, preceded any of Forester's published works, save his first *Bike World* article.[88]

By 1974, it was the official policy of the League of American Wheelmen that "the L.A.W. supports bike paths as separate facilities *only* where no public road exists, on bridges, to bypass or parallel limited access highways, or in special recreation and park areas."[89] Also in 1974, Harold Munn had read his paper before an ASCE conference and submitted it for publication. It described the central task of bicycle planning as convincing cyclists "to operate their bicycles as they do their automobiles." It was published in *Transportation Engineering* in 1975.[90] Again in 1974, Lawrence Walsh, a city employee, at San Jose, told a MAUDEP audience that

> [we] did not begin [our] bike route system until after the pilot efforts of Davis and Palo Alto, so we benefited from the successes and failures of those systems.... Only when the design of bikeways is based on the bicycle as a vehicle can engineering, enforcement, and education work in concert to produce a truly safe environment.[91]

And finally, at the same conference, Robert Shanteau of the Traffic Safety Research Corporation told his audience that "bicyclists can best be helped by including consideration of bottlenecks in transportation plans, assuring that existing problems are fixed and new ones are not created ... a resolved bottleneck lets bicyclists ride harmoniously, legally and safely with other traffic."[92] Again, these things were being actively discussed six months *before* Forester taught his first course at Foothills Community College, and eleven months *before* he self-published *Effective Cycling*. Almost all of the fundamental concepts behind vehicular cycling were already in circulation. The polemics of attribution aside, the core ideas of vehicular cycling were, in 1973–74, already out there, ripe for the picking.

Think back for a second to the contretemps over Robert Hurst's *The Art of Urban Cycling*. Both Hurst and Forester assumed, as a matter of course, that it was legitimate for Forester to pass judgment on what was or was not appropriate for the vehicular cycling canon, even if they did not agree about what that content should be. But remember, Effective Cycling is a set of specific intellectual properties that belong to one individual, while vehicular cycling is an amalgam of communal beliefs, opinions, best practices, and information that belongs to no one. Why do both men take for granted that there is any one individual who has some special gatekeeping authority over it?

Forester has just as much right to tell Hurst his ideas are bad as anyone else, and complete authority to decide if any of them will make it into *Effective Cycling*, the book, but he holds no privilege to decide if they should be considered a legitimate part of "vehicular cycling" by me, or you, or anyone else. Bluntly put, when it comes to the history of vehicular cycling, John Forester wasn't there at the start, he won't be there at finish, and for much of its history, he was either somewhere else, standing on the sidelines, or just too busy with trivial side-spats over 50-cent reflectors or handlebar hang-tags to be bothered.

On the other hand, the sheer marketing genius of marrying the still-somnolent anti-bikeways movement to the raging supernova of the CPSC controversy cannot be denied. As Jay Townley said, left to his own devices, Forester would have ended up an obscure bike club president somewhere. That is, his extremely polemical ideas didn't necessarily succeed because they were the only take on vehicular cycling available in 1974–75; as we have seen, they weren't. It shouldered its way to front of the pack because they had the best marketing hooks imaginable: fear and resentment.

Effective Cycling was vehicular cycling masterfully repackaged to make it emotionally indistinguishable from the alleged CPSC "threat" to high-quality imported bikes. It was the CPSC bicycle safety rules that were taking up page after page of the cycling magazines in 1973 and 1974, not bikeways. But by linking them together into a single indistinguishable identity called "government action," both wells could be poisoned together, even though the CPSC rules were effectively a dead issue by the end of 1974.[93] In November 1977, *Bicycling*'s Darryl Skrabak wrote that "those in government who have sought to lend a hand to bicyclists are likely to be discouraged from further efforts when the very people they have tried to help respond with criticism ... opposition is hardly the most desirable position to take in dealing with government.[94] But if your objective is to kill off *all* government involvement, the indiscriminate generation of discouragement is the most powerful tool available.

Finally, it must be kept in mind that for mainstream bicycle planners, specialized facilities were neither good nor evil. They were just unobtainable. In many cases, the compromises necessary to fit a facility into an available budget or physical space could result in a solution worse than simply implementing spot improvements or upgrading the roadway. Hence, they could either push vehicular cycling at their constituents or recommend that they give it up altogether. However, rejecting a bicycle facility because it can't be done, or done acceptably, is far different from objecting to it on ideology. As Dan Smith of DeLeuw, Cather & Co., who wrote much of the 1974–76 *Safety and Locational Criteria for Bicycles* report, told a MAUDEP conference:

> Some cyclists see the construction of independent trails as one facet of a ploy to simply get bikes off the roadway and out of the way of cars. They see similar problems with bike lanes.... Underlying all of the above is a belief that people who ride bicycles can and should achieve or approach the same level of bicycling proficiency that these serious cyclists do have.... This leads to the question of whether the opportunities of the few should be restricted to enhance the safety and opportunities of the many.... But there is a real question whether a substantial segment of the bicycling public can and will achieve a level of judgment and riding proficiency of the cycling elite. There has been a tendency for the most vocal spokesmen of the cycling elite to be accredited as a spokesman for the full cycling public ... elite cyclists have valid interests which should to some extent be provided for, but [planners must] also recognize that elite cyclists interests may conflict with that of the general cycling public.[95]

* * *

The degree to which Forester has been able to convince others he "invented" vehicular cycling is evident from the recollections of John Williams, who would later serve as the long-time editor of *Bicycle Forum*, about the origins of his path-breaking bike plan for the city of San Luis Obispo. Widely distributed by USDOT in the mid–1970s, it helped revolutionize thinking about what bicycle planning was, and how should be done.

At the time, Williams was winding up his undergraduate degree in architecture at CalPoly. "Two friends and I did the first San Luis Obispo bike plan in '69–'71 roughly," he recalls. "At that time there was a CalTrans plan that had been done by UCLA or someone." (This was *Bikeway Planning Criteria and Guidelines*, which pins down the date of Williams's memory more precisely to 1972.) "We put the first plan, based on the State's design info and presented our plan to the city council. They were impressed and allocated $5,000 for us to fill in the details." The city hired him in 1974 ("at $2.12 an hour") until he started his master's program in urban planning at the University of Waterloo. A friend dropped by his office in the basement of city hall "and mentioned that there was a poster on the wall in the hallway of the architecture building about a bikeway plan competition."[96]

This was the First Urban Bikeways Design Competition (UBDC-1), sponsored by the Urban Bikeway Design Collaborative, a consortium of mostly northeastern planning departments, based at the time at MIT. UDBC-1 had four categories of prizes (best amateur, best professional, best at promoting safety, best at promoting intermodal linkages). The judges represented a wide cross-section of philosophical approaches to bicycle planning, including Dan Burden, John Forester, Jerrold Kaplan, Jim Konski, Wesley Lum and Bill Wilkinson. Williams submitted the San Luis Obispo proposal (which he later referred to, tongue firmly in cheek, as the "Teen Angel" plan) in September 1974. It was, for its time, a radical concept, in that it eschewed the then-traditional methodology of equating a "bicycle plan" with a "bikeways plan." "In my opinion, bikeways are only a part of the solution, and as I became convinced during my analysis, certainly not the most important part," he wrote in the introduction."[97]

In fact, he argued that it was the tendency to confuse solution and problem that lay at the heart of many of the shortcomings in bicycle plans to date:

> I would venture to guess that most planners responsible for bicycle programs started with an initial statement like, "The problem is to design and construct bikeways in our city." Thus, they started with an initial problem statement that was in fact, much closer to a solution statement.... To me this seemed most presumptuous. When approaching a novel problem (that of dealing with the needs of bicyclists, in this

case), it is most destructive to the design or problem-solving process to start with an unquestioned assumption, particularly if it is not really made explicit.[98]

Instead, he continued, "I focused on improving streets for bicyclists, getting rid of bottlenecks, bad pavement, and so on, not to mention teaching people to cycle." In fact, his plan contained no bikeways element at all. "What I didn't like about [*Bikeway Planning Criteria and Guidelines*] was the emphasis on sidewalk bikeways," he later said. "As I put my plan together, riding around and looking at conditions, I couldn't see the value of sidewalk bikeways.... I was also pretty much of an Effective Cycling person."[99]

But here, Williams's memory is faulty: UBDC-1 was held in the first half of 1974, with the awards handed out at the San Diego MAUDEP conference in December. By early 1974, Forester had published only a handful of articles, and the only written piece Williams cites is Forester's "What about Bikeways?" article in the April 1973 issue of *Bike World*. Williams didn't use the phrase "Effective Cycling" in his plan because it didn't exist yet: Forester didn't start to use it until around December 1974, and his self-published book of that name didn't come out until a year after that.[100]

The primary shortcoming of Williams's plan was that it actually ended up recommending that the city do very little, and didn't promise much in the way of results. More space was devoted to education programs than to public-works activities, even though it recognized that these would have to be developed and implemented by the school system, over which the city had no control. The only engineering activities suggested were to increase the frequency and adjust the patterns of street sweeping; replace unsafe inlet grates; reduce the use of "Botts Dots"–type raised pavement markers; and delete two existing bike lanes because they did not meet current standards.

His primary recommendation regarding bikeways was that "the ones already constructed or planned should be used for an extensive evaluation program ... at that time action to extend the system or delete the lanes [entirely] should be taken." One reviewer commented that the plan "proceeds from a premise novel among bicycle transportation plan assumptions: that there are limits to what planning can do." That's certainly a kinder, gentler way of expressing the Forester-esque maxim "we're better off neglected."[101]

Williams himself distilled his plan down to one summary statement: "Bikeways can be the inexperienced cyclist's crutch; often they are the experienced cyclist's ball and chain ... just as a crutch may be a valuable aspect of our 'hurt leg' patient's recovery program, so may bikeways be a necessary *component* of the inexperienced cyclist's training program."[102] The possibility that someone might not see their inexperience and lack of dedication to cycling as a problem to be overcome, or that they might even prefer to stay "inexperienced," never seemed to have occurred to Williams. He identified nine cyclist user "types," Tourist 1–4; Family 1–2; Commuter 1–2. In no case did he identify any kind of involuntary or captive user subtype. The concept that someone would ride a bicycle because they had to, not because they wanted to, was apparently beyond comprehension. He was far more interested in removing balls and chains than in handing out crutches.[103]

CHAPTER 6

From "Bike Advocate" to "Transport Professional," 1977–1994

In May 1977, the CPSC and the USDOT convened the Bike-Ed '77 conference in Washington, D.C. It was probably the largest gathering of civil servants, consultants, and advocates working in the field of bicycle transport to date—215 attendees. It was also (arguably) the most significant event to that point in the history of American bicycle planning. Many of the professionals who would go on to guide the field of bicycle and pedestrian planning first met there, and at least two non-governmental organizations can directly trace their roots to it: the Bicycle Federation, later the National Center for Biking and Walking, publishers of the long-running policy/technical newsletter *Bicycle Forum*; and the Urban Scientific and Educational Research Corporation (USER).[1]

Three months earlier, Darryl Skrabak, *Bicycling*'s government affairs columnist, noted that "thousands of miles of bikeways [have been] paved, striped, and signed." The problem was that a lot of them didn't work well. "The unanticipated result was difficult to accept for many riders, particularly those who had worked hard to get bikeways built," he wrote. "The controversy caused the destruction of some bicyclist organizations and seriously drained others."[2]

Now, both government agencies and nongovernmental organizations were turning to other strategies. Skrabak, no government cheerleader over the prior three years, urged cyclists to move beyond blanket opposition and support these new alternatives. "Opposition is hardly the most desirable position to take in dealing with government ... [because] there is much that government can and should do." However, he admitted that "a difficulty in proposing alternative steps is that bicyclists are not yet agreed on what those steps are."

The largest and most frequent meetings up to this point had been the

MAUDEP conferences. But these were explicitly seminars on "the planning, design and implementation of facilities," and by the mid–1970s the bikeway wars were taking their toll. MAUDEP was running out of steam. Thomas May of the Pennsylvania DOT, himself an active club cyclist, told the 1976 conference that "unfortunately, the bicycle will probably never live up to its potential as a utilitarian transportation mode in the United States," and those with "strong inclinations to expand bicycle facilities should temper their capital investment with the knowledge that the usage will be modest in the immediate future and for some time to come." He noted that "every person who has tried bicycling for utilitarian purposes probably has assembled his own collection of horror stories." While training and experience can make urban cycling safe, keeping "the abilities, safe practices, and proper knowledge of motorists and bicyclists honed is a never-ending training process that must be continued."[3]

And that was the crux of the problem. While training and experience could make urban commuting safe, that was not the same as pleasant or convenient. Only one thing could do that, according to May: Type I fully separated bicycle facilities. "Class I bikeways present a solution, but in addition to other problems, their adoption in most downtown American cities does not seem politically and physically practical.... I believe this problem stifles destinational bicycling far more than is recognized and more than most potential bicyclists can or are willing to articulate." He concluded that "utilitarian biking at significant levels is just not around the corner."

Similarly, Larry Wuellner of the Missouri AAA (a pre–1969 pioneer in intelligent, if simple, bicycle safety programming) appeared to be giving up by 1976. "Presently, bicycling appears to be on the wrong road ... we cannot simply ask bicycle traffic to adapt and evolve. We must look beyond piecemeal projects and begin planning comprehensive programs ... if we ask the bicyclist to suffer his way onto the roads, he will likely become frustrated, combative and seldom attain the compatibility demanded for a successful traffic mix."[4]

By the time of the 1978 MAUDEP conference only eight of its 24 sessions dealt primarily with bicycling issues—the rest were given over to pedestrian planning. Even the eight cycling sessions mostly avoided what Michael Everett called "the bikeway controversy" by focusing on things like bicycle parking and bicycle-transit intermodalism.[5]

James Stacey of the city of Syracuse, New York, summed up the general air of pessimism when he told one audience that "little progress is being made in overcoming the gap between bikeways, planners and bicyclists, and the two sides seem to be locked in an endless dance around an either/or position: either we have bikeways everywhere, or we have none at all." Waiting in the wings were "traditional transportation engineers and planners" who resented "bikeways as taking needed funding away from standard highway projects," and who were hoping the bikeways controversy would provide the excuse they needed to effectively shut down bicycle programs entirely.[6]

"Greed may be the ultimate source of this program, but a more immediate root of the highway planner's fear may be a perceived threat to the professionalism and professional decisions of the planner," Stacey explained. As a result, funds originally earmarked for bikeways but put on hold as a result of the bikeway controversy would probably never be "diverted to more important facilities and programs, such as safety and bicyclists' training programs, lockers, showers, bus bike-carriers, increased road-maintenance for biking comfort and safety, and promotional programs." Instead, they would simply be returned to the general highway fund. Stacey summed up the problem as he saw it: "Most bicyclists and bike clubs show an abysmal lack of understanding about how the local city government, housing authorities, or state governments operate." The problem was becoming less one of "how can we get them to spend money for bikeways" than one of "how can we get them to spend money for *anything*?"

Bike-Ed '77, on the other hand, was the first bicycle advocacy conference to stake out ground entirely outside the topic of bikeways or facilities-based planning.[7] Unlike MAUDEP, it was primarily comprised of young turks, the up-and-comers in the world of bicycle planning. It is best known as place where Ken Cross debuted his landmark multi-city study of bicycle/motor vehicle accidents, the follow-up to his 1973 Santa Barbara study. Katie Moran, at that time still working for NHTSA, recalls that "he had agreed to preview the results of his landmark work ... six months before his report's final publication ... we all had had been hungry for solid guidance." Bill Wilkinson, who had just moved from Fairfax County to the U.S. Department of Transportation, noted that "it informed and influenced everything that followed related to bicycle safety education." Roger DiBrito, who later developed a unique program with Dan Burden for the Missoula school system, recalled: "Before Bike-Ed '77, most bike education programs consisted of a list of don'ts and a few coloring pages. Materials were designed to please motorists; the message was: stay out of the way. From [Ken's] talks and writings it was clear to me that we were called to teach children to avoid car crashes with knowledge and skill, not submission and fear."[8]

In an interview a few months later, Cross himself explained: "I personally don't think that bikeways are going to impact accidents very much one way or the other.... I'm personally not too sold on bike lanes as a means of accident reduction; but I don't think that's the only criterion on which to evaluate [them]." He agreed with James Stacey's assessment of the problem: "There's money to spend on bike lanes but not on other things, and there is no way to switch that around. Either you spend money on bike lanes or you don't spend any money at all ... people don't like to spend money on evaluation, they like to spend money on building things."[9]

A variety of different educational programs from around the country were presented at Bike-Ed '77 and discussed. Forester reviewed his Effective Cycling course. Although he acknowledged that in its current form it wasn't really suitable for children under 14, he explained that he was creating elementary and intermediate versions for younger riders, and suggested these would be suitable for use as a national standardized program, something along the lines of the British National Cycle Proficiency Scheme. "At the present time, there is no market that I can see for volunteer bicycle safety education," he told his audience. "You are not going to get people to come in and do this kind of thing."[10]

When the conference met in plenary session to make recommendations, the idea of modifying Effective Cycling into a universal school program was considered, but rejected: "While many people thought that John Forester's program was good in terms of its content and approach, there were questions about how it could be implemented on a national scale." Indeed, when they later appeared, the elementary and intermediate courses filled up 15 "jam-packed" course periods, required a certified instructor and two assistants, and could accommodate only 30 students per course.[11]

In general, the Bike-Ed '77 did not achieve its stated goal of "hammering out in two and one-half days a national strategy for bicycle education in the United States." Some of the attendees believed that doing so would result in government agencies concentrating on education to the exclusion of other program elements. Others expressed the concern that an overriding focus on safety would only reinforce an existing presumption that "bicycle" programs were essentially "safety" programs, with accident reduction becoming the overriding goal to the exclusion of everything else. Given inadequate resources or inflexible demands to demonstrate results, there would then be the temptation to turn "fewer accidents" into "less cycling" through fear or discouragement.[12]

But Bike-Ed '77 did have an immediate, if somewhat diffuse, impact on bicycle education programs. Lyle Brecht and Vince Darago, two original members of the Urban Bikeway Design Collaborative that organized the UDBC-1 and UDBC-2 competitions and published the *Bikeways Design Atlas*, formalized the loosely-knit collaborative into a new corporation called the Urban Scientific and Educational Research Corporation (USER). They were awarded a NHTSA contract to organize a series of ten bicycle safety workshops around the country, with Katie Moran acting as NHTSA's project manager. The workshops covered accident data collection and use, comprehensive planning, case studies and group discussions. One of these workshops was in Denver. Prodded into action by Brecht and Darago's workshop, the Mountain Bicyclists' Association organized a nine-hour "Basic Bicycling" course for adults covering the usual topics of on-street operations, bicycle maintenance and special situations and emergencies.[13]

NHTSA also awarded an $8,000 grant to Dan Burden and Roger DiBrito, a Missoula, Montana, physical education instructor, to expand a cyclist-training program that DiBrito had started in 1977 for the Missoula school system. The federally-funded version was offered for the first time in the spring of 1980 to third- fourth- and fifth-graders in two formats: a 12- and 20-lesson program. Both included two supervised street tours, but omitted maintenance instruction. The Missoula program was developed with the assumption that the instructors would be regular physical education teachers, not highly proficient cyclists. One of the strongest recommendations to come out of the pilot program was that the sponsor should provide the bicycles, as about a third of the students showed up on bikes too ill-fitting to be effectively used for the on-bike segments of the course. There was no measurable difference in demonstrated skill between those graduating from the 12- and the 20-class programs, but there was a positive correlation between improved skill and the percentage of total class time dedicated to on-bike instruction (as opposed to classroom work). The program was designed to be modified for the individual needs of each school system or other sponsor (such as a 4H chapter). "There must be some adaptation," Burden cautioned. "You can't take any program without changing it in some way."[14]

By 1987, the program had evolved into "Bike-Ed America," which was largely a proposal to create a nationwide 10-hour instruction program for children along the lines of the Missoula program and the British National Cycle Proficiency Scheme. It was spearheaded by Burden, who by now was state bicycle/pedestrian coordinator in Florida; DiBritio, who was still in Montana; and Bill Wilkinson at the Bicycle Federation in Washington. Florida and Arizona had already implemented safety programs that were somewhere between the Missoula program and the proposed new Bike-Ed America. In May 1987, the organizers had $54,000 in commitments, mostly from its first three customers—the states of Florida, Arizona, and Montana—but the startup budget was slightly over $100,000, with full implementation for the first three years projected at $380,000. That was big for an educational program, bicycle program money overall was very tight in the late 1980s, and the necessary money apparently did not materialize. Bike-Ed America never opened its doors.[15]

Burden and DiBrito's "you can't implement any program without expecting to change it for local conditions" approach to program development was contrary to Forester's Effective Cycling philosophy, which stressed that there was only one best way to teach cycling, and that it had not materially changed from the methods used in the 1930s by the British Cyclists' Touring Club. Forester's Effective Cycling program placed great emphasis on speed and strength. Describing his original course at the Foothills Community College in 1975, he explained that he did not introduce lane changing or vehicular-style left turns until the sixth week "because the students must all develop the horsepower," and boasted that the program's graduates' skill level "is as high as the most experienced cyclists around, men who have ridden hard for years."[16]

DeLeuw, Cather's Dan Smith, the manager for FHWA's *Safety and Locational Criteria for Bikeways* project, cautioned that while experienced cyclists may contend that the answer to all problems lay in proficiency development, "there is a real question whether a substantial segment of the bicycling public can and will achieve the level of judgment and riding proficiency of the cycling elite," and that "while arguments advanced by some elite spokesmen are based on the element of truth, in aggregate they constitute, not an impartial presentation of the facts, but a representation of the honest interests of a very special user group."[17] Michael Everett was more blunt:

> He [Forester] tells us that others can also become real cyclists, if they will only take his Effective Cycling course.... But he offers no substantive evidence that jamming in heavily traveled, high speed roads is not exceedingly dangerous no matter how it is done. Nor does he give any evidence that he can induce more than a trickle of cyclists to assume those risks.... He is more concerned about cycling life styles than the rights of other actual and potential cyclists.[18]

Dale and Donna Lott were even harsher:

> He [Forester] does not shrink from the fact that the needs of 98 percent of adults and 99 percent of children are neglected by public policy advocates. Rather, he believes that cycling is inherently elitist, that many will aspire but few will achieve, and that it should and must always be that way. He believes that now and always the rare sight of a doughty rider challenging taxis, trucks, and tornados on a featherweight 15-speed bicycle will inspire a murmured or silent, "there goes a real man," from every passerby.[19]

Actually, there was some relevant data starting to emerge that lent credence to the contention of Everett and the Lotts. Students in a half-semester long (eight week) course at the College of Staten Island, with mandatory "homework" riding assignments similar to those in Forester's Foothills Community College course, did increase their speed as a result of taking the class. However, the average improvement was about 12 percent. Generally, already strong cyclists showed the least improvement and inexperienced cyclists the most. Less proficient cyclists improved their "horsepower" in the range of 12 to 14 percent, while their more experienced classmates improved between 4 and 6 percent. This was hardly approaching Forester's Charles Atlas–like claim that proficiency training programs could crank out the equivalent of "the most experienced cyclists around, men who have ridden hard for years."[20]

* * *

In 1980, Katie Moran, now a consultant with the Mountain Bicyclists' Association in Denver, prepared what would become the first of two comprehensive documents that would close out the first "golden era" of American bicycle planning.[21] Both broke away from the previous focus on bikeways and looked much more toward the kind of comprehensive, vehicular cycling-based approach that John Williams outlined in his San Luis Obispo plan. Moran's report was *Bicycle Transportation for Energy Conservation*, prepared for the USDOT (with Bill Wilkinson as project manager), with funding provided through the National Energy Conservation Policy Act of 1978.

It was actually the second of two parallel studies. Six months earlier, in September 1979, Marda Fortmann Mayo (with Nina Dougherty Rowe as project manager) had prepared *Bicycling and Air Quality Information Document*, a 229-page report for the Environmental Protection Agency.[22] Section 108(f) of the Clean Air Act of 1977 required urban areas that were out of compliance with air quality standards (so-called "nonattainment areas") to prepare plans with "Reasonably Available Control Measures" that would bring them back into conformity, usually by reducing automobile emissions. Rowe's report outlined which bicycle measures would be permitted, and to what extent, in local and state attainment plans. Because the measures had to be "reasonably available," a pie-in-the-sky "if you'll give us enough money then we'll build it" bikeway plan wasn't considered acceptable. While bikeways were permitted, they had to be feasible, funded, effective as proposed, and implemented in conjunction with operational measures, such as parking facilities, showers, and other non-capital programs such as educational classes or enhanced roadway maintenance programs of the type Williams had described in his San Luis Obispo plan.

Moran's DOT report was the flip side of Mayo's EPA document. It was mandated under the National Energy Policy Act of 1978, which linked the Clean Air Act's pollution reduction mandate with a requirement to conserve energy. Section 682 of the Energy Policy Act required the Department of Transportation to commission a study on the energy conservation potential of the bicycle. In the end, both Rowe's clean air study and Moran's energy conservation study amounted to mode change feasibility analyses. They both sought to answer the question: Can people be induced to use transportation modes other than the single-occupant automobile, how much will it cost, and what are the best bets when it comes to spending money? The advantage of Moran's study was that it wasn't burdened with the requirement to fit its recommendations into the structure of the Clean Air Act's "Reasonably Available Control Measures," and then relate them with specific tailpipe emission reduction potentials. It could be more creative, if less pragmatic.

With that in mind, Moran's report was able to specify the development of a Comprehensive Bicycle Transportation Program (CBTP), largely focusing on utilitarian, point-to-point tripmaking. It identified three overall priorities: (1) increasing operator awareness and competence; (2) eliminating roadway surface and design hazards; and (3) increasing funding for operational bicycle program ("4-E") activities.[23] Although both reports said many of the same things, Moran's report was more succinct, more oriented toward the point of view of a transportation planner, and easier to follow. With only minor changes, its three goals have remained the three consensus objectives of American bicycle planning ever since. While a multitude of lesser priorities have come and gone over the years, or have reflected local circumstances, Moran's CBTP has formed the core of almost every state, regional, and local bicycle plan prepared since.[24]

Implementation, however, was, then as now, a different matter. Overall, the report recommended a $102 million national cycling action plan. Of this, $250,000 was proposed for an adult on-road bicycle training program. On the other hand, training at the elementary and intermediate level was left to local and state governments. Of the $102 million total plan budget, $100 million was proposed for financing through the then-existing Section 141 program, the successor to the original Section 217 of the 1973 highway act. Like Section 217, Section 141 permitted, but did not require, the expenditure of highway trust funds for alternative mode projects up to a maximum of $20 million per year.

This was only half the size of Section 217 ($40 million/yr), but no matter: the states had spent only about $24 million of the $200 million available over the five-year life of Section 217. The main reason for the low participation was twofold: first, most states didn't want to have to meet the 20 percent matching share requirement ($5.4 million of the $24 million that was spent), and second, they didn't want to divert any of their fixed allocation of 80 percent federal money away from traditional highway projects. Even after the Transportation Enhancement program was introduced in 1991 specifically to create a fund targeted at alternative, non-roadway uses that didn't compete with highway needs, some states chose to under-spend their allocation rather than put up a 20 percent match.[25]

Despite the success of the Missoula pilot program, and the willingness of at least three states to buy into what would eventually become Burden and DiBrito's Bike-Ed America program, no federal funding came through for any of the CBTP's sub-elements, including adult or juvenile education programs, and the United States never did implement a version of Britain's Cycle Proficiency Scheme. As the federal government began to retreat from its commitment to energy conservation and alternative transportation programs with the start of the Regan administration in 1980, Ralph Hirsch, national legislative program director of the L.A.W., summarized the situation:

> There is no [federal] money in 1982 for the bicycle grant program ... there is no money for the rails-to-trails program ... there is a sharp reduction in the highway safety program, under which a lot of bicycle-related state and local projects carried out, and the administration has proposed eliminating grants for bicycle and pedestrian safety projects altogether.... Conservation has become a dirty word in the Department of energy; environmental concerns are being subordinated to economics.[26]

And this continued to be the case from that point forward. There is a general belief that the Intermodal Surface Transportation and Efficiency Act of 1991 (ISTEA) represented a major reversal from the federal government's hands-off attitude toward alternative transportation. That may have been true to some extent for the facilities funded through the Transportation Enhancements program, but as Ron Engle of the National Highway Traffic Safety Administration explained to an audience in 1994, funding opportunities for "soft side" activities never really recovered:

> Everybody is talking about ISTEA as being the savior—yes indeed, Congress did give us ISTEA. They want to increase the amount of commuting, so forth and so on, trips by walking and biking. They also wanted to decrease casualties by 10 percent. But at the same Congress did that they also took away 70 percent of the funds that would go to pedestrian and bicycling safety and threw them away. So I think there's a message there from Congress that's just sort of like "Come here guys, but stand back." So many of those things that we would have available, and we planned to do this coming year, they're not going to happen. As a matter of fact, we don't have a bicycle safety program for the next couple of years.[27]

The second document that significantly defined American bicycle planning throughout the last two decades of the twentieth century was the *Guide to the Development of Bicycle Facilities*, produced by the American Association of State Highway and Transportation Officials (AASHTO) in 1981. UCLA had produced its *Bikeway Planning Criteria and Guidelines* for CalTrans in 1972, and between 1974 and 1976 the FHWA had followed this up with its five-volume *Safety and Locational Criteria for Bikeways*. The fifth volume of that series, 93 pages long and published in February 1976, contained its design and construction criteria. (A simultaneous manual of similar length contained the planning criteria.[28]) Even before it was completed, CalTrans decided that it needed a shorter, more focused manual for its design engineers. A California Bicycle Facilities Committee met from 1975 to 1978, and the new California design manual was issued in 1978. It, in turn, became the working outline upon which the FHWA staff built the initial draft of the proposed new *AASHTO Bicycle Guide*.

Ralph Hirsch first inveigled Congress to mandate that USDOT produce a new set of standards to replace the bulbous *Safety and Locational Criteria for Bikeways*. "Engineers like to pull off the shelf a book that has a recipe in it. If there is no recipe, or if the book has a recipe behind the state of the art, the product will be unsatisfactory," he explained. Once that was accomplished, the Department of Transportation assigned the task to the FHWA's bicycle programs office. The first draft was written by engineer Tom Jennings. After being sent out for review, during which time it received over a hundred written comments, it was revised by bicycle programs manager Richard Lemieux. Most of the engineers Lemieux contacted at AASHTO were not enthusiastic. "The people I worked with genuinely believe that highway users pay highway taxes and nobody else has a right to use that money," he complained. However, an important exception was Frank Francois, AASHTO's executive director, who, while not personally enthusiastic about cycling, realized that AASHTO's single-minded "we exist to serve the motoring public" focus would, in the coming decades, eventually doom the organization to social and political irrelevance unless it adopted a more flexible, far-sighted, multi-modal approach.[29]

AASHTO's *Policy on the Arterial Highways in Urban Areas* (the "Urban Greenbook") had been developed in 1957. By 1966, many parts of it were obsolete, and AASHTO had begun a comprehensive effort that year to update and expand it that took until 1973 to finish. The 1973 edition incorporated FHWA's so-called "PPM 50-9" mandate, requiring a defined planning process that identified the economic, social and environmental effect of each major highway project. The new version also included design criteria for mass transit, especially for buses on urban surface arterials and freeways. It was only natural, given the FHWA's inclusive planning directives in PPM-59, and the requirement that urban transit interface be built right into a road's basic geometrics, that some type of bicycle and pedestrian design guidance would have to either be added or appended to the Urban Greenbook. (The urban and highway greenbooks would eventually be merged into a single work, *A Policy on the Geometric Design of Highways and Streets, 1984*.[30])

After some harping and quibbling over liability details, the AASHTO executive committee approved the *Bicycle Guide* in October 1981. The hope was then to secure official FHWA acceptance, but that proved irrelevant, as it was AASHTO's seal of approval for use by each state's DOT that proved determinative. The *Guide* was even briefer than its CalTrans progenitor, only 31 pages long, mostly because only four pages were devoted to on-road facilities. The remainder was given over to off-road facilities, mostly recreational bike trails. In essence, Jennings and Lemieux had given up on the idea of recommending anything beyond rudimentary standards for on-street bicycle facilities, mostly due to a lack of consensus as to what should be recommended. "Bicycles can be expected to ride on almost all roadways," the new *Bicycle Guide* predicted, then suggested that when funds were limited, secure bicycle parking was probably a more cost-effective option, a recommendation taken straight from John Williams's San Luis Obispo plan.[31]

Cycle advocates and highway engineers were in agreement about one thing: while there was no harm in purely recreational facilities, provided they were designed well and not used as a subterfuge to ban cyclists from roadways, just broaching the subject of on-road facilities was a no-win situation, so why bother? Moreover, as one historian put it, this perspective "held sway throughout the late 1970s and 1980s because city officials found in vehicular cycling advocates the cheapest and easiest course of action to pursue." As urban planner James Stacey noted at the 1978 MAUDEP conference, "Given an equal choice between spending money on a facilities project or not, an official's decision is usually pretty easy to predict."[32]

An epilogue: The AASHTO *Bicycle Guide* was subsequently amended in 1991 and 1999. Neither was a substantial revision, and by 1999 it was still only 70 pages long. The National Cooperative Highway Research Program (NCHRP) of the Transportation Research Board issued extensive reports in 2004 and 2010 recommending updates to the *Bicycle Guide*, but in both cases AASHTO itself decided against any immediate revisions.[33]

As time went by, this created a gap in both technology and authority which was filled by improvisation and adhocracy. The same year that the first edition of the AASHTO *Bicycle Guide* came out, Donald Appleyard published a groundbreaking book, *Livable Streets*. It was inspired by two earlier works: Jane Jacobs's *The Death and Life of Great American Cities* (1961) and Colin Buchanan's lesser known *Traffic in Towns* (1963). Jacobs, who had successfully fought New York planning director Robert Moses's attempt to extend Fifth Avenue south through Washington Park and into lower Manhattan in the 1950s, could describe what made her Greenwich Village neighborhood so livable despite its age and location in the heart of a bustling city, but was at a loss to explain how its lessons could be applied to other neighborhoods.[34]

Buchanan, on the other hand, had been retained by the British Ministry of Transport and the Greater London Council to formulate a long-term transportation strategy for England's large cities, principally London. His report focused on a "zone and artery" system, with the zones emphasizing environmental quality, and the traffic immediately funneled onto a system of free-flowing arteries. Autos could move from one zone to another only via the arteries, but bicycles, busses and pedestrians would have greater permeability to move directly from one zone to another via pathways, overpasses, and tunnels. It was an original and brilliant plan, but the Tory government focused on the arteries and ignored the needs of the neighborhoods until the Labour governments of the 1970s shifted the transport ministry's priorities, at least until the Thatcher government took over. This was especially true in London, where the liberal Greater London Council took a lead role.[35]

Appleyard's book, which was the result of ten years' research, mostly in the San Francisco Bay area and in London, was widely recognized as pathbreaking, but for bicycle planners it did not have an immediate effect. As it became clear that American bicycle planning had settled on a long-term vehicular cycling paradigm, its dissenters either gave up in frustration and moved into other areas, or realized that the type of neighborhood improvement techniques being taught by Appleyard and others (such as Richard Unterman, a landscape architect teaching at the University of Washington–Seattle) could be slipped in under the radar as something other than "bicycle planning." Unterman, for example, named his book *Accommodating the Pedestrian*. It wasn't until one got to the subtitle "adapting towns and neighborhoods for walking and bicycling" that the message was communicated that this was a book about changing the built environment to the common advantage of both users:

> The bicycle commuters of the past mostly consisted of young, energetic, hearty bicyclists whose personality, character, nature and willingness to take chances allowed them to commute in our harsh urban environments. This author believes, based on European experiences and on the large number of potential bicyclists unwilling to brave those dangers, that the real need is to plan for accommodating more timid bicycle commuters.[36]

In this way, the rhetoric could be changed. The goal was now to improve the physical environment for pedestrians. Pedestrians have always used various types of augmentation devices: handcarts, "granny walkers," skateboards, even purloined grocery store carts. Bicycles are simply another of these "pedestrian augmentation devices." No need to make a big deal of it. One hears an echo of the exasperated retort of Dutch roadway engineer Tully Hendricks: "What do experienced cyclists think? What *is* an 'experienced' cyclist?"

Appleyard and Unterman's "liveable cities" work was a broadened, "big tent" form of bicycle planning, but with the name changed to avoid attracting the attention of the enthusiast cyclists who had traditionally dominated the process, and to avoid alienating the other constituent groups, such as homeowners' associations, elder rights groups, and neighborhood business associations, who did not identify with cyclists, and even found themselves intimidated or at odds with them.

Dan Burden, who had gone to work for the Bicycle Federation in the mid–1990s, recalled watching the office clear out when executive director Bill Wilkinson held up a work order for a walking-related project that the Federation had received from some agency, announcing that it needed a project manager. Nobody on the Federation's bicycle-oriented staff wanted to be involved.

Six years later, Burden, who got stuck with it, gave the Transportation Research Board's 2001 Distinguished Lecture—not on "bicycles" or on "pedestrians," but on "livable communities." Burden had become one of the most recognized and respected bicycle planners in America by dropping the word "bicycle" from his job title, his vocabulary and, most importantly, from his professional image. The youthful images of him grimly pushing a 10-speed touring bike along a quagmired Alaskan highway during the 1973 Hemistour were now relegated to the bottom of the drawer. By 2010, the job title of "bicycle planner" or "bicycle coordinator" had practically become an anachronism. Such professionals were now "complete streets coordinators" or "mobility enhancements planners." As such, one could implement a wide range of capital improvements to advance the overall functioning and quality of life in a local neighborhood—if it so happened that some of those design features looked and functioned an awful lot like a bicycle facility, well, life is just full of coincidences, isn't it?[37]

The bureaucratic gridlock at AASHTO in revising the *Bicycle Guide* not only concerned cycle advocates, but mainstream highway engineers as well. As each year went by, the failure to make the changes recommended in the Transportation Research Board's NCHRP reports put the *Guide* ever farther out of conformity with the Manual of Uniform Traffic Control Devices (MUTCD), which standardizes the configuration and placement of such things as pavement markings, street signs, and traffic signals. The MUTCD, unlike the *Guide*, has, since 1983, been accorded formal legal status under both the United States Code and the Code of Federal Regulations.[38]

Although the Code of Federal Regulations requires that the AASHTO *Guide to the Development of New Bicycle Facilities* "or equivalent guides developed in cooperation with state or local officials and acceptable to the division office of the FHWA" be used as the standard for the construction and design of bike routes, the term "bicycle routes" is left undefined. Thus, while adherence to the MUTCD is mandatory for each state, the AASHTO manuals, especially the *Bicycle Guide*, are stuck in a regulatory netherworld somewhere between advisory and mandatory.[39]

In March 2011, the National Association of City Traffic Officials (NACTO) issued its own manual, the *Urban Bikeway Design Guide*. Commentators noted that it was far less conservative than the 1999 AASHTO *Guide* in illustrating and discussing the range of treatments available, especially for on-road facilities. They were also surprised by the rapidity in which new editions appeared. (The second edition was issued eighteen months after the first, in September 2012.) Overlooked in all the excitement was that the NACTO *Guide* was, in actuality, an applications guide for devices and treatments already approved for the MUTCD. In fact, only two treatments in the NACTO *Guide* were not in the

MUTCD, and those were soon included by the Committee for Uniform Traffic Control Devices (the MUTCD steering committee) as "provisional" or "experimental" designs, a category that most of the NACTO designs had already gone through until data could be collected and their performance verified.[40]

In 2012, AASHTO finally released the fourth edition of its *Guide to the Development of Bicycle Facilities*. It had increased from 70 to 200 pages, but was still more conservative than the NACTO *Guide*, especially when it came to on-road treatments, where the AASHTO *Bicycle Guide* had always tread lightly. In a speech before an AASHTO meeting in February, 2013, outgoing transportation secretary Ray LaHood said that his department planned to abandon its dependence on state traffic officials to provide engineering leadership and would develop its own bicycle and pedestrian guides. The implication was that the department had grown dissatisfied with both AASHTO's lumbering process and its product, which after 13 years of work and two major studies, still failed to conform with the MUTCD. Whether this was sufficient to meet the "equivalent guides developed in cooperation with State or local officials and acceptable to the division office of the FHWA" condition in the Code of Federal Regulations that would thus allow local officials to substitute the NACTO manual for the AASHTO *Bicycle Guide* in its entirety is an unanswered question as this is being written. What appears certain is that in the long run, the "official" standard will be those issued by the Federal Highway Administration. AASHTO almost certainly managed to put itself out of the bicycle business, probably to its great relief.[41]

* * *

"Those in government who have sought to lend a hand to bicyclists are likely to be discouraged from further efforts when the very people they have tried to help respond with criticism," Darryl Skrabak famously noted in 1977. As the 1970s wore on, obtuseness and confusion became signature themes within both government agencies and bicycle advocacy organizations. In an environment where the most vocal and organized cyclists were increasingly able to express only what they were *against*, not what they were *for*, government agencies started to tune them out and turn to more receptive audiences. They knew that the weaker riders who had previously been shut out or shouted down by the club cyclists could be quietly ameliorated as a byproduct or spillover benefit of projects ostensibly used to meet other objectives. The key was to downplay or ignore such "externalities" during the planning process, then later treat them as an "accidental" or "incidental" result of the project. The re-positioning of many "bicycle planners" into "complete streets coordinators" or "neighborhood liveability coordinators," previously discussed, is just one symptom of this.

Another example is the widespread use of sidewalks as *de facto* sidepaths, facilitated through the installation of curb cuts or curb ramps. America's biggest and longest-lasting bicycle program succeeded beyond anyone's wildest dream simply because nobody ever thought of it as one. Starting in 1973, and for the next 40 years, local governments ended up installing universal systems of sidepaths with a nationwide price tag that, depending on how you do the math, could have cost as much as *480 billion dollars.* But it evaded controversy because everybody either overlooked or chose to ignore the clearly obvious impact it was having on cycling.

It was the result of the federal accessibility mandate initiated under Section 504 of the Rehabilitation Act of 1973, and expanded under the Americans with Disabilities Act (ADA) of 1990. Its formal designation was the "Federal Accessibility Guidelines for Public Walks and Rights-of-Ways," but it has always been known by a far more practical name: *the curb cut rule*. For the vast majority of cyclists, those of modest skill, or those who ride out of sheer necessity, the document that has affected them the most is not *Bicycle Transportation for Energy Conservation* or the *Guide to the Development of New Bicycle Facilities.* It isn't even a bicycle document. It is Section 504's most visible product, the *Uniform Federal Accessibility Standards* (UFAS). It makes sidewalks compatible for wheelchair use. It also turns them into *de facto* bikepaths.

It started in 1973 with two separate federal laws, Section 228 of the Federal Highway Act of 1973 and Section 504. The highway act required that all pedestrian ways constructed after July 1, 1976, built with full or partial federal funding, have curb cuts or ramps to accommodate people in wheelchairs. However, the real teeth were in Section 504. It was not necessary that a specific roadway project be federally funded to invoke the Section 228 requirement; all that was necessary was that a state's transportation budget *as a whole* have accepted federal funding. That, of course, meant every state, every project.

Moreover, the oversight authority for Section 504 wasn't given to USDOT, but to the Department of Justice, because 504 was a civil rights measure. The Federal Highway Administration and the state highway departments had always maintained a kind of go-along-to-get-along relationship with each other, especially through AASHTO, but the DOJ had no motivation to maintain chummy relationships with the state highway departments, and in the 1970s its civil rights division, quite frankly, didn't trust the states. In 1984, the federal government prepared the UFAS to standardize its own in-house practices, although most states ended up adopting it, because adherence to UFAS was *prima facie* proof that a state was meeting its 504 requirements.[42]

In 1990, Congress upped the ante by approving the Americans with Disabilities Act (ADA). Although revolutionary in many other areas, when it came to street sidewalks, it looked at first like there was little in the new law that wasn't already in Section 504. The ADA requirement that all facilities constructed after January 1992 be wheelchair-compliant was largely redundant, given that 504 already required this. Moreover, the new Americans with Disabilities Act Accessibilities Guidelines (ADAAG) for public sidewalks and crosswalks was largely taken from the UFAS. However, there were some important differences that were not immediately apparent. Under 504, curb cuts had to be installed when *curbs* were "constructed or replaced." The ADA required them when a *street* was "constructed or altered." Also, states and local governments had to prepare transition plans by 1995 for existing facilities that provided for retrofitting walkways serving public facilities. Everyone thought it would be the transition plans that would be the contentious part, but that proved not to be the case.[43]

After reviewing the law, the Pennsylvania Department of Transportation and the city of Philadelphia had settled on a policy of not installing curb cuts when they performed roadway resurfacing and reconstruction, unless: (1) the intersection was due for curb cut installation under its transition plan; or (2) the curbing was in such bad shape that it had to be replaced anyway. An advocacy group, Disabled in Action, sued the Pennsylvania DOT and the city of Philadelphia. A federal court ruled that if the pavement surface over which a crosswalk runs is being rebuilt, then it meets the definition of an "altered" street under the ADA and invokes the curb cut requirement, regardless of its status under the approved transition plan, because the language in the ADA, unlike Section 504, specified installation upon "construction or replacement" of the *street*, not the *curb*. The nationwide effect was to require that any road replacement or repair beyond mere pothole filling was going to trip the curb cut requirement.[44]

One reason for Pennsylvania's seemingly Scroog-ish policy is that prior to the TEA-21 transportation act of 1997, there was no federal money set aside to help state or local governments implement the curb cut mandate. TEA-21 allocated $33 billion between 1998 and 2003. There had previously been no money because nobody appreciated the magnitude of what Congress and the Department of Justice had done. As the U.S. Architectural and Transportation Barriers Compliance Board wrote, the ADA was intended to be flexible in its application: "In fact, existing facilities do not have to be made accessible if other methods of providing access are effective, *except for the installation of curb ramps, which are specifically required for program access.*" And, as the court had noted in the Pennsylvania case, the wording of the two acts taken together created a situation where "there is no general undue burden defense." Whatever you have to spend, you will spend, or you will lose all your federal transportation dollars.[45]

Compare the scope of the TEA-21 curb cut funding ($33 billion; 1998–2003) to the spending on bicycle and pedestrian projects under the federal Transportation Enhancements program ($3.17 billion; 1992–2004). Considering the entire life of the program between 1973 and fiscal year 2011, the Section 504/ADA walkway retrofit requirement has not only been the single largest nonmotorized transportation project undertaken in the United States, it is equal to, or larger than, the bicycle facilities programs in nations like Germany or the Netherlands. However, *it has never even been recognized as a program*. It was just something that evolved, incrementally, and by necessity. It is the classic example of a non-program program. A reasonable overall estimate is that Section 504 and ADA have led to the installation of about 55 million curb cuts in American urbanized areas over the last forty years at a total cost of between 165 to 485 *billion* dollars, depending on how costs are allocated.[46] If forced to make a single-point estimate, I would place the amount at about 330 billion dollars.

The first ADAAG manual was issued by the U.S. Architectural and Barriers Compliance Board in 1991. The current version of the ADAAG manual for accessible rights-of-way is far more extensive than is the current AASHTO *Guide to the Development of Bicycle Facilities*, and has become, for all intents and purposes, the default guide for the development of roadside "Radweg-style" bicycle facilities. After all, if a sidewalk is going to be safely used by someone in a standard or electric wheelchair, it is a pretty safe bet that it will work well enough for a bicycle user, provided he or she is willing to keep their speed under about ten or twelve mph, which is around 97 percent of the cyclists who prefer to use sidewalks.

Bicycle professionals and advocates alike may decry the use of sidewalks by the old, the young, the infirm, the timid, and even the inebriated or incompetent, but the fact is that with the universal installation of curb cuts, at least in urban areas, sidewalks are now America's bicycle facilities, and their very ubiquity has taken the pressure off state and local governments to "do something" for cyclists, because as far as the average low-skill cyclist is concerned, something *has* been done. It's not much, but it's not the street, either.

There is now a more-or-less unspoken pact between local politicians and those users the club cyclists consider the "great unwashed" that curb-ramped sidewalks are good enough, and as long as they are not banned from them too often, in too many places, then they won't make too much noise about demanding on-street bike lanes, let alone real honest-to-goodness bike paths. Thus, it's no wonder that club cyclists, at the same time they roll their eyes and make various snorting noises when the subject of sidewalk cycling comes up, would never in a thousand years dream of proactively agitating for sidewalk bans; in fact they generally fight them quite vigorously.

After all, the club cyclists know on which side their toast is buttered: if the masses with all their supposed cyclist inferiority complexes get pushed off into the streets, they are *not* going to go off running in search of the nearest Effective Cycling instructor to learn how to do a vehicular left turn. They will, instead, start screaming bloody murder for bike lanes and bike paths, no matter how jury-rigged, poorly engineered, or badly maintained they may end up being. And to get them, they would be willing to agree to mandatory use laws or most any other legislative compromise. Moreover, the club cyclists know that in this kind of battle, where the backs of the "great unwashed" are well and truly against the wall, and theirs are not, they would be out-manned, out-moneyed, and out-shouted, and the outcome could well pose a very real and very permanent threat to their type of high-performance road cycling. So rideable sidewalks for all are a compromise with which everyone has come to agree upon.

* * *

The other "stealth" American cycle-program, also a success story, has been bikes-on-bus service (BoB). Although the percentage of buses equipped with bike racks tripled between 2000 and 2010, from 27 to 72 percent (with New York City the only major city left totally unequipped), BoB service has been the Cinderella of American bicycle planning, largely ignored by mainstream bicycle planners and advocates. This is largely because BoB does not serve those cyclists most influential in formulating and monitoring government policy. In 2009, only 11 percent of regular adult sport cyclists came from households earning less than $25,000 per year, but 28 percent came from households earning $100,000 or more. Only 4 percent of regular adult sport cyclists were African-American and 4 percent were Hispanic.[47] In comparison, only 21 percent of BoB riders earned more than $30,000, and only 7 percent made $50,000 or more. African-Americans comprised 26 percents of BoB users and Hispanics 20.5 percent. Almost all were male. About two-thirds of service users were traveling to and from work.[48]

Because of these demographics, BoB has been ignored by bicycle advocates on both sides of the bikeways divide. In fact, its very success can be attributed to the fact that it was born and gestated outside of bicycle planning circles. Although most observers believe that its success was motivated by the need of transit agencies in low-density sunbelt urban areas to attract new riders at a low cost, much of its growth can be equally attributed to the private sector, to the engineering, technical support and vigorous marketing of commercial bike-rack manufacturers.

Bikes-on-bus and bikes-on-train service pre-dated the great 10-speed bike boom. More than a dozen transit agencies adopted some type of bikes-on-bus service in the 1960s and early 1970s, but often only for specialized services, and almost all were short-lived. Many were subsidized trial or pilot programs. In 1978, Seattle Metro Transit purchased rear-mounted racks for a few busses to shuttle bikes across the SR-520 bridge spanning Lake Washington that had no shoulders or bike lanes. The racks were purchased from a California firm and cost about a thousand dollars each. The rear racks held the bikes vertically and could carry four or five bikes, but had to be removed to access the engine and air conditioner bays, or to wash the buses. "There were only four stops where you could get off," recalled one user. "There were a few commuters at first, but I used it mostly on weekends on a bike loop from home, up the Burke-Gilman trail, and back around to [State Road] 520. The demise of rear mounted racks came quickly, if I remember, when a few people tried to ride for free by jumping on and hitching a ride on the rack when the driver wasn't looking."[49]

Similarly, AC Transit, based in Oakland, provided space inside select buses for the trip across the Oakland Bay Bridge which connected that city to San Francisco. The Lawrence Livermore Laboratory, east of Oakland, accommodated bikes on shuttle buses that ran between the Lab and the University of California main campus in Berkeley. Santa Barbara Metropolitan Transit initiated widespread BoB service starting in 1975 using towed bike trailers. Ridership reached about 41,000 trips per year before its subsidy was eliminated in the mid–1980s.[50]

The biggest problem was cartage technology. Transit agencies tried front racks, rear racks, trailers and internal stowage. Although rear racks were the most popular, none were found satisfactory. Front racks scraped the ground on dips, increased the clear distance needed on turns, and usually required that the front bike be removed before the rear bike could be added or taken off. Rear racks couldn't be seen or supervised by drivers adequately, and they blocked access to the service bays. The same was true for trailers. Trailers also added to problems with turning and made backing up a nightmare. Internal storage removed seating and wheelchair capacity.

Seattle began developing a front mounted rack in 1982. Seattle Metro credits one of their machinists, Bruce Hargin, with the design and tooling of the original model. It was modified in 1983–84 by fellow machinist Larry Whitney to ease removal for bus washing. Seattle stayed with their in-house design until 1993 when they turned to an outside supplier, Sportworks NW, who had solved the problem of making a rack that could be left on the bus during washing or quickly removed.

Portland Tri-Met and Phoenix Transit began large-scale test programs in 1991. The Phoenix program started by completely equipping three routes. At the end of the first six months, 1,404 riders per month were using the service.

At that point, it was decided to expand the service, one route at a time. By 1993 the decision was made to equip all 350 buses with racks manufactured in-house. They proved to be unsuitable for either Portland or Seattle, because they were designed for Phoenix's relatively flat terrain and hung too low, scraping on dips and the start of hills.[51]

It was at this point, in the early 1990s, that Sportworks NW entered the scene in a big way. Its two-bike rack was designed to bolt to the bus's frame under the front windshield, but immediately rose up a foot or so higher than the front bumper, thereby eliminating the "dip-scape" problem; it folded up easily; and each bike could be inserted and removed independently of the other. Every rack Seattle purchased after its Phase II installation and those Portland Tri-Met bought after its Phase III implementation were Sportworks products.

"[Seattle] Metro researched racks for several years attempting to find one they could fit on every bus in order to make the service universal and easy to use," but it was not able to realize this goal until after Sportworks and its competitors entered the market with significant economies of scale. "The Metro racks prior to '93 had several issues," recalls one Metro worker, "they were front loaders with swing away arms that required the cyclists in the front position to remove his or her cycle if the interior cycles were being removed ... then of, course there was the problem of washing the bus with the older rack."[52] Although several agencies manufactured their own racks in-house up to about 1995, after this, virtually all purchases were from private vendors, and Sportworks now supplies about 400 agencies.

This was the overlooked factor in the development of BoB service. As late as 1992, Case Study 9 ("Linking Bicycle Pedestrian Access with Transit") of the *National Bicycling and Walking Study* identified secure parking nodes ("bike and ride facilities") as the "basic prerequisite to successful bike-on-transit services." While it acknowledged that "bike-on-bus programs can significantly expand mobility for many people who lack automobiles and for those who live too far from available bus stops," it believed that any trip less than six miles in length "would not offer a significant travel time advantage to dual-mode travelers" barring some type of route obstacle. Bicycle planners were still thinking like, well, bicycle planners—trying to lure automobile drivers out of their cars and turn them into voluntary bicycle riders. They were not thinking like transit planners, who were used to working every day with an involuntary, captive user base. For transit planners, the question is not motivation, it's access—given the desperately small number of bus routes and stops you can afford to put on the street, how can you get the most number of patrons to and from each bus stop as cheaply as possible?[53]

After 1993, the private-sector rack manufacturers not only targeted the upper management of transit agencies with increasingly sophisticated marketing campaigns but also sent technicians and sample racks into transit garages. They became the principal carrier wave for disseminating technical know-how to mechanics and drivers about how the equipment should be installed, maintained and used. Active and retired drivers retained by the rack-makers helped prepare videos and give workshops reassuring drivers regarding the most common problems they would face: misinformed or confused customers; users marginally capable of lifting a bicycle or folding down a rack; handling customers when the rack was already full; dealing with a poorly installed bike partially demounting itself from the rack. All of these situations could be handled with the same aplomb they used everyday. Transit services learned one cheap and easy solution to the problem of full racks: make the advertising companies that supplied their bus benches or shelters supply a post and locking ring with every bench.

Surprisingly, it was a handful of transit planners, not bicycle advocates, that initially championed BoB service. Foremost among these was Michael Replogle and Elizabeth Drake. Replogle was a planner for the Maryland–National Capital Park and Planning Commission who began writing in the mid–1980s on the general topic of bicycle access to transit. BoB service was only a small part of his work, much of which examined the potential of improved parking systems to affect the ridership of rail systems, and was likely an outgrowth of the continued expansion of the Washington, D.C., Metro system into what was then the fringe areas of the capital city. Drake was a planner at several agencies over the years in the Phoenix metropolitan area. She had been interested in bicycle and pedestrian issues for many years (and was a participant at the Bike-Ed '77 Conference).

"Elizabeth was really the founding figure in Bikes-on-Bus," says Dan Burden.[54] Although, as has been noted, such services are disproportionately used by working-class nonwhite males, Phoenix turned to BoB service out of enlightened self-interest. The metro area is simply too disaggregated to cover adequately with regular line-haul service. In many areas, the distance between routes on the service grid is typically one-and-a-half to two miles, too far to walk. BoB allows at least one segment of the population, young employed males, to have nearly full access to the system. About one-quarter of BoB riders did not take the bus before they started utilizing BoB service. The reason most often cited by transit administrators for initiating BoB service is revenue augmentation. The second is the ability to make service accessible without having to add new transit routes or busses to the system. That has been a regular pattern with BoB system adoption.[55]

The role that the early promoters like Elizabeth Drake played was vital.

Transit services are conservative and their management is distrustful of anyone from outside their ranks. "I can remember in the '80s and early '90s transit agencies telling me, 'We can't implement this without a full feasibility study,'" Burden later recalled. "I'm going, 'Let's think about this. You are talking about spending $100,000 to study a program that will cost you $300,000 to implement. That's ridiculous. Save your money, fly down to Phoenix, take one of your drivers. Go talk to Elizabeth.' Phoenix Metro Transit used to complain about all the drivers from around the country out circling around in their parking lot in one of their rack-equipped busses, knocking down orange cones."[56]

After the 1990s, private companies, especially Sportworks NW in Seattle, took over that role. While Sportworks never bought their own bus, they did take the cheaper route of simply sending a couple of sample racks and a technician, bolting them to a potential customer's busses, and setting the drivers and bus hostellers loose. Once the fear element was gone, there were few negatives, customer frustration at full racks being the biggest complaint. In response, Sportworks introduced an easy-to-load 3-bike rack in the early 2000s.[57]

There has been very little coordination in bicycle planning between the "transit" and the "surface" elements of most bicycle plans. The biggest problem in the implementation of most bikeways plans is creating a connected grid of compatible routes. The goal is to be able to lay down a network of facilities, be they separated bicycle facilities, bike lanes, or adequate roadways. As the plan develops over time, the grid turns from "red" (links that are unsuitable for bicycle use) to "green" (highly compatible). But the job of turning those links from "red" to "green," either by improving the roadway system or by bypassing it with specialized bicycle facilities, is extraordinarily expensive and time consuming. In today's increasingly disaggregated urban areas, the goal of connectivity has become something of a holy grail, long sought, but always seemingly just out of grasp.

But if the network is not planned around the roadway system, but instead around the transit network, many urban areas already have a connected grid, because they have a fully bike-rack equipped transit system. The traditional carless transit customer can use the transit route network as the backbone of their "bicycling" system, riding only as far as the nearest transit stop, then taking the bus (or train) to as close to their destination as possible, riding only for the last link of their trip. The need for surface improvements, be they roadway upgrades or specialized facilities, radiates like the spokes of a wheel from each transit stop, and only extends as far as needed to distribute the trips to or from that transit stop.

Trying to "close the gaps" in roadway-based bicycle facilities grid over a low-density urban area of 100 to 200 square miles is a massive undertaking.

Moreover, given that the average journey-to-work trip is six to ten miles, but the average utility trip is only two to three, laying down a fully connected grid of bicycle-friendly routes that can service both types of trips simply can't be done. A workable grid would have to be so fine-meshed that it would, given the curvilinear, single-point-entry "superblock" neighborhood design of most sunbelt suburbs, be as dense as the roadway system itself.

The latest "great white hope" for surmounting this problem has been the so-called "electric bicycle," more accurately, the electric moped. The Velib bike-share system in Lyon, France, the first of the large-scale bike share programs, has gone to electric bikes for its second-generation equipment, and many believe this will be the future of bike-sharing, especially in North American sunbelt cities. Far cheaper is to use not a thousand or more compact electric motors; but fifty or seventy 400-cubic inch turbocharged natural-gas engines, each sitting in the back of a fifty-passenger, heated, air-conditioned, all-weather city bus.

CHAPTER 7

Unexpected Consequences, Big and Small, 1970–1983

Whether it was the lemming-like procession of urban "Yellow Bike" programs leaping off the cliff of economically suicidal mass theft trying to emulate the Amsterdam Provos' White Bikes of the 1970s (a program that existed only in the popular imagination of '60s urban protesters), or the American club cyclists' revolt of the mid–1970s (spurred on by the paralyzing fear that they would have to ride bikes laden with 50 cents' worth of plastic reflectors), American bicycle planning has always been the story of wildly gyrating mood swings, unexpected forces and unintended consequences. To be blunt, this has happened with predictable regularity because American cycle advocacy exists in a world of cognitive dissonance largely disconnected from political, social, technical or economic realities.

Cycle clubs and advocacy groups speak the language of "road rights" and "transportation equality," but club cyclists are the least likely demographic group to actually use their bicycles as transport, and for the most part they are uninterested in those groups who do. For them, the real issue (unspoken, of course) is the urgent need to maintain free and open access to the roadways for use as a recreational facility. One does not hear the American Street Festival Association or the National Street Stickball Federation framing their rhetoric as ancillary roadway users in terms of "rights," but bicycle organizations have no hesitation whatsoever about doing so.

On the other hand, there *is* a very legitimate question about whether a roadway system planned and built for rush-hour peak loads that occur only about 1,200 hours a year is being used to its maximum potential when all that excess capacity is kept vacant and denied to all other potential users for the other 7,500 hours a year. Instead, it is allowed to lie fallow, creating yawning canyons of concrete and asphalt. It is a real question, a legitimate question, but is it a *transportation* question? Likewise, even a quick survey of most low-density, sub-belt cities will reveal that the largest percentage of true transportation utility cyclists are low-skill, involuntary riders using the sidewalk system. Yet many Effective Cyclists see them as an embarrassment and would gladly support an effort to get rid of them, if only it could be done in a way that wouldn't threaten to boomerang back on them. Better to simply pretend they don't exist.

Even among the ardently pro-bikeways set, New York cyclist and writer Alexandra Gutierrez asks, "Are snobby cyclists their own worst enemies?... The driving principle behind most cycling policy is supposed to be inclusivity.... Yet the urbane cyclists pushing for these changes may be their own worst marketing problem. Bike culture is just too cool and clubby for its own good.... By continually framing bikeability as an urban issue, advocates are turning off otherwise sympathetic people in suburbs, exurbs and rural townships."[1]

But the divide is not always urban versus suburban. The bikelane installation projects pushed in New York under Mayor Michael Bloomberg's public works commissioner Janette Sadik-Kahn between 2007 and 2013 generated a vitriolic response far in excess of any actual adverse impact they may have generated. "The most important common denominator," observed *New York* reporter Matthew Shaer, "may be a strong preference for the city that *was* over the city that *may be*.... The bike lane fight has two sides: the blue-collar New Yorkers who have to drive to work and the coddled creative-class types who live close enough to commute on their Bianchis."[2]

Europe went through this 40 years ago. A trade unionist who had founded the Paris branch of the "Pedestrian Rights Association" in 1959 confessed ruefully that their intent to organize the disenfranchised and carless had failed woefully; instead, he now headed an organization of well-off urban professionals, 70 percent of whom were car-owning. He had, he acknowledged, never realized how many workers equated the idea of "the better life" with car ownership. What had emerged in the '60s and '70s within his organization was an amorphous urban subculture of enthusiastic pedestrians, cyclists and transit users that would soon coalesce around the new Green Party locals starting to organize in West Germany and the Netherlands.[3]

The irony was that even as he was complaining of his association's turn from a gritty labor-union based "worker's rights" mentality to a "Green Party chic" image, the Greens themselves were starting to fly apart. After their heyday in the 1983 parliamentary and local elections, the German central party started to split into two contesting factions. By 1989, Jutta Ditfurth, head of the Green's radical wing that saw parliamentary participation as a form of street theatre and was consequently uninterested in finding any kind of legislative common ground with the established parties, had been purged, and the leaders of the more coalition-minded "eco-green" wing gradually became co-oped into the liberal power structure. Like many American "neo-cons," who started out as campus radicals only to end up boardroom insiders, many became government ministers or corporate lobbyists: Joschka Fischer now works for Madeleine Albright's Stonebridge Group; Andrea Fischer is a lobbyist for the healthcare industry; Gunda Rostel joined a firm that designs electric powerplants, including nuclear reactors; and so on.[4]

When your basic premises rest upon a set of internal contradictions, unexpected consequences have to be expected. Returning to American bicycle planning, two of these have already been discussed. The first was the transformation of the average city sidewalk into a *de facto* bikeway through the Section 504/ADA sidewalk curb mandate. The second was the near-universal adoption of bikes-on-bus technology by American transit agencies, but through independent action or in consultation with their own professional organization, the American Public Transit Association (APTA) and not through extensive interaction with the bicycle planning establishment.

But there have been other, less visible, and often more ambiguous, unexpected consequences of adopting vehicular cycling as America's national bicycle planning standard. These include the inability of cycle advocates to create and maintain a stable non-governmental organization (NGO) to advocate for their interests along the lines of the Dutch ANWB, and the rise of a private sector in the business of vehicular cycling, initially in the publishing of "how-to" books, later in the development and teaching of "hands-on" courses. Much like the controversial privatization of prisons or charter schools (or, perhaps less dramatically, those ubiquitous private "traffic schools" offering a less-boring alternative to the stock government "ticket class," featuring entertainment themes from comedy central to punk rock), privatized vehicular cycling schools have become hot properties, and are sprouting like weeds. The only question is: are they better than what government bike programs and clubs are teaching now, and do they have hidden agendas?

* * *

In contrast to the successes of the ADAAG sidewalk program and bikes-on-bus, one of the more spectacular policy failures during the 1970s and '80s was inability of cycle advocates to create a stable non-profit advocacy organization with a full time, professional staff to represent their interests. As James Stacey, a planner with the city of Syracuse, lamented in 1978, "Most bicyclists and bike clubs show an abysmal lack of understanding about how ... governments operate separately and in concert. Improvement here would lead to more effective lobbying, granted that the bike advocates knew what they were after and are willing to present a strong, sustained effort."[5]

In late 1972, as the great bicycle boom was hitting full stride, Horace Huffman and Fred Smith of the Bicycle Manufacturers' Association (BMA) sent a memo to their fellow industry executives asking them to assist in the funding of a consumer organization. "Unless safer bike riding facilities are developed, adults could become disenchanted with the bicycle," they wrote, "we need local ordinances creating bikeways and bike paths ... a bike lobby is needed at every level if we are to attain our objective of bike path legislation and funding." Although the industry already had a trade group, the Bicycle Institute of America (BIA), that body "and each of us as individual manufacturers have to keep a very low profile in all these efforts. Trade associations and manufacturers frequently carry only negative influence." The solution, they concluded, was that "we must have a consumer lobby because this is the influence legislators respond to best."[6]

The BIA had two alternatives, Huffman and Smith believed: either fund an existing organization or start one of their own. The second alternative was quickly ruled out. "Some will say, let's start an organization specifically designed to achieve our objective. This alternative seems highly impractical to us in view of our limited resources," which they estimated at somewhere between sixteen- and twenty-thousand dollars per year. This quick dismissal is somewhat surprising, given how effective Bob Cleckner and Keith Kingbay had been throughout the '60s and early '70s in helping local clubs and governments achieve Huffman and Frank Schwinn's main priority, promoting bicycle facilities. However, for most of this time, Cleckner had been a one-man show, a roving ambassador for the American Youth Hostels, rather than the BIA. Kingbay was spending much of his time helping with the League of American Wheelmen and giving workshops and presentations arranged by Schwinn dealers and distributors. What Huffman and his fellow industrialists were now interested in was building up a full-time grass-roots membership-based cyclists' organization.

Going for a strategy of building up an already-existing organization left five candidates: the American Youth Hostels (AYH), the League of American Wheelmen (L.A.W.), the Amateur Bicycle League of America (ABLA), the Friends of Bikeology, and the National Safety Council (NSC). Bikeology was too small and new; the NSC wasn't interested in bicycle facilities, just education programs; and the ABLA was strictly a racing sanctioning body. That left the AYH and the L.A.W. The L.A.W. was the winner, for two reasons. First, while the larger and better organized of the two, the American Youth Hostels was "not solely interested in cycling. To get them to do what we want done would be difficult." In fact, the AYH was quite a large organization, with over one hundred hostels around the world. As Huffman pointed out, that was part of the problem: many AYH members joined just because they were going to Europe and wanted access to the inexpensive hostels. If they weren't planning to travel the following year, they let their memberships lapse. The AYH had a high turnover rate.

Second, the L.A.W. and the industry already went back together a long way. Despite claims to a lineage extending back to 1880, the L.A.W. had an on-and-off history. Founded in 1880, its membership peaked in 1898 at 101,000 during the first great bike boom, but declined rapidly thereafter. After 1904, it limped along as an old-timers club for high-wheeler riders, finally folding in 1924. It was resurrected in 1939 as a federation of bicycle clubs under the leadership of Jack Hansen, the president of the Chicago Cycle Supply, a bicycle and parts distributor affiliated with Schwinn. Its membership was always skewed towards clubs, not individuals, who tended to join only if they lived in a relatively remote location where there was no bicycle club. For example, in 1951 the L.A.W. membership was comprised of 400 clubs, but only 77 individuals. It carried on with annual financial assistance from the BIA until 1955, when Hansen's death precipitated another suspension of activity.[7]

It was revived again in 1964, its bank account intact. Like the 1939–55 organization, it was mainly an association of bicycle clubs in the upper Midwest and New England, and again with industry assistance, this time most of it funneled through Schwinn. It experienced phenomenal growth during the early '70s bike boom, but was sagging under its all-volunteer management structure, especially as it expanded from a Chicago-based group to a nationwide organization. It had no permanent headquarters, and by default, much of its leadership had fallen to the editor of its monthly magazine, the *L.A.W. Bulletin*, Phyllis Harmon, who lived near Chicago. In spite of this, Huffman and Smith wrote, "The L.A.W. is, in our opinion, a far better consumer organization for our lobbying needs than the others."[8]

In mid–1972, Schwinn and the Huffman Manufacturing Company had unilaterally pledged $16,000 to the L.A.W. so that the league's president, the Oregon-based Carroll Quimby, could hire a secretary and begin paying Harmon a salary. By February 1973, Huffman and Smith had put together a three year, $56,000 permanent financing package ($14,000 in 1973 and $21,000 in 1974 and 1975). This funding appears to have been made on top of the $16,000 "bridge" grant, of which $6,000 was paid in 1972 and $10,000 in 1973. Some or all of the bridge grant money—at least that part paid in 1973—appeared in the budget as guaranteed or pre-paid advertising to the *L.A.W. Bulletin*.[9] In June, Morgan Groves, an employee of the federal Office of Economic Opportunity in Dallas, was hired, and a new, permanent office was established in the Chicago suburb of Palentine.[10]

There was immediate conflict over the new funding, mostly because the L.A.W. leadership had never come to a consensus about what it was supposed to accomplish with the money. As Harmon later recalled, it was her understanding that it was to acquire permanent Chicago headquarters:

> The president had always been Chicago-based since 1964. Then it moved to Houston, then to Rockport, Massachusetts, then Paul Scharmberg in California, then Carroll Quimby up in the northeast.... Well, our base is here in Chicago, we can't keep changing our address every year, it's too confusing, nobody could keep up with the changes, so Schwinn and Huffy and Columbia, and so on, gave us money to set up an office here in Chicago and I went on salary then.[11]

This was considerably at odds with what Morgan Groves saw as his main priority of building up a larger, nationwide, member-services organization to replace the "federation of clubs" structure that had been the league's tradition since the day it was formed in 1880:

> The League had only an indirect relationship with its members. For a long time, you had to belong to a local club before you could join the L.A.W. The view of long-time members was that the League was an association of local clubs, but it had no strong club structure outside the Midwest and New England. All the new goals that were being developed in '73–'74 depended on direct, large-scale participation, not from clubs, but from the point-of-sale; goals like participation in national decision-making, lobbying, member services. You couldn't do that with 10,000 members.[12]

And in fact, Huffman's original December 1972 memo had stated that the BIA's finance committee should consider two goals when it evaluated the decision about whether to provide the grant to the L.A.W. First, the committee should "suggest changes to provide growth in membership and a more comprehensive lobbying effort for bike facilities, local state and national," and second, it should study the ways to "provide financing for the transition from an all-volunteer organization to a professionally managed organization."[13] Thus, it appeared that that both Harmon and Groves were right; the only question was which priority came first.

The basic problem was that the BIA simply didn't provide enough money to achieve both goals simultaneously. In 1973, the year the great bike boom began to ebb, the L.A.W. lost about $1,500 on gross revenues of $86,200, including the industry's $14,000 grant, and (probably) the $10,000 carry-over from the 1972 Schwinn/Huffy bridge grant that appears in the 1973 budget as additional advertising revenues in the *L.A.W. Bulletin*.[14]

It suffered from the same dilemma that had faced George Herbert Stancer at the Cyclist's Touring Club in England a half-century earlier: Was the L.A.W. a nationwide bike club that happened to put out a monthly magazine, or was it a cycle magazine publisher with a well-developed fan club network? The direct costs of getting out the *Bulletin* had been $26,020 in 1973. But that did not include Harmon's salary ($10,000) or the magazine's share of total overhead costs, such as office rent, telephones, office supplies, or administrative postage unrelated to shipping out each month's issue. When these are included, the *Bulletin*'s estimated gross cost for 1973 came to $45,588. Harmon sold $18,729 in advertising (including the bridge grant money), for a loss of $26,859, over 30 percent of the league's total annual expenses.[15]

But there is another way of looking at it. The league took in $39,719 in dues in 1973. If most or all of that is allocated to the *Bulletin*—that is, if dues are primarily considered magazine subscriptions, and only secondarily as membership fees supporting other activities—then the economics of the *Bulletin* makes sense, as does the older structure of the league. The idea that the L.A.W. was "merely an association of local bike clubs" that Groves complained about was indispensable because it was those local clubs that provided most of the hands-on activities that cyclists demanded, and provided most of the material with which Harmon filled the *Bulletin*. "The 1,700 plus riders that show up for TOSRV," wrote league director Ralph Galen, referring to Greg Siple and Dan Burden's Columbus-based tour, "don't show up for bike clinics. They travel thousands of cumulative miles for the rides, the fellowship on the rides, and [only] coincidentally for everything else."[16]

The league had two nationwide, multi-day events of its own, one in the summer and one in the winter. Both were actually organized by a sponsoring local bike club, with the league putting up initial working cash, and providing advertising, then splitting any resulting profits on a 50–50 basis. Only a small percentage of the membership (defined as those belonging to an L.A.W. affiliated local club) attended either in any given year. The biggest and most famous nationwide events, such as TOSRV and the Iowa cross-state ride RAGBRI, were actually bigger than any of the annual league get-togethers. Most cyclists belonged to an organization because they wanted access to its rides. Local clubs were by far the largest source of these. Primarily, the league was a networking organization whereby clubs could find out what big rides other clubs had coming up, and read what were essentially reviews of their events.

The problem was that few, if any, local clubs made joining the L.A.W. a prerequisite for joining their own group, and all that was required for a local club to be an L.A.W. affiliate was that it maintain five members who were L.A.W. members. While the *Bulletin*'s focus was on the affiliate clubs, their membership overlap with the L.A.W. was actually very small in almost every case. The league inherently did a better job of promoting local clubs than the local clubs did of promoting the league. It had been that way since 1880.[17] George Herbert Stancer had made sure there was no conflict between the duties of magazine editor and club executive director by holding onto both offices until he retired. In failing to do the same at the L.A.W., Groves ultimately guaranteed that his organization's effectiveness would be limited because of its own internal discord.

But most of all, as William Hoffman, who was on the league's board of directors at the time points out, the BIA grant was just too small to accomplish everything the BIA and the league's board of directors wanted:

> As I recall, the amount was $60K over three years. This was supposed to set up an office and pay the executive director's (Morgan's) salary (and benefits, I presume) over that time. Looking back, I don't see how it could have been done for that amount. Even if Morgan only got $15K a year, benefits would have added at least another 20 percent, bringing his share alone of the $60K to $54K. That would have left only $2K/year for rent and office expenses like utilities.[18]

Hoffman's estimates are a little off, but not enough to invalidate his point. The industry grant was $56,000 over three years, not $60,000. Groves's salary was $16,000 a year, but there were no benefits, at least not through the end of 1973, and it is doubtful if any were added afterwards, as membership revenues started dropping in 1974 as the bike boom waned.[19] The office rent was $2,040 per year. Groves's salary and rent thus totaled $54,000 over three years. General office expenses ran $16,300 per year and Harmon was being paid $10,000 per year, beginning in January 1973, six months before Groves started. It is unlikely the Schwinn/Huffman bridge financing was extended after the end of the 1973 fiscal year in December 1973. Therefore, the grant was only covering about half the total monthly overhead (personnel, rent, office expenses), with $1,556 per month coming in and $3,615 per month going out. This did not include costs budgeted to "Member Services" (mostly the direct costs of the *L.A.W. Bulletin* and the sale of century patches), which ran another $3,700 per month.[20]

However tempting it might have been, the league's financial situation did not lead Groves to bind the organization closer to the bicycle industry, particularly on the issue of bikeways, in exchange for financial gain. Although Horace Huffman sent a letter to Groves about a month after he moved to Chicago, gently prodding him to look into bikeways promotion, Huffman's highest priority was always fiscal and organizational soundness, not policy matters. Huffman would have liked the L.A.W. to become a little more active on bikeways; he insisted it be run like a business.[21]

Groves, for his part, expressed concern over the BIA's bikeway policies almost from the minute he walked in the door. Less than a week after starting work, he wrote league president Quimby: "The area of legislation will probably be critical for the next few years—particularly with regards to bikeways. We need to restudy our position to be sure we don't get bikeways and lose the right to the road." As discussed in detail in an earlier chapter, his two primary strategies to blunt any undue influence by the industry was first, to delegate policymaking to a new technical committee comprised of Robert Bond, Fred DeLong, Floyd Frazine, John Forester and Jim Konski. "I think the platform should represent the whole range of cyclists," he wrote Forester, but "it should put strong emphasis on forcing cyclists to gain the skills to use the roads properly."

Second, Groves sought financial independence through membership recruitment. As he wrote Forester, "The L.A.W. is in a precarious position in that the industry has put up some money to establish the central office, and I'm sure they're going to represent opposing our views. The only answer is going to in building our membership to the point that we can be completely free to oppose them whenever necessary."[22]

The committee's bikeway policy was sent to Groves in the fall of 1973, who passed it on to the executive committee, who in turn approved it late that year. Harmon published it in the *Bulletin* in January 1974. It was short and, at first glance, not particularly militant: "The L.A.W. supports bike paths as separate facilities only where no public road exists, on bridges, to bypass or parallel limited access highways, or in special recreation areas." But, as Ken Kolsbun of Bikeology pointed out in an editorial in the June 1974 issue of *Bicycling*, the policy's language presumably meant that the league opposed all on-street bikelanes. This was contrary to Bikeology's core goal of using bike facilities to promote the bicycle as a replacement for, not an adjunct to, the automobile. In a reply article, Groves denied that the league's antipathy to all bikeways was as strident as Kohlsbun claimed, but noted that "the state of the art in bikeway design is primitive. It will take at least 10 years of research and experimentation to even begin to approximate the sophistication of highway design."[23]

But even as this was happening, Groves and his organization were slipping apart. Later, Groves was blamed for excessive spending in pursuit of his vision of an expanded membership and a direct member-services structure, that is, one that was not dependent on the old "association of clubs" idea. "That was a flawed vision," recalls William Hoffman, a league boardmember at the time, "a mass organization. Too few of us, myself included, realized at the time how unrealistic this was."[24] However, it was less a vision than a desperate necessity. The "two headed monster" of financial and administrative problems caused by the unresolved division of power and control between the *L.A.W. Bulletin* and the operations side of the league was never really resolved.[25] Nor did the league ever achieve the kind of financial independence Groves sought. In reply to a suggestion by some board members that they use "trade" memberships as away to make the industry grant permanent, but hidden, he wrote:

> I am opposed to charging much higher dues to industrial members than to individuals and families, for at least a couple of reasons. First, I think we can achieve a large enough membership that we don't *need* a subsidy from the industry.... A second major reason for not wanting to pursue major dues contributions from the industry is that the L.A.W. needs to be able to maintain its independence and opportunity to oppose,

> where appropriate, the desires of the industry.... The industry has done a great deal for the League, and it's time now to show what we can do for ourselves.[26]

The league membership when Groves took over in 1973 was about 6,500. Over the course of the next decade, it never climbed higher than 14,000, and usually hovered around ten thousand.[27]

A final point of contention between Groves and Harmon in 1974–75 was Groves's enthusiasm about, and cooperation with, a new bicycle organization that Lys and Dan Burden were putting together in Montana called "Bikecentennial." Organized in 1973, Bikecentennial was planned as a five-month-trans–American tour to be held in the bicentennial year of 1976, using a common route and nightly stopping points. About 4,100 cyclists ultimately participated, split into about 300 different groups. To help Burden get the project up and on its feet, Groves provided him with the league's membership roster (which was published annually in book form and given to each member) and loaned him the league's map library, collected from local clubs. Harmon saw Burden's organization as competition and was incensed. Groves believed that it was the future: "I have the feeling that Bikecentennial is going to be, if Dan carries out the tremendous promise I see in it, kind of the bellweather for what's coming."[28]

Nobody is neutral about Dan Burden. His proponents laud him as a visionary and the ultimate communicator—"Dan can get through to anyone," Morgan Groves once said. His detractors call him an unfocused flake addicted to starting projects and making a splash, but who is temperamentally unsuited to the long, boring, tedious, thankless grind of bureaucratic minutia necessary to see any large-scale project through to completion. Both are a little bit true.

Dan and Lys Burden, along with the husband-and-wife duo of Greg and June Siple, had, for several years, helped with the two-day Tour of the Scioto River Valley (TOSRV) in Columbus, Ohio. TOSRV had been founded in 1962 by Greg Siple and his father, Charles, as their own personal two-day, 200-mile, out-and-back tour. Dan Burden joined in 1964, when about 45 riders participated. More importantly, Burden connected the Siples with Charlie Pace and the Columbus chapter of the American Youth Hostels at a time when the ride was becoming too big to remain an informal, *ad hoc* event. Starting in 1967, Pace became TOSRV's ride coordinator (and remained so for almost 25 years), and the Columbus AYH was the ride's sponsor. This would remain so until it became so big that the scale of finances and organization overwhelmed it, and TOSRV was spun off as its own non-profit corporation. By the early 1970s, TOSRV was already over 2,500 riders.

In 1972, the Burdens and the Siples embarked on the National Geographic–sponsored Hemistour, a lands-end-to-end bike tour from Alaska to Argentina.

The idea of a mass-participation transcontinental bike tour was Greg Siple's, but near Mexico City, the Burdens were forced to drop out of Hemistour when Dan contracted hepatitis. They had sent out a relatively small Bikecentennial mailing from Mexico City in June 1973. That fall, while Dan recovered and the Siples finished the Hemistour, Lys looked over possible routes. Carolyn Patterson, an assistant editor at National Geographic, donated $1,000 for the distribution of 10,000 flyers and a magazine ad. Each asked for a $10 donation. The money started trickling in. That December, a permanent headquarters was located in Missoula, Montana, where Dan was a college student. The BIA donated $2,000, then another $5,000. Ultimately, in May 1975, the American Revolution Bicentennial Commission designated it an official Bicentennial event and awarded a $26,700 grant.[29]

Bikecentennial was divided into separate tours of different lengths, each with eight to 15 riders. About 4,100 cyclists participated, 2,000 for the full coast-to-coast route. The organization provided highly detailed guide books and either nightly camping grounds or "bike inns" in church basements, gyms and other indoor facilities. Some groups were fully self-contained; others had their camping gear hauled from stop to stop. By 1975, there were 40 full-time staff members. Some were in the Missoula headquarters drafting and printing guide books and performing general administrative tasks, but many more were out in the field, researching routes, lining up camp grounds or inns, training group leaders, or troubleshooting. Many were recruited from AYH divisions, especially in Ohio and Montana.

Jim Sayer, current executive director of the organization (now known as the Adventure Cycling Association), boasts that "the organization had remained very focused on a clear mission to promote bicycle travel." John Schubert, technical editor of the organization's monthly magazine *Adventure Cycling*, has sometimes been critical of what he perceives as the L.A.W.'s wavering mission structure over the years: "Think about all the organizations that have come and gone since 1976 or metastasized beyond recognition." But Sayer's claim notwithstanding, the organization's purpose up to the end of 1976 was nothing so general as to "promote bicycle travel." Rather, it had a laser-like focus on developing and implementing a single, very large bicycling event. After that, it had no mission. It did have three options: (1) try to repeat the event; (2) disband; or (3) do something else.

Option one was not possible, fiscally or organizationally. But neither had Burden made plans for an organized demobilization or laid the foundation for any kind of mission change. What he had been doing was flying back-and-forth to Washington, D.C., to meet with a small group of beltway insiders to form a new political advocacy organization called the Bicycle Federation. Burden started easing himself out of the organization in late 1976, although he didn't formally quit as executive director until September 1977, four months after he had officially become the BikeFed's first director. Dave Prouty, a man without a background in bicycling but with strong non-profit management and finance skills, had been hired in November 1976 as Bikecentennial's number two man. He formally took over in August 1977, and is generally credited with saving the organization as revenues dropped to virtually nothing in 1977.[30]

To survive, Bikecentennial had to sell what it had on hand, which was its knowledge of America's bikeable back roads and its cartographic skills. It was a winning combination. After a little more than two years, Prouty turned the executive director's seat over to Gary McFadden, one of Burden's original recruits, who ran it successfully for the next 20 years. The Adventure Cycling Association continues as an apolitical organization, researching routes, making and selling maps, and acting as an information exchange for cyclotourists and tour operators.[31]

The original Bikecentennial was, for 30 months, an exemplar of how a bicycle organization could be formed, managed and funded. In terms of the money processed through its treasury, the donations it raised, the scale and scope of its organization—over twenty full-time staff in Missoula, hundreds of part-time employees in the field, dozens of pieces of equipment owned or leased (trucks, trailers and RVs, to say nothing of camping, cooking and office equipment)—it was light-years ahead of any other American bicycle organization, and probably would still be in the top two or three today.

Yet it was mobilized for a single, well-defined, six-month-long event with no overt political or social goals, and no plans to take advantage of its amassed goodwill or human or physical capital once it was completed. Part of the very reason for its success must be attributed to the fact that it was an adhocracy. During the entire time it was being conceptualized, planned and executed, its founders apparently never looked beyond the day the last rider would pull up at the West Coast. Many who were involved with it, including Greg Siple himself, described it as "a rolling Woodstock," and for the originators, that's what it was. But no "summer of love" can go on forever. The organization that Prouty and McFadden took over and ran, the present Adventure Cycling Association, is not, at heart, the same organization that the Burdens and the Siples created. It was as if Prouty and McFadden had acquired the shell of a ruined company at a bankruptcy sale—lots of good assets left, but the entity itself basically a shambles. What they put together was a very different organization doing a very different job in a very different way.

Morgan Groves's faith that Bikecentennial would be the "next coming thing" in nationwide bicycle organizations, the way out of the labyrinth of a moribund League of American Wheelmen, was misplaced. Bikecentennial worked because nobody worried about tomorrow. It had a single, well-defined purpose that everyone agreed upon. It was temporary, it was fun, and everyone enjoyed it while it lasted.

Burden moved to Washington to start the BikeFed in May 1977. He described it as "a central clearinghouse for ideas, workshops, and a need for a newsletter among professionals working in the field of bicycle transportation and bicycle recreation." Both Burden and Bill Wilkinson, who would become a later BikeFed executive director, claim that the organization was Burden's idea, and that he originated it.[32] However, despite Wilkinson's recollection that BikeFed had "no real industry presence until Dan recruited Horace Huffman for the board [about 1980]," both Schwinn and the BMA had extended grants to BikeFed in its first six months.

Some of the projects Burden described were already works-in-progress at Lyle Brecht and Vince Darago's Urban Scientific and Educational Research Corporation (USER), the successor to the MIT-based Urban Bikeway Design Collaborative that had organized the UBDC I and UBDC II planning and design competitions in 1973 and 1974. USER, working under the direction of Katie Moran at NHTSA, had already test run a two-day bicycle safety workshop in February 1978, and ten more in various cities around the country were being scheduled. Moreover, the newsletter that Burden described already existed: it was John Williams's *Cyclalateral Thinking*, an irregular publication that Williams had self-published since 1974, then USER had underwritten with their grant money for a couple of issues. When it came out under the BikeFed banner, Williams was still the editor, but the name was changed to *Bicycle Forum*.[33]

It is more likely that BikeFed had been in the works for some time, and was a meeting of four minds. The first three were Burden, whose impatience with mundane organizational (especially financial) matters was becoming apparent now that Bikecentennial's "big ride" summer was over; Bill Wilkinson at the U.S. Department of Transportation; and Katie Moran at the National Highway Traffic Safety Administration. Wilkinson and Moran had research dollars to spend, but too few places to spend it. They were limited to either "mainstream" traffic consultants who, with a few exceptions (Dan Smith at DeLeuw, Cather's San Francisco office being probably the most visible exception) didn't have much experience or interest in bicycle projects; or "bicycle experts" who either weren't very reliable, couldn't rein in their ideological biases, didn't know the government procurement ropes, or lacked the resources to do a professional-quality job.

The fourth and most important member of this group was Tedson Meyers. Meyers was an attorney who was just ending his tenure as a District of Columbia city councilor. He had also helped found the Washington Area Bicycle Alliance (WABA), which is still a model for many local cycle advocacy organizations. Both Wilkinson and Moran consider Meyers their mentor. If BikeFed owes its creation to any one individual, Meyers is probably that person. Because of his position on the council at that time, and because of Wilkinson and Moran's government employment, they couldn't afford to have their involvement advertised too widely, so Burden was assigned solo credit for its invention.[34] Meyers, Wilkinson and Moran may have been better off sticking with Lyle Brecht and Vince Darago's USER firm: Burden didn't stay at BikeFed long, leaving in 1979 to take a job as the bicycle and pedestrian coordinator for the Florida Department of Transportation. Except for *Bicycle Forum*, which John Williams was editing in Missoula, the organization became dormant.

The Bicycle Institute of America and the Bicycle Manufacturers' Association had been located in New York City for several decades, and for many years both had been directed by John Auerbach. But in 1975 the Federal Trade Commission filed a restraint of trade complaint against the BIA. This was the result of its umbrella-like structure. The BIA acted as the promotion and publicity organization for the entire American bicycle industry, and served as the "front office" for the industry's four trade groups, which handled the nitty-gritty lobbying tasks like arguing for better tariff rates, non-discriminatory trucking charges for bicycle-sized boxes, better product liability laws, and so on. These four trade groups were the Bicycle Manufacturers' Association (BMA); the Cycle Parts and Accessories Association (CPAA); and two organizations representing wholesale and retail bicycle dealers. As a result, the entire American industry was represented through trade groups that were, a little too directly, all interconnected through a single organization.

To avoid trouble, the industry agreed to break up the BIA into its five parts. The BIA would remain as the industry-wide promotion office. Each of the trade groups would go their own way as freestanding organizations. The BIA and the BMA moved to Washington. Auerbach stayed in New York to take over the parts association, the CPAA. As it turned out, the BIA and the BMA were the only two groups to survive the reorganization for any length of time; Auerbach retired about 1982.[35]

Wilkinson recalls that about a year after Burden left for Florida, the BMA leadership was advised by various groups to "get behind" BikeFed. Although Wilkinson declines to be specific, it appears that pressure came from either the emerging giant in the bicycle industry, Shimano, or from the trade group responsible for representing Japanese bicycle- and component-makers in the U.S., in which Shimano played a major role. Wilkinson and Katie Moran (who, by this time, had left NHTSA to become the executive director of the Mountain Bicyclists' Association in Denver) were jointly offered the executive directorship of a merged Bicycle Federation and Bicycle Institute of America in 1980.

They decided that Wilkinson would take over the BIA and Moran would move from the Mountain Bicyclists' Association to BikeFed. Gradually, as the American bicycle industry shrank, the importance of the BIA/BMA as an industry trade group was also reduced. In 1984, both the Bicycle Manufactures' Association and the Bicycle Institute of America ceased operation, leaving only BikeFed. Several firms independently put up the money so that Wilkinson could transfer from the BIA to BikeFed.

In late 1984 or early 1985, the surviving BMA member firms, Shimano, and several other bicycle and component importers were invited to join a new trade promotional firm. The industry leaders selected two organizations to run it. BikeFed was asked to do public promotion and outreach, and a nationwide for-profit consultant was hired to handle administration, membership, lobbying, and other industry-specific tasks. A year or so later the consultants withdrew when money became scarce and BikeFed took over everything, with the industry-specific tasks dropped and only public promotion and outreach remaining. The Bicycle Institute of America name was owned by the BMA's old law firm, and the BikeFed board asked that it be transferred to them. The firm agreed and since late 1985 the Bicycle Federation and its successors have owned the BIA name. BikeFed later changed its name to the National Center for Bicycling and Walking (NCBW). Moran left bicycle-pedestrian work for other endeavors in the 1990s; Wilkinson remained with NCBW until he retired in 2008. In 1999, a new trade group, Bikes Belong, was formed by Richard and John Burke of the Trek Bicycle Corporation.[36]

Bikes Belong both provides funding assistance to membership organizations and lobbies on matters of interest to the industry, some of which overlap with consumer interests (highway funding) and some that do not (tariffs, product liability laws), according to executive director Tim Blumenthal. In this day and age, is industry support necessary to keep a membership-oriented consumer organization going? "No, it's not crucial, but the seven or eight groups that have been successful [over the last decade] *have* all received industry support ... the only objection to industry support has been among a small group of old schoolers. There has been no tension at all between the newer boards and staffers."[37]

Blumenthal believes that the biggest challenge facing nationwide membership-based clubs is diversity. That's not any kind of policy bias, it's simply a matter of non-profit Business Administration 101:

> One of the biggest challenges facing membership bicycle organizations is to close the huge gap between the number of advocates and the number of people who ride, even if occasionally. The ratio is about 150 or 200 to one; occasional cyclists to advocates.

> Much of this comes because cycling is a relatively spontaneous, unencumbered activity. There have been only about seven or eight groups that have been successful in developing and sustaining an organizational base. Not many are successful that aren't diverse. Only the strongest, which are diverse, can survive bad economic times.

The history of the oldest organization, the L.A.W., tends to support his theory. Formed in 1880, it skyrocketed to 101,000 members during the great bicycle boom, but fell just as rapidly, collapsing to less than ten thousand members by 1905. Its secretary, Abbot Bassett, kept it going by changing it to an old-timers club. He was among the longest-lived of the high-wheel riders, so when he died in 1924 there wasn't much of a league left to die with him. It was revived in the late 1930s in the Chicago area, but it was never a large organization, averaging about 500 members in the early 1950s, most of those as members of local clubs; only about 75 were individuals. In 1954–55, a deep recession year for American manufacturers due to the imposition of favorable tariffs for British imports, the league folded. The third revival, from about 1963 on, nearly came to disaster after 1973 when revenues fell precipitously when the great bike boom collapsed.

The league has since had a financial crisis almost every time there has been a severe economic recession. This is a common feature of individual-membership hobby-interest organizations. The current board and staff are trying to avoid further repetitions of this cycle by seeking out revenues from long-term institutional grants and municipal and corporate memberships, while keeping income from individual membership fees at or below the one-third mark. Once completed, this would move the L.A.W. away from being an individual-membership hobby-interest organization to a public policy/political activist organization with individual contributions or donations defined through annual "memberships" that promote the donor's sense of identification with the organization and its goals. Examples of organizations operating under this type of model include Greenpeace, the World Wildlife Fund and Doctors Without Borders.[38]

Blumenthal finally notes that "if the older cycling membership organization had continued to act the same way they acted from in the 1970s [after Morgan Groves left] through the 1980s, they would be out of business."[39]

* * *

Considering how much emphasis vehicular cycling has always placed on the role of education, especially adult education, it is mystifying why it took so long before it dawned on book publishers that there was money to be made out of bicycle education textbooks. Although this is one of those topics that does not fit neatly within the 1968–91 timeframe, it is a fascinating case study worthy of attention.

As noted earlier, the first published edition of *Effective Cycling* appeared in late 1975. About half of its "cycling technique" sections were revamped versions of the articles that had appeared in *Bike World* between December 1973 and April 1974. Much of the rest was the material Forester had assembled in 1974 for his work on the SCR-47 California state bicycle committee. A subcommittee (apparently mostly Forester) reviewed all available cyclist educational programs, both domestic and foreign, and submitted a report to the main committee. It went largely unused in the final report, according to Forester. But in the process, he had amassed a considerable body of information, and it was this material (especially, as noted earlier, Fred DeLong's 1968–71 AYH program) that formed much of the basis of *Effective Cycling*.[40]

But at the same time, Forester had been doing a lot of propaganda pieces for the California Association of Bicycle Organizations (CABO) and his own mailings, and as *Bike World* reviewer William Saunders noted, "This book is as much a political manifesto as an instruction manual." For that reason, no publisher would touch it, and so Forester cranked it out himself on a mimeograph machine in his garage.[41] The best overall description was written by *Bicycling*'s Darryl Skrabak, who had been generally very sympathetic to Forester's cause over the years:

> There is about Forester's directions the attitude of airplane pilots, motor racers, athletes—those who live by their skills and wits. If your wits aren't sharp or you make an error, these types feel, you are exposed to a possibility of penalty. One pays for ones mistakes. The Forester biking style is like that. You get out there with the motors and you mix with it, and as long as you do it right, you're okay. To those who would protest such an attitude, Forester responds: what else is there? The motor vehicles are on the road, and yes, they can be dangerous. But if we would be on the road, we cannot evade them. We join motor traffic on the best terms we can manage or we stay home.[42]

In 1976, Forester lent the use of the Effective Cycling course to the League of American Wheelmen at no cost as its official program. However, he retained ownership of the firm that published *Effective Cycling*, thus profiting from the sale of each copy of the textbook. He had earlier said that the Effective Cycling course was unsuitable for absolute beginners, as "it is impractical to teach a class of persons who cannot ride at all, because developing the ability to balance and steer is an intuitive thing that is learned but not taught, like running."[43]

But on the other hand, Forester's 30-plus hour program proved to be overkill when applied solely to a class of already proficient L.A.W. cyclotourists. About 1981, League Effective Cycling Committee chair Bill Frey became convinced that "we needed a standardized examination that could be used to define what was required knowledge for earning the Effective Cyclist patch. Several

ECIs [Effective Cycling Instructors] including myself put such an examination together and have continued to improve on the first version. This is the so-called National EC examination." Frey noted that most league members who took a shorter 20-hour version of the Effective Cycling course that the league's "EC" Committee had developed had no problem passing the final exam and subsequent road test, but "shorter courses for beginners, like the 20-hour one I just taught, do not permit a beginning student to pass the test." Another problem was the process for admitting new trainees to the Effective Cycling instructors' program and moving them through to final certification, which Frey called "intimidating." Frey's successor as EC committee chair, John Jefferson, was even more blunt: "Cumbersome procedures involve as much as a month or more between inquiry and a reply, a process which may have to be repeated several times. We have been criticized in circles, including some of the board of directors, as being elitist."[44]

In fact, Forester had intentionally designed it this way. "I knew that I had to be very selective in order get instructors who already knew vehicular cycling and felt in their bones that vehicular cycling was right." In other words, students that were amenable to total indoctrination into the Forester way of thinking, and who could be counted on to not water it down to a generalized vehicular-style adult cycling class by incorporating elements from, say, DeLong's Philadelphia AYH program or Ken Cross's hazard recognition studies. "So I set up a system for considering applicants," Forester later recalled:

> I developed a lengthy questionnaire that elicited, as much as I could, of the applicant's cycling history, type of cycling, and views about cycling. I insisted on evaluations from other responsible persons in the cycling world, mailed to me directly from the originator in response to a question sheet I sent out. Using this method, I was able to select applicants whom I thought had the necessary attitude.[45]

As a result, the league's Effective Cycling instructor's program crawled along at a snail's pace, so there was often nobody to teach the league's Effective Cycling patch-earning course at its regional events. Between 1977 and mid–1985, only 240 individuals had been accepted into the instructor's program, and of these only 140 had completed it. By 1986, the number of active instructors had actually decreased, to around 118, and fewer than ten new instructor trainee applications had been received, approved, and the students assigned to advisors.[46]

The program became even more problematic in late 1983 when Forester was voted out of his seat as California district representative on the league's board of directors. Forester did not prohibit the use of his materials, but it appears that he allowed them to go out of print. In 1985, the chair of the league's Effective Cycling committee, John Jefferson, informed the board that the program had "suffered in the past from many things," but that "lack of materials is the most prominent." However, an agreement had been arranged that "instructors in training have his [Forester's] written permission to copy other third editions [of *Effective Cycling*] to meet present needs until printed copies of the fourth edition are available." Jefferson noted that at that time "the text, *Effective Cycling*, [has been] out of print many years."[47]

MIT professor David Gordon Wilson convinced MIT Press to publish a trade edition of *Effective Cycling*. Although the MIT "fourth edition" carried a 1984 copyright date, as Jefferson's report indicates, it was not widely available until late 1985.[48] By this time many league Effective Cycling instructors had quietly switched to John S. Allen's 1981 book, or more typically, had created their own "copy shop" compendiums from excerpts out of the third edition of *Effective Cycling*, magazine articles, Allen's book and other sources. The seed had been planted among the league's board that it might make more sense (to say nothing of more dollars) to produce their own educational curriculum.

Forester finally had enough of the league and prohibited it from using his Effective Cycling trademarks in 1992. This was not considered a major disaster by the board. In fact, *Effective Cycling* had by now become something of an embarrassment, the cranky musings of an *enfant terrible* grown old. The league sliced up the material and renamed it Bike Ed, after the nationwide youth's education project that Dan Burden and Roger DiBrito had proposed back in 1987, probably in the hopes of being able to attract sponsorship money, and carried on as before.

The first *commercial* attempt to take on *Effective Cycling* didn't get far. In 1979, Signpost Press, a specialty publisher of outdoor books in the Seattle area, released Frederick Wolfe's *The Bicycle: A Commuting Alternative*.[49] It was a transitional work, handicapped in two ways. First, probably for reasons of economy, it was produced in a small format barely bigger than a mass-market paperback, limiting both the text and the clarity of the photographs. Second, only 62 pages were given over to the section covering on-the-road situations, and these were organized in an encyclopedic format, as capsule comments arranged alphabetically by topic—"bumps," "heavy traffic," "left turns," etc. Generally, the message hewed to a middle-of-the-road "soft" vehicular cycling line. Rather bizarrely, however, the accompanying photographs almost all illustrated various types of bike lanes, paths, over- and under-passes, and other specialized facilities. The text discussions that cried out for illustrating (changing lanes in traffic, making one-step left turns), were completely ignored, while many of the bikeway illustrations were irrelevant to what was being discussed in the text (and were, to be honest, sometimes pretty sad examples of bikeway engineering).

The overall impression was that of publisher who had been thinking along one story-board (bikeways) while the author was writing a book according to a very different script (efficient riding in traffic). When the book segued to topics like parking and multi-modal (bikes-on-bus) use, the text and illustrations meshed together. It was clear that some publishers, even those specializing in outdoor sports, were not yet willing to release a book that showed photographs of cyclists changing lanes and making left turns in traffic on heavily-trafficked multi-lane arterial streets, even when the technique was being explained in some detail by an experienced, big-city bicycle coordinator. In short, it was a dud. "The last time I read anything so dull and wordy, it was an anthropology text," complained *Bicycling's* John Schubert, "if I didn't know better, I'd conclude that's it's less hassle to buy a car."[50]

A year later, Rodale Press, *Bicycling*'s publisher, released John S. Allen's *The Complete Book of Bicycle Commuting*. This was a winner. Starting as a contributor to *Bike World* in 1976 Allen had become a regular writer for *Bicycling*, which, by this time, was being edited by James McCullagh and assistants John Schubert and Susan Weaver. "Around 1979 Rodale had been sent a proposal for a commuting book, but it didn't look very promising, and editors McCullagh and Schubert turned to me," Allen recalls.[51]

Probably the two biggest differences between *The Complete Book of Bicycle Commuting* and *Effective Cycling* was that, first, Allen included three levels of skill, experience, and assertiveness, making no categorical statements as to which one was "better" or "worse." However, he did gently urge riders to advance themselves up through the categories as quickly as practical, because he believed "Level 3" riding to be the most comfortable and useful. Second, his approach could be described as "rationally assertive" as opposed to Forester's "aggressively defensive driving." "Use courtesy when you can, and be assertive if you must," is Allen's "one rule to remember." Although he was never openly critical of Allen's work, Forester did dismiss it as "a book much like *Effective Cycling*, but much simpler," which is an inversion of the truth. *Effective Cycling*, when all its polemics and repair-manual advice are stripped away, is a fairly simple book, not much more than the series of magazine articles upon which it was based, while Allen's book, with its three-tier system and more sophisticated use of graphics, clearly shows itself as the second-generation product. To his credit, Allen notes the advantages he had, acknowledging Forester's book as the pioneering foundation upon which he could build.[52]

Ultimately, 20,000 copies of *The Complete Book of Bicycle Commuting* were printed and Rodale Press ran excerpts from it for two years in *Bicycling*. They never published a second edition, which is a shame, because Allen's book is without a doubt the best work on cycling techniques that has ever been done. Some of the material was adapted for use in another book, *Glen's New Complete Bicycle*

Manual, a publication of Crown Books, when Allen edited a major overhaul of it in 1987.

In 1996, the British government released its first *National Cycling Strategy*, with an overall goal of doubling the level of cycling and 18 specific objectives. Much like the report *Bicycle Transportation for Energy Conservation* that Katie Moran wrote for the U.S. Environmental Protection Agency and the Department of Transportation back in 1980, the *National Cycle Strategy* contained a broad vision, ambitious goals, and not even a pretense of an implementation plan. The fine print revealed that almost all of the nationwide achievements were actually expected to be reached by aggregating the initiatives made (and paid for) by local governments. In essence, it was a bold plan predicated on aggressive action by parties who were never part of the process.[53]

However, one exception was a national commitment to develop a National Cycle Training Project for adults to complement RoSPA's National Cycle Proficiency Scheme for children and teens, now almost a half-century old and about to be renamed *Bikeability*. In an irony harkening back to the controversies of the late 1930s, the Cyclists' Touring Club submitted its bid as the prime contractor for the development and administration of the adult program, and won.[54]

They in turn subcontracted to John Franklin, who had written a book called *Cyclecraft* in 1988. He later explained that he had developed it primarily by combining elements of Forester's *Effective Cycling* with RoSPA's already-existing training manual for motorcycle road-craft. After input by a National Cycle Training Project advisory committee and the National Transportation Laboratory, Franklin issued a completely revised *Cyclecraft* in 1997 and an instructor's manual, both published by the Government Stationery Office. A further updated version was issued in 2007 and a North American version (switched from "keep left" to "keep right") was released two years later.[55]

"*Cyclecraft* is not concerned with setting an example to others," Franklin stated. "Although a skilled rider will often do this as a matter of course, a cyclist is too vulnerable to follow rigid rules irrespective of risk." Like Allen's *Complete Book of Bicycle Commuting*, it defines three levels of cycle proficiency, and the book is divided into the skills that a cyclist should develop and apply at each level of proficiency. Each subsection is coded to the skill level it is intended for, so there is no shock when a rank beginner opens the book and sees a diagram of a cyclist moving left through two lanes of heavy traffic to set herself up for a left turn. Conversely, the advanced cyclist knows that some "Level 1" techniques may end up being discarded as she moves up in skill, speed, confidence and assertiveness.

Cyclecraft became the textbook for Canada's national bicycle safety program, CAN-Bike, and League of American Bicyclists now had a textbook that was virtually purpose-built for Bike Ed and its league cycling instructor (LCI) program. But a funny thing happened on the way to the bicycle school: the league figured out that money could be made off a good bicycle education textbook. (The North American *Cyclecraft* was a hefty $36 for a medium-sized trade paperback.) So after using Franklin's book as its "official" text for four years, in 2013 the league brought out its own book, *Street Smarts*, a compendium edited by executive director Andy Clarke.

Although it never published a second edition of *The Complete Book of Bicycle Commuting*, in 1987 Rodale Press approached Allen about condensing its material into a booklet and online publication for use by the Commonwealth of Pennsylvania, Rodale's home state. It was published later that year as *The Bicycle Driver's Handbook*. In 2001, Allen licensed the Pennsylvania material back from Rodale, updated and improved it, then published it as *Bicycling Street Smarts*. Working with a Cambridge publisher, Rubel BikeMaps, Allen specializes in customizing the 48-page booklet, adapting it to the traffic laws of an individual state. At least one organization, the Florida Bicycle Association, uses it as the textbook for their bicycle proficiency training course. There are about a dozen custom versions in addition to a generic publication. "Editions in French, German, and Spanish are in the works," Allen notes.[56] So after almost 20 years when the League of American Wheelmen and other organizations had to hold their noses and use *Effective Cycling* even though they found it overpriced, underwritten, and offensive, simply because there wasn't anything else out there, the bicycle education textbook business is now a highly competitive and, at least for one or two organizations, an apparently fairly lucrative business.

David Henderson, bicycle-pedestrian coordinator of the Miami Area Metropolitan Planning Organization, points out that there is more to these programs than the textbook. In fact, he believes the material itself is not all that critical: "There's no problem getting your hands on decent bicycle education course material. It's the delivery system that counts. If the program doesn't have an established system of logistics for instructors, equipment, and facilities, and the program isn't consistent with the system's resource limitations, it's not going anywhere." For example, Forester's program, in its original 33-hour guise, was so time and resource intensive that it never could be scaled up to a national level, despite the many efforts to do so.

On the other hand, the texts are generally limited in that they are still basically just compilations of club cycling wisdom. "There's no professional research feedback loop of 'develop, teach, monitor, measure, evaluate, modify' the way there is in pedestrian safety programs," Henderson notes. He points to the millions of dollars that are going to medical schools and university highway safety institutes to develop pedestrian programs, but relatively little to bicycle programs "outside of safe routes to school," because bicycle clubs and bicycle advisory boards won't support it. "They've got *Effective Cycling*, or *Bicycling Street Smarts*, or whatever, teaching that a skilled, assertive cyclist with a high mileage base is a safe cyclist, and that's what they want to hear."[57]

As lucrative as the "textbooks" are a newer generation of "do-it-yourself" books that do not aspire to the completeness and objectivity of *CycleCraft* or the *Complete Book of Bicycle Commuting*. Robert Hurst's 2004 book *The Art of Urban Cycling* (republished unrevised in 2007 as *The Art of Cycling*, no doubt to broaden its target audience), was commented on in an earlier section. Hurst was (and apparently still is) a bike messenger in Denver, although he later told an interviewer that he never participated in critical mass rides and was rarely involved in any of the radical-bike politics for which messengers are supposedly associated, a connection originating more from the overheated halls of academia than the typically drab offices of most big-city messenger firms.[58]

As was previously discussed, the most notable feature of Hurst's book is that he swears undying fealty to *Effective Cycling*, proceeds to explain that his work is simply an extension of Forester's book to an urban environment, and not a refutation or replacement for it, and then proceeds to demolish many of its most cherished (but least substantial) myths. He rationalizes his book by arguing that there is the need for a work that "goes beyond" *Effective Cycling* by, alternatively, explaining that it merely covers situations that Forester could never have foreseen forty years ago ("one of the big problems with the vehicular-cycling principle, or any principle of cycling, for that matter, is that it fails to account adequately for the complexities, details, and chaos of city streets ... indeed, much has changed since the concept was formally introduced"), and, on the other hand, arguing that Forester's "true" message has been distorted by unfaithful followers who, over the years, have degraded his intent:

> While Forester's advice is usually quite sound, a large number of cyclists have added a militant, confrontational tone to the framework of his message. They have taken the vehicular-cycling principle and bastardized it. Through their riding habits in traffic which are often deliberately, theatrically antagonistic, they seek to make some kind of point to their special audience of other road users. One is never quite sure exactly what that point is.[59]

From a practical standpoint, there wasn't all that much difference between *Effective Cycling* and *The Art of [Urban] Cycling*, and Hurst's argument that his book was just a specialized application of Forester's book to dense, inner-city areas was a fairly pragmatic one. Hurst didn't spend much time bothering with such things as bike lanes, because in his world, they were just covered with off-loading trucks and double parked cars anyway. Got a car at a four-way stop that can't make up its mind to cut you off or wait? Turn right. It'll blow through, then you do a shallow u-turn 50 feet down the street from the intersection. Come up on a jammed downtown block? Probably better to take to the sidewalk for 600 feet than try to snake your way through. Hardly meltdown material. But Forester himself repeatedly said that *Effective Cycling* was "everything you really need to know to ride every day, under any conditions for whatever purpose you desire," so if you wrote a guide on how to organize a bicycle expedition to the south pole and back and it said anything more than "go read *Effective Cycling*," you should probably expect to get slammed in a Forester review.[60]

Dave Glowacz took a straighter path to get to the same place in his *Urban Bikers' Tricks and Tips.* It's hard to find a really substantive difference between Hurst and Glowacz's books (reviewers made a big thing about his advice on the best way to break a car windshield with a U-lok, but he advised doing it only if your back was really, truly up against the wall). Probably the two biggest differences were that it had a lot more graphics, including step-by-step instructions on how to use a front-end bike-on-bus rack, a very original and good idea. Both Hurst and Glowacz's books were clearly aimed at the big-city market, a glaring deficiency in *Effective Cycling* that Forester never attempted to correct, as he frequently admitted that his program was targeted at suburban cyclists who rode out of choice, not need.[61]

Hurst and Glowatz's books should be considered a sample, not a complete enumeration, of a new sub-genre of urban-oriented cycling "how-to" books: small trade paperbacks of two hundred or so pages, brief, to the point, much like the "mainstream" education manuals such as Franklin's *Cyclecraft* or the League of American Bicyclists' *Street Smarts*, but shorter, snazzier, more to the point, made less comprehensive by omitting rural recreational riding and touring. Like cycling itself in the beginning of the 21st century, they were getting more specialized; cyclists wanted their bikes for specific chores, not to pursue an all-around hobby. As James McCullagh observed in 1978, *Effective Cycling* may consist of "everything you really need to know," anywhere, anytime, anyplace, but *that* audience of cyclists was rapidly shrinking. It was now a matter of "what do I need to know to get there *now*," not tomorrow, not in eleven weeks, *now*.[62]

Conclusions

What, then, can we take from the long two-decade period in the history of American bicycle planning lasting from 1969 to 1991?

1. The study of the political history of bicycle planning is in its infancy, so almost every historical categorization and definition is still flexible and contingent.

Even the time period initially selected, 1969 to 1991, turns out to be less determinative than one would think. The year 1969 was originally selected to open this study because it was the start of the 10-speed bike boom of 1969–73, when adult bicycle riding became a highly visible nationwide activity. The closing year of 1991 was chosen because that was when the second edition of the American Association of State Highway and Transportation Officials' (AASHTO) *Guide to the Development of New Bicycle Facilities*, was published and the federal ISTEA Highway Act enacted. The *Guide* is widely believed to be the document that institutionalized vehicular cycling into the planning and engineering policies and procedures of most state highway departments. The first (1982) edition was equivocal as to the Association's position on the development of on-road bicycle facilities, but the second edition laid out a clear policy that the *existing* roadway system, in a largely unaltered condition, should serve as the primary system for conveying bicycle traffic.

The ISTEA transportation funding act created the Transportation Enhancements program, which, for the first time, earmarked funds for alternative, ameliorative, and compensatory projects, including bicycle and pedestrian projects not directly associated with a roadway facility. More importantly, it required metropolitan planning organizations and state transportation departments to plan on a fully intermodal basis. ISTEA did not require that states and localities "go intermodal," but it did for transportation what environmental impact statements had done under the National Environmental Policy Act (NEPA) of 1969.

NEPA did not require that an agency select the least environmentally invasive alternative, but it did require an environment impact statement that spelled out all the feasible alternatives and fully explained the impacts of each. Similarly, ISTEA required that state DOTs and MPOs identify how their various long-term strategies would affect mobility across the full range of modes, but in the end, did not bind them to anything other than their historical goal of minimizing aggregate traffic delay.[1]

But while some states and MPOs took transit and alternative modes seriously and others did not, they at least had to *state* their policy in black-and-white for everyone to see, and very few DOTs and MPOs wanted be on record as saying that they simply did not give a damn about the fate of cyclists or pedestrians on their roadways (although one or two initially came close). State highway departments are large, lumbering ships to turn, but ISTEA eventually did start to change attitudes towards alternative modes planning almost everywhere, and for this reason it can be considered a convenient break-point between eras in American bicycle planning.

But both these opening and closing dates should be seen as generalized guidelines, and good arguments can be made for setting different mileposts. As we have seen, significant efforts were made well before 1969 to provide for bicycle use in a number of different ways. Bob Cleckner and Keith Kingbay were working as activists and lobbyists on behalf of organizations such as the American Youth Hostels (AYH), the League of American Wheelmen (L.A.W.), and the Bicycle Institute of America (BIA) as early as 1963 or 1964. Mostly this was in the area of bikeways, but in the case of the AYH, it also included safety programs. Fred DeLong, acting through the Philadelphia chapter of the AYH, the Pennsylvania division of the L.A.W. and *Bicycling* magazine, had developed a cyclist safety course by 1969 that within two or three years had become fairly sophisticated. As early as 1969 the Safety Committee of the L.A.W. had copied several sets of a projector slide show of DeLong's course for distribution to local bicycle clubs.[2]

Thus far, it has been assumed that the only American bicycle advocacy efforts of any significance before 1968 were industry-based, and focused solely on promoting bikeways. It is clear that a diversity of activities were occurring earlier and were broader in scope and location than originally thought. Many of these can legitimately be considered at least progenitors of vehicular cycling. American bicycle advocacy before 1970 is not well understood nor fully researched. It is likely that further investigation will yield even more evidence of advocacy, education and government program efforts from before the great 10-speed bike boom that can legitimately lay claim to belonging within this same category.

Similarly, it is not clear how meaningful it is to bring down the historical curtain at 1991. True, the AASHTO *Bicycle Guide* remained little changed for another twenty years. It was updated in 1999, but not fundamentally revised until 2012. But keep in mind that the *Guide* was simply an annex to AASHTO's master document, the *Greenbook*, its policy on the planning, design and construction of streets and highways. During the years that the AASHTO *Bicycle Guide* was in hibernation, the most important companion document to the *Greenbook*, the *Manual of Uniform Traffic Control Devices* (MUTCD), administered by a different organization, the National Committee for Uniform Traffic Control Devices (NCUTCD), was undergoing a process of continuous refinement that included significant alterations to its standards for bicycle and pedestrian safety markings and devices, many to coordinate such devices with traffic control measures such as traffic circles, intersection neckdowns, chicanes, and diverters.

AASHTO has always been an organization dominated by the concerns and interests of rural highway builders; its most influential early figure, "Chief" Thomas McDonald, was formerly the Iowa state highway engineer. The "T" in its name (as in "*and Transportation* Officials") was reluctantly added only in the 1970s. NACTO, the National Association of City Transportation Officials, was formed in 1995 as an alternative to AASHTO by big-city transportation and public-works directors frustrated by a process developed during the 1920s and 1930s to block direct communications between metropolitan transportation officials by forcing information and authority to flow through state highway departments. Many state DOTs had (and some still have) an anti-urban bias, and they could not help but favor the construction of rural highways when the federal government was offering to underwrite them with 80 and 90 percent matching funds.[3]

The NCUTCD, on the other hand, tended to do a better job of balancing rural and urban transport concerns. Therefore, over the years, AASHTO and the NCUTCD tended to drift apart, as did their respective publications, the *Manual of Uniform Traffic Control Devices* and the AASHTO *Guide to the Development of Bicycle Facilities*. In 2011, when NACTO first issued its own bicycle facility guide, it could claim legitimacy for its more aggressive standards through the MUTCD by pointing out that its designs did nothing but apply already-approved designs and features (even if only given provisional status) in the MUTCD.

The final steps in this schism occurred in early 2013 when NACTO said that it would follow up its bicycle guide with an urban streets *Greenbook*, prompting the federal Department of Transportation to announce that it would investigate the possibility of having the Federal Highway Administration take over the process of issuing roadway design standards for urban areas.[4] The unresolved question is whether these proposed FHWA standards will apply only to urban local streets, or whether AASHTO and its highway *Greenbook* will, in its entirety, be sent packing out of America's great cities, which will then adopt standards largely unrelated to the traditional rural-based highway designs that emerged in the 1930s—that is, whether they will return to something more akin to what Miller McClintock was recommending almost a century ago.

The fear of Francis Francois, AASHTO's long-time executive director, was that if his organization did not step out of Chief McDonald's long and deep shadow and become a more modern, urbanized, and multi-modal association, it would fade into irrelevancy or become replaced by another professional organization. As historian Mark Rose notes, by the 1970s "as Americans attempted to shape policies capable of dealing with rapid change in cities, in the economy, and in perceptions of neighborhood and environmental integrity, political leaders determined that a national highway program was no longer viable. As a result road engineers lost their authority."[5]

So, like most historical studies, it is simply not possible to delineate hard-and-fast boundaries when this chronicle begins and ends. It is, at best, a snapshot. Similarly, it is hard to gather together a bundle of often loosely-related (occasionally, completely unrelated) events, motivations and circumstances under the single umbrella of "bicycle history." In some cases, actors were unaware of each other until many years after the start of our period. In other cases, participants worked together, but later fell out with each other. It was very common in bicycle advocacy for actors to become bored, frustrated, or (having achieved their immediate goal) disinterested in the political aspects of cycling, but to remain quite active in the recreational and social side. Morgan Groves, for example, after leaving the League of American Wheelmen in 1975 and the National Committee on Uniform Traffic Laws and Ordinances in 1976, opened a bicycle store, collected antique bicycles, and remained a dedicated club rider up to his death in 2011. Finally, issues likewise carried on unrelated lives until they became linked by a sudden change of circumstances, differing perceptions, or raw opportunism.

All of the above notwithstanding, some robust, continuous, identifiable conclusions can be drawn from this "long two decade" period in the history of American bicycle planning.

2. Vehicular cycling is a unique, indigenous American style of bicycle planning.

At various times it has been known under other generic labels, including bicyclism, vehicular inclusion of cycling, and bicycle driving. It has also gone (and now goes) by various proprietary names and trademarks, including Effective Cycling, Street Smarts, Smart Cycling, CAN-Bike, Bikeability, and Cyclecraft.

While each has had its own particular shade of meaning, all have usually shared four common elements. They are: (1) a primary emphasis on cyclist proficiency; (2) a reliance on the existing roadway network to provide its basic infrastructure system; (3) a reliance on the standard (or at most, a barely modified) motor vehicle code; (4) a preference for programmatic government activities such as safety classes or "pot hole hotlines" over capital improvement projects such as bikeways or trails; or, alternatively, a desire that government have no involvement in cycling matters whatsoever, usually based on ideological grounds.

While some facets of vehicular cycling can be traced back to the anti-bikeway and anti-taillight programs of the British Cyclists' Touring Club (CTC) of the 1930s, these similarities are more coincidental than causal. The CTC's efforts derived more from the fact that its monthly magazine, the *CTC Gazette*, required a large subsidy from the club's general revenues. To guarantee the provision of these funds, its editor, George Herbert Stancer, felt it necessary to control both the club and the magazine in tandem, which he did by serving as both the magazine's editor and the club's secretary. To ensure that the club's officers and members would not question this structure, Stancer used his power as club secretary to generate and maintain controversies that really were of little actual objective importance to sport cyclists, thereby justifying the size, importance, and expense of the *Gazette*. When Stancer ceased to dominate the CTC, so did the *Gazette*, and so did the role of the grinding, never-ending, irreconcilable, nonnegotiable bicycle politics that drained and exhausted the club into a state of near-death by the early 1960s.

Nor can the origins of vehicular cycling can be traced to the early American cyclists of the late–19th century. Although the League of American Wheelmen was formed in 1880 to a large extent to fight for the road rights of cyclists, and while they did realize some early successes in large eastern-seaboard cities, most of their energy was soon dissipated into internecine battles over sectional representation, membership eligibility, and especially racing. The good-roads movement was used by the league's executive board as much to decentralize autonomy to its state chapters while preserving itself as a national organization as it was an ideological campaign. In the end, much of its work as a good-roads organization was undone by the "color bar" issue and continued racing controversies and was carried on by other, composite organizations such as the Good Roads League. In the end, "good roads" was an issue decided largely by the creation of postal rural free delivery and a federalized highway funding structure, not through the efforts of the cyclists or their league.

The origins of American vehicular cycling can, instead, be found in the traffic planning work of William Phelps Eno and Miller McClintock of the 1920s. Both men rejected a deterministic "hard" engineering approach that assumed that motor vehicle drivers could never be made cooperative, rational, or safe. Eno believed that without clear, logical traffic regulations, drivers would act as a "mob," but if carefully crafted, and made uniform in nature and application, drivers could be as rationalized as an infantry brigade on a parade ground. While not as idealistic as Eno, McClintock believed that traffic improvement did ultimately resolve itself down to driver improvement. All measures, whether in the form of education, enforcement or engineering, had to be targeted at improving the driver and his responses to the environment. Most importantly, engineering, in the form of capital improvements, would be just so much wasted money if they did not serve the fundamental purpose of assisting the driver to do what he already wanted to do. In other words, engineering that was planned from the start to be purely coercive in nature would never succeed, because it could always, in the end, be overcome. But by World War II, the general traffic philosophies of both Eno and McClintock were disfavor as civil engineers built roads designed so that they could only be used "as the engineer intended them to be used," the modern interstate highways being the best example.

3. Credit for the name "vehicular cycling," as well as the first relatively complete articulation of its basic principles, must go to Harold C. Munn.

Munn, a Los Angeles engineer for the California Department of Transportation, read his paper, "Bicycles and Traffic," before a conference of the American Society of Civil Engineers, and submitted it to their *Transportation Engineering Journal* in November 1974. "The task," he wrote, "is to convince [cyclists] to operate their bicycles as they do their automobiles." It was published in the journal *Transportation Engineering* in November 1975. In December 1973, at the Orlando MAUDEP conference, John Forester was advocating specialized facilities—bicycle boulevards—because he considered it more important that a way be found to allow cyclists to avoid stop signs than it was that they be treated as the full legal equivalents to automobiles. (By late 1974 or early 1975 he had changed his mind about this, mostly by coming to the conclusion that the Uniform Vehicle Code only required cyclists to treat stop signs as yield signs.) However, leaving aside specific nomenclature and privileged "buzz phrases," clearly identifiable elements of what we now call vehicular cycling can be traced to the works of at least nine different authors during the years 1969–1975. Vehicular cycling is a vernacular, communal intellectual property without a single identifiable source of time, place, or originator.

4. Vehicular cycling is something government does, not something cyclists do.

Vehicular cycling is not an educational program, a philosophy of cycling, or a riding method. There are now many educational programs that claim to teach "vehicular cycling." All this means is that such a course teaches the student to ride in a roadway environment in which no special provision has been made for bicycle use. It is the government policy upon which this assumption is based that truly comprises vehicular cycling: i.e., it is unrealistic to expect that any significant public effort can and will be made to provide for bikeways or other roadway modifications any time in the foreseeable future, so cyclists are themselves responsible for their own safety and welfare.

As stated in the introduction, it is irrelevant whether one believes that this is a good thing or a bad thing. The League of American Bicyclists (L.A.B.), for example, teaches a multi-week vehicular cycling class while at the same time strongly advocating for the local provision of bike lanes and other capital improvements. The British Cyclists' Touring Club now does the same. While there is no ideological contradiction between the two in the eyes of their respective boards of directors, staffs and most members, some believe that this Janus-faced approach undercuts the club's credibility in their appeal for safer roadways and separated paths. Vehicular cycling-type courses reinforce the bias held by many government transportation planners and highway professionals that organized cyclists prefer skills enhancement training to bikeways, and that the clubs have the capacity to act effectively on their own initiative to address the problem without any need to resort to government action. At a minimum, such education programs reinforce a belief among bureaucrats and elected officials that improving the roadway for bicycle use need not be a top priority, and that even in an environment of benign neglect, cyclists will manage to get by. Thus, the cycling organizations unintentionally provide the political justification needed by policymakers for not diverting highway funds away from traditional motor vehicle capacity improvements.

On the other hand, in the case of the L.A.B., the dissonance between its role as a nationwide sponsor of vehicular cycling instruction and a nationwide bikeways advocacy organization has led to internal conflict between those who believe that an organization that teaches vehicular cycling should not, at the same time, be advocating anything other than the use of unmodified roadways. Others believe that vehicular cycling instruction is simply a pragmatic answer to a real, immediate problem of cyclist safety, and should not be used to inculcate students with political opinions about public policy, or to make judgments about the legitimacy of low-skill or occasional cyclists. In general, the L.A.B. has responded to the schism by forsaking its most elitist members, taking the position that it represents cyclists across the entire spectrum of skills and interests, even those who will likely never be interested in joining the organization, making up for the revenues lost from individual membership fees through foundation grants and sponsorships from corporations and municipalities.

5. Modern vehicular cycling is broad-based, organic and vernacular. It cannot be attributed to any one "inventor," "developer," or "leader." That being said, some observations as to its most salient features can be made:

a. *Education and proficiency training.* The earliest cyclist proficiency training classes can be traced back to the work of Fred DeLong at the Philadelphia Council of the American Youth Hostels about 1968–69. The L.A.W. duplicated a slide show illustrating DeLong's Philadelphia course in 1969 for distribution to local cycle clubs. It began to run as a monthly feature in *Bicycling* magazine in April 1970. These went as high as Part 10 by May 1971, and irregular updates continued to appear as late as November 1972. DeLong's program was heavily influenced by his observations about rural and urban bicycle use in France. His work was never fully collated into a single source, but some of it appeared in his 1974 book, *DeLong's Guide to Bicycles and Bicycling.*[6]

John Forester collected the information in DeLong's program and other bicycle education material for a subcommittee report he prepared for the SCR-47 California statewide bicycle committee report in 1974. He combined this material with four articles he wrote for *Bike World* magazine between December 1973 and April 1974 to create classroom instructional material for a course he taught at Foothills Community College starting in June 1975. The first version of the book *Effective Cycling* that was available for sale to the public was a self-published, mimeographed, comb-bound volume of about 200 pages issued in November 1975. It remained self-published until 1984 when the first trade edition was published.

The League of American Wheelmen used *Effective Cycling* and the *Effective Cycling Instructors' Manual* from about 1977 until 1992. However, as early as 1981, members of the league's EC Committee began modifying the course content, largely because ten to 12 of the course's original 33 hours was felt to duplicate information already familiar to the regular cyclotourists that largely comprised the league's membership. In 1992, Forester revoked the league's permission to use his material, so it developed its own program, called Bike Ed, later Smart Cycling. In 2009, the league adopted John Franklin's *Cyclecraft* as its text. *Cyclecraft* was originally written in 1988 and later modified for North American use. In 2013, the league developed its own textbook, entitled *Smart Cycling.*

In 1981, Rodale Press published the best commercially available book, John S. Allen's *The Complete Book of Bicycle Commuting.* No instructional program was ever developed around this work, but in 1988, Allen and Rodale Press developed Bicycling Street Smarts, with material extracted from the 1981 book. Allen purchased this material and continues to update and actively market it to state departments of transportation and statewide bicycle organizations as a 48-page booklet customized to reflect a given state's laws. There are about a dozen or so of these customized manuals and a generalized version. At least one state bicycle organization uses *Bicycling Street Smarts* as the text for its adult bike safety classes.

b. *Reliance on the normal roadway system as opposed to specialized bikeways.* Opposition to urban bicycle facilities was articulated as early as November 1972 by Fred DeLong in *Bicycling*; December 1972 by Jim Konski at the first MAUDEP conference (his speech was reprinted in June 1973 in *Bicycling*); in February 1973 by John Forester in *Bike World*; and in May 1973 by Bill Wilkinson at the Bicycles USA conference in Cambridge, Massachusetts.[7] In June 1974, Morgan Groves, L.A.W. executive director, issued a policy statement in the *L.A.W. Bulletin* on behalf of the league's board stating that it was the league's policy to support paths "only where no public road exists, on bridges, to [bypass freeways], or in special recreation and park areas." This policy had been developed through a special committee that Groves had assembled in the fall of 1973 that included both Fred DeLong and John Forester and was approved by the L.A.W. board in January 1974.

By 1975–76, John Williams's bikeway-less "Teen Angel" bicycle for the city of San Luis Obispo was being widely distributed by USDOT as a model to be emulated. In 1977, *Bicycling*'s Darryl Skrabak wrote that the urban bikeway movement was effectively dead. After 1979, the MAUDEP conferences were discontinued because there was so little interest among bicycle planners in bikeways development.[8]

c. *Suspicion of any bicycle-specific traffic law or regulation.* Although the earliest successes in American bicycle advocacy were in the area of legislative changes, this area has also been among the most problematic, because the stated goals of the activist club cyclists were often not their actual goals. (It may be more accurate to say that their stated goals were not their ultimate goals.) In January 1975, Richard Rogers of Caltrans received a formal opinion of the California attorney general's office interpretating of the state's then-current "ride to the right" statute, which was virtually identical to the language in the nationwide Uniform Vehicle Code. The attorney general's opinion stated that in spite of its literal language, the statute should be interpreted to mean that cyclists could leave the right-hand edge of the road, but only in a limited number of circumstances, including making a vehicular-style left turn, to overtake other, slower vehicles, and to avoid an obstacle.[9]

The National Committee on Uniform Traffic Laws and Ordinances

(NCUTLO) appointed the four-member Michael Panel to recommend bicycling-related changes to the Uniform Vehicle Code. It reported its findings in January 1975. The Panel made three primary recommendations. The first was that a bicycle should be included within the definition of a "vehicle." The second was that both the "ride to the right" and "mandatory sidepath" regulations be deleted in their entirety. The California state bikeways committee, on the other hand, ended up recommending that their existing "ride-to-the-right" statute be changed by adding six new bicycle-specific exceptions.

At its July 1975 meeting, the NCUTLO approved only the amendment that redefined the bicycle as a vehicle. In 1979, it modified the "ride to the right" rule by adding the same six exceptions that the California bicycle committee had developed five years earlier, although using different specific language. However, it again rejected any change to the mandatory sidepath rule. In 1983, it finally approved the amendment to delete the mandatory sidepath provision.[10]

Surprisingly, there has never been unanimous support among cycle advocates for these changes, especially the change redefining a bicycle as a vehicle. The prior language made bicycles subject to all of the rights and duties of a vehicle, except for those provisions "which by their nature can have no application." Some Effective Cycling adherents argue that the cyclist himself should have the sole legal power to determine if a given provision "by its nature can have no application," a so-called subjective legal interpretation. This logic has been most frequently applied to the argument that a cyclist need not come to a full stop for stop signs and (less often asserted) red lights. But by their nature, traffic ordinances do not lend themselves to subjective interpretation, and in no known case has a subjective interpretation defense ("I determined that I stopped for that stop sign to the extent appropriate for a cyclist of my degree of skill and experience to carry out the essential purposes of the stop sign law") ever been upheld.

6. Bicycle transportation planning during the 1970s was comprised of three separate approaches, only two of which still remain. The "third stream" of bicycle planning, based on the belief that without dedicated bicycle facilities cycling could not remain viable, died out by 1981.

Much of the historical fog suffusing the early years of American bicycle planning has emanated from the basic belief that there were two contending schools of bicycle planning in the 1970s: bikeway advocates and anti-bikeway vehicular cyclists. A review of the literature from this period indicates that this simply was not the case. There were, instead, three clearly defined schools of bicycle planning: (1) a relatively small group of strident vehicular cyclists; (2)

a broadly inclusive school of pragmatists, best described as "middle-of-the-road," who, after the initial spate of bikeway construction stimulated by the Land and Water Conservation Act from 1969 to 1975, realized that European-style bikeway planning models could not be automatically transferred to American circumstances without extensive re-evaluation; and (3) an actively redistributionist "third stream" that adamantly supported specialized bikeways development along a northern European (especially Dutch) model, strongly opposed any policy that demanded even a modicum of cyclist proficiency, and was vehemently anti-elitist in outlook. These "third stream" planners and advocates were not in the least reluctant to admit that their designs would impair high-skill cyclists, even to the point of endangering the continued viability of cycling as a sporting activity. But by the time of the first AASHTO *Bicycle Guide* in 1981 (and probably some two to four years sooner), this "third stream" had all but ceased to exist.

7. Thus, what emerged at the end of the 1970s was a single, broad, centrist school of American bicycle planning that could either be described as "non-ideological vehicular cycling" or more simply "pragmatic-eclectic."

Where there had once been an active leftist "third-stream" school, there was now an equally enthusiastic, but also equally marginal, libertarian Effective Cycling school. Mainstream transportation planners and engineers, who had originally been sympathetic with the third stream bicycle planners because they offered the vague promise of getting cyclists off the roadway and onto relatively low-cost Radweg-style sidepaths, now switched their support to the vehicular cyclists because their program was predicated on unaltered roadways, thereby placing the responsibility for safety solely on the cyclists themselves. Thus, no capital expenditures on bicycle-related projects was required. From the perspective of the mainstream roadway engineer, vehicular cycling held the promise of something for nothing; the only role for the traffic engineer was to build more roads, and build them to current roadway standards. What could be easier? Since the time of the Roman empire, field-level bureaucrats have always been more than happy to let the locals call down their own devisive, self-defeating decisions upon themselves, turning away in amazement with a mild shrug and a murmured, "I wash my hands of it."

Even those remaining instructors and administrators who today use the Effective Cycling training material no longer have any reservations about editing down the material, glossing over or omitting entirely sections they believe are obsolete, incorrect, or (most often), just plain irrelevant. As a result, most vehicular cyclists who still consider themselves Effective Cyclists have become "cafeteria" effective cyclists. They, like Robert Hurst of *The Art of Urban Cycling*, give little thought to the ideological implications of cutting through a parking lot or taking a back street. The same is true for Effective Cycling instructors: time and resources are limited, and whether one prefers to wear a rain suit or a cape and spats, or prefers a mountain bike to a road bike, it simply does not matter.

Today, as was the case in 1985, bicycle professionals are vehicular cyclists because they have to be: with no meaningful funding for adequate urban bicycle facilities in sight, they have no choice. The funding that does exist is sporadic, often unplanned and usually spent for political, not technical, reasons. A shocking amount of it is simply wasted. Vehicular cycling remains the predominant mode of planning in 2014 Mackay for the same reason it became the predominant mode 30 years ago: it adheres to what has become, by bitter experience, the basic rule of American bicycle planning: "First, do no harm."

Chapter Notes

Introduction

1. Anne Katrin Ebert, "Cycling Towards the Nation: The Use of the Bicycle in Germany and the Netherlands, 1880–1940," *European Review of History* 2, 3 (2003): 347–64; Jennifer Bonham and Peter Cox, "The Disruptive Traveler? A Foucauldian Analysis of Cycleways," *Road and Transport Research* 19, 2 (2010): 42–53; Ruth Oldenziel and Adri Albert de la Bruhèze, "Contested Spaces: Bicycle Lanes in Europe, 1920–1995," *Transfers* 1, 2 (Summer 2011): 29–49; Tiina Männistö-Funk, The Crossroads of Technology and Tradition: Vernacular Bicycles in Rural Finland, 1880–1910," *Technology and Culture* 52, 4 (October 2011): 733–56; Anna-Maria Rautio and Lars Östlund "Starvation Strings and the Public Good: Development of a Swedish Bike Trail Network in the Early Twentieth Century," *Journal of Transport History* 33, 1 (June 2012): 42–63; Martin Emanuel, "Constructing the Cyclist: Ideology and Representations in Urban Traffic Planning in Stockholm, 1930–70," *Journal of Transport History* 33,1 (June 2012): 67–91; Anne-Katrin Ebert, "When Cycling Gets Political: Building Cycle Paths in Germany and the Netherlands, 1910–40," *Journal of Transport History* 33, 1 (June 2012): 115–37; Manuel Stoffers, "Cycling as Heritage: Representing the History of Cycling in the Netherlands," *Journal of Transport History* 33, 1 (June 2012): 92–114; Peter Cox, "A Denial of Our Boasted Civilization: Cyclists' Views Over Road Use in Britain, 1926–1935," *Transfers* 2, 3 (Winter 2012): 4–30; Dave Horton, Paul Horton, and Peter Cox, eds. *Cycling and Society* (Aldershot, UK: Ashgate, 2007).

2. Wiebie Bijker, *Of Bicycles, Bakelites and Bulbs: Towards a Theory of Sociotechnical Change* (Cambridge, MA: MIT Press): 9–11; Gary Sanderson, Index to the Proceeding of the International Cycle History Conference, 1 (1990) through 20 (2009) (manuscript, 2011).

3. Rolf Monheim, "Policy Issues in Promoting the Green Modes," in *The Greening of Urban Transport*, ed. Rodney Tolley (London: Belhaven Press, 1990): 134–58.

4. Oldenziel and de la Bruhèze, "Contested Spaces: Bicycle Lanes in Europe," 36.

5. For a strongly pro-facilities view, see John Pucher and Ralph Buehler, eds. *City Cycling* (Cambridge, MA: MIT Press, 2012).

6. Robert Sommer and Dale Lott, "The Bicycle Era: Bikeways in Action, the Davis Experience," 117, *Federal Register* 10830–833 (April 19, 1971) (emphasis in original).

7. Bicycle use to 1920: Clay McShane, *Down the Asphalt Path: The Automobile and the American City* (New York: Columbia University Press, 1994), Chapters 1–4. Dramatic increase in sales after 1969: A. Trent Germano, *et al.*, "The Emerging needs of Bicycle Transportation," *Transportation Research Record* 436 (1973): 8–18.

8. *Guide for the Development of New Bicycle Facilities* (Washington, D.C.: AASHTO, 1991), 2–3.

9. See, for example, Jeff Mapes, *Pedaling Revolution: How Cyclists are Changing American Cities* (Corvallis: University of Oregon Press, 2009); Zack Furness, *One Less Car: Bicycling and the Politics of Automobility* (Philadelphia: Temple University Press, 2010).

10. In addition to Mapes, *Pedaling Revolution*, and Furness, *One Less Car*, cited immediately above, see Robert Hurst, *The Art of Cycling: A Guide to Bicycling in 21st Century America* (Guilford, CT: Falcon Guides, 2007). This contains a good, relatively non-partisan discussion of the ideological division among cyclists.

11. The term *satisficing*, also known as *bounded rationality*, was coined by the economist Herbert Simon in the 1950s. The general concept is that, in the real world, as opposed to pure rational choice economic models, decision-making itself is an activity requiring time and money, so resources

must be allocated between the act of reaching a decision and actually implementing it. Thus, solutions that quickly and cheaply present themselves as "good enough" to get the job done tend to be favored because they leave more resources free for implementation. See Herbert A. Simon, "A Behavioral Model of Rational Choice," *Quarterly Journal of Economics* 69 (1955): 99–118.

12. Spending on all levels of government per million vehicle miles traveled was $11,400 in 1967; it dropped to a low of $4,489 in 1989, and remained flat until 2004 when it started increasing slightly, reaching $5,628 in 2010. Since then it has resumed its decline. Source: author's calculations, based on "Funding for Highways and Disposition of Highway User Revenue," http://www.fhwa.dot.dot.gov/policyinformation/statistics.cfm.

13. Even after 1991, when states began to be offered specially earmarked funds for bicycle and pedestrian projects at an 80–20 federal-state matching ratio, several states declined their apportionment rather than come up with a 20 percent matching share.

14. Blake Gumprecht, *The American College Town* (Amherst: University of Massachusetts Press, 2008), 145–88 (regarding the debate over whether Davis "is no longer a progressive community," but is "deeply conservative" due to wealth and need to protect inflated property values).

15. Robert L. Beisner, *Dean Acheson: A Life in the Cold War* (New York: Oxford University Press, 2006), 489.

16. James E. Stacey, "Bridging the Gap Between Bikeway Planners and Bicyclists," in *Proceedings of the Seminar/Workshop on Planning, Design and Implementation of Bicycle and Pedestrian Facilities, Chicago, July 19–21, 1978* (New York, MAUDEP, n. d. [1978]), 203–09.

17. Charles Floyd, "The Future of the Bicycle as a Mode of Transportation in the United States," *Traffic Quarterly* 31, 1 (January 1977): 139–53; *Transportation Enhancements: Summary of Nationwide Spending as of FY 2009* (Washington, D.C.: National Transportation Enhancements Clearinghouse, 2010).

18. Michael A. Replogle, *National Bicycling and Walking Study: Case Study 9, Linking Bicycle/Pedestrian Facilities with Transit* (Washington, D.C.: Federal Highway Administration, 1992, Report No. FHWA-PD-93-012).

19. Christopher Haglin, *A Return on Investment Analysis of Bikes-on-Bus Programs* (Tampa: Center for Urban Transportation Research, University of South Florida, 2005).

20. Jennifer, Toole, *et al.*, *Revising the Guide for the Development of New Bicycle Facilities: Final Report* (Washington, D.C.: Transportation Research Board, 2010, Report No. NCHRP 15-37FR).

21. John Forester, *Effective Cycling* (Cambridge: MIT Press, 7th ed. 2012), 693. If you disagree with Forester, he believes you suffer from "Cyclist Inferiority Phobia," which he asserts, starting with the 2012 seventh edition of *Effective Cycling*, meets the criteria established in DSM-IV for a specific phobia (300.29). It should be noted that falsely accusing someone of mental illness can constitute defamation *per se* in some states, and thus, accusing a specific, named individual of "Cyclist Inferiority Phobia," may now subject one to liability for libel or defamation.

Chapter 1

1. Charles E. Pratt, "Our First Bicycle Club," *Wheelman* 1, 6 (March 1883): 401–12.

2. Karl Kron [Lyman H. Bagg], *Ten Thousand Miles on a Bicycle* (New York: the author, 1887): 140–141; Ross D. Petty, "The Impact of the Sport of Bicycle Riding on Safety Law," *American Business Law Journal* 35, 2 (Winter 1998): 185–224.

3. Clay McShane, *Down the Asphalt Path* (New York: Columbia University Press, 1994), 118; Charles E. Pratt, "The L.A.W. and Legal Rights," *Outing* 7 (January 1886): 454–56; Petty, "The Impact of the Sport of Bicycle Riding on Safety Law," 185–200.

4. The story of the Central Park bike ban is taken from the following sources: Philip P. Mason, *The League of American Wheelmen and the Good-Roads Movement, 1880–1905* (Doctoral dissertation, University of Michigan, 1957), 30–42; Gregory C. Lisa, "Bicyclists and Bureaucrats: The League of American Wheelmen and the Public Choice Theory Applied," *Georgetown Law Review* 84 (1995): 373–98; Kron, 92–95; *In re Wright, et al.*, 63 How. 345 (S.C.N.Y.C. 1882); and *In re Wright, Foster and Walker*, 65 How. 119 (S.C.N.Y.C., 1883).

5. For a fuller treatment of this somewhat iconoclastic view, see Bruce Epperson, *Peddling Bicycles to America: The Rise of an Industry* (Jefferson, NC: McFarland, 2010), chapters 4 and 6.

6. Petty, "The Impact of the Sport of Bicycle Riding on Safety Law," 212–20; Lisa, "Bicyclists and Bureaucrats," 373–80; Mason, *passim*.

7. Kron, 624–27; Thomas C. Burr, "Markets as Producers and Consumers: The French and U.S. National Markets, 1875–1910" (Ph.D. Dissertation, University of California at Davis, 2005), 87.

8. "I guess a certain number of these men": "Testimony of William S. Kelly" in *Transcript of Witnesses, January 23, 1888, Pressy v. H. B. Smith Mfg. Co.*, 19 A. 618 (N.J. App. 1889), 49; Hagley Museum and Library, Wilmington, Delaware (hereafter referred to as *Pressy v. Smith* Case File). "We always objected to these expenses": "Testimony of C. H. Chickering," in *Pressy v. Smith* Case File, 517.

9. Kron, 627.

10. George D. Gideon, "A Defense of the Two-Class System in Bicycle Racing," *Harper's Weekly* 39 (March 1895): 286.

11. Letter from David J. Post to Sam A. Miles, June 27, 1891, Pope/Hartford Papers, Connecticut State Library, Hartford, Connecticut.

12. Mason, 47; Glen Norcliffe, *The Ride to Modernity: The Bicycle in Canada, 1869–1900* (Toronto: University of Toronto Press, 2001), 197.

13. *American Athlete and Cycle Trades Review*, 4, 2 (January 2, 1889): 109.

14. "Killed by Negroes," *Cycle Age and Trade Review* 20 (November 23, 1899): 107.

15. Mason, 69–71, 76.

16. Horatio Sawyer Earle, *The Autobiography of "By Gum" Earle* (Lansing: State Review Publishing, 1929), 42–48.

17. Sterling Elliott, "The League of American Wheelmen: Its Origin, Growth, and Prospects," *Harper's Weekly* 39 (March 1895): 284–86; *American Athlete and Cycle Trades Review* 5, 38 (November 22, 1889): 576; "The League and Politics," *American Athlete and Cycle Trades Review* 5, 36 (November 8, 1889): 547.

18. "The farmers must bear": *Engineering News* 30 (December 1893): 30. "Give the farmer a fair price": "The Editor's Table," *Good Roads* 1 (April 1892): 224.

19. Letter from H. S. Robinson to Roy Stone, Bureau of Public Roads Inquiry, February 3, 1893, Record Group 30.1.1, File 67 (Records of the Bureau of Public Roads), National Archives, Archives II Facility, College Park, MD. (Hereafter: 30.1.1/67 BPR Papers, Archives II.)

20. "L.A.W. National Assembly," *Wheel and Cycling Trade Review* 6 (February 1891): 681; Mason, 108; *Wheel and Cycling Trade Review* 8 (December 1891): 525.

21. Potter was not selected to any office in the new Good-Roads League, formed in November 1892, although he remained active in the L.A.W.: Epperson, *Peddling Bicycles to America*: 97–98, 258, 41n.

22. Letter from James Dunn to Roy Stone, July 27, 1892, RG 30.1.2/2 67 BPR Papers, Archives II.

23. Andrew Ritchie, *Major Taylor: The Extraordinary Career of a Champion Bicycle Racer* (San Francisco: Bicycle Books, 1988), 38–39; citing *Bicycling World*, June 3, 1892.

24. *Wheel & Cycle Trades Review* (November 27, 1891): 435; *Bicycling World and L.A.W. Bulletin* (June 3, 1892): 1065; *Bicycling World and L.A.W. Bulletin* (July 8, 1892): 1272.

25. "Meeting of the National Assembly," *American Athlete and Cycle Trades Review* 11, 8 (February 24, 1893): 159.

26. Mason, 136–39.

27. Richard F. Weingroff, *Portrait of a General: General Roy Stone* (Unpublished Manuscript, Federal Highway Administration, U.S. Department of Transportation, 2003), 30–39; Letter from J. Sterling Morton to Roy Stone, date unknown [c. October 1893], RG30.1.2/2 Box 66 BPR Papers, National Archives II; Mason, 150.

28. William Stull Holt, *The Bureau of Public Roads: Its History, Activities, and Organization* (Baltimore: Institute for Government Research Service, 1923), 9.

29. Mason, 202.

30. Lisa, "Bicyclists and Bureaucrats," 395. Although the Department of Agriculture and the Post Office did not reach a formal agreement until 1906, they were working together on the RFD-roads issue as early as 1896: Mason, 207.

31. Elliott, "The League of American Wheelmen," 286.

32. Mason, 217.

33. "News of the Cyclers," *New York Times* (June 5, 1898); "Gossip of the Cyclers," *New York Times* (August 28, 1898); Mason, 217.

34. Evan Frist, "The Path Not Taken: The Rise of America's Cycle Paths and the Fall of Urban Cycling," in *Cycle History 20: Proceedings of the 20th International Cycling History Conference, Freehold*, ed. Gary Sanderson (n.l. John Pinkerton Memorial Publishing Fund, 2010), 67–72.; James Longhurst, "The Sidepath Not Taken: Bicycles, Taxes, and the Rhetoric of the Public Good in the 1890s," *Journal of Policy History* 25, 4 (2013): 557–85.

35. "Good Roads Workers," *Brooklyn Eagle* (April 3, 1898), 19.

36. Ibid.

37. Frist, "The Path Not Taken," 69–70.

38. Coney Island: Frist, 558; Denver and Minneapolis: Longhurst, *passim*.

39. Isaac B. Potter, "Side Paths," *LAW Bulletin* 24, 2 (1896): 51

40. Longhurst, 569.

41. Ross Petty, "Post-Boom Bicycling in Minneapolis: Counting Transportation Use," in *Cycle History 20: Proceedings of the 20th International Cycling History Conference, Freehold*, ed. Gary Sanderson (n.l. John Pinkerton Memorial Publishing Fund, 2010), 73–80.

42. Minneapolis state legislation: Longhurst, 573. Longhurst reports that the Minnesota tag-sale law was enacted in 1901, but Petty provides sales figures for 1900 and photograph of a 1900 badge. It thus appears the law was enacted in February 1900: Petty, "Post-Boom Cycling in Minneapolis," 76–77.

43. *Ellis v. Frazier*, 63 P. 642 (Or. 1901).

44. *Porter, et al. v. Shields, et al.*, 49 A. 785 (Penn. 1901).

45. There is very little literature on the administrative-organizational dynamics of high-

way building in the pre-federal era. Among the best is Michael R. Fein, *Paving the Way: New York Road Building and the American State, 1880–1956* (Lawrence: University Press of Kansas, 2008).

46. *People v. Bruce*, 63 P. 519 (Wash. 1901).

47. Petty, 76–77; Longhurst, 574–77.

48. L.A.W. membership numbers: Mason, 217. But not blacks. The "whites only" provision remained in the constitution well into the 20th century, unenforced, because there were not enough members to enact a constitutional amendment.

49. Longhurst, 574.

50. David Blanke, *Hell on Wheels: The Promise and Peril of America's Car Culture, 1900–1940* (Lawrence: University Press of Kansas, 2007), 142; Daniel M. Albert, "Order Out of Chaos: Automobile Safety, Technology, and Society, 1925–1965" (Ph.D. dissertation, University of Michigan, 1997), Section II.

51. William P. Eno, *The Science of Traffic Regulation, 1899–1920* (Washington, D.C.: the author, 1920), 3; John A. Montgomery, *Eno: The Man and the Foundation* (Westport, CT: Eno Foundation, 1988), *passim*. The state of New York did adopt a "keep right" ordinance for turnpikes and highways in 1801, but it did not apply to cities.

52. Peter D. Norton, *Fighting Traffic: The Dawn of the Motor Age in the American City* (Cambridge: MIT Press, 2008), 50–53. Norton asserts that Eno's rules placed a high priority on speed. I do not agree, although I do concur that Eno did highly value continuous movement, so preferred rotary intersections over street lights and stop signs: Eno, *The Science of Traffic Regulation*: *passim*; William P. Eno, *Simplification of Highway Traffic* (Washington, D.C.: Eno Foundation, 1929), *passim*; Montgomery, *Eno: The Man and the Foundation*, 120.

53. "ProBicycle: Bicycle Advocacy by Cyclists for Cyclists," at http://probicycle.com. Thanks to Zack Furness for bringing this website and its contents to my attention. The problem with such a totalistic formulation is that "vehicle" is a virtually undefined term under the Model Code. It applies equally to an automobile, an oxcart, or a riding lawn mower. As will be discussed in greater detail later, all it means from a legal standpoint is that any section of the traffic code that refers to a "vehicle" includes a bicycle, while a section referring to a "motor vehicle" does not.

54. Miller McClintock, *Street Traffic Control* (New York: McGraw-Hill, 1925), 168.

55. Scott Bottles, *Los Angeles and the Automobile: The Making of the Modern City* (Berkeley: University of California Press, 1987), 116–17. This is also discussed in McClintock's *Street Traffic Control*.

56. McClintock, 118–19.

57. Quoted in untitled photo caption, *Texas Parade* 2, 2 (July 1937): 4.

58. 3-E's: Edward A. Tenney, *The Highway Jungle: The Story of the Public Safety Movement and the Failure of Driver Education in the Public Schools* (New York: Exposition Press, 1962), 20–25. Whitney wrote a book: *Albert W. Whitney, Man and the Motor Car* (New York: J. J. Little and Ives, 1936).

59. Blanke, 125–32. Whitney did not consider civil suits, as it was assumed at this time that an appropriate liability insurance network would render litigation moot.

60. Albert, *Order Out of Chaos*, 58–70; Morton Keller and Phyllis Keller, *Making Harvard Modern: The Rise of America's University* (New York: Oxford University Press, 2001), 79.

61. Blanke, 152.

62. Population growth along fringe: Mark S. Foster, *From Streetcar to Superhighway: American City Planners and Urban Transportation, 1900–1940* (Philadelphia: Temple University Press, 1981), 15. Urban horse population: Kenneth T. Jackson, *Crabgrass Frontier: The Suburbanization of the United States* (New York: Oxford University Press, 1985), 184.

63. Foster, *From Streetcar to Superhighway*, 89.

64. On the issue of incremental (what economists call "marginal") advantage and distribution of costs, *see*, in general, Charles L. Wright, *Fast Wheels, Slow Traffic: Urban Transportation Choices* (Philadelphia: Temple University Press, 1992) and Bottles, *Los Angeles and the Automobile: The Making of the Modern City*.

65. Norton, *Fighting Traffic: The Dawn of the Motor Age in the American City*, *passim*; Clay McShane, *Down the Asphalt Path: The Automobile and American City* (New York: Columbia University Press, 1994), 176, 202. There is no clear proof one way or the other that this "suburban serendipity" effect carried over to cyclists, but due to the fact that before 1965 "cyclist" and "child" were highly correlated, the quantitative safety effects on child pedestrians and cyclists likely moved together.

66. Bruce Epperson, "Review of Peter D. Norton's *Fighting Traffic*," *Technology and Culture* 50, 1 (January 2009): 235–36.

67. McShane, 202.

68. Oscar Newman, *Defensible Space: Crime Prevention Through Urban Design* (New York: Macmillan, 1972).

69. Foster, 146.

Chapter 2

1. Volker Briese, "From Cycling Lanes to Compulsory Bike Path: Bicycle Path Construction in Germany, 1897–1940" in *Cycle History 5:*

The Proceedings of the Fifth International Cycle History Conference, Cambridge, England, ed. Rob Van der Plas (San Francisco: Bicycle Books, 1995), 123–128.

2. Briese, 124–26; Anne-Katrin Ebert, "When Cycling Gets Political: Building Cycle Paths in Germany and the Netherlands, 1910–40," *Journal of Transport History* 33, 1 (June 2012): 115–137; Ruth Oldenziel and Adri Albert de la Bruheze, "Contested Spaces: Bicycle Lanes in Europe, 1900–1995," *Transfers* 1, 2 (Summer 2011): 29–49.

3. Ebert, 120–22; 125–27; Oldenziel and de la Bruheze, 35–38; Rüdiger Rabenstein, "The History of the German Workers' Cycling Association, Solidarity," in *Cycle History 11: Proceedings of the 11th International Cycle History Conference, Osaka,* ed. Andrew Ritchie and Rob van der Plas (San Francisco: Van der Plas Publications, 2001), 160–168.

4. Ebert, 125–27.

5. Timan Bracher, "Germany," in *The Bicycle and City Traffic,* ed. Hugh McClintock (London: Belhaven Press), 175–189. Briese, "From Cycling Lanes to Compulsory Bike Path," 126. See also Oldenziel and de la Bruheze, 37.

6. Manuel Stoffers, "Cycling as Heritage: Representing the History of Cycling in the Netherlands," *Journal of Transport History* 33, 1 (June 2012): 92–114.

7. Gijs Mom, "Roads Without Rails: European Highway-Network Building and the Desire for Long-Range Motorized Mobility," *Technology and Culture* 46, 4 (October 2005): 745–72; Ebert, 116–18; Oldenziel and de la Bruheze, 34.

8. Pete Jordan, *In the City of Bikes: the Story of the Amsterdam Cyclist* (New York: Harper Perennial, 2013), 55–56.

9. Most unpopular tax ever levied: Jordan, 66. Intended only for revenue enhancement: Stoffers, "Cycling as Heritage," 102–03; 109; Ebert, 123–25.

10. Most unpopular tax, and like a bicycle auction: Jordan, 68–69; later modification to tax: Ebert, 123–25.

11. Ton Welleman, "An Efficient Means of Transport: Experiences With Cycling Transport Policy in the Netherlands," in *Planning for Cycling: Principles, Practice and Solutions for Urban Planners,* ed. Hugh McClintock (Cambridge, UK: Woodhead, 2002), 192–208.

12. Ebert, 130 (Table 1).

13. Stoffers, "Cycling as Heritage: Representing the History of Cycling in the Netherlands," 105–106; Ebert, 129–31.

14. Jordan, 180–81.

15. Martin Emanuel, "Constructing the Cyclist: Ideology and Representations in Urban Traffic Planning in Stockholm, 1930–70," *Journal of Transport History* 33, 1 (June 2012): 67–91. Emanuel is quoting from a 1933 book by Dahlberg, *Cykelbanor och cykeltrafik.*

16. Emanuel, "Constructing the Cyclist: Ideology and Representations," 71 and 17n. Emanuel is citing the 1936 *Regionplan for Stockholm,* 149.

17. Emanuel, "Constructing the Cyclist: Ideology and Representations," 81.

18. Anna Maria Rautio and Lars Östlund, "Starvation Strings and the Public Good: Development of a Swedish Bike Trail Network in the Early Twentieth Century," *Journal of Transport History* 33, 1 (June 2012): 42–63.

19. Peter Cox, "A Denial of our Boasted Civilization: Cyclists' Views on Conflicts Over Road Use in Britain, 1926–1935," *Transfers* 2, 3 (Winter 2012): 4–30.

20. Thirty-eight thousand members: William Oakley, *Winged Wheel: The History of the First Hundred Years of the Cyclists' Touring Club* (Galdalming: CTC, 1977), 27, 41; sales of 1.4 million in 1938: Roger Lloyd-Jones and M. J. Lewis, *Raleigh and the British Bicycle Industry* (Aldershot, UK: Ashgate, 2000), 202.

21. Oakley, 28, 44–46, 176. In 1963, the *Gazette* was spun off as a self-supporting, semi-independent commercial magazine, *Cycletouring;* Cox, "A Denial of Our Boasted Civilization," 30.

22. Oakley, 33.

23. Peter Walker, "75 Years After the UK's First Cycle Lane Opened, the Same Debate Rages On," *The Environment Guardian Online,* www.environmentguardian.co.uk (posted December 13, 2009).

24. Oakley, 77–78.

25. Walker, "75 Years After the UK's First Cycle Lane Opened"; Michael D. Everett, "The Bikeway Controversy," in *Proceedings of the Seminar/Workshop on Planning, Design and Implementation of Bicycle and Pedestrian Facilities, Chicago, July 19–21* (1977) (New York: MAUDEP, n. d. [1978]), 42–49. Everett is quoting from the *CTC Gazette,* July 1938.

26. Oakley, 180–81.

27. John Franklin, "National Cycle Training Project: Cheltenham Address, May 2002," http://www.cyclecraft.com/articles/index/; John Franklin, "Segregation: Are We Moving Away From Cycling Safety?" *TEC: Traffic Engineering and Control* (April 2002): 23–27, at http://www.cyclecraft.com/articles/index/; Cox, "A Denial of Our Boasted Civilisation," 24.

28. Per Lundin, "Mediators of Modernity: Planning experts and the Making of the Car Friendly City in Europe," in *Urban Machinery: Inside Modern European Cities,* ed. Mikael Hard and Thomas J. Misa (Cambridge: MIT Press, 2008), 257–79.

29. Bracher, 185–87; Oldenziel and de la Bruheze, 39.

30. Bracher, 176.
31. Ibid., 186–87.
32. Jordan, 238–39.
33. Oldenziel and de la Bruheze, 37.
34. Stoffers, "Cycling as Heritage," 92; Jordan, 272.
35. Oldenziel and de la Bruheze, 37. Eindoven peaked at about 37–38 percent in 1983, fell again to 32 percent in 1992, and then started a slow increase. The data ends in 1995.
36. Mom, "Roads Without Rails," 767–69.
37. The story of Provos' White Bicycle Program is taken from Jordan, Chapters 16 and 17.
38. Jordan, 317 (emphasis in original).
39. La Rochelle succeeded: Susan A. Saheen, Stacey Guzman and Hua Zhang, "Bikesharing Across the Globe," in *City Cycling*, ed. John Pucher and Ralph Buehler (Cambridge: MIT Press, 2012), 183–210. La Rochelle failed: Jordan, 318.
40. Thomas Krag, "Urban Cycling in Copenhagen," in *Planning for Cycling: Principles, Practice and Solutions for Urban Planners*, ed. Hugh McClintock (Cambridge, UK: Woodhead, 2002), 223–36.
41. Copenhagen: Shaheen, Guzman and Zhag, "Bikesharing Across the Globe," 186–88; American cities: Jordan, 318–21; Paul DeMaio, "Bike Sharing: Its History, Models of Provision, and Future," *Journal of Public Transportation* 13, 4 (2009): 41–56.
42. Mom, "Roads Without Rails," 768–69.
43. Daniel Yergen, *The Prize: The Epic Quest for Oil, Money and Power* (New York: Simon & Schuster, 1991), 613–32.
44. Welleman, "An Efficient Means of Transport," 195.
45. Krag, "Urban Cycling in Denmark," 224–25. Woonervern: Tom Vanderbilt, *Traffic: Why We Drive the Way We Do* (New York: Knopf, 2008), 188–91.
46. Martin Kroon, "Traffic and Environmental Policy in the Netherlands," in *The Greening of Urban Transport: Planning for Walking and Cycling in Western Cities*, ed. Rodney Tolley (London: Belhaven Press, 1990), 113–33; Jan Hartman, "The Delft Bicycle Network," in *The Greening of Urban Transport: Planning for Walking and Cycling in Western Cities*, ed. Rodney Tolley (London: Belhaven Press, 1990), 193–200; Gerrit van Werven, "Groningen, Netherlands," in *The Bicycle in City Traffic*, ed. Hugh McClintock (London: Belhaven Press, 1992), 154–64.
47. Jordan, 376.
48. Emanuel, "Constructing the Cyclist," 82. Emanuel translates the name of the KSC (Kommittén för Svensk Cykelpropaganda) literally as the "Committee for Swedish Cycle Propaganda." In English, *propaganda* is a synonym for *disinformation* (and can only be used as a noun, not interchangeably as a noun and verb), so I have substituted the less literal but probably more accurate *promotion*.
49. Robert Fishman, *Urban Utopias in the Twentieth Century* (New York: Basic Books, 1977), Chapter 7.
50. E. C. Claxton, "The Future of the Bicycle in a Modern Society," *Royal Society for the Encouragement of Arts, Manufacturers and Commerce Journal* 116, 5138 (January 1968): 114–34.
51. Claxton, "The Future of the Bicycle in a Modern Society," 131 (comments of Ernest Marples).
52. Ibid. (comments of E. C. Caxton).
53. John Forester, "How to Gain Access Without Using Ketchup," *Bicycling* 22, 9 (November/December 1981): 44–45; John Forester, "Bicycling Transportation and the Problem of Evil" (unpublished speech manuscript, October 22, 2007), www.johnforester.com. In 1971, Marples, with the family silver and jewels in tow, caught the midnight ferry to Calais, one step ahead of Inland Revenue enforcement agents, having neglected to pay his annual income tax for over a decade. He spent the rest of his days in a rather sullen continental exile.
54. Hugh McClintock, "Planning for the Bicycle in Newer and Older Towns in Cities" in *The Bicycle and City Traffic*, ed. Hugh McClintock (London: Belhaven Press, 1992), 40–61.
55. Hugh McClintock, "Post-War Traffic Planning and Special Provision for the Bicycle," in *The Bicycle in City Traffic*, ed. Hugh McClintock (London: Belhaven Press, 1992), 19–39; Hugh McClintock, "Planning for the Bicycle in Urban Britain: an Assessment of Experience and Issues," in *The Greening of Urban Transport: Planning for Walking and Cycling in Western Cities*, ed. Rodney Tolley, (London: Belhaven Press, 1990), 201–17.
56. Hugh McClintock, "The Development of UK Cycling Policy," in *Planning for Cycling: Principles, Practice and Solutions for Urban Planners*, ed. Hugh McClintock (Cambridge, UK, 2002), 17–35; Hugh McClintock, "Nottingham" in *Planning for Cycling: Principles, Practice and Solutions for Urban Planners*, ed. Hugh McClintock (Cambridge, UK, 2002), 171–91; Robert Cervero, *Suburban Gridlock* (New Brunswick: Rutgers University Press, 1988).
57. Laura Golbuff and Rachel Aldred, *Cycling Policy in the UK* (London: University of East London, n. d. [2010]), 16.
58. Golbuff and Aldred, *Cycling Policy in the UK*, 17.
59. Ibid., 22.
60. Michael Yeates, "Making Space for Cyclists: A Matter of Speed?" in *Planning for Cycling: Principles, Practice and Solutions for Urban Planners*, ed. Hugh McClintock (Cambridge, UK, 2002), 50–71.

61. Yeates, "Making Space for Cyclists: A Matter of Speed?" 60.

62. Marilyn Johnson, Jennie Oxley, and Max Cameron, *Cycling Bunch Riding: A Review of the Literature* (Victoria: Monash University, 2009, Monash Univ. Accident Research Ctr. Report No. 285); City of Bayside, *Bayside City Council Bicycle Strategy* (2003); T. Burridge, P. Lajbcygier, and M. Lema, *Draft Response to Bayside City Council Bicycle Strategy* (Melbourne: David Locke and Associates/PBAI Australia, 2003).

Chapter 3

1. Efforts to find industries to generate dollar flows to England: John Lewis Gaddis: *George F. Kennan: An American Life* (New York: Penguin Press, 2011), 361–62; Tony Judt, *Postwar: A History of Europe Since 1945* (New York: Penguin, 2005), 160–161; 356–57. Change in tariff rates and resulting change in British and American bicycles: "Bicycle Makers Seek Tariff Help," *New York Times* (August 22, 1954), F1; Ross Petty, "Peddling Schwinn Bicycles: Marketing Lessons from the Leading Post-WWII U.S. Bicycle Brand," *Quinnipiac University CHARM Symposium Papers 2007*, 162–71. The tariff rate for lightweight bicycles, the most popular import category, was lowered to 7.5 percent. For the other three categories it was lowered to 15 percent. These rates were adjusted to 11.25 percent for lightweights and 22.5 percent for the others in 1955. *See* Petty.

2. "The thing we fought": transcript of author's interview with Norman Clarke, April 5, 1998, 6–7. For the purposes of this book, the Bicycle Institute of America (BIA) and the Bicycle Manufacturers' Association (BMA) are synonymous. After World War II, the BIA served as the umbrella group for the bicycle trades. It was comprised of four subsidiaries for bicycle makers, parts makers, distributors, and retailers. In 1968, Schwinn exited the BIA over disagreements about the role that mass merchandisers (Sears, Montgomery Ward, etc.) should play in the organization, but continued to work in close coordination with it. About 1975, the BIA disaggregated into its four constituent groups, with the BMA becoming the most visible entity and the most prominent supporter of the BIA. The BMA discontinued operations in 1984 as the American cycle industry contracted: author's interview with William C. Wilkinson III, former executive director, BIA, July 17, 2008; email from former Schwinn vice-president Jay Townley to the author, April 11, 2013.

3. Interview with Norman Clarke, 12–14. Keith Kingbay, *Inside Bicycling* (Chicago: Henry Regnery Co., 1976), 9.

4. Interview with Norman Clarke, 14; "League of American Wheelmen Financial Statement, June 15, 1951"; "League of American Wheelmen Financial Statement, October 30, 1951," http://john-s-allen.com/Biklg1965-/index.htm.

5. Dick Teresi, *Popular Mechanics Book of Bikes and Bicycling* (New York: Hearst Corp., 1975), 196–97.

6. Gary Toth and Brendan Crain interview with Dan Burden, Andy Clarke, and Charlie Gandy: www.pps.org/blog/after-30-years-of-bikeped-advocacy-how-far-have-we-come/htm.

7. Toth and Crain interview with Burden, Clarke, and Gandy; "Bob Cleckner," *Journal of Health, Physical Education and Recreation* (April 1965), 35; emails from Jay Townley to the author, April 11, 2013 and April 17, 2013. Frank V. Schwinn (1920–88) is frequently misattributed as "Frank Schwinn, Jr." His father's name was Frank W. Schwinn (1894–1963).

8. John S. Allen, "The League of American Wheelmen/Bicyclists in the 20th Century," in *Cycle History 20: Proceedings of the 20th International Cycle History Conference, Freehold*, ed. Gary Sanderson (n.l.: John Pinkerton Memorial Fund, 2010), 114–22; "League of American Wheelmen: Cash Receipts and Disbursements, 1-1-73 through 12-31-73," http://john-s-allen.com/Biklg1965-/correspondence/1973/ Board_correspondence.pdf.

9. Kingbay, *Inside Bicycling*, 11; emails from Jay Townley to the author, April 11 and 17, 2013.

10. Interview with Norman A. Clarke, 12. Schwinn introduced an 8-speed in 1963 and a 10-speed the following year: author's interview with Jay Townley, May 23, 2009.

11. The sales of derailleur-geared bicycles was 610,000 in 1969, 3.5 million in 1975: Frank J. Berto, "The Great American Bicycle Boom," in *Cycle History 10: Proceedings of the 10th International Cycle History Conference, Nijmegan*, ed. Hans Erhard Lessing and Andrew Ritchie (San Francisco: Van der Plas Publications, 2000), 133–48. The original source of this theory appears to be a strategic plan prepared by a consultant for Schwinn in 1978.

12. E. Peter Hoffman, "200,000 Miles of Bikeways," in *The Best of Bicycling*, ed. Harley M. Leete (New York: Trident Press, 1970), 287–290; "Third Annual L.A.W. Winter Rendezvous," *L.A.W. Bulletin* (February 1969): 3.

13. Hoffman, "200,000 Miles of Bikeways," 288–90.

14. "Bob Cleckner," 35; John B. Corgel and Charles Floyd, "Toward a New Direction in Bicycle Transportation Policy," *Traffic Quarterly* 33, 2 (April 1979): 297–310.

15. Tom Lewis, *Divided Highways. Building the Interstate Highways, Transforming American Life* (New York: Viking, 1997); Mark H. Rose, *Interstate: Express Highway Politics, 1939–1989*

(Knoxville: University of Tennessee Press, 2nd ed. 1990).

16. Corgel and Floyd, "Toward a New Direction in Bicycle Transportation Policy," 302–10.

17. W. L. Cook, *Bike Trails and Facilities—A Guide to Their Design, Construction and Operation* (New York: BIA, 1965, rev. ed. 1969); "Trails Seminar," *Bicycling*, 12, 5 (May 1971): 26.

18. Joe Kossak, "Hatboro Wizard Speaks," *Bike World* 3, 10 (October 1974): 10; Fred DeLong, *DeLong's Guide to Bicycles and Bicycling* (Radnor, PA: Chilton, 1974), *passim*; Fred DeLong, "I.S.O. Technical Committee TC-149 (Cycles), An Overview," *Bicycling* 15, 7 (July 1974): 72–77.

19. DeLong booklet: "Untitled," *L.A.W. Bulletin* (July 1969): 6; riding to the right: Fred DeLong, "From the Safety Committee," *L.A.W. Bulletin* (December 1969): 1–2; Fred DeLong, "Report of the Safety Committee, 1969," http://john-s-allen.com/Bikelg1965-/board._meetings/1983–12%20Board%20meeting/B.pdf.

20. Fred DeLong, "Safety: A Bicyclist Proficiency Course," *Bicycling* 11, 3 (April 1970): 22–23, 32; Fred Delong, "Cyclist Safety and Proficiency Course: Part 10, Club Riding and Touring Skills," *Bicycling* 12, 5 (May 1971): 20–21; Fred Delong, "Bicycle Proficiency: Where on the Road?" *Bicycling* 13, 11 (November 1972): 36–37.

21. Fred DeLong, *DeLong's Guide to Bicycles and Bicycling*, 178–244, quotation on 203. John Forester, *Effective Cycling* (Palo Alto: Custom Cycle Fitments, 1975), section 3.3.1.

22. Fred DeLong, "Cyclists in Traffic," *Bicycling* 15, 2 (February 1974): 28–30.

23. Forester, *Effective Cycling*, section 3.3.1.

24. Delong, "Bicycle Proficiency: Where on the Road?" 36.

25. Fred DeLong, "The Bicycle's Place on the Road: Another Viewpoint," *Bicycling* 9, 7 (July 1973): 20.

26. *Bikeway Planning Criteria and Guidelines* (Los Angeles: UCLA-ITTE, 1972). The legislative mandate was Assembly Concurrent Resolution 26 (1971); "The Bicycle Era" (reprint of Robert Sommer and Dale Lott, "Bikeways in Action, the Davis Experience"), 117; *Congressional Record* 10830–833 (April 19, 1971).

27. The efficacy of these designs depends: *Bikeway Planning Criteria and Guidelines*, 108; cyclists make left turns: Robert Sommer and Dale F. Lott, Behavioral Evaluation of a Bikeway System," in *Proceedings of the Northwestern Undergraduate Conference on Environmental Behavior* (Amherst: Institute for Man and the Environment, 1974), 12–17.

28. Ralph B. Hirsch, *Facilities and Services Needed to Support Bicycle Commuting into Center City Philadelphia* (Philadelphia: Philadelphia Bicycle Coalition/Environmental Protection Agency, June 1973), 2, 13, 27.

29. The author is personally familiar with a situation where the alternative proposals for the extension of an existing elevated rail system in a large metropolitan area were studied about 120 times over 30 years before circumstances changed sufficiently to facilitate implementing one two-mile extension.

30. Bill Wilkinson, "Construction, Maintenance, and Enforcement on the George Washington Memorial Parkway Pathway," in *Bicycles USA: Proceedings, May 7–8, 1973* (Cambridge: USDOT, Transportation Systems Center, n. d. [1973]), 40–42.

31. The story of the 1973 Santa Barbara accident study comes from two sources: "Bicycle Forum Interviews Ken Cross," *Bicycle Forum* 2 (Fall 1978): 2–10; "How Friends and Colleagues Remember Ken," at the website of the Association of Pedestrian and Bicycle Professional (www.abpb.org), under "Ken Cross Research Scholarship."

32. "Bicycle Forum Interviews Ken Cross," 3; Ken Cross, "Bicycle/Motor Vehicle Accident Types," *Bike Ed 77: Conference Report May 4–6, 1977* (No Location [Washington, D.C.]: Lawrence Johnson & Assoc./CPSC/USDOT, 1977, Report No. CE 014–066.) Cross's presentation is on pages 44–59. Letter from Ralph Hirsch to Morgan Groves, November 12, 1975, http://john-s-allen.com/Biklg1965 /correspondence /1973/More_LAW_Correspondence.pdf.

33. Dean Hayward, "Hot Program from Hawaii," *Bicycling* 21, 9 (November/December 1980): 90–91, 106–07.

34. The following is taken from two sources: James L. Konski, "It's Up to You," *Bicycling* 9, 6 (June 1973): 20–23, a reprint of Konski's December 1972 MAUDEP address, and James L. Konski, "Anticipation and Control of Hazards," in *Bicycles USA: Proceedings, May 7–8, 1973* (Cambridge: USDOT, Transportation Systems Center, n. d. [1973]): 26–28.

35. Eric Hirst, "Bicycles, Cars and Energy," *Transportation Quarterly* 28, 3 (October 1974): 573–84; Eric Hirst, *Energy Use for Bicycling* (Oak Ridge, TN: Oak Ridge National Laboratory, February 1974, Report No. ORNL-NSF-EP-65). Commuting times and distances: Anthony Downs, *Stuck in Traffic: Coping With Peak Hour Traffic* (Washington, D.C.: Brookings Institution, 1992), 17–20. These are 1982 data.

36. Harold Munn, "Bicycles and Traffic," *Transportation Engineering Journal* 101, TE4 (November 1975): 753–62; active with Los Angeles Wheelmen: "Bike Lanes" [letter of Hal Munn], *Bicycle Forum* 35 (January 1994): 2–3.

37. Thus, Forester's activities at the time were being financially supported by the League of American Wheelmen and the BIA through CABO. CABO history and findings: Alan Wachtel, "A

History of CABO," *Bicycle USA* (December 1980): 12–14. History of SCR-47: Richard Rogers, *SCR 47 Statewide Bicycle Committee: Final Report, February 10, 1975* (Sacramento: CalTrans, 1975), 3; Darryl Scrabak, "Bike Law: Trend Setting Report on Bike Law Emerges in California," *Bicycling* 16, 6 (June 1975): 72–75; Darryl Scrabak, "NCUTLO Spells Power," *Bicycling* 16, 12 (December 1975): 55–59.

38. Opinion of the Florida Attorney General AGO 84–10 (January 26, 1984).

39. Harold Michael, *et al.*, *Report of the Panel on Bicycle Laws and Supplementary Agenda for the Subcommittee on Operations, January 27, 1974* (Washington, D.C.: NCULTO, 1974); Scrabak, "NCUTLO Spells Power," 55–56. Truckload of materials: author's interview with Morgan Groves, November 12, 2007.

40. Memo from Marion Embrick to the Oregon Committee of the Judiciary, April 1974, Re: Comparison of Uniform Vehicle Code and Oregon Law, 5–6.

41. Michael, *et al.*, Report of the Panel on Bicycle Laws and Supplementary Agenda, 1–10.

42. Ibid., 19.

43. Ibid., 21.

44. Scrabak, "NCUTLO Spells Power," 55–56; Nina Dougherty Rowe, "Cyclists' Rights to the Road: Improving but Still Poor," *Bicycling* 2, 3 (April 1981): 24–26.

45. Memo from Deputy Attorney General Frank A. Iwama to Richard Rogers, CalTrans, January 21, 1975 (Attorney General's Opinion No. CV 74/224 IL) (Attached as "Appendix C" to Rogers, *et al.*, *SCR 47 Statewide Bicycle Committee Final Report*).

46. Readers shouldn't be shocked at this type of legal clash; it happens all the time. There is even a specialty area within legal studies, "conflict of laws," to study such contradictions and figure out how to systematically resolve them.

47. Memo from Iwama to Rogers, January 21, 1975, in Rogers, *et al.*, *SCR 47 Statewide Bicycle Committee Final Report.*

48. Rogers, *SCR 47 Statewide Bicycle Committee Final Report*; Wachtel, "A History of Cabo," 13. The 1969 version of the UVC gave local governments the authority to enact local regulations through the *Model Traffic Ordinance* in subsection 15–1202(a)(8), but specified a complete set of its own regulations in subsection 11–1201 *et. seq.*

49. Morgan Groves, "Good News from the NCUTLO," *Bicycling* 16, 1 (January 1975): 6–7; Skrabak, "NCUTLO Spells Power," 58–59; Rowe, "Cyclists' Rights to the Road," 24, 26; "Update" [letter of Ralph B. Hirsch], *Bicycling* 22, 8 (September/October 1981): 40.

50. Wachtel, "A History of CABO," 14.

Chapter 4

1. Blake Gumprect, *The American College Town* (Amherst: University of Massachusetts Press, 2008), 144–54; Theodore J. Buehler, *Fifty Years of Bicycle Policy in Davis, CA* (Davis: Institute for Transportation Studies, June 2007), 20–21.

2. Robert Sommer, "Bikeway Research at the University of California-Davis in the 1960s," in *Cycle History 16: Proceedings of the 16th Annual Cycle History Conference, Davis*, ed. Andrew Ritchie (San Francisco; Van der Plas Publications, 2005), 47–51; author's interview with Donna Lott, November 19, 2007; Buehler, *Fifty Years of Bicycle Policy in Davis, California*, 26.

3. Gumprect, *The American College Town*, 146–148. Theodore J. Buehler and Susan Handy, *Fifty Years of Bicycle Policy in Davis, California*; *Transportation Research Record* 2074 (2008), 52–57. Gumprect is skeptical of the "political skirmish" argument; Buehler and Handy subscribe to it.

4. Sommer, "Bikeway Research at the University of California-Davis," 48–49; Interview with Donna Lott.

5. Sommer, "Bikeway Research at the University of California-Davis in the 1960s," 47.

6. Robert Sommer and Dale F. Lott, "The Bicycle Era: Bikeways in Action, The Davis Experience," 117 *Congressional Record* (April 19, 1971), H10830–833; David Takemoto-Weerts, "Evolution of a Cyclist-Friendly Community," in *Cycle History 16: Proceedings of the 16th Annual Cycle History Conference, Davis*, ed. Andrew Ritchie (San Francisco: Van der Plas Publications, 2005), 11–15; Buehler and Handy, *Fifty Years of Bicycle Policy in Davis, California*, 53–56.

7. Robert Sommer and Dale F. Lott, "Behavioral Evaluation of a Bikeway System," in *Proceedings of the Northeastern Undergraduate Conference on Environmental Behavior* (Amherst: Institute for Man and the Environment, 1974), 12–17; Deleuw, Cather and Co., *City of Davis/University of California Bicycle Circulation and Safety Study* (San Francisco: Deleuw, Cather and Co., August 1972), 27.

8. Sommer and Lott, "Bikeways in Action," H10830; Sommer and Lott, "Behavioral Evaluation of a Bikeway System," 15–17; Author's interview with Ted T. Noguchi, December 12, 2011; Takemoto-Weerts, "Evolution of a Cyclist-Friendly Community," 13.

9. Sommer and Lott, "Bikeways in Action," H10830; Gary Fisher, *et al.*, *Bikeway Planning Criteria and Guidelines* (Los Angeles: UCLA-ITTE, 1972).

10. Sommer, "Bikeway Research at the University of California-Davis," 48. Sommer is quoting from a document Ramey wrote.

11. UCLA faculty member Dr. Gary Fischer is not the Gary Fischer of mountain-bike fame.

12. Robert Sommer, "Point of View: Bikeways, More Research, Less Rhetoric," *Bicycling* 14, 11 (November 1973): 48.

13. John Forester, "Toy Bicycle Mentality in Government," *Bicycling* 14, 9 (September 1973): 52–54; Sommer, "Bikeways, More Research, Less Rhetoric," 48. Lott quote: Jeff Mapes, 125. Lott is referring to John Forester, who frequently mentions his participation in the L.A. Double Century (200 miles) during the late 1960s and early 1970s.

14. Tully Hendricks, "Opening Remarks: Question and Answer Session," ThinkBike Workshop, Miami, Florida, July 12, 2011.

15. Buehler and Handy, *Fifty Years of Bicycle Policy in Davis, California*, 55.

16. Dan Smith, *Bikeways: The State of the Art* (Washington, D.C.: DeLeuw, Cather/FHWA, 1974), 18.

17. Dan Smith, *Safety and Locational Criteria for Bikeways, User Manual*, Vol. 2 (Washington, D.C.: FHWA, 1976), 14.

18. Takemoto-Weerts, "Evolution of a Cyclist-Friendly Community," 12.

19. Buehler and Handy, *Fifty Years of Bicycle Policy in Davis, California*, 56.

20. Robert H. Wortman, "Bikeway Hazards" in *Proceedings of the Fourth National Seminar on the Planning Design and Implementation of Bicycle and Pedestrian Facilities, December 4–6, 1975, New Orleans* (New York: ASCE, 1975), 320–25.

21. "Basically the research ended": Buehler, *Fifty Years of Bicycle Policy in Davis, California*, 67. "Because so little research": Sommer, "Bikeway Research at the University of California-Davis," 48.

22. "Only cyclists know": John Forester, "Cycling to Overcome the Cyclist Inferiority Complex: Key Element in Training for Cycling Transportation Engineering," in *Proceedings of the Seminar/Workshop on Planning, Design and Implementation of Bicycles and Pedestrian Facilities, Palo Alto, July 6–8, 1977* (Berkeley: University of California/MAUDEP, 1978), 154–166, quote on 164.

23. For an excellent example of the clash between the "black woolies" and the "white lab coats" (with the latter clearly prevailing), see Dale Lott, Timothy Tardiff, and Donna Lott, "Evaluation by Experienced Riders of a New Bicycle Lane in an Established Bikeway System," John Forester, "Discussion," and Lott, Tardiff, and Lott, "Authors' Closure," all *Transportation Research Record* 683 (1978), 40–52.

24. BIA funding: Memo from H. M. Huffman and F. C. Smith to American Bicycle Manufacturers, n. d. [c. late 1972], http://john-s-allen.com/Biklg1965-/correspondence/1973/Board_correspondence.pdf. Anti-Bikeway: Anon. [Ken Kolsbun], "Point of View: An Anti-Bikeways Movement," *Bicycling* 15, 6 (June 1974): 77–79.

25. John Finley Scott, "The Cycling Community: Who Leads, Who Follows, A Reply to Bob Sommer," *Bicycling* 18, 11 (November 1977): 12, 68–69; John Finley Scott, "The City of Bicycles: Can the Davis Model Work Elsewhere?" *California Bicyclist* (October 1984): n.p. Accident rates of men and women: Jerrold A. Kaplan, *Characteristics of the Regular Adult Bicycle User* (M.S. Thesis, University of Maryland, 1975), 62. In 1997, William A. Moritz duplicated Kaplan's survey as closely as possible and got the same results: William Mortitz, "Survey of North American Bicycle Commuters: Design and Aggregate Results," *Transportation Research Record 1578* (Washington, D.C.: Transportation Research Board, 1997), 91–101.

26. John Finley Scott, "The American College Sorority: Its Role in Class and Ethic Endogamy," *American Sociology Review* 30, 4 (August 1965): 514–27, quote on 522.

27. Interview with anonymous UC-Davis research associate of the 1970s, who later returned as an employee. Scott was murdered in 2006 by an itinerant landscaper living temporarily at his rural home outside Davis. His body was not recovered for over two years, long after his killer had been captured and convicted.

28. Robert Sommer, "Building Bridges Between Communities of Cyclists," *Bicycling* 18, 8 (August 1977): 70–72.

29. Interview with Donna Lott, November 2007.

30. Weintraub quote: Mapes, 130; Buehler and Handy, *Fifty Years of Bicycle Policy in Davis, California*, 57. Bustos quote on 76.

31. Susan Handy, Eva Heinen, and Kevin J. Krizek, "Cycling in Small Cities," in *City Cycling*, ed. John Pucher and Ralph Buehler (Cambridge: MIT Press, 2012), 257–86; Mapes, 131. As near as can be determined from the GO Boulder numbers, Boulder City has 97,000 residents, not counting 30,000 students (who are census residents of their parents' home towns) and 37,500 workers who commute each day from out of town. Out of 97,000 residents, the workforce comprises about 53,500, so 11,200 commute by bicycle. It's possible that the 21 percent figure (11,200) was reached by rolling back in the proportion of the 30,000 students who cycle. More recently, GO Boulder has claimed a more modest 9.9 percent mode share: "Boulder," *American Bicyclist—2010 Bicycle Friendly America Issue* (2010): 9.

32. Carl Abbott and Joy Margheim, "Imaging Portland's Urban Growth Boundary," *Journal of the American Planning Association* 74, 2 (Spring 2008): 196–208.

33. Yizhao Yang, "A Tale of Two Cities: Physical Form and Neighborhood Satisfaction in Metropolitan Portland and Charlotte," *Journal of the American Planning Association* 74, 3 (Summer 2008): 307–23.

34. Donald Appleyard, *Livable Streets* (Berkeley: University of California Press, 1981).

35. Charles M. Tiebout, "A Pure Theory of Local Expenditures," *The Journal of Political Economy* 64, 5 (October 1956): 416–24.

36. Jane Duckwall, "Former Oregonian Likes That We Have Fewer Bikes," *Charlotte Observer* (February 19, 2006).

37. Abbott and Margheim, "Imaging Portland's Urban Growth Boundary," 206.

38. Mapes, 150.

39. Mapes, Chapter 5; Hal Bernton, "State Senate Deadlock Kills Columbia Crossing," *Seattle Times* (July 1, 2013).

40. Jeff Manning, "Traffic Estimates on Columbia River Crossing Further Muddy the Financial Picture," *Oregonian* (July 19, 2011); Joseph Rose, "Most Portland, Vancouver Drivers Would Dodge Columbia River Crossing's Interstate 5 Toll, Poll Finds," *Oregonian* (November 30, 2012).

41. Angie Cradock, *et al.*, "Factors Associated with Federal Transportation Funding for Local Pedestrian and Bicycle Programming and Facilities," *Journal of Public Health Policy* 30 (2009): S38–S72. Through the calendar year of 2010, $8.17 billion had been obligated and $7.1 billion had actually been spent on 24,811 projects. Of this, 62.1 percent was obligated for bike-ped projects of various kinds and 15.5 percent was obligated for landscaping and the acquisition of scenic corridors. *Transportation Enhancements: Summary of Nationwide Spending as of FY 2008* (Washington, D.C.: National Transportation Enhancements Clearinghouse, May 2010), 2–4.

42. Joshua Miller, *Results of 2010–11 Campus Travel Survey* (Davis: UC-Davis Institute of Transportation Studies, 2011, Report No. UCD-ITS-RR-11–08), Tables 2, 12, 13, 14, 15, 25.

43. Commuting data and Sommer/Takemoto-Wertz editorials: Buehler and Handy, *Fifty Years of Bicycle Policy in Davis, California*, 57. Proposed Fifth Street modifications: Gumprecht, The American College Town, 181–88. Takemoto-Weerts quote: Takemoto Weerts, "Evolution of Cyclist Friendly Community," 14.

Chapter 5

1. John Forester, "Bikelane Countermeasures: Preserving Cyclists' Rights and Safety in a Motor-Minded World," in *Proceedings of the Seminar on Planning, Design and Implementation of Bicycle/ Pedestrian Facilities, San Diego, December 1974* (New York, ASCE, 1975), 33–41.

2. Lee Foster, "Meek Little Creatures? The Political Phenomenon of the Menlo Park Bicycle Festival," *Bicycling* 13, 1 (January 1972): 14–15; Clifford Franz, "Organized Bicycling and Urban Bikeways," in *Proceedings of the Pedestrian/Bicycle Planning and Design Seminar, San Francisco, December 13–15, 1972* (Berkeley: ITTE, 1973), 237–38.

3. Author's interview with Ted T. Noguchi, December 12, 2011; "The ABC's of Creating a Bike Route System," *Bicycling* 13, 7 (July 1972): 18–19.

4. Michael D. Everett, "The Bikeway Controversy," in *Proceedings of the Seminar/Workshop on Planning, Design and Implementation of Bicycle and Pedestrian Facilities, Chicago, July 19–21* (New York: MAUDEP, n. d. [1978]), 42–49.

5. Ordinance 2652, Section 8: "Any person riding or operating a bicycle upon any street where a bicycle lane or path appropriate to his direction of travel is established and officially designated shall ride or operate such bicycle only in such bicycle lane or path or on the sidewalk where otherwise allowed by the Palo Alto Municipal Code..."

6. Interview with Ted Noguchi; Palo Alto Resolution 4441 (April 19, 1971); Palo Alto Ordinance 2652 (April 24, 1972); repealed by Palo Alto Ordinance 2771 (February 11, 1974).

7. Jack Murphy, "Public View of Bicycle Facilities," in *Proceedings of the Pedestrian/Bicycle Planning and Design Seminar, San Francisco, December 13–15, 1972* (Berkeley: ITTE, 1973): 234–36.

8. "Transcript of Testimony, Mr. John Forester, October 1, 1993," *Johnson v. Derby Cycle Co., et al.* Superior Court of New Jersey, ESX-L-16063–89, at 11. Forester was apparently cited in January or February 1973 for not obeying the sidepath law (see flyer entitled "Cyclists for Reopening Our Streets," dated February 6, 1973, http://john-s-allen.com/Biklg1965-/correspondence/1973/Board_correspondence.pdf, but it may have been for making an illegal turn: John Forester, "What about Bikeways?" *Bike World* 2, 2 (February 1973): 36–37.

9. Wilbur Smith and Associates, *Palo Alto Bicycle Transportation Plan* (May 2003): 3.

10. Forester article: "What about Bikeways?" 36–37. An arcane kind of guy: author's interview with Morgan Groves, November 12, 2007. Can't argue without being rude: letter from C. S. Forester to Francis Perkins, April 22, 1949, C. S. Forester Papers, Humanities Research Center, University of Texas, Austin. Being vague: "Transcript of Testimony, Mr. John Forester, October 1, 1993," 11, 13, 16. Reconnaissance run: letter from John Forester to Morgan Groves, http://john-s-allen.com/Biklg1965-/correspondence/1973/Board_correspondence.pdf.

11. Used to call at night: author's interview with Ted Noguchi; practically everybody: John Forester, *Effective Cycling* (Cambridge, MIT Press, 1993), xi.

12. John Forester, *Novelist & Storyteller: The Life of C. S. Forester* (Lemon Grove, CA: the author, 2000): II, 579, 687–90.

13. Forester, "Planning for Cyclists as They See Themselves Instead of as Motorists See Them," 323–24.

14. Some of the lanes had apparently been replaced with boulevards as early as the fall of 1973: Letter from John Forester to Clifford Franz, October 3, 1973, http://john-s-allen.com/Biklg1965-/correspondence/1973/ More_LAW_Correspondence.pdf.

15. Forester objected to bicycles as vehicles: John Forester, "How to Gain Access Without Using Ketchup," *Bicycling* 22, 9 (November/December 1981): 44–45; Carl Bianchi and John Schubert, "Controversy in Great Potato: Idaho's New Rolling Stop Law," *Bicycling* 24, 3 (March 1980): 192, 195; "Report of Legislative Committee," *Minutes of Meeting of the Board of Directors of the League of American Wheelman, Baltimore, December 10–11, 1983*, http://john-s-allen.com/Biklg1965-/board._meetings/1983-12%20 Board%20 meeting/B.pdf. The ultimate solution the NCUTLO reached was simply to limit the applicability of many sections, such as tailgating and street racing, to "motor vehicles." Hence, a bicycle cannot illegally tailgate another bicycle under the UVC. Whether a bicycle can illegally tailgate a motor vehicle under the UVC language has been subject to disparate court interpretations in several states.

16. Forester, "How to Gain Access Without Using Ketchup," 44–45; John Forester, "Bicycling Transportation and the Problem of Evil" (unpublished manuscript, October 22, 2007), www.johnforester.com.

17. To be precise, a violator would have available in court the affirmative defense of irrational or unreasonable application of the ordinance.

18. Bianchi and Schubert, "Controversy in Great Potato: Idaho's New Rolling Stop Law," 192, 195. Author's interview with Morgan Groves, November 12, 2007; John S. Allen's transcript of his interview with Morgan Groves, October 31, 2009.

19. Letter from John Forester to Morgan Groves, October 31, 1973, http://john-s-allen.com/ Biklg1965-/correspondence/1973/More_LAW_Correspondence.pdf.

20. *Hodel v. Indiana*, 452 U.S. 314 (1981).

21. United States v. Caroline Products Co., 304 U.S. 144, 158 (1938).

22. FCC v. Beach Communications, Inc., 508 U.S. 307, 315 (1993).

23. John Forester, *Effective Cycling* (Cambridge: MIT Press, 7th ed. 2012): 691–94; Bianchi and Schubert, "Controversy in the Great Potato," 195.

24. *Bicycle Standard BMA/6: Safety Standards for Regular Bicycles* (New York: BMA, 1970; revised edition 1972; 2nd revised edition 1974).

25. *National Commission on Product Safety, Final Report to the President, Volume 1* (Washington, D.C.: National Commission on Product Safety, 1970), 18–20. Ross D. Petty, "The Consumer Product Safety Commission's Promulgation of a Bicycle Safety Standard, *Journal of Product Liability* 10 (1987): 25–50; Ross D. Petty, "The Impact of the Sport of Bicycle Riding on Safety Law," *American Business Law Journal* 35, 2 (Winter 1998): 185–224; Fred DeLong, "New Bicycle Safety and Performance Standards," *Bicycling* 6, 12 (December 1970): 26–27.

26. Food and Drug Administration, *Staff Analysis of Bicycle Accidents and Injuries* (Washington, D.C.: Food and Drug Administration, 1972, NTIS Report No. PB-207–665).

27. FDA banning order: 38 Federal Register 12300–313 (May 10, 1973). Too much timidity: Teresa M. Schwartz, "The Consumer Product Safety Commission: A Flawed Product of the Consumer Decade," *George Washington Law Review* 51 (1982): 32–95, on 38. New legislation more stringent than old: *Forester et al. v. Consumer Product Safety Commission*, 559 F.2d 774, 11n, 22n (D.C. Cir. 1977).

28. April Stockard and Don Stockard, "Bike Law: Our Rights and Reasons," *Bicycling* 9, 7 (July 1973): 41–42.

29. "Comments and Recommendations of the Schwinn Bicycle Company," *Consumer Product Safety Act Amendments: Hearings on H.R. 5361 and H.R. 6107*, 94th Cong. (Washington, D.C.: Government Printing Office, 1994, No. 94–30), 36–37.

30. 39 Federal Register 26100 (July 16, 1974).

31. "Statement of Thomas F. Shannon, Bicycle Manufacturers Association," *Consumer Product Safety Commission Oversight: Hearings on S. 644 and S. 1000*, 94th Cong. 145–49, (Washington, D.C.: Government Printing Office, 1975, serial no. 94–12), 146.

32. Fred DeLong, "International Bicycle Standards: An Update," *Bicycling* 16, 1 (January 1975): 62–65; interview with Jay Townley, May 23, 2009.

33. "Statement of Thomas F. Shannon," Consumer Product Safety Commission Oversight: Hearings on S. 644 and S. 1000, 146–48.

34. Norman Clarke, "There Outta be a Law," in *Proceedings of the Seminar on Bicycle/Pedestrian Planning and Design, December 12–14, 1974* [sic, s.b. 1973] (New York: ASCE, 1974), 550–51.

35. "Comments and Recommendations of the Schwinn Bicycle Company," *Product Safety Act*

Amendments: Hearings on H.R. 5361 and H.R. 6107, 26; "A Quick Digest of Laws to Watch," *Bicycling* 15, 4 (April 1974): 8.

36. "Statement of Jay Townley," Consumer Product Safety Commission Oversight: Hearings on S. 644 and S. 1000, 128.

37. Forester, "What about Bikeways?" 36–37; Jim Konski, "It's Up to You," *Bicycling* 9, 6 (June 1973) 20–23; Fred DeLong, "The Bicycle's Place on the Road: Another Viewpoint," *Bicycling* 9, 7 (July 1973): 20, "Hooray for Fred DeLong" (multiple letters to the editor), *Bicycling* 14, 9 (September 1973): 6, 61.

38. John Forester, "Toy Bike Syndrome," *Bike World* 2, 5, (October 1973): 24–26. A shorter, heavily edited version was published as John Forester, "Point of View: The Toy Bike Mentality in Government," *Bicycling* 14, 9 (September 1973): 52–53.

39. Townley quote: author's interview with Jay Townley; Taylor quote: author's interview with Dorris Taylor, November 5, 2007; Forester quote: John Forester, "Planning for Cyclists as They See Themselves Instead of as Motorists See Them," 315–27; Groves quote: letter from Morgan Groves to John Forester, November 20, 1973; http://john-s-allen.com/Biklg1965-/correspondence/1973/Board_correspondence.pdf; "it is no use": The F.D.A. Versus You, *Bike World* 2, 5 (October 1973): 3.

40. "What they plan to enforce": letter from William Hoffman to Morgan Groves, August 1, 1973, http://john-s-allen.com/Biklg1965-/correspondence/1973/Board_correspondence.pdf. Morgan Groves believed: interview with Morgan Groves; letter from Morgan Groves to Carroll Quimby, August 2, 1973, letter from Morgan Groves to John Forester, November 6, 1973, both http://john-s-allen.com/Biklg1965-/correspondence/1973/Board_correspondence.pdf. Nina Cornell, Roger Noll, and Barry Weingast, "Safety Regulation," in *Setting National Priorities: the Next Ten Years*, ed. Henry Owen and Charles L. Schultze (Washington, D.C.: Brookings Institution, 1976), 457–508.

41. Dick Teresi, *The Popular Mechanics Book of Bike and Bicycling* (New York: Hearst Corp., 1975), 31.

42. 38 Federal Register 12300 (May 10, 1973); 41 Federal Register 4144 (January 28, 1976); *Bicycle Standard BMA/6* (1972 version): section 5.1; letter from Leon Taylor to Richard Simpson, CPSC, copy to Morgan Groves, November 28, 1973, http://john-s-allen.com/Biklg1965-/correspondence/1973/ Board_correspondence.pdf. Admittedly, some deep discounters continued to insist on selling "in the box" with assembly as an extra-cost option; product liability litigation largely drove them to standardized pre-sale assembly by the 1980s.

43. Letter from Norman Clarke to the author, February 3, 1998. BMA/6 Safety Standard for Regular Bicycles: section 7.2.1; Teresi, *The Popular Mechanics Book of Bike and Bicycling*: 139.

44. Petty, "The Consumer Product Safety Commission's Promulgation of a Bicycle Safety Standard," 37; email from Ross Petty to the author, September 17, 2007; Fred DeLong, "Editor's Notes: CPSC Standards," *Bicycling* 3, 4 (April 1974): 6. John Forester privately acknowledged the CPSC engineers' concerns about poorly made Taiwanese bicycles: letter from John Forester to "Cliff," [Clifford Franz], with copy to Morgan Groves, October 3, 1973, http://john-s-allen.com/Biklg1965-/correspondence/1973/Board_correspondence.pdf.

45. "Letter from the Chambre Syndicale du Cycle, and the Syndicate des Fabricants d'Equipments et de Pieces Pour Cycle et Motocycles," and "letter from William H. Lucking, attorney for Raleigh of America," *Consumer Product Safety Act Amendments: Hearings on H.R. 5361 and H.R. 6107*, 266–69.

46. Letter from Morgan Groves to John Forester, November 20, 1973, http://john-s-allen.com/Biklg1965-/correspondence/1973/Board_correspondence.pdf; Forester, "Planning for Cyclists as They See Themselves Instead of as Motorists See Them," 324.

47. Letter from Morgan Groves to Carroll Quimby, August 2, 1973; letter from Morgan Groves to John Forester, November 6, 1973, both http://john-s-allen.com/Biklg1965-/correspondence/1973/Board_correspondence.pdf.

48. Letter from Morgan Groves, to John Forester, November 6, 1973, http://john-s-allen.com/Biklg1965-/correspondence/1973/Board_correspondence.pdf.

49. Memo from Morgan Groves to Carroll Quimby, Robert Reid and Phil Menninger, L.A.W. executive committee, August 7, 1974; letter from Morgan Groves to John Forester, November 6, 1973, both http://john-s-allen.com/Biklg1965-/correspondence/1973/Board_correspondence.pdf. Letter from John Forester to Morgan Groves, November 14, 1973, http://john-s-allen.com/Biklg1965-/correspondence/1973/ More_LAW_Correspondence.pdf.

50. Letter from Morgan Groves to John Forester, November 6, 1973; letter from Morgan Groves to John Forester, November 20, 1973, both http://john-s-allen.com/Biklg1965-/correspondence/1973/ Board_correspondence.pdf. Letter from John Forester to Morgan Groves, November 14, 1973, http://john-s-allen.com/Biklg1965 /correspondence/1973/More_LAW_Correspondence.pdf.

51. Final version of rules: 39 *Federal Register* 26100–111 (July 16, 1974); Darryl Skrabak, "Bike

Law: The CPSC Regulations Go to Court," *Bike World* 17, 4 (April 1976): 23, 56–61. A regular bike would pass: DeLong, "Editor's Notes: CPSC Standards," 6.

52. "Testimony of Richard O. Simpson," Consumer Product Safety Act Amendments: Hearings on H.R. 5361 and H.R. 6107, 181.

53. Ross Petty, "Regulation vs. the Market: The Case of Bicycle Safety (Part I)," *Risk* 2 (1991): 77–87 (1991); Ross Petty, "Regulation vs. the Market: The Case of Bicycle Safety (Part II)," *Risk* 2 (1991): 93–120.

54. "Testimony of Richard O. Simpson," Product Safety Act Amendments: Hearings on H.R. 5361 and H.R. 6107, 181.

55. CPSC rejected application: 39 *Federal Register* 31943–944 (September 3, 1974); may have misread: *Forester*, 559 F.2d 774, 22n.

56. Postponed indefinitely: 39 *Federal Register* 43436 (December 16, 1974); interview with Jay Townley.

57. "The CPSC obtained the services": Forester, *Bicycle Transportation* (Cambridge: MIT Press, 1983), 366. "A well-known cyclist with a long history" and "Fred should have told": Forester, *Effective Cycling* (1993): 523.

58. DeLong quotes: Beinhorn, "*Bike World* Interview: Fred Delong," 8, Townley quote: interview with Jay Townley.

59. Already decided to sue: letter from John Forester to "Cliff," [Clifford Franz], October 3, 1973, http://john-s-allen.com/Biklg1965-/correspondence/1973/Board_correspondence.pdf; elicit useful material: John Forester, "Logic Lost in CPSC Ruling," *Bike World* 5, 7 (July 1976): 7.

60. *Forester v. CPSC*, 559 F.2d 774, at 775; "Statement of Jay Townley and John R. F. Baer," Consumer Product Safety Commission Oversight: Hearings on S. 644 and S. 1000, 132–33.

61. Skrabak, "CPSC Regulations Go to Court," 59; interview with Jay Townley.

62. Paul Hill, "Bicycle Laws and Regulations," *Bike World* 5, 2 (February 1976): 28–31.

63. Probably to try to recover attorney's fees and costs.

64. Believed CPSC would be limited to children's bicycles: "Agenda for NUTCLO Subcommittee on Operations Meeting, 22–24 February 1978," as attached to CPSC Advisory Opinion No. 269 (1978). Initially argued in favor of headlights: *Forester v. CPSC*, 559 F.2d, 774, 797.

65. Forester quote: Forester, "What About Bikeways?" 36; Taylor quote: interview with Dorris Taylor; headlamps dropped from final brief: *Forester v. CPSC*, 559 F.2d 774, 797.

66. *Forester v. CPSC*, 559 F.2d 774, on 789–99.

67. Interview with Jay Townley.

68. The keys to understanding these points are located in footnotes 11 and 22 of the *Forester* court opinion.

69. *Forester v. CPSC*, 559 F.2d 774, n. 11 and n. 22; *and see Hearings on H.R. 5361 and H.R. 6107, supra* note 67, on 180–82 (testimony of Richard O. Simpson).

70. *R. B. Jarts, Inc. v. Richardson*, 438 F.2d 846 (2nd Cir. 1971).

71. In the five years after the *Forester v. CPSC* decision, the so-called "body count" issue was cited in almost a hundred separate legal cases.

72. Interview with Jay Townley.

73. *Forester v. CPSC*, 559 F.2d, 774, 788.

74. "Deposition of Mr. John Forester," *Johnson v. Darby Cycle Co. et al.*, (Sup. Ct. New Jersey, Essex Co. ESX-L-16063–89, 1993), Vol. 2 of 3, 39–41.

75. Petty, "The Impact of the Sport of Bicycle Riding on Safety Law," 220–21; Petty, "Regulation vs. the Market: The Case of Bicycle Safety (Part I)," 82–84; interview with Jay Townley.

76. Darryl Skrabak, "Bike Law: Bicycle Advocates, Where they Stand Now," *Bicycling* 18, 2 (February 1977): 50–51.

77. Forester, "Toy Bike Syndrome," 26. Forester admirers like to boast that their basic philosophy is "same road, same rights." Based on their frequently disingenuous interpretations of "same," I would propose that "we're better off neglected" far better captures both the emotional sprit and intellectual philosophy of Effective Cycling.

78. Richard Rogers, ed., *SCR 47 Statewide Bicycle Committee Final Report: February 10, 1975* (Sacramento: California Dept. of Transportation, 1975); letter from Ralph Hirsch, Bicycle and Pedestrian Transportation Research Center, to Morgan Groves, League of American Wheelmen, November 12, 1975, http://john-s-allen.com/Biklg1965-/correspondence/1973/More_LAW_Correspondence.pdf; Alan Wachtel, "A History of CABO," *Bicycle USA* (December 1980): 12–14.

79. John Forester, "Teaching the Proper Use of Bicycle Facilities," in *Proceedings of the Fourth National Seminar on Planning Design and Implementation of Bicycle and Pedestrian Facilities* (New York: ASCE, 1975), 533–44; John Forester, Effective Cycling (1975).

80. John Forester, "Letter to the Editor," *Transportation Law Journal* 39, 1 (Fall 2011): 31–51.

81. Gary Toth and Brendan Crain interview notes of Morgan Groves interview by John S. Allen, October 31, 2009. Gary Toth, Dan Burden, Andy Clarke, and Charlie Gandy: www.pps.org/blog/after-30-years-of-bikeped-advocacy-how-far-have-we-come/.

82. James C. McCullagh, "The Politics of Cycling Space," *Bicycling* 19, 11 (November 1978): 10–13.

83. Interview with Jay Townley.

84. Email from John S. Allen to the author, January, 27, 2012.

85. Robert Hurst, *The Art of Cycling* (Guilford, MT: FalconGuides, 2007 [2004]), xv.

86. John Forester, "Traffic Cyclists as Performance Artists: A Review of the Art of Cycling," 9–10, http://www.johnforester.com/articles/.

87. David G. Bromley, "Dramatic Dénouements," in *Cults, Religion and Violence*, ed. David G. Bromley and J. Gordon Melton (Cambridge, UK: Cambridge University Press, 2002), 1–10. John Forester, "Bicycling, Transportation and the Problem of Evil" (an address to the Preserving the American Dream Conference, October 2007), 8, http://www.johnforester.com/articles/.

88. Fred Delong, "Bicycle Proficiency: Where on the Road?" *Bicycling* 13, 11 (November 1972): 36; James Konski, "Its Up to You," *Bicycling* 9, 6 (June 1973): 20–23; Bill Wilkinson, "Construction, Maintenance, and Enforcement on the George Washington Memorial Parkway Pathway" in *Bicycles USA: Proceedings, May 7–8, 1973* (Cambridge, MA: USDOT, Transportation Systems Center, n. d. [1973]), 40–42.

89. Ken Kolsbun, "Point of View: An Anti-Bikeway Movement," *Bicycling* 15, 6 (June 1974): 78–79.

90. Harold Munn, "Bicycles and Traffic," *Transportation Engineering Journal* 101:TE4 (November 1975): 753–62.

91. Lawrence B. Walsh, "Factors in Bikeway Design," in Proceedings of the Seminar on Planning, Design and Implementation of Bicycle/Pedestrian Facilities, San Diego, December 1974 (New York: ASCE, 1975), 308–11.

92. Robert M. Shanteau, "Bicycle Bottlenecks: Bicycle Planning from a Bicyclist's Point of View" in *Proceedings of the Seminar on Planning, Design and Implementation of Bicycle/Pedestrian Facilities, San Diego, December 1974* (New York: ASCE, 1975), 240–54.

93. Dead issue by late 1974: Fred DeLong, "Editor's Notes: CPSC Standards," *Bicycling* 15, 4 (April 1974): 6; Fred DeLong, "Bucking the Authorities," *Bicycling* 15, 11 (November 1974): 42–43; Paul Hill, "Bicycle Laws and Regulations," *Bike World* (February 1976): 28–31.

94. Darryl Skrabak, "Bicycle Activists: Where They Stand Now," *Bicycling* 18, 2 (February 1977): 50–51.

95. Daniel T. Smith, "Experienced Bicyclists and the Bikeway Controversy," in *Proceedings of the Seminar on Planning, Design and Implementation of Bicycle/Pedestrian Facilities, San Diego, [Dec. 4–6] 1974* (Berkeley: ITTE, 1975), 434–43.

96. Emails from John Williams to the author, December 12 and 13, 2011.

97. John Williams, "San Luis Obispo," in *Bikeway Design Atlas: Urban Bikeway Design Competition* (Cambridge, MA: Urban Bikeway Design Collaborative, January 1975), 26–52, quote on 36.

98. Ibid., 35.

99. Emails from John Williams to the author, December 12 and 13, 2011.

100. UBDC awards at MAUDEP: Wes Lum, "1974 Urban Bikeway Design Competition Awards," in *Proceedings of the Seminar on Planning, Design and Implementation of Bicycle/Pedestrian Facilities, San Diego [Dec. 4–6] 1974* (Berkeley: ITTE, 1975): 418–23; Nina Dougherty Rowe, "Three Promising Bicycle Organizations," *Bicycling* 19, 2 (February 1978): 58–60. The first published use of the phrase "Effective Cycling" I have been able to find is: Forester, "Bikelane Countermeasures: Preserving Cyclists' Rights and Safety in a Motor-Minded World," 41. It was tacked on at the end of a paper presented at a December 1974 conference, undefined, as a slogan, suggesting that it was of very recent origin.

101. Williams, "San Luis Obispo," 35. Proceeds from a novel premise: Darryl Skrabak, "Bike Law: The Bikeway Backlash," *Bicycling* 16, 9 (September 1975): 25–28.

102. Williams, "San Luis Obispo," 36.

103. In subsequent years, Williams moderated his views and became far more inclusionary in his thinking. He attributes this change primarily to his having worked with Ellen Fletcher and Ted Noguchi, who together converted the first flawed Palo Alto bikeway system into its highly refined "bicycle boulevard" system. However, he continued to be a vocal opponent of badly designed or badly built facilities installed for their own sake: email from John Williams to the author, December 13, 2011.

Chapter 6

1. A sampling of current and soon-to-be bicycle planning notables included Dan Burden, Bruce Burgess, Phil Burke, Ken Cross, Elizabeth Drake, John Fegan, John Forester, Gihon Jordon, Phyllis Harmon, Eileen Kadesh, Ed Kearney, Keith Kingbay, Don LaFond, Katie Moran, Tom Pendleton, Nina Dougherty Rowe, John Schubert, Bill Wilkinson, and Curtis Yates: *Bike Ed '77 A Conference Report, May 4–6, 1977*, Report CE014-066: Appendix 2. NGOs: Nina Dougherty Rowe, "Three Promising Bicycle Organizations," *Bicycling* 19, 2 (February 1978): 58–60.

2. Darryl Skrabak, "Bike Law: The Bikeway Backlash," *Bicycling* 16, 9 (September 1975): 25–28; Darryl Skrabak: "Bicycle Activists: Where they Stand Now," *Bicycling* 18, 2 (February 1977): 50–51.

3. Thomas H. May, "The Limited Future of Bicycling in the USA," in MAUDEP *Proceedings of the Seminar/Workshop on Planning, Design and*

Implementation of Bicycle and Pedestrian Facilities, Toronto, July 14–16, 1977 [sic, s.b. 1976], ed. Walter Craft (New York: MAUDEP, 1977), 392–405.

4. Larry Wuellner, "Safety—Bicycling's Cul-de-Sac?" in *MAUDEP Proceedings of the Seminar/Workshop on Planning, Design and Implementation of Bicycle and Pedestrian Facilities, Toronto, July 14–16, 1977 [sic, s.b. 1976]*, ed. Walter Craft (New York: MAUDEP, 1977), 505–11.

5. Michael D. Everett, "The Bikeway Controversy" and Ronald Thompson, "Introduction: Bikeway Issues," in *Proceedings of the Seminar/Workshop on Planning, Design and Implementation of Bicycle and Pedestrian Facilities, Chicago, July 19–21, 1978* (New York: MAUDEP, n. d. [1978]), 42–47 (Everett) and 202 (Thompson).

6. James E. Stacey, "Bridging the Gap Between Bikeway Planners and Bicyclists," in *Proceedings of the Seminar/Workshop on Planning, Design and Implementation of Bicycle and Pedestrian Facilities, Chicago, July 19–21 1978* (New York: MAUDEP, n. d. [1978]), 203–09.

7. Skrabak, "Bicycle Activists: Where They Stand Now," 50–51; Darryl Skrabak, "Rules are Being Made, Why Not be There?" *Bicycling* 18, 4 (April 1977): 80–81.

8. "How Friends and Colleagues Remember Ken Cross," at "Ken Cross Research Scholarship," www.http.//abpb.org. Wilkinson at USDOT: "Looking at People," *Bike World* 7, 6 (June 1977): 41.

9. "Bicycle Forum Interviews Ken Cross," *Bicycle Forum* 2 (Fall 1978): 2–10.

10. John Forester, *Effective Cycling* (Palo Alto: Custom Cycle Fitments, 1975): 4.6–1.

11. *Bike Ed '77: A Conference Report*, 69–70, 83; "jam packed": John Forester, *Bicycle Transportation* (Cambridge: MIT Press, 1983), 188; instructor and two assistants: John Forester, *Effective Cycling* (Cambridge: MIT Press, 1984), 305.

12. *Bike Ed '77: A Conference Report*, 89.

13. USER contract: Rowe, "Three Promising Bicycle Organizations," 59–60. Denver biking course: James C. McCullagh, "Coming of Age: There is More to Our New Look than Shiny New Clothes," *Bicycling* 22, 2 (March 1981): 6.

14. Judi Lawson Wallace, "Our Legacy to the Young—Teaching Them the Bike is Not a Toy," *Bicycling* 22, 6 (July 1981): 45, 47, 122–24.

15. "Bike-Ed America Proposal," appended to "A Proposal for Increased Involvement by the League of American Wheelmen in Bicycle Safety Instruction for Children," http://john-s-allen.com/Biklg1965-/board._meetings/1983-12%20Board%20meeting/B.pdf.

16. John Forester, "Teaching the Proper Use of Bicycle Facilities," in *Proceedings of the Fourth National Seminar on Planning, Design and Implementation of Bicycle and Pedestrian Facilities, New Orleans, [December 4–6] 1976* (New York: ASCE, 1975): 533–43, quotes on 540, 543–44.

17. Daniel T. Smith, Jr., "Experienced Bicyclists and the Bikeway Controversy," in *Proceedings of the Seminar on Planning, Design and Implementation of Bicycle and Pedestrian Facilities, San Diego, [December 4–6] 1974* (New York: ITTE, 1974): 434–43, quotes on 443, 436.

18. Michael Everett, "The Bikeway Controversy" in *MAUDEP Proceedings of the Seminar on Planning, Design and Implementation of Bicycle and Pedestrian Facilities, Chicago, July 19–21* (New York: MAUDEP, 1978), 42–50, quote on 49–50.

19. Dale and Donna Lott, "Authors' Closure," in Dale Lott, Timothy Tardiff, and Donna Lott, "Evaluation by Experienced Riders of a New Bicycle Lane in an Established Bikeway System," *Transportation Research Record* 683 (1978): 46.

20. Najim Jabbar, "Practical Advice: Speed Program," *Bike World* 8, 6 (November/December 1979): 8. The improvement for "less proficient" cyclists can only be estimated, because a high proportion dropped out before completion of the trial in the "before" scenario, and some in both the "before" and "after."

21. Katie Moran, *et al.*, *Bicycle Transportation for Energy Conservation: Technical Report* (Washington, D.C.: USDOT, May 1980, Report No. DOT-P-80-092). The "golden era" was the relatively generous period of federal financing for research, planning and development that originated with the great bicycle boom of 1969–73, which peaked with the energy crises of 1973 and 1979, and ended with the barren years of the Reagan administration, 1981–89, and the deep recession of the early years of the subsequent Bush administration (1989–93). Its drought ended with the ISTEA Highway Act of 1991.

22. Marda Fortmann Mayo, *et al.*, *Bicycling and Air Quality Information Document* (Washington, D.C.: Environmental Protection Agency, September 1979, Report No. 68-01-4946).

23. Engineering Education, Enforcement, and Encouragement. With the exception of the last of these, this was the same "3-E" program that the National Safety Council initiated in 1915. See David Blanke, *Hell on Wheels: The Promise and Peril America's Car Culture, 1900–1940* (Lawrence: University Press of Kansas), 127.

24. Moran, Bicycle Transportation for Energy Conservation: Technical Report, 4–5.

25. Ibid., 92–106.

26. Ralph Hirsch, "A Washington Report," *Bicycling* 23, 4 (May 1982): 40–42.

27. U.S. Product Safety Commission, *Chairman's Conference on Nighttime Bicycle Safety, Bethesda, November 9, 1994*, at www.cpsc.gov/FOIA/meetings/mtg95/nighttimebike.pdf.

28. Dan T. Smith and Deleuw, Cather & Co.,

Safety and Locational Criteria for Bikeways: Users Manual Vol. 1, Facilities Locational Criteria (Washington, D.C.: FHWA, 1976). Report No. FHWA-RD-75-113; *Safety and Locational Criteria for Bikeways: Users Manual Vol. 2, Design and Safety Criteria* (Washington, D.C.: FHWA, 1976). Report No. FHWA-RD-75-114.

29. John Schubert, "What Should a Bicycle Facility Be?" *Bicycling* 23, 5 (June 1982): 45–47. In 1994, as a young transportation planner, the author personally heard Frank Francois say at a meeting of the Transportation Research Board that "if AASHTO does not take the unique concerns of urban transportation more seriously, we [AASHTO] will lose the big-city transportation directors and their elected officials to a new organization." He was scoffed at, but with the founding of NACTO (the National Association of City Transportation Officials) as an alternative to AASHTO some 15 years later, he was eventually proven right.

30. Edward Weiner, *Urban Transportation Planning in the United States: A Historical Overview* (Westport: Praeger, 1999): 80–86.

31. Schubert, "What Should a Bicycle Facility Be?" 45–47; Jennifer Toole, *Revising the Guide for the Development New Bicycle Facilities: Final Report* (Washington, D.C.: Transportation Research Board, 2010, Report No. NCHRP 15–37FR), 3.

32. AASHTO, *Guide for the Development of New Bicycle Facilities*, 2–3; Stacey, "Bridging the Gap Between Bikeway Planners and Bicyclists," 203–209; Zack Furness, *One Less Car: Bicycling and the Politics of Automobility* (Philadelphia: Temple University Press, 2010), 71.

33. "Background," in Toole, *Revising the AASHTO Guide for the Development of Bicycle Facilities: Final Report.*

34. Donald Appleyard, *Livable Streets* (Berkeley: University of California Press, 1981); Jane Jacobs, *The Death and Life of Great American Cities* (New York: Random House, 1961). One criticism of Jacobs is that her only interest was preserving the historical privileges of wealthy urbanites against public intrusion, *i.e.*, that she was an American Bourbonist uninterested in the bigger picture of urban distress. This criticism is not entirely undeserved.

35. Colin Buchanan, *Traffic in Towns* (London: Her Majesty's Stationery Office, 1963).

36. Richard K. Unterman, *Accommodating the Pedestrian: Adapting Towns and Neighborhoods for Walking and Bicycling* (New York: Van Nostrand Reinhold, 1984), 63.

37. Gary Toth and Brendan Crain interview with Dan Burden, Andy Clarke, and Charlie Gandy: www.pps.org/blog/after-30-years-of-bikeped-advocacy-how-far-have-we-come/. Dan Burden, "Building Communities with Transportation," *Transportation Research Record* 1773 (2001), 5–20.

38. The MUTCD is the national standard for all "traffic control devices installed on any street, highway, or bicycle trail open to the public" under Title 23, sections 109(d) and 402(a) of the U.S. Code and Title 23, sections 601–03, CFR. Title 23, section 652.13 of the CFR makes the AASHTO Guide "or equivalent guides developed in cooperation with state or local officials and acceptable to the division office of the FHWA" the standard for the construction and design of bike routes. For MUTCD notice-and-comment rulemaking, *see also* 48 Federal Register 46776 (October 14, 1983) and 51 Federal Register 16834 (May 7, 1986).

39. Several states have adopted the MUTCD with their own local supplements, as they are permitted to do.

40. *Urban Bikeway Design Guide* (Washington, D.C.: NACTO, 2011, 2nd edition, 2012). Tanya Snyder, "NACTO Beats the Clock with Quick Update of Bike Guide," D.C. Streetsblog, June 19, 2012. Last viewed: April 11, 2013. Tanya Snyder, "U.S. DOT to Challenge AASHTO Supremacy on Bike/Ped Safety Standards," February 28, 2013. Last viewed: April 11, 2013. Both http: //dcstreets blog.org/category/other-organizations/.

41. Snyder, "U.S. DOT to Challenge AASHTO Supremacy on Bike/Ped Safety Standards."

42. Section 228: 23 U.S.C. §402(b)(1)(D); 49 C.F.R. 27.75; 44 Federal Register 31468 (May 31, 1979). Section 504: 29 U.S.C. §794(a), 49 C.F.R. 27, pt. 27.

43. 42 U.S.C. 12131–12164; 28 C.F.R. 35.150–151. Those wanting to learn the most about these laws (in the most painless way possible) should consult two sources: *Accessible Sidewalks and Street Crossings* (the *ADAAG Manual*), by the U.S. Architectural and Barriers Compliance Board, available online by searching for "PROWguide.pdf," and *Kinney v. Yerusalem*, 9 F.3d 1067 (3rd Cir 1993).

44. *Kinney v. Yerusalem*, 9 F.3d 1067 (3rd Cir. 1993).

45. U. S. Architectural and Barriers Compliance Board, *Accessible Sidewalks and Street Crossings* (the *ADAAG Manual*) (Washington, D.C.: Federal Highway Authority, 2001), available online by searching for PROWguide.pdf.

46. That is, how many curb cut installations can be chalked up to the overall costs of building a brand new roadway or overhauling an existing roadway to such an extent that the curbs have to be ripped out anyway, and how many curb cuts are stand-alone projects undertaken solely because of the section 504/ADA mandate. Transportation enhancements spending: Angie L. Craddock, *et al.*, "Factors Associated with Federal Transportation Funding for Local Pedestrian and Bicycle

Programming and Facilities," *Journal of Public Health Policy* 30 (2009): S38-S72, esp. Table 1 (S51). 55 million curb cuts: estimation based on total U.S. urbanized land area of 92,480 sq. mi. (2000), 48 to 128 arterial and collector intersections per square mile, and 4 or 8 curb cuts per intersection. Cost estimates range between $2,000 and $12,000 per curb cut, depending if the cut was part of a pre-existing curb reconstruction or a free-standing project. My single-point cost estimate is $333.543 billion, which assumes that 10 percent of curb cut projects were stand-alone, and 33 percent were accelerated.

47. Data on regular cyclists: "Year in Review," *Bicycle Retailer and Industry News* 19, 11 (July 1, 2010): 1, 3. The source data is the National Sporting Goods Association Annual Data Survey.

48. Christopher Hagelin, *A Return on Investment Analysis of Bikes-on-Bus Programs* (Tampa: Center for Urban Transportation Research, University of South Florida, 2005), 52–68.

49. "RiziBeo," quoting "Brian," in "History of the Bus Bike Rack," http://rikibeo.wordpresscom/2009/02/18/history-of-thebus-bike-rack/. Last accessed: August 1, 2013.

50. Michael A. Replogle, *Public Transportation: New Links to Suburban Transit Markets* (Washington, D.C.: Bicycle Federation, 1983); John T. Doolittle, Jr., and Ellen Kret Porter, *Transit Cooperative Research Program Synthesis 4: Integration of Bicycle and Transit* (Washington, D.C.: TRB/National Academy Press, 1994); John Pucher and Ralph Buehler, "Integration of Cycling with Public Transportation," in City Cycling, ed. John Pucher and Ralph Buehler (Cambridge: MIT Press, 2012), 157–81.

51. Doolittle, Jr., and Porter, *Transit Cooperative Research Program Synthesis 4: Integration of Bicycle and Transit*, 13–14.

52. "RiziBeo," quoting "Florb," in "History of the Bus Bike Rack," http://rikibeo.wordpresscom/2009/02/18/history-of-thebus-bike-rack/. Last accessed: August 1, 2013.

53. Michael Replogle, *National Bicycling and Walking Study: Case Study 9, Linking Bicycle/Pedestrian Facilities with Transit* (Washington, D.C.: Federal Highway Administration, 1992), 136–38.

54. Author's interview with Dan Burden, August 1, 2007.

55. Hagelin, *A Return on Investment Analysis of Bikes-on-Bus Programs*, 60.

56. Interview with Dan Burden, August 2, 2007.

57. Author's interview with Dan Burden; Hagelin, *A Return on Investment Analysis of Bikes-on-Bus Programs*, 60.

Chapter 7

1. Alexandra Gutierrez, "The Bicycle Grief," *American Prospect* 21, 2 (March 2010): 6–7.

2. Matthew Shaer, "Not Quite Copenhagen," *New York* (March 28, 2011): 34–39, 91–92.

3. Brian Ladd, *Autophobia* (Chicago: University of Chicago Press, 2008), 148.

4. Joachim Jachnow, "What's Become of the German Greens?" *New Left Review* 81 (2nd Ser.) (May/June 2013): 94–117.

5. James E. Stacey, "Bridging the Gap Between Bikeway Planners and Bicyclists," in *Proceedings of the Seminar/Workshop on Planning, Design and Implementation of Bicycle and Pedestrian Facilities, Chicago, July 19–21 1978* (New York: MAUDEP, n. d. [1978]): 203–09.

6. Memo from Horace Huffman and Fred C. Smith to the American Bicycle Manufactures, n. d. (c. December 1972), http://john-s-allen.com/Biklg1965-/correspondence/1973/Board_correspondence.pdf.

7. Memo from Huffman and Smith to The American Bicycle Manufactures, n. d.; letter from Ray Burch to Carroll Quimby, January 15, 1973, both http://john-s-allen.com/Biklg1965-/correspondence/1973/ Board_correspondence.pdf; John S. Allen, "The League of American Wheelmen/Bicyclists in the 20th Century," in *Cycle History 20: Proceedings of the 20th International Cycle History Conference, Freehold*, ed. Gary Sanderson (n.l.: John Pinkerton Memorial Fund, 2010), 114–22. BIA assistance during 1939–55 and membership structure: "League of American Wheelmen, Inc. Financial Statement, June 15, 1951" and "League of American Wheelmen, Inc. Financial Statement, October 30, 1951," http://john-s-allen.com/Biklg1965-/board._meetings/1983–12%20Board%20meeting/B.pdf.

8. Memo from Huffman and Smith to The American Bicycle Manufactures, n. d., http://john-s-allen.com/Biklg1965-/correspondence/1973/Board_correspondence.pdf.

9. Only the $14,000 BIA/Schwinn/Raleigh contribution appears on the L.A.W.'s budget for the calendar year of 1973. However, the advertising income for the *L.A.W. Bulletin* was exactly $10,000 over budget, while the *Bulletin* editor's salary was not included in the budget, creating a $7,000 overage. The Schwinn/Huffman donation was probably included in the budget in the form of "advertising revenues." Why Harman's salary was not included in the budget is a mystery.

10. Unilaterally donated: Memo from Huffman and Smith to the American Bicycle Manufactures, n. d. Plan announced: Letter from Horace Huffman to Carroll Quimby, February 15, 1973, with attached blank press release. An initial $52K program announced in February was later

augmented by $4K donated by Raleigh: memo from Horace Huffman to Morgan Groves, August 28, 1973. Groves hired: letter from Ray Birch to Carroll Quimby, June 28, 1973. All of the above, http://john-s-allen.com/Biklg1965-/correspondence/1973/Board_correspondence.pdf . Groves's background: author's interview with Morgan Groves, November 12, 2007. The 1973 year-end budget summary indicates "donations" of $14,000, suggesting that only the funds in the three-year BIA plan were transferred, and none of the "interim" Schwinn/Huffman funds were: "League of American Wheelmen: Cash Receipts and Disbursements, 1-1-73 through 12–31-73," http://john-s-allen.com/Biklg1965-/board._meetings/1983–12%20Board%20meeting/B.pdf.

11. John S. Allen interview of Phyllis Harmon, January 16, 2006, Tape #2 at 4:17; 17:49, http://john-s-allen.com/labdocs/interviews/index.htm.

12. Author's interview with Morgan Groves, November 12, 2007; notes of John S. Allen's interview of Morgan Groves (with annotations by William Hoffman), October 31, 2009, http://john-s-allen.com/labdocs/interviews/ index.htm.

13. Memo from Huffman and Smith to The American Bicycle Manufactures, n. d. http://john-s-allen.com/Biklg1965-/correspondence/1973/ Board_correspondence.pdf.

14. See note 9; "League of American Wheelmen: Cash Receipts and Disbursements, 1–1–73 through 12–31–73," n. d. This would have made industry support about 32 percent of total revenues, a level consistent with the trend in the early 1950s.

15. Ibid.

16. Letter from Ralph Galen to Tom Owen, August 7, 1973, http://john-s-allen.com/Biklg1965-/correspondence/1973/Board_correspondence.pdf.

17. Memo to Morgan Groves from Leon Taylor, http://john-s-allen.com/Biklg1965-/correspondence /1973/Board_correspondence.pdf.

18. Annotations provided by William Hoffman to notes of John S. Allen's interview of Morgan Groves, October 31, 2009, http://john-s-allen.com/labdocs/interviews/index.htm.

19. Salary was $16,000 and no benefits: letter from Carroll Quimby to Morgan Groves, May 10, 1973, http://john-s-allen.com/Biklg1965-/correspondence/1973/Board_correspondence.pdf.

20. Harmon paid $10,000/year: John S. Allen interview of Phyllis Harmon, January 16, 2006, Tape #2 at 17:49, http://john-s-allen.com/labdocs/interviews/index.htm. L.A.W. 1973 finances: "League of American Wheelmen: Cash Receipts and Disbursements, 1-1-73 through 12–31-73," http://john-s-allen.com/Biklg1965-/correspondence/1973/ Board_correspondence.pdf.

21. Bikeways: letter from Horace Huffman to Morgan Groves, August 31, 1973. Businesslike manner: letter from Horace Huffman to Carroll Quimby, October 29, 1973, both http://john-s-allen.com/Biklg1965-/correspondence/1973/Board_correspondence.pdf.

22. Letter from Morgan Groves to Carroll Quimby, August 2, 1973; letter from Morgan Groves to John Forester, November 6, 1973, both http://john-s-allen.com/Biklg1965-/correspondence/1973/ Board_correspondence.pdf.

23. Ken Kohnsbun, "Point of View: An Anti-Bikeway Movement," *Bicycling* 15, 6 (June 1974): 77–79; Morgan Groves, "Point of View: Is L.A.W. Anti-Bikeway?" *Bicycling* 15, 8 (August 1974): 66–68.

24. Notes of John S. Allen's interview of Morgan Groves (with annotations by William Hoffman): October 31, 2009, http://john-s-allen.com/labdocs/interviews/htm.

25. Memo from H. M. Huffman to Morgan Groves re: Problem Areas in L.A.W., October 10, 1973, http://john-s-allen.com/Biklg1965-/correspondence/1973/Board_correspondence.pdf.

26. Memo from Morgan Groves to Carroll Quimby, August 7, 1973, http://john-s-allen.com/Biklg1965-/correspondence/1973/Board_correspondence.pdf.

27. "Winter Board Meeting, December 10–11, 1983," http://john-s-allen.com/Biklg1965-/board._meetings/1983–12%20Board%20meeting/B.pdf.

28. Harmon's concern's about Groves's cooperation with Burden: John S. Allen interview of Phyllis Harmon, January 16, 2006, Tape #2 at 20:24, http://john-s-allen.com/labdocs/interviews/htm; notes of John S. Allen's interview of Morgan Groves (with annotations by William Hoffman): October 31, 2009, http://john-s-allen.com/labdocs/interviewshtm/. Burden's belief that Bikecentennial was the future: Morgan Groves interview with the author, November 12, 2007. Groves quote: "*Bike World* Interview: Morgan Groves," 10.

29. This and the following paragraphs describing Bikecentennial are taken from four sources: Tom Miller, "*Bike World* Interview: Dan Burden," *Bike World* 3, 4 (April 1974): 8–10; Dan D'Ambrosio, "Our History" (1996), *Adventure Cyclist* online, www.adventurecycling.org; Dan D'Ambrosio, "Thirty Years: A History of Adventure Cycling Association," *Adventure Cyclist* 33, 7 (July 2006): 10–19.

30. There is some obscurity about when Burden left Bikecentennial. The two "official" histories, written by Dan D'Ambrosio, clearly try to give the impression that Burden left the organization in mid–1976. D'Ambrosio, "Our History" (1996) *Adventure Cyclist* online, www.adventurecycling.org; D'Ambrosio, "Thirty Years: A History

of Adventure Cycling Association," 19. However, an NHTSA report, dated July 1977 and co-written by Bruce Burgess and Dan Burden, in which the Bikecentennial safety statistics are given, states that Burden, now residing in Washington, is still affiliated with the organization: *Bicycle Safety Highway Users Information Report* (Washington, D.C.: Federal Highway Administration, 1978), 9. A news brief in the September 1977 issue of *Bike World* announces that Dave Prouty succeeded Burden as Bikecentennial executive director: "Looking at People," *Bike World* 7, 9 (September 1977): 40. In its May 1978 issue, *Bicycling* stated that Burden had started the BikeFed in Washington, D.C. the previous May—that is, in May 1977: Rowe, "Three Promising Bicycle Organizations," 58–59. Thus, it appears that Burden was executive director of both Bikecentennial and BikeFed from about May to September of 1977.

31. In 1984, Prouty was hired by the United States Cycling Federation and managed it until shortly after the 1986 world's cycling championships in Colorado Springs. Although almost all his comments regarding Bikecentennial are supportive, his scathing 1988 memoir of his USCF years, *In Spite of Us*, is undoubtedly the single-best commentary on the sad state of American bicycle NGO politics—not just in the racing sector, but everything—ever written. David Prouty, *In Spite of Us: My Education in the Big and Little Games of Amateur and Olympic Sports in the U.S.* (Brattleboro: VeloPress, 1988).

32. Burden claims: Rowe, "Three Promising Bicycle Organizations," 58. Wilkinson claims: author's interview with Bill Wilkinson, July 17, 2008.

33. Wilkinson's recollections: author's interview with Bill Wilkinson, July 17, 2008. BikeFed had grants: Rowe, "Three Promising Bicycle Organizations," 59.

34. Tedson Meyers, "The New Federalism: Here's One Organization that Beat Reagan to the Punch," *Bicycling* 23, 6 (June 1982): 150–52; author's interview with Bill Wilkinson, July 17, 2008; Rowe, "Three Promising Bicycle Organizations," 58–59.

35. Author's interview with Bill Wilkinson, July 17, 2008; author's interview with Norman A. Clarke, April 5, 1998; author's interview with Tim Blumenthal, October 6, 2009; Jason Norman, "First and Most Prominent Advocate John Auerbach Dies," *Bicycle Retailer and Industry News* (April 15, 2007): 20.

36. Author's interview with Bill Wilkinson, July 17, 2008.

37. Author's interview with Tim Blumenthal, executive director, Bikes Belong Coalition, October 5, 2009.

38. League history: John S. Allen, "The League of American Wheelmen/Bicyclists in the 20th Century," in *Cycle History 20: Proceedings of the 20th International Cycle History Conference, Freehold*, ed. Gary Sanderson (n.l.: John Pinkerton Memorial Fund, 2010), 114–22.

39. Blumenthal interview.

40. John Forester, *Effective Cycling* (1975); Darryl Skrabak, "Bike Law: Trend Setting Report on Bike Law Emerges in California," *Bicycling* 16, 6 (June 1975): 72–75; Darryl Skrabak, "Book Review: John Forester Writes a Bike Book," *Bicycling* 17, 3 (March 1976): 82–83.

41. William Saunders, "Book Review: Master Cyclist's Winning Textbook," *Bike World* 4, 11 (November 1975): 57–58.

42. Skrabak, "Book Review: John Forester Writes a Bike Book," 83.

43. John Forester, "Teaching the Proper Use of Bicycle Facilities," in *Proceedings of the Fourth National Seminar on Planning Design and Implementation of Bicycle and Pedestrian Facilities, [December 4–6] 1975, New Orleans* (New York: ASCE, 1976): 533–44, quote on 535.

44. Memo from Bill Frey to L.A.W./Bicycle USA Board of Directors, re: Status of Effective Cycling Program, June 22, 1985; Memo from John W. Jefferson to L.A.W./Bicycle USA Board of Directors re: Status of the Effective Cycling Program, and Appendix "D," November 9, 1985, updated December 11, 1985, both http://john-s-allen.com/Biklg1965-/board._meetings/1983-12%20Board%20meeting/B.pdf.

45. John Forester, "History of the Effective Cycling Program," http://www.johnforester.com/Articles/Education/ ECHistory.htm.

46. Memo from Bill Frey to L.A.W./Bicycle USA Board of Directors, re: Status of Effective Cycling Program, June 22, 1985, http://john-s-allen.com/Biklg1965-/board._meetings/1983-12%20Board%20meeting/B.pdf.

47. Memo from John W. Jefferson to L.A.W./Bicycle USA Board of Directors re: Status of the Effective Cycling Program, and Appendix "D," November 9, 1985, updated December 11, 1985, http://john-s-allen.com/Biklg1965-/board._meetings/1983-12%20Board%20meeting/B.pdf.

48. David Gordon Wilson's influence: "Transcript of Testimony of Mr. John Forrester [sic], October 4, 1993" *Johnson v. Derby Cycle Co. et al.*, Sup. Ct. of New Jersey, Essex Co., ESX-L-16063-89, Pt. 2 of 3, on 53.

49. Frederick L. Wolfe, *The Bicycle: A Commuting Alternative* (Edmonds, WA: Signpost Books, 1979).

50. John Schubert, "Review: The Bicycle, A Commuting Alternative," *Bicycling* 21, 3 (April 1980): 90–91.

51. This may have been Fred Wolfe's book.

52. John S. Allen, *The Complete Book of Bicycle Commuting* (Emmaus, PA: Rodale Press, 1981); email from John Allen to the author, January 25, 2012. Aggressively defensive cycling: John Forester, "Toy Bike Syndrome," *Bike World* 2, 5 (October 1973): 24–27, on 27; use courtesy when you can: John S. Allen, "Assertive Cycling," *Bicycling* 23, 7 (July 1982): 59–63; Forester quote: "Transcript of Testimony of Mr. John Forrester [sic], *Johnson v. Derby Cycle Co. et al.*, Sup. Ct. of New Jersey, Essex Co., ESX-L-16063–89, Pt. 2 of 3: Pt. 2 of 3, 54.

53. Laura Golbuff and Rachel Aldred, *Cycling Policy in the UK: A Historical and Thematic Overview* (London: University of East London, n. d. [2011]): 15.

54. John Franklin, "National Cycle Training Project: An Introduction to the Project Given in Cheltenham, May 2002," at www.lesberries.co.uk/cycling/htm.

55. John Franklin, *Cyclecraft: North American Edition* (n.l.: TSO, 2009).

56. Excerpts from *The Complete Book of Bicycle Commuting* ran almost monthly from December 1980 to September 1982, and less frequently thereafter. Clarence W. Coles, Harold T. Glenn and John S. Allen, *Glenn's New Complete Bicycle Manual* (New York: Crown, 1987); John S. Allen, *Street Smarts* (Florida Version), (Gainesville: Florida Bicycle Association, 2001); email from John Allen to the author, January 25, 2012.

57. Email from David Henderson to the author, March 21, 2013.

58. For a more extended critique of the "academic slumming" aspects of messenger studies, see Bruce Epperson, "A New Class of Cyclists: Banham's Bicycle and the Two-Wheeled World it Didn't Create," *Mobilities* 8, 2 (2013): 238–51, esp. 245–47.

59. One of the big problems: Robert Hurst, *The Art of Cycling* (Guilford, CT: FalconGuides, 2007), 64. While Forester's advice is usually: Hurst, *The Art of Cycling*, 64.

60. Everything you really need: James C. McCullagh, "The Politics of Cycling Space," *Bicycling* 19, 11 (November 1978): 10–11.

61. Dave Glowacz, *Urban Bikers' Tricks and Tips* (Chicago: Wordspace Press, 2010); John Forester, "Bicycling, Transportation and the Problem of Evil" (an address to the Preserving the American Dream Conference, October 2007), 8, at http://www.johnforester.com/articles/ .

62. McCullaugh, "The Politics of Cycling Space," 10–11.

Conclusions

1. Ralph Hirsch, "A Washington Report," *Bicycling* 23, 4 (May 1982): 40–42. It is a well-known anecdote among environmental planners and lawyers that under NEPA, an environmental impact statement can identify the outcome of "Option A" as the end of all life on earth, and the statement can still go right ahead and identify Option A as the preferred alternative. Whether the project will subsequently survive a court challenge from an adversely impacted group is another matter.

2. Minutes of L.A.W. Board of Directors, June 22, 1969, at http://john-s-allen.com/Biklg1965-/board.meetings/1983–12%20Board%20meeting/B.pdf

3. See, for example: Mark Rose, *Interstate: Express Highway Politics, 1939–1989* (Knoxville: University of Tennessee Press, 1979); Tom Lewis, *Divided Highways: Building the Interstate Highways, Transforming American Life* (New York: Viking, 1997); Owen D. Gutfreund, *Twentieth-Century Sprawl: Highways and the Reshaping of the American Landscape* (New York: Oxford University Press, 2004): Michael R. Fein, *Paving the Way: New York Roadbuilding and the American State, 1880–1956* (Lawrence: University Press of Kansas, 2008).

4. Tanya Snyder, "U.S. DOT to Challenge AASHTO Supremacy on Bike/Ped Safety Standards," February 28, 2013, at http: //dcstreetsblog.org/category/other-organizations/htm.

5. John Schubert, "What Should a Bicycle Facility Be?" *Bicycling* 23, 5 (June 1982): 45–47; Rose, *Interstate: Express Highway Politics, 1939–1989*: 117.

6. Fred DeLong, "Safety: A Bicycling Proficiency Course," *Bicycling* 11, 3 (April 1970): 22–23, 33; Fred DeLong, Cycling Safety and Proficiency Course: Part 10, Club Riding and Touring Skills," *Bicycling* 12, 5 (May 1971): 20–21; Fred DeLong, "Bicycle Proficiency: Where on the Road?" *Bicycling* 13, 11 (November 1972): 36–37; Fred DeLong, *DeLong's Guide to Bicycles and Bicycling* (Radnor, PA: Chilton Books, 1974): Chapter 12.

7. Fred DeLong, "Bicycle Proficiency: Where on the Road?" *Bicycling* 13, 11 (November 1972): 36–37; Fred DeLong, "The Bicycle's Place on the Road: Another Viewpoint," *Bicycling* 9, 7 (July 1973): 20; John Forester, "What About Bikeways," *Bike World*, 2, 2 (February 1973): 36–37; Bill Wilkinson, "Construction, Maintenance and Enforcement on the George Washington Memorial Parkway Path," in *Bicycles USA Conference, [May 7–8] 1973, Cambridge* (Washington, D.C.: USDOT, 1973), 40–42; Jim Konski, "It's Up to You," *Bicycling* 9, 6 (June 1973): 20–23;

8. Morgan Groves, "Point of View: Is L.A.W. Anti-Bikeway?" *Bicycling* 15, 8 (August 1974): 66–68; John Williams, "San Luis Obispo," in *Bikeway Design Atlas: Urban Bikeway Design Competition* (Cambridge, MA: Urban Bikeway Design Collaborative, January 1975), 26–52; notes of Morgan Groves interview by John S. Allen, October 31, 2009; Darryl Skrabak, "Bicycle Activists: Where They Stand Now," *Bicycling* 18, 2 (February 1977): 50–51.

9. Memo from Deputy Attorney General Frank A. Iwama to Richard Rogers, CalTrans, January 21, 1975 (AG Op. No. CV 74/224 IL) in Rogers, *et al. SCR 47 Statewide Bicycle Committee Final Report*).

10. Nina Dougherty Rowe, "Cyclists' Rights to the Road: Improving but Still Poor," *Bicycling* 2, 3 (April 1981): 24–26. Morgan Groves, "Good News from the NCUTLO," *Bicycling* 16, 1 (January 1975): 6–7; "Update" [letter of Ralph B. Hirsch], *Bicycling* 22, 8 (September/October 1981): 40.

Bibliography

Published Sources

Abbott, Carl, and Joy Margheim. "Imaging Portland's Urban Growth Boundary." *Journal of the American Planning Association* 74, 2 (Spring 2008): 196–208.

"The ABC's of Creating a Bike Route System." *Bicycling* 13, 7 (July 1972): 18–19.

Albert, Daniel M. *Order Out of Chaos: Automobile Safety, Technology, and Society, 1925–1965.* Ph.D. dissertation, University of Michigan, 1997.

Allen, John S. "Assertive Cycling." *Bicycling* 23, 7 (July 1982): 59–63.

_____. *The Complete Book of Bicycle Commuting.* Emmaus, PA: Rodale Press, 1981.

_____. "The League of American Wheelmen/Bicyclists in the 20th Century." In *Cycle History 20: Proceedings of the 20th International Cycle History Conference, Freehold,* ed. Gary Sanderson (n. p.: John Pinkerton Memorial Fund, 2010): 114–22.

_____. *Street Smarts* (Florida Version). Gainesville: Florida Bicycle Association, 2001.

Appleyard, Donald. *Livable Streets.* Berkeley: University of California Press, 1981.

Bayside, City of. *Bayside City Council Bicycle Strategy.* Bayside: Bayside Public Safety Department, 2003.

Beinhorn, George. "*Bike World* Interview: Fred DeLong." *Bike World* 3, 3 (March 1974): 8–9.

_____. "*Bike World* Interview: Morgan Groves." *Bike World* 3, 7 (July 1974): 8–9.

Beisner, Robert L. *Dean Acheson: A Life in the Cold War.* New York: Oxford University Press, 2006.

Bernton, Hal. "State Senate Deadlock Kills Columbia Crossing." *Seattle Times,* July 1, 2013.

Berto, Frank J. "The Great American Bicycle Boom." In *Cycle History 10: Proceedings of the 10th International Cycle History Conference, Nijmegan,* ed. Hans Erhard Lessing and Andrew Ritchie (San Francisco: Van der Plas Publications, 2000): 133–48.

"*Bicycle Forum* Interviews Ken Cross." *Bicycle Forum* 2 (Fall 1978): 2–10.

"Bicycle Makers Seek Tariff Help." *New York Times,* August 22, 1954, F1.

Bijker, Wiebe. *Of Bicycles, Bakelites and Bulbs: Towards a Theory of Sociotechnical Change.* Cambridge: MIT Press, 1995.

Bike Ed '77: A Conference Report, May 4–6, 1977. Washington, D.C.: CPSC/USDOT, 1977, Report No. CE014–066.

Bicycle Standard BMA/6: Safety Standards for Regular Bicycles. New York: BMA, 1970, 1972, 1974.

Blanke, David. *Hell on Wheels: The Promise and Peril of America's Car Culture, 1900–1940.* Lawrence: University of Kansas Press, 2007.

"Bob Cleckner." *Journal of Health, Physical Education and Recreation* (April 1965): 35.

Bonham, Jennifer, and Peter Cox. "The Disruptive Traveler? A Foucauldian Analysis of Cycleways," *Road and Transport Research* 19, 2 (2010): 42–53.

Bottles, Scott. *Los Angeles and the Automobile: the Making of the Modern City.* Berkeley: University of California Press, 1987.

Bracher, Tilman. "Germany." In *The Bicycle and City Traffic,* edited by Hugh McClintock, 175–89. London: Belhaven Press, 1992.

Briese, Volker. "From Cycling Lanes to Compulsory Bike Path: Bicycle Path Construction in Germany, 1897–1940." In *Cycle History 5: The Proceedings of the Fifth International Cycle History Conference, Cambridge, England,* edited by Rob Van der Plas, 123–28. San Francisco: Bicycle Books, 1995.

Bromley, David G. "Dramatic Denouments." In *Cults, Religion and Violence,* edited by David G. Bromley, and J. Gordon Melton, 1–10. Cambridge, UK: Cambridge University Press, 2002.

Buchanan, Colin. *Traffic in Towns.* London: Her Majesty's Stationery Office, 1963.

Buehler, Theodore J. *Fifty Years of Bicycle Policy in Davis, California*. Davis: Institute for Transportation Studies, June, 2007.

Buehler, Theodore J., and Susan Handy. "Fifty Years of Bicycle Policy in Davis, California." *Transportation Research Record* 2074 (2008): 52–57.

Burden, Dan. "Building Communities with Transportation." *Transportation Research Record* 1773 (2001): 5–20.

Burgess, Bruce, and Dan Burden. *Bicycle Safety Highway Users Information Report*. Washington: Federal Highway Administration, 1978, Report No. DOT HS-803 206.

Burr, Thomas C. *Markets as Producers and Consumers: The French and U.S. National Markets, 1875–1910*. Ph.D. Dissertation, University of California at Davis, 2005.

Burridge T., P. Lajbcygier, and M. Lema. *Draft Response to Bayside City Council Bicycle Strategy*. Melbourne: David Locke and Associates/PBAI Australia, 2003.

Cervero, Robert. *Suburban Gridlock*. New Brunswick, NJ: Rutgers University Press, 1988.

Clarke, Norman. "There Outta be a Law." In *Proceedings of the Seminar on Bicycle/Pedestrian Planning and Design, December 12–14 1974* (*sic*, s.b. 1973), 550–51. New York: ASCE, 1974.

Claxton, E. C. "The Future of the Bicycle in a Modern Society." *Royal Society for the Encouragement of Arts, Manufacturers and Commerce Journal* 116, 5138 (January 1968): 114–34. Paper and discussion by E. Marples, A. Moulton, and others.

Coles, Clarence W., Harold T. Glenn, and John S. Allen. *Glenn's New Complete Bicycle Manual*. New York: Crown, 1987.

Consumer Product Safety Act Amendments: Hearings on H.R. 5361 and H.R. 6107, 94th Congress. Washington: Government Printing Office, 1994, No. 94–30.

Consumer Product Safety Commission Oversight: Hearings on S. 644 and S. 1000, 94th Congress. Washington: Government Printing Office, 1975, No. 94–12.

Cook, W. L. *Bike Trails and Facilities—A Guide to their Design, Construction and Operation*. New York: Bicycle Institute of America, 1965, 1969.

Corgel, John B., and Charles Floyd. "Toward a New Direction in Bicycle Transportation Policy." *Traffic Quarterly* 33, 2 (April 1979): 297–310.

Cornell, Nina, Roger Noll, and Barry Weingast. "Safety Regulation." In *Setting National Priorities: The Next Ten Years*, edited by Henry Owen and Charles L. Schultze, 457–508. Washington, D.C.: Brookings Institution, 1976.

Cox, Peter. "A Denial of Our Boasted Civilization: Cyclists' Views Over Road Use in Britain, 1926–1935." *Transfers* 2, 3 (Winter 2012): 4–30.

Craddock, Angie L., et al. "Factors Associated with Federal Transportation Funding for Local Pedestrian and Bicycle Programming and Facilities." *Journal of Public Health Policy* 30 (2009): S38–S72.

Cross, Ken. "Bicycle/Motor Vehicle Accident Types." In *Bike Ed 77: Conference Report May 4–6, 1977*, 44–59. Washington: CPSC/USDOT, 1977, Report No. CE 014–066.

D'Ambrosio, Dan. "Thirty Years: A History of Adventure Cycling Association." *Adventure Cyclist* 33, 7 (July 2006): 10–19.

Deleuw, Cather, and Company. *City of Davis/University of California Bicycle Circulation and Safety Study*. San Francisco: The author, August 1972, 27.

Delong, Fred. "Bicycle Proficiency: Where on the Road?" *Bicycling* 13, 11 (November 1972): 36–37.

_____. "The Bicycle's Place on the Road: Another Viewpoint." *Bicycling* 9, 7 (July 1973): 20.

_____. "Bucking the Authorities." *Bicycling* 15, 11 (November 1974): 42–43.

_____. "Cyclist Safety and Proficiency Course: Part 10, Club Riding and Touring Skills." *Bicycling* 12, 5 (May 1971): 20–21.

_____. "Cyclists in Traffic." *Bicycling* 15, 2 (February, 1974): 28–29.

_____. *DeLong's Guide to Bicycles and Bicycling*. Radnor, PA: Chilton, 1974.

_____. "Editor's Notes: CPSC Standards." *Bicycling* 15, 4 (April 1974): 6.

_____. "From the Safety Committee." *L. A. W. Bulletin* (December 1969): 1–2.

_____. "International Bicycle Standards: An Update." *Bicycling* 16, 1 (January 1975): 62–65.

_____. "I. S. O. Technical Committee TC-149 (Cycles), an Overview." *Bicycling* 15, 7 (July 1974): 72–77.

_____. "Lights and Reflectorization for Bicycles, the Laws and the Codes." *Bicycling* 15, 9 (September 1974): 20–21.

_____. "New Bicycle Safety and Performance Standards." *Bicycling* 6, 12 (December 1970): 26–27.

_____. "Performance Tests for Coaster Brakes." *Bicycling* 13, 10 (October 1972): 50–53.

_____. "A Purist Changes His Mind." *Bicycling* 18, 5 (May 1977), 60–61.

_____. "Safety: A Bicyclist Proficiency Course." *Bicycling* 11, 3 (April 1970): 22–23, 32.

DeMaio, Paul. "Bike Sharing: Its History, Models of Provision, and Future." *Journal of Public Transportation* 13, 4 (2009): 41–56.

Doolittle, Jr., John T., and Ellen Kret Porter. *Transit Cooperative Research Program Synthesis 4: Integration of Bicycle and Transit*. Washington, D.C.: TRB/National Academy Press, 1994.

Downs, Anthony. *Stuck in Traffic: Coping with Peak Hour Traffic.* Washington, D.C.: Brookings Institution, 1992.

Duckwall, Jane. "Former Oregonian Likes That We Have Fewer Bikes." *Charlotte* (NC) *Observer*, February 19, 2006.

Earle, Horatio Sawyer. *The Autobiography of "By Gum" Earle.* Lansing, MI: State Review Publishing, 1929.

Ebert, Anne Katrin. "Cycling Towards the Nation: The Use of the Bicycle in Germany and the Netherlands, 1880–1940." *European Review of History* 2, 3 (2003): 347–64.

_____. "When Cycling Gets Political: Building Cycle Paths in Germany and the Netherlands, 1910–40." *Journal of Transport History* 33, 1 (June 2012): 115–37.

"The Editor's Table." *Good Roads* 1 (April 1892): 224.

Elliott, Sterling. "The League of American Wheelmen: Its Origin, Growth, and Prospects." *Harper's Weekly* 39 (March 1895): 284–86.

Emanuel, Martin. "Constructing the Cyclist: Ideology and Representations in Urban Traffic Planning in Stockholm, 1930–70." *Journal of Transport History* 33,1 (June 2012): 67–91.

Embrick, Marion. *Comparison of Uniform Vehicle Code and Oregon Law* (State of Oregon Committee on Judiciary Reference Paper, April 1974).

Eno, William P. *The Science of Traffic Regulation, 1899–1920.* Washington, D.C.: The author, 1920.

_____. *Simplification of Highway Traffic.* Washington, D.C.: Eno Foundation, 1929.

Epperson, Bruce D. "The Great Schism: Federal Bicycle Safety Regulation and the Unraveling of American Bicycle Planning." *Transportation Law Journal* 37, 2 (Summer 2010): 73–118.

_____. *Peddling Bicycles to America: The Rise of an Industry.* Jefferson, NC: McFarland, 2010.

_____. "Review of Peter D. Norton's Fighting Traffic." *Technology and Culture* 50, 1 (January 2009): 235–36.

Everett, Michael D. "The Bikeway Controversy." In *Proceedings of the Seminar/Workshop on Planning, Design and Implementation of Bicycle and Pedestrian Facilities, Chicago, July 19–21*, 42–49. New York: MAUDEP, n. d. (1978).

_____. "Commuter Demand for Bicycle Transportation in the United States." *Transportation Quarterly* 28, 3 (October 1974): 585–601.

_____. "Counterattack." [letter] *Bike World* 5, 5 (May 1976): 63–64.

"The FDA Versus You." *Bike World* (October 1973): 3.

Fisher, Gary, et al. *Bikeway Planning Criteria and Guidelines.* Los Angeles: UCLA Institute for Traffic and Transportation Engineering, 1972.

Fishman, Robert. *Urban Utopias in the Twentieth Century.* New York: Basic Books, 1977.

Food and Drug Administration. *Staff Analysis of Bicycle Accidents and Injuries.* Washington, D.C.: USFDA, 1972, Report No. NTIS PB-207–665.

Forester, John. *Bicycle Transportation.* Cambridge, MA: MIT Press, 1983.

_____. "Bikelane Countermeasures: Preserving Cyclists' Rights and Safety in a Motor-Minded World." In *Proceedings of the Seminar on Planning, Design and Implementation of Bicycle/Pedestrian Facilities, San Diego, Dec. 1974*, 33–41. New York: ASCE, 1975.

_____. *Effective Cycling.* 2nd edition, Palo Alto: Custom Cycle Fitments, 1975; 5th edition, Cambridge, MA: MIT Press, 1984; 6th edition Cambridge, MA: MIT Press, 1993; 7th edition Cambridge, MA: MIT Press, 2012.

_____. "How to Gain Access Without Using Ketchup," *Bicycling* 22, 9 (November/December 1981): 44–45.

_____. "Letter to the Editor." *Transportation Law Journal* 39, 1 (Fall 2011): 31–51.

_____. "Logic Lost in CPSC Ruling." *Bike World* 5, 7 (July 1976): 7.

_____. *Novelist & Storyteller: The Life of C. S. Forester* (two volumes). Lemon Grove, CA: The author, 2000.

_____. "Planning for Cyclists as They See Themselves Instead of as Motorists See Them." In *Proceedings of the Seminar on Bicycle Pedestrian Planning and Design, December 12–14, 1974* (*sic*, s.b. 1973), 315–330. New York: ASCE, 1974.

_____. "Point of View: The Toy Bike Mentality in Government." *Bicycling* 14, 9 (September 1973): 52–53.

_____. "Teaching the Proper Use of Bicycle Facilities." In *Proceedings of the Fourth National Seminar on Planning, Design and Implementation of Bicycle and Pedestrian Facilities, New Orleans, December 4–6, 1976*, 533–543. New York: ASCE, 1975.

_____. "Toy Bike Syndrome." *Bike World* 2, 5 (October 1973): 24–27.

_____. "What About Bikeways?" *Bike World* 2, 2 (February 1973): 36–37.

Foster, Lee. "Meek Little Creatures? The Political Phenomenon of the Menlo Park Bicycle Festival." *Bicycling* 13, 1 (January 1972): 14–15.

Foster, Mark S. *From Streetcar to Superhighway: American City Planners and Urban Transportation 1900–1940.* Philadelphia: Temple University Press, 1981.

Franklin, John. *Cyclecraft: North American Edition.* Blue Ridge Summit, PA: TSO, 2009.

_____. "Segregation: Are We Moving Away from Cycling Safety?" *TEC: Traffic Engineering and Control* (April 2002): 23–27.

Franz, Clifford. "Organized Bicycling and Urban Bikeways." In *Proceedings of the Pedestrian/Bicycle Planning and Design Seminar, San Francisco, December 13–15, 1972*, 237–238. Berkeley: ITTE, 1973.

Frist, Evan. "The Path Not Taken: The Rise of America's Cycle Paths and the Fall of Urban Cycling." In *Cycle History 20: Proceedings of the 20th International Cycling History Conference, Freehold*, ed. Gary Sanderson (n.l., John Pinkerton Memorial Publishing Fund, 2010): 67–72.

Furness, Zack. *One Less Car: Bicycling and the Politics of Automobility*. Philadelphia: Temple University Press, 2010.

Gaddis, John Lewis. *George F. Kennan: An American Life*. New York: Penguin Press, 2011.

Germano, A. Trent, et al. "The Emerging Needs of Bicycle Transportation." *Transportation Research Record* 436 (1973): 8–18.

Gideon, George D. "A Defense of the Two-Class System in Bicycle Racing." *Harper's Weekly* 39 (March 1895).

Glowacz, Dave. *Urban Bikers' Tricks and Tips* (3d ed.). Chicago: Wordspace Press, 2010.

Golbuff, Laura, and Rachel Aldred. *Cycling Policy in the UK*. London: University of East London, n. d. (2010), 16.

"Good Road Workers." *Brooklyn Eagle*, April 3, 1898.

"Gossip of the Cyclers." *New York Times*, August 28, 1898.

Groves, Morgan. "Good News from the NCUTLO," *Bicycling* 16, 1 (January 1975): 6–7.

_____. "Point of View: Is L. A. W. Anti-Bikeway?" *Bicycling* 15, 8 (August 1974): 66–68.

Guide for the Development of Bicycle Facilities. Washington, D.C.: AASHTO, 1982.

Guide for the Development of New Bicycle Facilities. Washington, D.C.: AASHTO, 1991.

Gumprecht, Blake. *The American College Town*. Amherst: University of Massachusetts Press, 2008.

Gutierrez, Alexandra. "The Bicycle Grief." *American Prospect* 21, 2 (March 2010): 6–7.

Hagelin, Christopher. *A Return on Investment Analysis of Bikes-on-Bus Programs* Tampa: Center for Urban Transportation Research, University of South Florida, 2005.

Handy, Susan, Eva Heinen, and Kevin J. Krizek. "Cycling in Small Cities." In *City Cycling*, edited by John Pucher and Ralph Buehler, 257–86. Cambridge, MA: MIT Press, 2012.

Hartman, Jan. "The Delft Bicycle Network." In *The Greening of Urban Transport: Planning for Walking and Cycling in Western Cities*, edited by Rodney Tolley, 193–200. London: Belhaven Press, 1990.

Hayward, Dean. "Hot Program from Hawaii," *Bicycling* 21, 9 (November/December 1980): 90–91, 106–07.

Hill, Paul. "Bicycle Laws and Regulations." *Bike World* 5, 2 (February 1976): 28–31.

Hirsch, Ralph B. *Facilities and Services Needed to Support Bicycle Commuting into Center City Philadelphia*. Philadelphia: Philadelphia Bicycle Coalition/ USEPA, June 1973.

_____. "Update," *Bicycling* 22, 8 (September/October 1981): 40.

_____. "A Washington Report," *Bicycling* 23, 4 (May 1982): 40–42.

Hirst, Eric. "Bicycles, Cars and Energy." *Transportation Quarterly* 28, 3 (October 1974): 573–84.

_____. *Energy Use for Bicycling*. Oak Ridge, TN: Oak Ridge National Laboratory, February 1974. Report No. ORNL-NSF-EP-65.

Hoffman, E. Peter. "200,000 Miles of Bikeways." In *The Best of Bicycling*, edited by Harley M. Leete, 287–290. New York: Trident Press, 1970.

Holt, William Stull. *The Bureau of Public Roads: Its History, Activities, and Organization*. Baltimore, MD: Institute for Government Research Service, 1923.

Horton, Dave, Paul Horton, and Peter Cox, eds. *Cycling and Society*. Aldershot, UK: Ashgate, 2007.

Hurst, Robert. *The Art of Cycling: A Guide to Bicycling in 21st Century America* (2nd edition). Guilford, CT: Falcon Guides, 2007.

Jabbar, Najim. "Practical Advice: Speed Program." *Bike World* 8, 6 (November/December 1979): 8.

Jachnow, Joachim. "What's Become of the German Greens?" *New Left Review* 81 (2nd Ser.) (May/June 2013): 94–117.

Jackson, Kenneth T. *Crabgrass Frontier: The Suburbanization of the United States*. New York: Oxford University Press, 1985.

Jacobs, Jane. *The Death and Life of Great American Cities*. New York: Random House, 1961.

Johnson, Marilyn, Jennie Oxley, and Max Cameron. *Cyclist Bunch Riding: A Review of the Literature* (Accident Research Ctr. Report No. 285). Melbourne: Monash University, 2009.

Jordan, Pete. *In the City of Bikes: the Story of the Amsterdam Cyclist*. New York: Harper Perennial, 2013.

Judt, Tony. *Postwar: A History of Europe Since 1945*. New York: Penguin, 2005.

Kaplan, Jerrold A. *Characteristics of the Regular Adult Bicycle User*. M.S. Thesis, University of Maryland, 1975.

Keller, Morton, and Phyllis Keller. *Making Harvard Modern: The Rise of America's University*. New York: Oxford University Press, 2001.

"Killed by Negroes." *Cycle Age and Trade Review* 20 (November 23, 1899): 107.

Kingbay, Keith. *Inside Bicycling*. Chicago: Henry Regnery Company, 1976.

Kolsbun, Ken. "Point of View: An Anti-Bikeways Movement." *Bicycling* 15, 6 (June 1974): 77–79.

Konski, James L. "Anticipation and Control of Hazards." In *Bicycles USA: Proceedings, May 7–8, 1973*, 26–28. Cambridge, MA: USDOT, Transportation Systems Center, n. d. [1973].

_____. "It's Up to You." *Bicycling* 9, 6 (June 1973): 20–23.

Kossak, Joe. "Hatboro Wizard Speaks." *Bike World* 3, 10 (October 1974): 10.

Krag, Thomas. "Urban Cycling in Copenhagen." In *Planning for Cycling: Principles, Practice and Solutions for Urban Planners*, edited by Hugh McClintock, 223–36. Cambridge, UK: Woodhead Publishing, 2002.

Kron, Karl [Lyman H. Bagg]. *Ten Thousand Miles on a Bicycle*. New York: The author, 1887.

Kroon, Martin. "Traffic and Environmental Policy in the Netherlands." In *The Greening of Urban Transport: Planning for Walking and Cycling in Western Cities*, edited by Rodney Tolley, 113–133. London: Belhaven Press, 1990.

Ladd, Brian. *Autophobia*. Chicago: University of Chicago Press, 2008.

"L.A.W. National Assembly." *Wheel and Cycling Trade Review* 6 (February 1891): 681.

"The League and Politics." *American Athlete and Cycle Trades Review* 5, 36 (November 8, 1889): 547.

Lemov, Penelope. "Buck Rogers Doesn't Live Here Anymore." *Governing* (November 1989): 17–19.

Lewis, Tom. *Divided Highways: Building the Interstate Highways, Transforming American Life*. New York: Viking, 1997.

Lisa, Gregory C. "Bicyclists and Bureaucrats: The League of American Wheelmen and the Public Choice Theory Applied." *Georgetown Law Review* 84 (1995): 373–98.

Lloyd-Jones, Roger, and M. J. Lewis. *Raleigh and the British Bicycle Industry*. Aldershot, UK: Ashgate, 2000.

Longhurst, James. "The Sidepath Not Taken: Bicycles, Taxes, and the Rhetoric of the Public Good in the 1890s." *Journal of Policy History* 25, 4 (2013): 557–85.

Lott, Dale, Timothy Tardiff, and Donna Lott. "Authors' Closure." In "Evaluation by Experienced Riders of a New Bicycle Lane in an Established Bikeway System." *Transportation Research Record* 683 (1978): 46.

"Looking at People." *Bike World* 7, 9 (September 1977): 40.

Lum, Wes. "1974 Urban Bikeway Design Competition Awards." In *Proceedings of the Seminar on Planning, Design and Implementation of Bicycle/Pedestrian Facilities, San Diego [Dec. 4–6] 1974* (Berkeley: ITTE, 1975): 418–23.

Lundin, Per. "Mediators of Modernity: Planning Experts and the Making of the Car Friendly City in Europe." In *Urban Machinery: Inside Modern European Cities*, edited by Mikael Hard and Thomas J. Misa, 257–79. Cambridge, MA: MIT Press, 2008.

McClintock, Hugh. "The Development of UK Cycling Policy." In *Planning for Cycling: Principles, Practice and Solutions for Urban Planners*, edited by Hugh McClintock, 17–35. Cambridge, UK, 2002.

_____. "Nottingham." In *Planning for Cycling: Principles, Practice and Solutions for Urban Planners*, edited by Hugh McClintock, 171–91. Cambridge, UK, 2002.

_____. "Planning for the Bicycle in Newer and Older Towns in Cities." In *The Bicycle and City Traffic*, edited by Hugh McClintock, 40–61. London: Belhaven Press, 1992.

_____. "Planning for the Bicycle in Urban Britain: an Assessment of Experience and Issues." In *The Greening of Urban Transport: Planning for Walking and Cycling in Western Cities*, edited by Rodney Tolley, 201–217. London: Belhaven Press, 1990.

_____. "Post-War Traffic Planning and Special Provision for the Bicycle." In *The Bicycle in City Traffic*, edited by Hugh McClintock, 19–39. London: Belhaven Press, 1992.

McClintock, Miller. *Street Traffic Control*. New York: McGraw-Hill, 1925.

McCullough, James C. "Coming of Age: There is More to Our New Look than Shiny New Clothes." *Bicycling* 22, 2 (March 1981): 6.

_____. "The Politics of Cycling Space." *Bicycling* 19, 11 (November 1978): 10.

McShane, Clay. *Down the Asphalt Path: The Automobile and the American City*. New York: Columbia University Press, 1994.

Manning, Jeff. "Traffic Estimates on Columbia River Crossing Further Muddy the Financial Picture." *Oregonian*, July 19, 2011.

Mannisto-Funk, Tiina. "The Crossroads of Technology and Tradition: Vernacular Bicycles in Rural Finland, 1880–1910." *Technology and Culture* 52, 4 (October 2011): 733–56.

Mapes, Jeff. *Pedaling Revolution: How Cyclists are Changing American Cities*. Corvallis: University of Oregon Press, 2009.

Mason, Philip P. *The League of American Wheelmen and the Good-Roads Movement, 1880–1905*. Doctoral dissertation, University of Michigan, 1957.

Mayo, Marda Fortmann, et al. *Bicycling and Air Quality Information Document*. Report No. EPA 68–01–4946. Washington: Environmental Protection Agency, September 1979.

"Meeting of the National Assembly." *American Athlete and Cycle Trades Review* 11, 8 (February 24, 1893): 159.

Meyers, Tedson. "The New Federalism: Here's One Organization that Beat Reagan to the Punch." *Bicycling* 23, 6 (June 1982): 150–52.

Michael, Harold, et al. *Report of the Panel on Bicycle Laws and Supplementary Agenda for the Subcommittee on Operations, January 27, 1975*. Washington, D.C.: National Committee on Uniform Traffic Laws and Ordinances, 1975.

Miller, Tom. "*Bike World* Interview: Dan Burden." *Bike World* 3, 4 (April 1974): 8–10.

Mom, Gijs. "Roads Without Rails: European Highway-Network Building and the Desire for Long-Range Motorized Mobility." *Technology and Culture* 46, 4 (October 2005): 745–72.

Monheim, Rolf. "Policy Issues in Promoting the Green Modes." In *The Greening of Urban Transport*, edited by Rodney Tolley, 134–58. London: Belhaven Press, 1990.

Monkerud, Don. "A Cyclist Who Pedals Politics." *Bike World* 8, 5 (September/October 1979): 38–41.

Montgomery, John A. *Eno: The Man and the Foundation*. Westport, CT: Eno Foundation, 1988.

Moran, Katie. *Bicycle Transportation for Energy Conservation: Technical Report*. Report No. DOT-P-80-092. Washington, D.C.: U.S. Department of Transportation, May 1980.

Mortitz, William. "Survey of North American Bicycle Commuters: Design and Aggregate Results." *Transportation Research Record 1578*. Washington, D.C.: Transportation Research Board, 1997.

Munn, Harold C. "Bicycles and Traffic." *Transportation Engineering Journal* 101: TE4 (November 1975): 753–62.

_____. "Bike Lanes" [letter], *Bicycle Forum* 35 (January 1994): 2–3.

Murphy, Jack. "Public View of Bicycle Facilities." In *Proceedings of the Pedestrian/Bicycle Planning and Design Seminar, San Francisco, December 13–15, 1972*. Berkeley, CA: ITTE, 1973.

National Commission on Product Safety, Final Report to the President, Volume 1. Washington: National Commission on Product Safety, 1970.

Newman, Oscar. *Defensible Space: Crime Prevention Through Urban Design*. New York: Macmillan, 1972.

"News of the Cyclers." *New York Times*, June 5, 1898.

Norcliffe, Glen. *The Ride to Modernity: The Bicycle in Canada, 1869–1900*. Toronto: University of Toronto Press, 2001.

Norman, Jason. "First and Most Prominent Advocate John Auerbach Dies." *Bicycle Retailer and Industry News*, April 15, 2007.

Norton, Peter D. *Fighting Traffic: The Dawn of the Motor Age in the American City*. Cambridge, MA: MIT Press, 2008.

Oakley, William. *Winged Wheel: The History of the First Hundred Years of the Cyclists' Touring Club*. Godalming, UK: CTC, 1977.

Oldenziel, Ruth, and Adri Albert de la Bruhèze. "Contested Spaces: Bicycle Lanes in Europe, 1920–1995." *Transfers* 1, 2 (Summer 2011): 29–49.

Petersen, Grant. *Just Ride: A Radically Practical Guide to Riding Your Bike*. New York: Workman, 2012.

Petty, Ross D. "The Consumer Product Safety Commission's Promulgation of a Bicycle Safety Standard." *Journal of Product Liability* 10 (1987): 25–50.

_____. "The Impact of the Sport of Bicycle Riding on Safety Law." *American Business Law Journal* 35, 2 (Winter 1998): 185–224.

_____. "Peddling Schwinn Bicycles: Marketing Lessons from the Leading Post-WWII U.S. Bicycle Brand." *Quinnipiac University CHARM Symposium Papers 2007*: 162–71.

_____. "Post-Boom Bicycling in Minneapolis: Counting Transportation Use." In *Cycle History 20: Proceedings of the 20th International Cycling History Conference, Freehold*, ed. Gary Sanderson (n.l., John Pinkerton Memorial Publishing Fund, 2010): 73–80.

_____. "Regulation vs. the Market: The Case of Bicycle Safety (Part I)." *Risk* 2 (1991): 77–87.

_____. "Regulation vs. the Market: The Case of Bicycle Safety (Part II)." *Risk* 2 (1991): 93–120.

Potter, Isaac B. "Side Paths." *LAW Bulletin* 24, 2 (1896): 51.

Pratt, Charles E. "The L. A. W and Legal Rights," *Outing* 7 (January 1886): 454–56.

_____. "Our First Bicycle Club." *Wheelman* 1, 6 (March 1883): 401–12.

Prouty, Dave. *In Spite of Us*. Brattleboro, VT: Velopress Books, 1988.

"A Quick Digest of Laws to Watch." *Bicycling* 15, 4 (April 1974): 8.

Rabenstein, Rüdiger. "The History of the German Workers' Cycling Association, Solidarity." In *Cycle History 11: Proceedings of the 11th International Cycle History Conference, Osaka*, edited by Andrew Ritchie and Rob van der Plas, 160–68. San Francisco: Van der Plas Publications, 2001.

Rautio, Anna-Maria, and Lars Östlund. "Starvation Strings and the Public Good: Development of a Swedish Bike Trail Network in the Early Twentieth Century." *Journal of Transport History* 33, 1 (June 2012): 42–63.

Replogle, Michael A. *National Bicycling and Walking Study: Case Study 9, Linking Bicycle/Pedestrian Facilities with Transit*. Report No. FHWA-

PD-93-012. Washington: Federal Highway Administration, 1992.
_____. *Public Transportation: New Links to Suburban Transit Markets*. Washington, D.C.: Bicycle Federation, 1983.
Ritchie, Andrew. *Major Taylor: The Extraordinary Career of a Champion Bicycle Racer*. San Francisco: Bicycle Books, 1988.
Rogers, Richard, et al. *SCR 47 Statewide Bicycle Committee: Final Report, February 10, 1975*. Sacramento: CalTrans, 1975.
Rose, Joseph. "Most Portland, Vancouver Drivers Would Dodge Columbia River Crossing's Interstate 5 Toll, Poll Finds." *Oregonian*, November 30, 2012.
Rose, Mark H. *Interstate: Express Highway Politics, 1939–1989* (2nd edition). Knoxville: University of Tennessee Press, 1990.
Rowe, Nina Dougherty. "The League of American Wheelmen Legislative Program." *Bicycling* 19, 3 (March 1978): 26, 88.
_____. "Three Promising Bicycle Organizations." *Bicycling* 19, 2 (February 1978): 58–60.
Sanderson, Gary. *Index to the Proceeding of the International Cycle History Conference, 1 (1990) through 20 (2009)* (manuscript, 2011).
Schubert, John. "What Should a Bicycle Facility Be?" *Bicycling* 23, 5 (June 1982): 45–47.
Scott, John Finley. "The American College Sorority: Its Role in Class and Ethic Endogamy." *American Sociology Review* 30, 4 (August 1965): 514–27.
_____. "The City of Bicycles: Can the Davis Model Work Elsewhere?" *California Bicyclist* (October 1984): n. p.
_____. "The Cycling Community: Who Leads, Who Follows, a Reply to Bob Sommer." *Bicycling* 18, 11 (November 1977): 12, 68–69.
Shaer, Matthew. "Not Quite Copenhagen." *New York* (March 28, 2011): 34–39, 91–92.
Shanteau, Robert M. "Bicycle Bottlenecks: Bicycle Planning from a Bicyclist's Point of View." In *Proceedings of the Seminar on Planning, Design and Implementation of Bicycle/Pedestrian Facilities, San Diego, December 1974*. 240–254. New York: ASCE, 1975.
Simon, Herbert A. "A Behavioral Model of Rational Choice." *Quarterly Journal of Economics* 69 (1955): 99–118.
Skrabak, Darryl. "Bicycle Activists: Where They Stand Now." *Bicycling* 18, 2 (February 1977): 50–51.
_____. "Bike Law: The Bikeway Backlash." *Bicycling* 16, 9 (September 1975): 25–28.
_____. "Bike Law: Trend Setting Report on Bike Law Emerges in California." *Bicycling* 16, 6 (June 1975): 72–75.
_____. "Experienced Bicyclists and the Bikeway Controversy." In *Proceedings of the Seminar on Planning, Design and Implementation of Bicycle/Pedestrian Facilities, San Diego, Dec. 4–6, 1974*, 434–43. Berkeley, CA: Institute of Transportation and Traffic Engineering, 1975.
_____. "John Forester Writes a Bike Book." *Bicycling* 17, 3 (March 1976): 82–83.
_____. "NCUTLO Spells Power." *Bicycling* 16, 12 (December 1975): 55–59.
_____. "Rules are Being Made, Why Not be there?" *Bicycling* 18, 4 (April 1977): 80–81.
Smith, Dan T., and Cather DeLeuw. *Bikeways: The State of the Art*. Washington, D.C.: FHWA, 1974.
_____. *Safety and Locational Criteria for Bikeways: Final Report*. Report No. FHWA-RD-75–112. Washington: FHWA, 1975.
_____. *Safety and Locational Criteria for Bikeways: Users Manual Vol. 1, Facilities Locational Criteria*. Report No. FHWA-RD-75–113. Washington, D.C.: FHWA, 1976.
_____. *Safety and Locational Criteria for Bikeways: Users Manual Vol. 2, Design and Safety Criteria*. Report No. FHWA-RD-75–114. Washington: FHWA, 1976.
Sommer, Robert. "Bikeway Research at the University of California-Davis in the 1960s." In *Cycle History 16: Proceedings of the 16th Annual Cycle History Conference, Davis*, edited by Andrew Ritchie, 47–51. San Francisco: Van der Plas, 2005.
_____. "Building Bridges Between Communities of Cyclists." *Bicycling* 18, 8 (August 1977): 70–72.
_____. "Point of View: Bikeways, More Research, Less Rhetoric." *Bicycling* 14, 11 (November 1973): 48.
Sommer, Robert, and Dale Lott. "Behavioral Evaluation of a Bikeway System." In *Proceedings of the Northwestern Undergraduate Conference on Environmental Behavior*, 12–17. Amherst, MA: Institute for Man and the Environment, 1974.
_____. "Bikeways in Action, the Davis Experience." *Congressional Record*, 92nd Cong, 1st Sess. April 19, 1971: 10830–833. The article is combined with other material under the overall title, "The Bicycle Era."
Stacey, James E. "Bridging the Gap Between Bikeway Planners and Bicyclists." In *Proceedings of the Seminar/Workshop on Planning, Design and Implementation of Bicycle and Pedestrian Facilities, Chicago, July 19–21 1978*, 203–09. New York: MAUDEP, n. d. [1978].
Stockard, April, and Don Stockard. "Bike Law: Our Rights and Reasons." *Bicycling* 9, 7 (July, 1973): 41–42.
Stoffers, Manuel. "Cycling as Heritage: Representing the History of Cycling in the Netherlands." *Journal of Transport History* 33, 1 (June 2012): 92–114.
Takemoto-Weerts, David. "Evolution of a Cyclist-

Friendly Community." In *Cycle History 16: Proceedings of the 16th Annual Cycle History Conference, Davis*, edited by Andrew Ritchie, 11–15. San Francisco: Van der Plas, 2005.

Tenney, Edward A. *The Highway Jungle: The Story of the Public Safety Movement and the Failure of Driver Education in the Public Schools.* New York: Exposition Press, 1962.

"Third Annual L.A.W. Winter Rendezvous," *L.A.W. Bulletin* (February 1969): 3.

Thompson, Ronald. "Introduction: Bikeway Issues." In *Proceedings of the Seminar/Workshop on Planning, Design and Implementation of Bicycle and Pedestrian Facilities, Chicago, July 19–21 1978*, 202. New York: MAUDEP, n. d. [1978].

Toole, Jennifer, et al. *Revising the Guide for the Development New Bicycle Facilities: Final Report.* Report No. NCHRP 15–37FR. Washington, D.C.: Transportation Research Board, 2010.

"Trails Seminar." *Bicycling* 12, 5 (May 1971): 26.

Transportation Enhancements: Summary of Nationwide Spending as of FY 2009. Washington, D.C.: National Transportation Enhancements Clearinghouse, 2010.

United States Architectural and Barriers Compliance Board. *Accessible Sidewalks and Street Crossings* [ADAAG Manual]. Washington: FHWA, 2001.

Unterman, Richard K. *Accommodating the Pedestrian: Adapting Towns and Neighborhoods for Walking and Bicycling.* New York: Van Nostrand Reinhold, 1984.

"Untitled." *L.A.W. Bulletin* (July 1969): 6.

"Untitled." *Texas Parade* 2, 2 (July 1937): 4.

Urban Bikeway Design Guide. Washington, D.C.: NACTO, 2011.

Urban Bikeway Design Guide (2d edition). Washington, D.C.: NACTO, 2012.

van Werven, Gerrit. "Groningen, Netherlands." In *The Bicycle in City Traffic*, edited by Hugh McClintock, 154–64. London: Belhaven Press, 1992.

Vanderbilt, Tom. *Traffic: Why We Drive the Way We Do.* New York: Knopf, 2008.

Wachtel, Alan. "A History of CABO." *Bicycle USA* (December 1980): 12–14.

Wallace, Judi Lawson. "Our Legacy to the Young—Teaching Them the Bike is Not a Toy." *Bicycling* 22, 6 (July 1981): 45, 47, 122–24.

Walsh, Lawrence B. "Factors in Bikeway Design." In *Proceedings of the Seminar on Planning, Design and Implementation of Bicycle/Pedestrian Facilities, San Diego, December 1974*, 308–311. New York, ASCE, 1975.

Weiner, Edward. *Urban Transportation Planning in the United States: A Historical Overview.* Westport, CT: Praeger, 1999.

Weingroff, Richard F. *Portrait of a General: General Roy Stone* (Unpublished Manuscript, Federal Highway Administration, U.S. Department of Transportation, 2003).

Welleman, Ton. "An Efficient Means of Transport: Experiences with Cycling Transport Policy in the Netherlands." In *Planning for Cycling: Principles, Practice and Solutions for Urban Planners*, edited by Hugh McClintock, 192–208. Cambridge, UK: Woodhead, 2002.

Whitney, Albert W. *Man and the Motor Car.* New York: J. J. Little and Ives, 1936.

Wilkinson, Bill. "Construction, Maintenance, and Enforcement on the George Washington Memorial Parkway Pathway." In *Bicycles USA: Proceedings, May 7–8, 1973*, 40–42. Cambridge, MA: USDOT, Transportation Systems Center, n. d. [1973].

Williams, John. "Bikepaths and the Law" [letter], *Bike World* 3, 1 (January 1974): 50.

_____. "San Luis Obispo." In *Bikeway Design Atlas: Urban Bikeway Design Competition*, 26–52. Cambridge, MA: Urban Bikeway Design Collaborative, January 1975.

Wolfe, Frederick L. *The Bicycle: A Commuting Alternative.* Edmonds, WA: Signpost Books, 1979.

Wortman, Robert H. "Bikeway Hazards." In *Proceedings of the Fourth National Seminar on the Planning Design and Implementation of Bicycle and Pedestrian Facilities, December 4–6, 1975, New Orleans*, 320–325. New York: ASCE, 1975.

Wright, Charles L. *Fast Wheels, Slow Traffic: Urban Transportation Choices.* Philadelphia: Temple University Press, 1992.

"Year in Review." *Bicycle Retailer and Industry News* 19, 11 (July 1, 2010): 1–3.

Yang, Yizhao. "A Tale of Two Cities: Physical Form and Neighborhood Satisfaction in Metropolitan Portland and Charlotte." *Journal of the American Planning Association* 74, 3 (Summer 2008): 307–23.

Yeates, Michael. "Making Space for Cyclists: A Matter of Speed?" In *Planning for Cycling: Principles, Practice and Solutions for Urban Planners*, edited by Hugh McClintock, 50–71. Cambridge, UK: 2002.

Yergen, Daniel. *The Prize: The Epic Quest for Oil, Money and Power.* New York: Simon & Schuster, 1991.

Websites and Online Articles

Allen, John S. "Interview of Phyllis Harmon, January 16, 2006, Tapes 1–3" (audio) http://john-s-allen.com/labdocs/interviews/.

D'Ambrosio, Dan. "Our History. (1996) *Adventure Cyclist* online, http://www.adventurecycling.org.

Forester, John. "Bicycling, Transportation and the Problem of Evil" (an address to the Preserving the American Dream Conference, October 2007). http://www.johnforester.com/articles/. Last viewed: April 11, 2010.

_____. "History of the Effective Cycling Program." http://www.johnforester.com/articles/Education/ECHistory.htm. Last viewed: December 10, 2013.

_____. "Traffic Cyclists as Performance Artists: A Review of the Art of Cycling." http://www.johnforester.com/articles/. Last viewed: March 2, 2011.

Franklin, John. "National Cycle Training Project: An Introduction to the Project Given in Cheltenham, May 2002," http://www.lesberries.co.uk/cycling/. Last viewed: December 6, 2011.

_____. "National Cycle Training Project: Cheltenham Address, May 2002." http://www.cyclecraft.com/articles/index/. Last viewed: December 6, 2011.

"How Friends and Colleagues Remember Ken." Website of the Association of Pedestrian and Bicycle Professional (http://www.abpb.org), under "Ken Cross Research Scholarship." Last viewed: December 1, 2011.

"ProBicycle: Bicycle Advocacy by Cyclists for Cyclists," http://probicycle.com.

"RiziBeo," "History of the Bus Bike Rack," http://rikibeo.wordpresscom/2009/02/18/history-ofthebus-bike-rack/. Last viewed: August 1, 2013.

Snyder, Tanya. "*NACTO Beats the Clock with Quick Update* of Bike Guide," D.C. Streetsblog, June 19, 2012. http: //dcstreetsblog.org/category/other-organizations/. Last viewed: April 11, 2013.

_____. "U.S. DOT to Challenge AASHTO Supremacy on Bike/Ped Safety Standards," D.C. Streetsblog, February 28, 2013. http: //dcstreetsblog.org/category/other-organizations/. Last viewed: April 11, 2013.

Toth, Gary, and Brendan Crain. "Interview with Dan Burden, Andy Clarke, and Charlie Gandy." http://www.pps.org/blog/after-30-years-of-bikeped-advocacy-how-far-have-we-come/. Last viewed: July 7, 2012.

United States Product Safety Commission. *Chairman's Conference on Nighttime Bicycle Safety, Bethesda, November 9, 1994.* http://*www.cpsc.gov/FOIA/meetings/mtg95/ nighttimebike.pdf.*

Walker, Peter. "75 Years After the UK's First Cycle Lane Opened, the Same Debate Rages On," *The Environment Guardian Online*, December 13, 2009, http://www.environmentguardian.co.uk. Last viewed: September 3, 2011.

Legal Cases

Ellis v. Frasier, 63 P. 642 (Or. 1901)

FCC v. Beach Communications, Inc., 508 U.S. 307 (1993)

Forester et al. v. Consumer Product Safety Commission, 559 F.2d 774 (D.C., c. 1977)

Hodel v. Indiana, 452 U.S. 314 (1981)

In re Wright, et al., 63 How. 345 (S.C.N.Y.C. 1882)

In re Wright, Foster and Walker, 65 How. 119 (S.C.N.Y.C. 1883)

Johnson v. Derby Cycle Co. et al., ESX-L-16063–89 (Sp. Ct. New Jersey, Essex Co., 1989)

People v. Bruce, 63, P. 519 (Wash. 1901)

Porter, et al. v. Shields, et al., 49 A. 785 (Penn. 1901)

Pressy v. H. B. Smith Mfg. Co., 19 A. 618 (N. J. App., 1889)

R. B. Jarts, Inc. v. Richardson, 438 F.2d 846 (2d Cir., 1971)

United States v. Caroline Products Co., 304 U.S. 144 (1938)

Interviews

Blumenthal, Tim. October 5, 2009.

Burden, Dan, August 1–2, 2007.

Clarke, Norman. April 5, 1998.

Forester, Geoffrey. September 19, 2009.

Groves, Morgan. November 12, 2007.

Groves, Morgan. (By John S. Allen). October 31, 2009.

Harmon, Phyllis. (By John S. Allen). January 16, 2006.

Lott, Donna. November 19, 2007.

Noguchi, Ted. December 12, 2011.

Taylor, Dorris. November 5, 2007.

Townley, Jay. May 23, 2009.

Wilkinson, William C., III. July 17, 2008.

Index